MASCULINITY IN AMERICAN POLITICS

Masculinity in American Politics

Edited by
Monika L. McDermott *and* Dan Cassino

NEW YORK UNIVERSITY PRESS
New York

NEW YORK UNIVERSITY PRESS
New York
www.nyupress.org

Library of Congress Cataloging-in-Publication Data
Names: McDermott, Monika L., 1966–   editor. | Cassino, Dan, 1980–   editor.
Title: Masculinity in American politics / edited by Monika L. McDermott
and Dan Cassino.Description: New York : New York University Press, 2025. |
Includes bibliographical references and index.
Identifiers: LCCN 2024013750 (print) | LCCN 2024013751 (ebook) |
ISBN 9781479830688 (hardback) | ISBN 9781479830701 (paperback) |
ISBN 9781479830718 (ebook) | ISBN 9781479830725 (ebook other)
Subjects: LCSH: Masculinity—Political aspects—United States. |
Sexrole—Political aspects—United States. | Political culture—United States. |
Political candidates—United States—Public opinion. |Politicians—
United States—Public opinion.
Classification: LCC HQ1090.3 .M345 2025 (print) | LCC HQ1090.3 (ebook) |
DDC 155.3—dc23/eng/20240411
LC record available at https://lccn.loc.gov/2024013750
LC ebook record available at https://lccn.loc.gov/2024013751

This book is printed on acid-free paper, and its binding materials are chosen for strength and durability. We strive to use environmentally responsible suppliers and materials to the greatest extent possible in publishing our books.

Manufactured in the United States of America

10 9 8 7 6 5 4 3 2 1

Also available as an ebook

CONTENTS

Introduction

Masculinity and Politics

MONIKA L. MCDERMOTT AND DAN CASSINO

Finally, a president with some balls.
—T-shirts spotted at Trump rallies (Hesse 2020)

For President Donald Trump, extreme masculinity was a defining feature of his persona and his behavior both on the campaign trail and in office. But Trump was far from the first president to accentuate masculinity in his politics, nor is he likely to be the last. Consider Teddy Roosevelt's "unabashed paean to violence, and a desperate fashioning of masculinity into political culture" (Watts 2003, 2), or, more recently, George W. Bush's "swagger of privileged Texas masculinity" (Tuathail 2003, 863). These are only three examples of presidents who paraded their masculinity both on the campaign trail and in office, but there are many more, including Ronald Reagan and Lyndon Baines Johnson, both of whom cultivated an outdoorsy, cowboy image, though Reagan's portrayal was somewhat more genteel than Johnson's infamous foul mouth and bullying behavior.

Masculinity can also play a role in presidential campaigns when it is noticeably absent. Michael Dukakis's campaign photo op riding around in a military tank and looking "silly" was "one of the biggest mistakes in a campaign of many mistakes" (Devlin 1989, 397). Similarly, John Kerry taking part in an "elitist" sport—windsurfing—while wearing a "mildly effeminate" bodysuit (Christiansen 2017, 173) bolstered the image of him as not being tough enough for the job.

While these examples all arise from the highly visible arena of the US presidency, assertions and contestations of masculinity claims can be found across all levels of the political system, among candidates and voters, in elections local and national. Masculinity is not new to US politics—but what *is* new is the effort made by political science and other fields to apply the relatively long history of masculinity research to the political world. Psychology and sociology have been analyzing and measuring masculinity and its effects for decades, but they rarely pay any attention to potential political effects. Political science, as a field, has largely ignored masculinity until very recently.

Studying, understanding, and analyzing masculinity have been priorities in the fields of psychology, sociology, and gender studies for at least a decade, and, in some cases (especially psychology), multiple decades. What these studies show is that masculinity, in its many forms, helps to predict attitudes and behaviors not only for men but also for women. Masculinity has been found to impact aspects of American life as diverse as mental health and help seeking, domestic violence, physical health disparities, and educational success.

We can also see the importance of masculinity in the wide range of journals that publish articles on the topic. The most notable are the specific journals *Men & Masculinities*, and *Psychology of Men & Masculinities* (well-above-average impact factors of 3.893 and 3.971 respectively). Masculinity is also a common topic in broader gender journals like *Journal of Gender Studies* (824 research or review articles contain the term "masculinity" as of this writing), as well as broad disciplinary journals such as the *Sociological Review* (1,459 research articles) and the *Journal of Social Psychology* (397 research articles).

Masculinity and Politics

Despite the attention given to masculinity in other disciplines, few studies in political science have chosen to follow this path of inquiry to date (for in-depth exceptions, see McDermott 2016; Cassino and Besen-Cassino 2021). Political science has almost exclusively focused on the effects of biological sex on political attitudes and behavior—an outdated way of looking at gender. More and more, researchers are interested in going beyond the simple sex dichotomy and looking at gendered personalities as well as societal gender roles and norms and their influence.

One of the problems in analyzing masculinity in the social sciences is that few scholars agree on exactly what it is. What scholars *can* agree on (though political science is rather late to the game on this one as well) is that it is distinct from biological sex. While the terms "gender" and "sex" have traditionally been used interchangeably in political science—with "gender" being the more frequently employed phrase, used to mean "sex"—sociology and psychology have stronger traditions of trying to at least discuss distinctions between the two (e.g., Unger and Crawford 1993). No field of study seems to be completely settled, however, as even biological scientists felt the need to define the distinction between the terms as recently as 2005:

> These words have specifically different etymologies and meanings. In the most basic sense, sex is biologically determined, and gender is culturally determined. The noun sex includes the structural, functional, and behavioral characteristics of living things determined by sex chromosomes. Sex (noun) is derived from the Latin word "sexus," meaning either of two divisions of organic nature distinguished as male or female, respectively (*Oxford English Dictionary* 1989). According to the Oxford English Dictionary, sex (noun) has a definition as "the sum of those differences in the structure and function of the reproductive organs on the ground of which beings are distinguished as male and female, and of the other physiological differences consequent on these; the class of phenomena with which these differences are concerned." Gender can be thought of as the behavioral, cultural, or psychological traits typically associated with one sex. Gender (noun) is derived from the Latin word "genus" referring to kind or race. Gender (noun) is defined as "a kind, sort, or class referring to the common sort of people." It is through an understanding of these principal definitions that scientists can apply these terms in a specific manner to sex-based research. (Torgrimson and Minson 2005, 785–86)

Torgrimson and Minson's (2005) difference is the one that many political scientists—at least those working in gender research—as well as psychologists and sociologists have recently come to adopt: sex is about biology, while gender is about culture and socialization. This is also the distinction we make in this volume. Masculinity, then, is a gendered aspect of an individual, rather than anything biologically related. While most research finds that men tend to score more highly than women do on various measures of masculinity (see, e.g., chapter 1 of this volume), masculinity is not restricted to men regardless of how it is measured (unless specifically measured only among men).

Pulling together top scholars across disciplines and methods—qualitative, quantitative, experimental, and theoretical—to analyze masculinity and politics, this volume helps fill this large gap in research on American politics and masculinity and create a narrative around it. Part of this narrative is the wide range of measurements used in studying masculinity that can lead to researchers looking at very similar subjects and talking past each other. Masculinity has become a catchall term for different aspects of gendered identities. For example, masculine personalities are not necessarily the same as masculine self-perceptions, and separate measures are used to capture each. While different chapters in this volume make use of different scales or constructs, like the Bem Sex Role Inventory (BSRI), or hegemonic masculinity, they are all seen and treated as one deep-rooted ideal manifested or expressed in different ways. As a result, they are all of a piece.

Another part of this narrative comes from the effects that masculinity, in its many forms, can have on politics. What existing sociological and psychological research has shown us is that gender is central to the way that both men and women structure their social worlds, and that it plays out in multiple ways. Importantly, because gender is not sex, both women and men can hold and assert masculine traits, beliefs, and behaviors, and they often do so. Masculinity may even impact men and women differently, interacting with sex in complicated ways.

This narrative also includes how other forms of identity interact with masculinity to influence politics. Social identity theory teaches us that demographic, cultural, and social aspects of society and individuals are all important to attitudes, behaviors, and judgments. Specifically, both race and sex and their intersections with gender are an integral part of the story. Much of the literature that *does* exist on politics and masculinity focuses on men alone (e.g., Kimmel 2017; Ashcraft 2022). Additionally, given the difficulty and expense of national samples with substantial minority representation, there is little research into how Black and Latino/a/x voters or candidates are affected by masculinities. This volume contains various chapters that address these gaps as well.

While the focus of this volume is on masculinity, we do not dismiss the power of femininity in politics. From existing research, we know that gender is central to politics, but the research and evidence in political science is primarily on the feminine aspects of being a woman. The gendered roles that women play affect their individual voting behavior, their likelihood to be politically active, their political ambition, and even their success when running for office. Masculinity, however, is rarely subject to scrutiny in political science but has as much potential to explain individual and institutional behavior as do femininity and feminine roles. While masculinity and femininity are neither opposites nor mutually exclusive, there is no reason to believe that one plays a role while the other does not.

Moreover, masculinity is an important factor in many areas of interest to political scientists and analysts, including, but not limited to political socialization, potential candidate ambition, the running of campaigns, individual vote choices, and the effects of masculinity on political attitudes and beliefs ranging from political knowledge to estimation and understanding of candidate issue positions. Herein lies the strength of this volume: the quality and variety of contributions all around the central, largely unexamined topic of masculinity and politics.[1]

The Structure and Contents of the Volume

While the contributions to the edited volume encompass a variety of methods and disciplines, they all arise from the same theoretical understanding. It draws from psychology (e.g., Alfred Adler); from sociology (e.g., Judith Butler); and from political science, in applications of social identity theory (e.g., David Sears, Leonie Huddy). But the modern, cross-disciplinary study of masculinities seeks to incorporate many of these into a single, larger understanding of people's gender identities. Often, the similarities between the understandings of social scientists studying gender are obscured by differences in terminology and methods, but we have worked to bring together authors that have proven themselves able to talk about these issues across disciplinary lines. This is not a volume in which we present competing views about issues within the field of interest, but rather one in which the authors draw from the same roots and, often, each other, in applying a unified understanding of a puzzle. And, as with a puzzle, those pieces work together to form a larger picture.

The book is divided into two main topic areas that progress from concept to application within each. The first area—chapter 1 by McDermott and Jones—focuses on concepts and measurement of masculinity in the sociological, psychological, and limited political science traditions, all of which have had a significant impact on development of masculinity as we currently understand it. It addresses differences in the literature and measurement of masculinity and helps to distinguish between standard measures and their applications, including gendered personalities, masculinity ideology, and social identity measures. The inclusion of techniques and concepts from diverse fields helps to show ways that we can bridge these gaps, and build toward a new, more inclusive understanding of the field that transcends disciplinary boundaries, and it allows us to apply the findings of other fields into the study of masculinity in political science.

This first part of the volume then proceeds to look at how masculinity matters to American politics and elections from the standpoint of the masculinized political system in America and how it affects candidates and their campaigns. In chapter 2, Zoe M. Oxley, Jill S. Greenlee, Mirya R. Holman, Angela L. Bos, and J. Celeste Lay analyze a unique dataset of the pictures children draw when asked to draw a political leader, and how masculine the children's descriptions of the pictures are. Chapter 3, by Nichole M. Bauer, Eugene Lee-Johnson, and Dan Qi presents a new dataset (drawn from the Wesleyan Media Project archives) that looks at the gendered nature—specifically the assertions of masculinity—in campaigns by women of color, relative to white women, in both advertising content and images. Chapter 4 is a first, experimental look at ableist stereotypes and masculinity as it affects candidates—using Pennsylvania senator John Fetterman as a model. Specifically, the experiment tests whether voters view a candidate who suffers from mental or physical illness (or both) as less masculine than average and whether this affects electability.

The second portion of the book focuses on individual citizens and voters and the way their own masculine profiles affect their attitudes and behaviors, progressing from more general studies to more specific applications. As with other parts of the volume, the chapters in this section deal with some of the key questions around political behavior and gender. It begins with an overview by Christina Pao and Nate Roundy in chapter 5 of existing research on gender (masculinity and femininity) and American politics. This is followed by chapter 6, in which Catherine Bolzendahl, Canton Winer, and Tara Warner analyze the role that hegemonic masculinity, specifically, plays in ideological beliefs in America, demonstrating that conservatism is driven by hegemonic gendered beliefs. Next, in chapter 7, Nathaniel E. C. Schermerhorn and Theresa K. Vescio consider the unique role that masculinity ideology played in support for Donald Trump in both 2016 and 2020, but not in support for either of his general election opponents.

Chapters 8 and 9 both deal with men and masculinity, specifically, and masculine security and expression, albeit in very different contexts. In chapter 8, Sarah H. DiMuccio and Eric D. Knowles pull together many of their existing findings regarding how threats to masculinity lead men to support more aggressive policies and politicians. Chapter 9, by Ivelisse Cuevas-Molina and Dan Cassino, analyzes a unique dataset of men in Newark, New Jersey, that contains large samples of men of color and allows the authors to examine the intersection of race and masculinity in detail, and how race and masculinity relate to political efficacy in areas with differing racial and ethnic makeups.

The next chapters dig more deeply into specific political and cross-disciplinary questions. For example, chapter 10, by Carl J. Palmer and Rolfe Daus Peterson, contains an analysis of the link between masculinity and the traditional "gender gap" in political knowledge—taking this question beyond the binary sex distinction for the first time and analyzing the role of both femininity and masculinity among men, women, and political knowledge primarily using the BSRI. Also using the BSRI, in chapter 11, Leonie Huddy and Maggie K. Martin analyze multiple datasets to disentangle the relationship among sex, empathy, and femininity/masculinity.

Chapters 12 and 13 look at specific groups and their masculinities. In chapter 12, Amanda Bittner and Elizabeth Goodyear-Grant use original survey data from America and Canada to analyze the levels of hypermasculinity in each system, and how they relate to different policy preferences between citizens of the two countries. Chapter 13 looks at an understudied group: Generation Z. In this chapter, Melissa Deckman takes on the task of analyzing this famously gender-fluid generation and how their masculine and feminine outlooks and political attitudes defy traditional models of gendered expectations, especially when it comes to what she defines as "toxic masculinity": the extreme gendered expectations that society can put on American men.

As is evident from these very brief synopses, the topics covered in this volume are all related in important ways, but they also provide distinctively informative and important results that speak to our larger understanding of masculinity (and, in some cases, femininity) in American politics. Putting this volume together was both an extremely easy and extremely difficult task. To our surprise, almost everyone we approached with the idea of contributing to this volume was eager to (and in the end did) participate, resulting in the great number of projects we are able to offer from such astounding scholars. At the same time, as discussed (and to be covered in much more detail in chapter 1), definitions of masculinity abound at a rate close to the number of scholars who write about it. We in this volume have made every attempt to understand the underlying concepts at work here and to define our terms as consistently as possible when analyzing the same ideas. Again, chapter 1 will help provide the road map for readers to follow in deciphering the varied measures at work, and what, precisely, they are measuring. In the end, we hope that readers not only learn much more about masculinity and its importance in US (and Canadian) politics but that they also find the contributed pieces as exciting, novel, and important as we the editors and all the contributors do.

NOTE

1 We need to state at the outset that in this volume, and in much of *social* science, our interest in the concept of masculinity is in its role as an *independent* variable: meaning, what impact masculinity has on the world of politics. The study of masculinity as a *dependent* variable—why some individuals are more masculine or less masculine, for reasons such as heritability or testosterone levels—is largely divorced from politics, and as such will not be discussed here. For research of this latter type, see, for example, Knafo, Iervolino, and Plomin (2005); Lippa (2005); and Van Anders (2013).

PART 1

Masculinity and the Political World

1

Measuring Masculinity across Disciplines

MONIKA L. MCDERMOTT AND DAVID R. JONES

There is no single definition of masculinity in modern culture, even within modern American culture alone. It is therefore more appropriate to talk about "masculinities" in the plural than "masculinity" as a solo concept (Connell and Messerschmidt 2005). Reflecting the multiple conceptual definitions of masculinity, a plentiful supply of measures exists that each aim to capture masculinity—and its frequently considered counterpart, femininity—in its various forms. In some ways, this multiplicity is a good thing. Masculinity is a nuanced concept, and its study should not impose artificially rigid limitations on methods of measurement. At the same time, however, as masculinity becomes increasingly important to examining American politics, understanding the varying forms is crucial.

The purpose of social science is to organize and systematize knowledge to facilitate greater common understanding (Gerring 2011). This goal is fundamentally threatened to the extent that—in the extreme case—each discipline or study uses its own name for, or own unique measure of, a common concept. For example, when the results of studies disagree about what effects "masculinity" has on a specific outcome variable, it becomes impossible to know whether the differing results are reflective of a weak or inconsistent underlying relationship or are merely attributable to different measurement strategies.

Rather than accumulating knowledge, a broad field of study that lacks common understanding regarding names, definitions, and measures of common concepts risks having scholars speak past each other. To date, this is happening among the fields of sociology, psychology, and political science when it comes to the study of masculinities. Each discipline, and sometimes even different scholars within a single discipline, is having separate, mostly *intra*disciplinary dialogues about these different concepts and measures. Cross-pollination from one field to another is also relatively rare.

Because of the need for some consistency in order to begin to reach common understandings about masculinity, this chapter has the vital, if lofty, goal of sorting through some of the more prominent concepts and measures. This is an attempt to create structure and order and, where possible, speak to overlap among the disciplines and their treatments of the broader concept. Such an analysis does not yet exist and is thereby all the more central to understanding where the current field of study stands, and how we can move forward overall, specifically in this volume.

The chapter proceeds in three main parts. First, it looks at the history of the early development of conceptions and measurements of masculinity. Second, it identifies and discusses five main concepts currently in use in the study of masculinity and the measures commonly associated with each: masculine personality traits, "hegemonic" or ideal masculinity, masculinity ideology, toxic masculinity, and masculine gendered identity. The final section analyzes the amount of correlation and overlap among the standard measures of these concepts. The chapter concludes with a brief discussion that helps to inform the use of the term masculinity, and accompanying measures, that will be used in the remainder of this volume.

Early Conceptions of Masculinity

The multifaceted concept of masculinity can be traced back at least as far as ancient Greece. Historians and theorists who discuss masculinity often refer to the Greek term *andreia*, which refers to masculinity as a military ideal, or courage on the battlefield. Being masculine meant being armed and trained in a military style (Cartledge 2013). While courage, or *andreia*, was an important, common element of masculinity across ancient Greece, Scott Rubarth (2014) notes that differences also existed among different states and cultures within Greece—namely, Athenian, Spartan, and Stoic societies. These differences were largely political in nature, as they were driven by alternative attitudes toward military service and political participation.

For Athenians, patriarchy was also an important element of masculinity (Rubarth 2014), with a man's role as head of household seen as vital to his identity. In Sparta, by contrast, women were the heads of household, as men, and preadult boys, belonged in the army. Spartan women were largely left to their own devices to make decisions about the household, land, and most of what was within that realm. Political participation is another area of sharp distinctions. Athenians were orators and intellectuals, and participating in the running of the state was an essential male role. In Sparta, on the other hand, oration and intellectualism were disdained and discouraged, to the point of driving artists and intellectuals out of the region. The Stoics straddled a middle ground of sorts: appreciating intellectual thought, but not for the purpose of personal gain, more for the goal of wisdom. To be a man among the Stoics was to be a sage.

These societies in ancient Greece also differed in the extent to which they distinguished between being biologically male and having traits that would traditionally be considered as masculine. The Athenians, who kept their wives in a solidly subservient state, never considered that there could be a difference between the two concepts. The Stoics did not treat women as the Athenians did, as subservient, but nevertheless did not see a distinction between being male and being masculine. In Sparta, however, where women were free to exercise power, gain wealth, and rule their lands autonomously, masculine characteristics were not distinct to men, apart from courage (*andreia*), as war was a world for men alone. The Spartans were certainly ahead of their time in making this distinction—it would take psychology until the twentieth century to grasp the possibility of both women and men having masculine and feminine traits. It would take political science much longer.

All of these distinctions are relevant to our attempts to define masculinity in the more modern period. What masculinity *is*, exactly, remains a hot topic of debate, in both psychology and sociology. It should come as no surprise, then, that none other than the father of psychoanalysis, Sigmund Freud, was drawn to the idea of masculinity (and femininity) in his studies of human behavior. While in Freud's work, masculinity largely centers around sexual desire and sexual behavior (as does much of his work generally), he does acknowledge that there is a sociological aspect to the concept, and that masculinity and femininity may not track perfectly with, and may even transcend, their classifications in biology and psychology (Freud 1915, 219n1). Adler extended the idea of the separation of masculinity and femininity even further, theorizing that women may take on masculine characteristics in order to compete with men, while men dominate women—assert their masculinity—in order to avoid any feelings of femininity or inferiority (see Ansbacher and Ansbacher 1956). Adler's ideas would be prophetic for future psychological studies of masculinity.

At the beginning of the twentieth century, the first real efforts at systematic measurement of masculinity (and femininity) as a psychological or sociological phenomenon were made. In 1936, Lewis Terman and Catharine Cox Miles established one of the first widely accepted, and long-lived methods for measuring masculinity and femininity, dubbed the "M-F scale." Their goal was to create a scale with two poles—masculine and feminine—on which individuals *of both sexes* could be placed. This scale could then be used to determine the degree to which men and women differed along this continuum. In doing so, they were among the first researchers to use measures of attitudes and interests to test the idea that biology may not be the determinative distinction between masculinity and femininity, and that there might be some underlying measure on which some men were more masculine than others.

Terman and Miles's M-F test kicked off a productive decade or more of additional tests by other psychologists to attempt to measure masculinity and femininity. Among some of the more notable were the masculine/feminine portion of the Minnesota Multiphasic Personality Inventory (MMPI), the masculine (anti-feminine) portion of the Guilford-Martin Inventory of Factors (GAMIN; Guilford and Martin 1943), and the Strong Vocational Interest Blank (SVIB) measure of women and men (Strong 1936), to name a few. This increase in psychological measures attempting to define and capture elements of masculinity and femininity also led to research that compared these various measures. For the most part, these comparative studies find that while the measures frequently correlate with each other, they do not necessarily capture the same aspects of masculinity and femininity. That did not, however, dampen their use in psychological research. The Terman and Miles test alone was applied to individual factors as diverse as psychopathy (Bosselman and Skorodin 1940) and mechanical and clerical abilities (Lee 1952).

One thing these tests of the first half of the twentieth century had in common was their primary goal of distinguishing between the sexes. Whether on personal interests, vocation preferences, or abilities, all were trying to find the elusive explanation for what made men, men, and women, women. It would be a couple of decades before scholars would truly begin to question whether the concepts of masculinity and femininity, merely as items to distinguish between the sexes, were truly useful or valid for explaining other phenomena. In a 1973 essay reviewing the current state of M-F measures—including those of Terman and Miles, Strong, the MMPI, and GAMIN, Anne Constantinople (1973)—came to two primary conclusions. First, the concepts of M-F are multidimensional and not necessarily measured adequately in a single scale. Despite what researchers had been doing to that point, there was sufficient evidence that M-F was not a bipolar concept. Second, basing M-F measures solely on their ability to distinguish differences between the sexes calls into question the utility of any such measure.

More Recent Developments in the Study of Masculinity

Constantinople's (1973) diagnosis presaged (just barely) a dramatic change in the way psychologists and others were trying to measure masculinity and femininity. Rather than trying to merely find ways, other than biology, to distinguish between the sexes, new measures began to focus on two major questions. First, what is the model of ideal masculinity (positive or negative), and how close is anyone to it? Second, how much do individuals of *either* sex—not just men alone—conform to the behaviors and characteristics associated with masculinity?

The Gendered Personality Traits Approach

Around the same time of Constantinople's (1973) piece, psychological researchers began to look at personality traits and the extent to which they reflected masculinity and femininity as measures of these gendered phenomena. These measures were largely based on a slightly earlier, in-depth essay by David Bakan (1966), which argued that human beings are made up of two distinct types of characteristics: those that are self-oriented and those that are other-oriented. Bakan dubs these two orientations "agency" and "communion," respectively. Agency is about independence and looking out for oneself, while communion is about looking out for others. To Bakan, in order to be psychologically healthy, any individual needs a mixture of both sets of characteristics. Psychologists were quick to take up this distinction and use it as the basis for new measures of masculinity and femininity—perhaps as Bakan intended. As he wrote: "I propose for consideration that what we have been referring to as agency is more characteristically masculine, and what we have been referring to as communion is more characteristically feminine" (1966, 110).

While both Constantinople and Bakan were talking about masculinity and femininity as multidimensional concepts, what psychologists seized upon at that time was the personality element of this agency/communion divide. In particular, psychologist Sandra Bem (1974) developed a measure of psychological masculinity, femininity, and androgyny that is still in use today.[1] Bem's measure (the Bem Sex Role Inventory, hereafter the BSRI) was based on the idea that masculinity and femininity are not simply two poles on a single, unidimensional scale (as represented in the M-F conception and critiqued by Constantinople). Rather, masculinity and femininity are more properly conceptualized as each forming their own, largely independent dimension, each of which can apply to both men and women, with androgyny reflecting the extent to which an individual of any sex rates highly on both dimensions.

Another equally important contention by Bem was that "the sex-typed person [is] someone who has internalized society's sex-typed standards of desirable behavior for men and women" (1974, 155). In other words, people could either be sex-typed, conforming to society's expectations for their sex role, or they could deviate through nonconformity. Bem's intent to measure whether or not an individual's personality traits fit society's expectations for their sex was new to the field, which had previously been focused on measuring how different men were from women. To do this, she created a battery of traits that were societally understood—according to surveys Bem conducted at the time—as either masculine or feminine. To measure masculinity and femininity among any sample, these traits are presented to survey respondents without any gendered labels, and individuals are asked to rate how well each trait describes themselves. The results measure the extent to which any individual of either sex fits the traits that society deems "appropriate" for their sex role. This was not a measure of the difference between men and women, but rather a measure of the difference between an individual's self-reported traits and society's expectations for their traits based on their sex.

Concurrent with, but separate from, Bem's development of the BSRI was development of the Personal Attributes Questionnaire (PAQ) by Spence, Helmreich, and Stapp (1974). The PAQ was designed to capture the same two basic elements within any individual that Bakan and Bem also both discuss: the tendency to be either self- or other-oriented, dubbed by Spence and colleagues as instrumental and expressive, respectively. Instrumentality is to be self-directed and self-oriented, while expressiveness is marked by compassion and understanding toward others (other-oriented). While Spence and her fellow researchers initially equated instrumentality and expressiveness with masculinity and femininity—even dubbing their scales with an M or F, for masculine and feminine—Spence later argued that their measures captured more than simply these gendered personality concepts and argued for the labels of agency and communion instead (Spence 1993). The measures are still popularly referred to, however, as masculinity and femininity (Hoffman 2001).

It is hard to overstate the importance of these developments in the measurement of masculinity and femininity: a move toward ideal—or at least traditional—types, and, more importantly, an allowance for crossover measurement of both sets of traits among both sexes, something that would become central to psychological measures that came after. Together, these developments resulted in independent masculinity and femininity measures for individuals, rather than placement on a bipolar M-F scale.[2]

This shift from existing differences between the sexes to individual differences on ideal types for each sex became, briefly, the new definition for masculinity and femininity, and the BSRI became the dominant measure for this. Whether male or female, a person was considered very masculine (or to have a "masculine personality") if they scored high on masculinity traits but low on femininity traits. In similar fashion, a highly feminine individual was someone who scored high on femininity and low on masculinity. While Bem also included "neutral items" on the original test for the scale construction, they were not intended to measure androgyny. Androgyny was instead measured as the extent to which an individual conformed to both masculine and feminine ideal types (high on both sets of traits), regardless of biological sex.

While the BSRI has been primarily used in psychological research, it has, more recently, found a home in political science as well. The most extensive, though not the first, use of the BSRI to examine potential political effects can be found in McDermott's (2016) book on femininity and masculinity in political behavior. Prior to McDermott, Rosenwasser and Dean (1989) used the BSRI in experiments to find that political offices at all levels (local, state, and national) were seen as more masculine than feminine, and that when it came to the presidency, masculine presidential tasks—like fighting terrorism and dealing with a military crisis—were rated as significantly more important to the job of president than were feminine tasks like educational and racial issues. Before this, Hershey (1977) used the BSRI to find that, among other things, feminine men were more likely to consider women for political office than were masculine or androgynous men, but women of all types were statistically equally likely to support women for political office. McDermott's (2016) use of the BSRI built on this existing research to analyze how individuals' femininity and masculinity influence their vote choice, political participation, and judgments about women's roles.

The personality traits approach (also called the sex roles approach) still has some devotees in the research world, and the measures still serve an important purpose. If one wants to know about an individual's adherence to their prescribed sex role, these measures—especially the BSRI—facilitate that. For example, the chapter in this volume by Huddy and McDonnell employs the BSRI to analyze individuals' willingness to vote for a male candidate with more feminine traits over a more masculine one. The chapter by Oxley and her colleagues also makes use of the BSRI, as well as the PAQ, to define masculine traits. At the same time, however, the traits approach came under direct scrutiny and criticism as a measure of masculinity (and femininity) in the 1980s, and, as such, was not the end of the story.

The future usefulness of personality measures such as the BSRI and PAQ remains in question. As gender dynamics and roles in society change, so too may expectations. In an attempt to foretell the future, Diekman and Eagly (2000) asked college students samples to project how gender-stereotypical men and women would be in the years 2025 and 2050 and found that, in terms of personality, people expect both women and men to become significantly more nontraditional as time passes. Women are expected to become less feminine and more masculine, and men are projected as becoming more feminine and less masculine. While this does not negate the use of gendered personality measures, it may shed new light or interpretation on them.

The Concept of "Hegemonic Masculinity"

The discipline of sociology has taken a different approach to the study and conception of masculinity. R.W. Connell's groundbreaking work on masculinity began with her 1987 book, *Gender and Power*, where she laid out her conception of "hegemonic masculinity," which revolves largely around gender relations, rather than roles or traits investigated by psychologists. According to Connell, there is no single form of masculinity, but multiple masculinities that fall into a sort of hierarchy, with the hegemonic form at the top. Hegemonic men (she initially conceptualized masculinity as purely a biologically male issue) are those who are, in any given society and at any given time, at the top of the gender hierarchy; they are the ideal type of "man" for that culture. Hegemonic masculinity "embodied the currently most honored way of being a man, it required all other men to position themselves in relation to it" (Connell and Messerschmidt 2005, 832). In addition, hegemonic masculinity required the subordination of women to men, possibly with the cooperation of women (or, at least, heterosexual women). Connell never argued that most men, or even many, fit the hegemonic model, merely that it exists as a model toward which a man can strive, or to which he can compare himself.

This formulation of hegemonic masculinity became central to the burgeoning academic field of masculinity studies (Connell and Messerschmidt 2005), especially within sociology. It was used in a wide range of areas, including men's health, ethnography, law, and even sexual politics (Segal 1993). It was not without critics, however, and Connell and Messerschmidt updated and refined the theory in 2005. In their defense of the concept, the authors concede that the hegemonic masculinity model does need to consider additional aspects, including more agency for women.

Regardless of any criticisms of the theory, however, the term "hegemonic masculinity" has become a catchall for many social scientists—sociologists, psychologists, and, very recently, political scientists—looking to measure masculinity in its most dominant or ideal form. Whether or not these usages fit with the original conception of the term is up for debate. Messerschmidt (2012) finds that some studies abide by the original gendered power imbalance formulation by Connell, while others use the term to study masculine traits in a range of ways, many of which do not conform to the original conceptualization. The reality is, however, that the term has largely been co-opted by the social sciences, for good or ill, to study masculinity in a large variety of ways. Notably, one of these ways draws on the general theory of hegemonic masculinity to develop the concept and measure of masculinity ideology, as explained in the next section.

The Bolzendahl, Winer, and Warner chapter in this volume is an example of a study that does incorporate the important aspects of hegemonic masculinity noted by both Connell (1987) and Messerschmidt (2012). The authors rely on a combination of multidimensional aspects of masculinity including a gender power dynamic, to look at different levels of masculinity (in their terms, "Rejectors," "Protectors," and "Hegemonics") and ideological leanings.

The Concept and Measure of Masculinity Ideology

The most recent developments in measuring masculinity have largely centered around the idea of a "masculinity ideology." This is distinct from the traits-based approaches of the 1970s and is intends instead to capture the extent to which an individual ascribes to the sociocultural ideal of masculinity. It changes the concept of masculinity from an inward adherence to masculine personality traits as an individual to an outward appreciation for masculine attitudes and behaviors in men generally. Put another way, it is the extent to which an individual believes that the idealized form of masculinity put forward in concepts like "hegemonic masculinity" are personally and socially desirable. Indeed, it is this outward-facing aspect that leads proponents of this concept to label it an "ideology," as opposed to a personality.

Thompson and Pleck (1986), a sociologist and a psychologist, were among the first to attempt to measure masculinity ideology. They define it as "the social norms that prescribe and proscribe what men should feel and do. It is a sensitizing concept that summarizes the general social expectations men face, and these norms can be operationally assessed by examining attitudes toward the array of prescriptions and proscriptions men encounter because of their sex" (531).

In theorizing this measure, the authors distinguish between what they call "descriptive norms" and "sociocultural norms" (531). They dismiss descriptive norms as trait-oriented approaches, those that try to distinguish among the personality traits (which they equate with stereotypes) held by men (and women)—presumably including the BSRI. They define the difference between the two types of norms as the difference between what men *are* and what they *should be*, respectively. The latter they deem as the proper measure of masculinity.

Using a college student sample, Thompson and Pleck asked males the extent to which they agreed or disagreed with fifty-seven different statements about men's expected behavior. Through factor analysis, they identified three dimensions of men's expected behaviors, which they called "status," "toughness," and "anti-femininity." The result was a twenty-six-item measure of conformity to the male role. This is not to say that the students endorsed all of these traditional norms—merely that the norms formed a reliable measure of what masculinity, or the preferred male role, could be.

In 1992, Thompson, Pleck, and Ferreira took on their first analysis of what they then dubbed "measures of masculinity ideology." By this, they meant the sociocultural role norms that men face. At that point, multiple measures of this type of masculinity ideology had been developed. Most of these measurement efforts included women in their studies as well, acknowledging that views on male role norms could influence attitudes and behavior among both men and women. A follow-up analysis by Thompson and Bennett (2015) looked at a host of more modern, time-tested measures, including the Male Role Norms Inventory (MRNI) created by Levant and colleagues (1992), which the review dubbed "one of the most commonly used measures of masculinity ideologies" (4).[3]

The MRNI was also intended to measure the masculine ideal by gauging prescriptive norms in an absolute, rather than sex-relative, sense. As with Thompson and Pleck (1986), and, to some extent, Connell (1987), masculinity became about the ideal, leaving behind previous decades of measuring masculinity as men relative to women (e.g., M-F and sex-distinguishing traits) or as a sex-role identity (e.g., BSRI). As Levant and colleagues (1992) explain it, the MRNI is more in line with the idea of gender strain, which is the extent to which one believes in the absolute masculine ideal, or "the absolute norms for the male role" (326), which can cause individual strain for those who do not conform.[4] In their earliest attempt (1992) to identify a multidimensional measure that adequately captures male role norms, the result was a three-factor structure, with one factor that held many substructures (such as anti-femininity and achievement/status), and then two more factors of aggression and self-reliance, respectively. Overall, their measure bears strong similarities to Thompson and Pleck's (1986) original measure, although the MRNI has distinct and meaningful subfactors and has largely eclipsed Thompson and Pleck's measure in applied research.

Levant continued to develop the MRNI over time, analyzing not only the quality of the measure and its application but also shorter forms of the measure, and importantly, its applicability to women and invariance across the sexes. An important piece in this research arrived in 2019, when McDermott, Levant, and colleagues released the MRNI Very Brief (MRNI-VB) measure (2019) and tested that it had acceptable levels of invariance across men and women (2020), measuring "traditional masculinity ideology" (sometimes referred to as TMI) well among both sexes while correlating with important concepts like sexism and rape myth.

Multiple authors in this volume use some type of masculinity ideology measure in their analyses. For example, Vescio and Schermerhorn use the original Thompson and Pleck (1986) measure of masculinity ideology in their chapter analyzing possible connections between masculinity and other traits, like social dominance orientation and authoritarianism.

The Concept and Measure of "Toxic Masculinity"

Another modern conceptual twist in measuring masculinity based on male role norms is the idea of toxic masculinity. The idea along with debates surrounding its definition and legitimacy have been around since at least the 1970s, coinciding with feminism and the rise of the men's empowerment (mythopoetic) movement (de Boise 2019). It was not until the late 2010s, however, that the term caught on—especially in America—and became part of the political lexicon. According to a ProQuest US Newstream search for newspaper references to the term "toxic masculinity" and the stem "politic," the first use was in 1999, with only three uses between that date and 2015. From 2016 to October 2023, the term was used in a political context in 920 newspaper articles. The rise of Donald Trump and his specific presentation of masculinity—including his language about grabbing women—spoke to many as toxic. The #MeToo movement also boosted the popularity of the term.

While social scientists—primarily sociologists and psychologists—had, by 2016, been debating the term and its meaning for decades, measurement was elusive. In 2019, Parent, Gobble, and Rochlen were among the first to use the term in a quantitative analysis: as an element that could influence individual behavior and attitudes—namely, depression. The researchers' definition was that toxic masculinity was a "subset" of hegemonic masculinity and was specifically: "characterized by a drive to dominate and by endorsement of misogynistic and homophobic views" (2019, 278). Their definition stemmed from earlier work by Parent and Moradi (2011), analyzing structure of the Conformity to Masculine Norms Inventory (CMNI). Originally formulated by Mahalik and colleagues (2000) and Ludlow and Mahalik (2001), the CMNI was a measure aimed at capturing *adherence*, or conformity, to the elements of the male role norms. This focus on conformity to role norms differs from both the BSRI's focus on personality traits and the MRNI's focus on endorsement of certain masculine behaviors.[5]

In their analysis of the validity of the full CMNI structure, Parent and Moradi (2011) find low correlations among many of the subscales of the measure, and between some of the subscales and the overall measure, resulting in questions of validity. Notably, they find that the strongest correlations between the subscales and the overall measure are for the Power over Women subscale, the Heterosexual Presentation subscale, and the Winning subscale. As they note, the connection of these three items is consistent with feminist theory on some of the key dangers of masculinity. It is these three items that Parent and Moradi point to as comprising toxic masculinity (2011).

There is very limited scholarly work, to date, on toxic masculinity in American politics. In an international study, Daddow and Hertner (2019) use a measure to examine the toxic masculinity of two European political parties that resembles Parent and Moradi's (2011) emphasis on sexism, heterosexism, and winning. And, in this volume, Melissa Deckman creates a toxic masculinity scale for Gen Z men and women that addresses the aspect of conformity but differs in that it asks survey respondents about whether they believe there are negative consequences that stem from expecting men to conform to traditional masculinity.

Masculine Self-Identity and Centrality

One element common to all of the measures of masculinity discussed previously in this section is that each depends on the *researchers'* definitions of what "masculine" means (based on societal stereotypes). But this leaves out a potentially important aspect of a person's gender: their own gendered sense of self. For example, a person with personality traits that happen to produce a low masculinity score on the BSRI may nevertheless consider themselves to be very masculine and feel it is an important part of their identity.[6]

The distinction between objective and subjective identity is clearly important (see Huddy 2013). In political science—or, more precisely, political psychology—it is well established that a person's self-identity is often a better predictor of their political attitudes and behavior than is their objective group membership. Consider partisanship, for example. The best predictor of how someone will vote in an upcoming election is not the party they last voted for nor the party with which they are officially registered; rather, the best vote predictor is a person's *self-identification* with a party (Campbell et al. 1960).

The literature highlights two key aspects of a person's gendered sense of self as it applies to the study of masculinity. The first aspect is the degree to which one consciously identifies as being masculine; we refer to this as "masculine self-identity." The second aspect is the degree to which being masculine is important to one's sense of self. We refer to this as "masculine centrality." We discuss each of these in turn.

Sociologists Magliozzi, Saperstein, and Westbrook (2016) were among the first scholars to note that while most surveys allow respondents to self-identify their biological sex (e.g., male, female) they historically have not allowed respondents to explicitly self-identify their degree of masculinity or femininity. To correct this, they propose that survey researchers ask all respondents to rate themselves on a seven-point masculinity scale (0 = not at all; 6 = very) as well as a separate femininity scale. As with other measures of masculinity, their findings demonstrate significant heterogeneity within each sex. In their study, only 36 percent of women rated themselves as "not at all" masculine, and only 28 percent of men rated themselves as "very" masculine. In political science, Cassino and Bessen-Cassino (2021) employ similar measures. Other works in this field ask respondents to place themselves on a single, bipolar masculinity-to-femininity scale (e.g., Bittner and Goodyear-Grant 2017; Cassino 2020). However, the authors of these latter pieces acknowledge that using a bipolar measure could be problematic, especially given past findings that gender is multidimensional, as discussed previously (e.g., Constantinople 1973).

Even among a group of individuals who all see themselves as masculine, it is possible that, for some, this categorization is not incorporated into their sense of who they are as a person, while for others it feels deeply important, or central. An analogous situation might be that among some people who self-identify as Catholic, this designation carries no emotional attachment, while for others it is very important. This concept of identity centrality—measured by the self-rated importance of that identity—has a long history in the field of psychology (Stryker and Serpe 1994).

In gender studies, one version of identity centrality is the degree to which men think "being a man" is important to them, and women think "being a woman" is important to them (e.g., Cassino and Bessen-Cassino 2020; Deaux and LaFrance 1998; Cameron 2001; Tate, Bettergarcia, and Brent 2015). Though they may not employ this terminology, we would argue that such studies are essentially measuring *sex* centrality:

the importance of one's grouping as a man or woman. But, in theory, there exists another version which we would call *gender* centrality: the importance to one's sense of self of "being masculine" or "being feminine." Although our review of the literature did not uncover any empirical research using this particular version, we believe that such a measure is consistent with the broader literature on centrality and deserves further investigation by gender scholars.

This gendered self-identity approach appears in this volume in chapters by Bittner and Goodyear-Grant, and Cassino and Cuevas-Molina. The former looks at gendered identity—specifically masculinity—and the influences it has on political attitudes between Americans and Canadians, while the latter analyzes the impact of masculine/feminine self-identity—along with political efficacy, and racial and ethnic identity—among men in Newark, New Jersey.

A Side Note: Gendered Physical Attributes and Masculinity

In addition to behaviors and beliefs associated with masculinity, scholars have also studied physical characteristics that society associates with masculinity, albeit not in depth, to date. Physical attributes commonly associated with masculinity include aspects of bone structure (big, strong jaw and brow), facial expression (anger, disgust; see, e.g., Hess et al. 2009), and vocal timbre (low pitch). This attention to physical features is consistent with Ritter's (2007) contention that gender as a social categorization has a dimorphic core.

In political science, the focus of most of these studies revolves around the physical characteristics of a politician: how citizens may use this information to make behavioral or policy inferences about the politician and how it affects the politician's electability. For example, Klofstad, Anderson, and Nowicki (2015) find that voters prefer leaders with lower-pitched voices because they are perceived as being stronger and more competent, possessing greater physical prowess, and having higher integrity. Carpinella and her colleagues (2016) find that more masculine facial features increase support for male Democratic candidates and decrease support for male Republican candidates. Other research shows that a preference for candidates with masculine faces is affected by environmental context, increasing in the context of war or other conflict, and decreasing in times of peace (e.g., Spisak et al. 2012). Although not yet commonly used in political science research, scholars in other fields, such as biology, have developed quantitative measures of masculine (dimorphic) facial features, such as facial width-to-height ratio (for a critique and discussion, see, e.g., Lefevre et al. 2012) that can help to inform such research.

This volume does not contain a chapter dedicated to the topic of such physical manifestations of masculinity in politics as its focus is solely on respondents' personalities and attitudes. Nevertheless, we believe that this is an important area of research in gendered politics and look forward to further developments.

Quantitative Analysis of Masculinity Measures

With so many different conceptions of masculinity, an important question arises about the relative overlap versus distinctiveness of their corresponding measures. Specifically: Are the standard measures used to capture the four basic concepts discussed above—masculine personality, masculinity ideology, toxic masculinity, and masculine gendered identity—actually measuring different concepts, or are they merely slight variations on one central theme?

In this section, we analyze measures of these four basic concepts using two original national surveys of Americans. The first was conducted March 15–26, 2021 among a representative sample of 805 adult Americans nationally, and the second was fielded June 4–9, 2021 among a representative sample of 745 white, non-Hispanic adults nationwide. Both surveys contain men and women. Each was conducted using Qualtrics' panel of web survey vendors. Opt-in panels such as this are not optimal for survey methodological purity, but they have been shown to accurately measure relationships between variables (Vavreck and Rivers 2008) and even approximate the results of random sample surveys (Walter et al. 2019).

This analysis will proceed in three parts. First, we will analyze any overlap, or shared variance, among the four main measures of masculinity cited above to determine if each measure is capturing a separate construct. We will then proceed to analyze intersectionality within the measures. That is, we will look at how these measures of masculinity and their relationships to one another are affected by sex. Finally we will analyze the relationship, if any, these measures have with race and ethnicity.

Relationships among Masculinity Measures

As a first simple step, we need to describe the specific measurement strategy we are using to represent each of these four concepts. They are relatively straightforward, relying on the traditional strategies found in the literature we have discussed.

To measure masculine personality traits, we use the BSRI-M short form masculinity scale (Bem 1981), consisting of ten masculine traits. To measure masculinity ideology, we use the MRNI-VB scale developed by McDermott, Levant, and colleagues (2019). As a toxic masculinity measure, we follow the guidance of Parent and Moradi (2011) and use the nine best-fitting items of the CMNI representing winning, hetero-sexism, and power over women (based on a CMNI analysis by Levant and colleagues, 2020). This results in a measure that is only a portion of the CMNI, the portion that Parent and Moradi point to as toxic.

To represent masculine self-identity and centrality, we draw on this work to develop three alternative measures. The first measure captures masculine self-identity using the simple question asked by Cassino and Besen-Cassino (2020) of how masculine one considers oneself—though, unlike these authors (and similar to Magliozzi, Saperstein, and Westbrook 2016), we ask it of men and women alike, given past findings that both men and women can see themselves as having masculine elements (e.g., Magliozzi, Saperstein, and Westbrook 2016). Second, as one measure of centrality, we ask how important it is to the respondent that "others" see them as masculine. Third, we create an additional measure of centrality, building off a question asking respondents how important their "gendered identity (masculine/feminine)" is to them as a person. Using other questions in the survey, we are able to recode this original question into a pseudomeasure of how important *masculine* (not feminine) identity is to them. This measure's constructions starts by determining whether the respondent prefers to be seen as masculine or as feminine.[7] Then, for those who prefer being seen as masculine, we use their self-placement on the *gendered* identity self-importance question as a proxy measure of how important their (preferred) *masculine* identity is to them. For those who prefer to be seen as feminine, we recode their responses to the original gendered identity self-importance question all to zero (to indicate that a masculine identity is not important to them). After this recoding, the combined measure provides a rough indicator, for all respondents, of how important (or central) their masculine identity is to them personally, if they have one.

All the variables analyzed are scaled to range from 0 to 1, where 0 is least masculine (or not at all masculine) and those coded 1 are the most masculine possible (in terms of each measure) individuals. The elements that make up the various indices were randomly ordered for each respondent. Wording for all survey questions is available in this volume's online appendix. Not every variable is consistently available for analysis in both survey datasets. The masculine personality and masculinity ideology variables, along with the masculine importance version of the masculine identity variable, are included in both surveys. Toxic masculinity is included only in the second survey, and the self-identity version of masculine identity (and thereby the interactive version) are only in the first survey. Table 1.1 summarizes the mapping of measures to concepts and our surveys.

TABLE 1.1: Concepts and measures

Concept	Summary description	Measure (# of items)†	Survey
Masculine personality	Degree to which one holds personality traits that society has traditionally expected males to hold	BSRI-M, Short Form (10)	1, 2
Masculinity ideology	Degree to which one believes that, in general, male attitudes and behaviors should conform to traditional norms	MRNI–VB (5)	1, 2
Toxic masculinity	Degree to which one's own attitudes conform to traditional expectations of masculinity re: winning, heterosexism, and power over women	Toxic subset of CMNI (9)	2
Masculine identity	Degree to which one (a) self-identifies as masculine; (b) believes it is important that others see them as masculine; (c) considers masculine group identity to be important to them	MI—self (a) (1) MI—imp (b) (1) MI—group ID (c) (1)*	(a) 1 (b) 1, 2 (c) 1, 2

†For brief item descriptions, see table 1.4. *This measure is comprised of multiple items but is interactive, not an index.

TABLE 1.2: Masculinity correlation matrix for survey 1

	MRNI-VB	MI-self	MI-imp	MI-group ID	Mean	S.D.	Index α
BSRI-M	0.30*	0.26*	0.29*	0.17*	0.62	0.17	0.83
MRNI-VB		0.31*	0.49*	0.27*	0.39	0.26	0.83
MI-self			0.69*	0.53*	0.45	0.33	—
MI-imp				0.63*	0.31	0.35	—
MI-group ID				—	0.26	0.38	—

* p ≤ .05 (two-tailed); N = 805

TABLE 1.3: Masculinity correlation matrix for survey 2

	MRNI-VB	Toxic	MI-imp	MI-group ID	Mean	S.D.	Index α
BSRI-M	0.27*	0.31*	0.28*	0.09*	0.61	0.17	0.86
MRNI-VB		0.73*	0.49*	0.24*	0.39	0.27	0.88
Toxic			0.48*	0.24*	0.37	0.25	0.91
MI-imp				0.55*	0.41	0.31	—
MI-group ID				—	0.21	0.35	—

* p ≤ .05 (two-tailed); N = 745 (white, non-Hispanic only)

As a first look at the data, tables 1.2 and 1.3 present correlations among the variables present in each survey. The right side of the tables also report the means and standard deviations for each variable, and the Cronbach's alphas for variables that are indices built from multiple items (to measure their internal consistency).

As both tables demonstrate, all the masculinity measures are significantly related to one another. In fact, the sizes of the correlations are surprisingly consistent between the two surveys, given the different samples (all Americans and non-Hispanic white Americans, respectively) and time frames. In both, the BSRI and the MRNI are correlated somewhat, but not very strongly (r ≤ .30). The BSRI continues this moderate relationship with each of the masculine identity measures. The MRNI and self-rated masculinity correlation (table 1.2 only), and its correlations with the MI-group ID (both tables) are also at this moderate level. The correlations between the MRNI and masculinity importance are much stronger, however, hovering just below .50. Toxic masculinity, which only appears in survey 2, is very strongly correlated with the MRNI (.73), and moderately correlated with importance of masculine identity (.48)—just as the MRNI is. It is no surprise to see the toxic measure correlating highly with, and displaying similar patterns to, the MRNI in these data, because the literature has previously found that the full CMNI battery—from which toxic masculinity is taken here—and the MRNI also correlate highly, despite their somewhat different measurement goals (Levant et al. 2009; see also note 4 above).

The conclusions we can draw from these simple correlations are largely in line with what we might have expected from the concepts we have discussed. Notably, the BSRI is mostly its own entity, with low shared variance with each of the other measures. This is understandable since it is the only measure that captures an individual's inherent masculine traits. In contrast, the MRNI and toxic measures are the most highly correlated, which may reflect the fact that both measures are about *attitudes* regarding male or masculine norms. Masculine identity importance displays a moderate relationship with both MRNI and toxicity. The moderate level of overlap among the MRNI, toxic masculinity and the MI variables is understandable as identity may be more inward looking than role attitudes. The importance variable's stronger correlations with these measures likely reflects that it is an outward, performative attitude—how individuals would like others to see them, which fits with the MRNI's role strain logic.

To further analyze the measures, we next conduct a factor analysis on all the components of the indices and each of the stand-alone variables to determine whether they truly are measuring distinct underlying elements, or whether they are mostly capturing one well of basic masculinity.[8] Table 1.4 contains the results of the factor analysis for survey 2. We present the results from survey 2 here in order to include the toxicity measure (the factor analysis for survey 1 is presented in table A1.1 in the online appendix). For visual clarity, all tables display only the primary factor loading for each item (unless the item loads equally onto two factors).

The analysis results in a five-factor solution that gives us important validation for the differences between the measures tested. The BSRI

TABLE 1.4: Factor analysis of masculinity components for survey 2

	Variable	Factor				
		1	2	3	4	5
BSRI-M	Leadership ability		0.74			
	Aggressive	0.61				
	Dominant	0.58				
	Willing to take a stand		0.80			
	Defends own beliefs		0.71			
	Willing to take risks		0.63			
	Forceful	0.57				
	Strong personality		0.78			
	Assertive		0.69			
	Independent		0.70			
MRNI-VB	Men should not be too quick to tell others that they care about them			0.70		
	I think a young man should try to be physically tough, even if he's not big			0.76		
	A man should always be the boss			0.69		
	Boys should prefer to play with trucks rather than dolls			0.75		
	Men should watch football games instead of soap operas			0.76		
Toxic (partial CMNI)	For me, the best feeling in the world comes from winning	0.62				
	I will do anything to win	0.75				
	In general, I must get my way	0.78				
	It would be awful if people thought I was gay				0.81	
	I would get angry if people thought I was gay				0.84	
	I would be furious if someone thought I was gay				0.80	
	I love it when men are in charge of women	0.58				
	The women in my life should obey me	0.70				
	Things tend to be better when men are in charge	0.51				
MI	Importance					0.69
	Group ID					0.91

largely loads onto one factor (no. 2)—a factor that no items from any other measure load onto. Similarly, the elements of the MRNI form their own factor (no. 3). And, despite only having three variables included, self-identity loads neatly onto its own factor (no. 5). These results provide important confirmation for the idea that these measures are each capturing largely unique concepts. There are, however, some surprising findings as well. First, not all the BSRI elements load solely onto one factor, as they have done in the past (e.g., McDermott 2016). Three of the measures within the index—aggressive, dominant, and forceful—are in a different factor. Notably, they load onto the same factor (no. 1) as six of the nine toxic masculinity elements, the winning elements and the power over women elements. Clearly, over time, the stronger, more forceful masculine traits of the BSRI have come to be considered similar to toxicity. The toxic measure itself does not load onto a single factor either. The heterosexism elements all load onto their own factor (no. 4), calling into question whether winning, power over women, and heterosexism form a reliable measure of toxic masculinity.

The result of this analysis is an underlying structure with five groups: basic masculine traits centered around self-confidence; support for masculine role norms; aggressive or otherwise toxic masculine traits; masculine identity; and heterosexism. The analysis also raises questions about the conceptual and statistical validity of the BSRI in its traditional form, and our definition (from Parent and Moradi, 2011) of "toxic masculinity." There is a good chance that the combination of the #MeToo movement, the broad acceptance of gay marriage, and the presidency of Donald Trump have impacted people's own conceptions of the traits and elements involved. As noted, the term exploded onto the political scene just around 2016 and beyond, after much of the research discussed in the previous section was already complete. Certainly, further, future analysis of changes in masculinity and its multiple concepts is warranted.

As we would expect from the extensive research done on these various masculinity measures, they do measure distinct concepts, even though they are also correlated in a logical way. At the same time, we should also keep in mind that the factor analyses indicate some unexpected differences in underlying structure of some of the measures—namely, the BSRI and the toxic masculinity measure—which raise questions about the *validity* of these measures. While tables 1.2 and 1.3 show high levels of measure reliability (alphas), it appears that both the BSRI-M and the toxic masculinity measure are each multidimensional, contrary to expectations from existing research. Additionally, it is somewhat unclear exactly what the masculine identity measures are capturing. The purpose of this chapter is not to reinvent the wheel. Nevertheless, future research into these specific concepts and their measures should consider their potential multidimensionality. At this point, we move on to analyzing these measures and their validity among subgroups that are important in gender analysis.

Sex and Masculinity Measures

Biological sex presents, naturally, the first and most important subgroup for analysis when it comes to gendered measurements. Since sex has been conflated with gender for so long, analyzing the extent to which these measures capture elements within both women and men is essential. The existing literature has demonstrated that both the BSRI and the MRNI are reliable and valid measures among both sexes. While the literature has not examined this issue as closely for measures of masculine identity, there is good reason to believe that women and men can both see themselves as masculine in a self-identification question. While we would not expect women to place themselves as high as men do, or to place the same importance on being seen as masculine, there is no reason the measure should not be valid among both women and men.

Toxic masculinity, however, is inherently different from these other three measures. Because the measure is taken from the CMNI, which is meant to measure conformity to masculine norms, it does not necessarily readily apply to women, despite our (and the literature's) contention that masculinity measures are important among all sexes. For example, while a woman might rate herself highly on "wanting to win," we would not expect the same woman to rate herself highly on the "believing men should be superior to women" item. In fact, we might logically expect these two items to correlate negatively for a woman. As a result, we will focus primarily on the measures in survey 1 when it comes to sex differences. Table 1.5 contains the correlation matrix for women and men separately on the BSRI, MRNI-VB, and the masculine identity measures.

TABLE 1.5: Masculinity correlation matrix for survey 1, by sex of respondent

Women	MRNI-VB	MI-self	MI-imp	MI-group ID	Mean	S.D.	Index α
BSRI-M	0.23*	0.17*	0.22*	0.06	0.60	0.17	0.83
MRNI-VB		0.10*	0.37*	0.19*	0.32	0.26	0.83
MI-self			0.56*	0.24*	0.25	0.26	—
MI-imp				0.41*	0.14	0.26	—
MI-group ID				—	0.04	0.16	—
Men							
BSRI-M	0.33*	0.28*	0.28*	0.13*	0.65[a]	0.17	0.84
MRNI-VB		0.31*	0.49*	0.13*	0.46[a]	0.25	0.80
MI-self			0.51*	0.26*	0.68[b]	0.24	
MI-imp				0.48*	0.52[b]	0.33	
MI-group ID				—	0.49[b]	0.40	

* p ≤ . 05 (two-tailed) correlation; [a] means t-test between sexes; [b] crosstab γ between sexes. N = 805

The correlations of the masculinity measures among women only and those among men only display patterns that are largely consistent with each other and in comparison to the overall sample (table 1.2). In all groups, the BSRI generally has the weakest correlations with all other measures, whereas the MRNI has relatively strong correlations with masculine identity importance. The masculine identity measures are all consistently correlated with each other, although at different levels of strength (the group ID measure and the self-rating have the least variance in common). That said, the correlations are weaker among women than they are among men, across the board. Additionally, and as expected, the column for means shows that women score significantly lower on all of the measures than do men, although on the BSRI they come substantively close. This latter observation is consistent with recent findings elsewhere in the literature (e.g., Donnelly and Twenge, 2017).

Similarly, a factor analysis for survey 1 conducted separately for women and men provides the same four-factor solution within each sex as found in the main analysis of survey 1 (full results presented in the appendix, table A1.3). The single difference between women and men is that for men, the BSRI trait of assertive loads onto both BSRI-based factors (the basic and the toxic) rather than just the more toxic one. Taken together, these results emphasize the consistency in the applicability of the concepts and measurements of masculinity across both sexes. Although women score significantly lower on these measures than men in absolute terms, the same underlying structural distinctions are visible among women as among men. Women are generally less masculine than men, but their masculinity seems to be made up of the same components.

Race, Ethnicity, and Masculinity Measures

Scholars frequently emphasize that masculinity is culturally dependent (Kimmel and Messner 1992). While research tends to generalize masculinity to the norms that hold among white males, this does not mean these norms hold true for individuals of differing cultures—even differing cultures within the United States. This is an especially open question when it comes to racial culture. Research into masculinity has long acknowledged the different context in which Black men in America are raised, and how that context can impact their perceptions and performance of masculinity. As William Oliver (1989) explains: "Due to their membership in a racial group that has been systematically denied equal access to political and economic power, as well as educational and employment opportunities, a substantial number of Black males lack the skills and resources that are necessary to successfully enact the traditional male role" (20).

Given this stark reality, there is always a chance that, in America, Black men and other men of color who have experienced a different male culture and different contexts, may not be accurately represented or measured by the standard masculinity measures covered in this chapter. The same could also be said of women of color. While we do not have the resources to conduct extensive testing of culture-specific measures, which others have done (for a recent example, see Unnever and Chouhy 2021), what we can do is examine the extent to which the measures in our survey are answered by individuals of color in similar ways to whites.

For this analysis we will again be using survey 1 as it is the only one of our two surveys that contains a representative sample of all races. While our sample sizes are small (103 US residents who are Black, and 143 who are Latino/a/x, we still think that an exploratory analysis is worthwhile.[9] If the results find that none of these measures follow consistent correlational or factorial structure patterns among individuals of color compared to whites, then the broader conclusion about these measures may need to be considered as only valid among whites. Certainly, it is not inconceivable that we might find differences. After all, existing studies have found that Blacks tend to score higher on some masculinity measures, specifically the BSRI-M (McDermott 2016, though not significantly), and the MRNI (Levant, Majors, and Kelley 1998).

Because we are replicating our analysis for three different racial and ethnic subgroups, our detailed tables are presented in the appendix (tables A1.4-A1.6 and A1.7-A1.9). Here, we will summarize our comparison of the correlation patterns and the factor structures across all three groups. We focus first on the correlations. One difference across the three groups is the average magnitude of the correlations. For whites, the sizes of the correlations are slightly larger than their respective counterparts in the full sample in table 1.2. For Blacks and for Latino/as, the magnitudes are a bit smaller than among their counterparts in table 1.2, and among whites. In a few cases, they do not reach statistical significance, but this could also be due in part to the smaller number of cases. Despite these important differences in magnitudes, the *pattern* of the correlations is highly similar across all three groups. For the most part, just as in table 1.2, with each of the three groups BSRI-M has the lowest correlations with the other variables, MRNI correlates at slightly higher levels with the MI measures, and the SI measures are, for the most part, correlated strongly with each other. The only minor exception to this pattern is that among Blacks, the BSRI correlates with the MI-group ID measure at the same level as the MRNI. Overall, while most of these measures correlate more strongly to each other among whites, the ranking of which measures correlate more highly than others is strikingly similar across all three racial and ethnic groups.

The factor analysis also displays substantial commonality across these groups. Specifically, it produces the same four-factor model for whites, Blacks, and Latino/as it did for the overall sample in survey 1, with two small exceptions. First, among whites the BSRI assertive trait loads onto the more aggressive BSRI measures (as it did among men). For both Blacks and Latinos assertiveness remains among the less toxic of the

BSRI measures. In another twist, for Black respondents the BSRI element of "willing to take risks" fits into the more toxic factor of BSRI elements that we saw in the full-sample analysis (factor 1 in table 1.1). This could well be reflective of the unfortunate position into which Blacks are put in America, and as a result, taking risks may be a more dangerous or toxic proposition than it is for whites and Latino/as. Overall, however, the similarity among the models is again striking, and it is supportive of the idea that, at least on these measures, all three racial/ethnic groups answer the questions in a similarly structured way.

Discussion and Conclusion

The goal of this volume is to establish how and why masculinity, in its various forms, is important to both the practice and study of American politics. Americans have a long history of preferring masculine characteristics in their leaders and socializing their children into a masculine view of politics, as the analyses in the remainder of this part of the volume demonstrate. Additionally, masculinity influences a wide array of individual political beliefs, attitudes, and behavior, as the chapters in part 2 show. These analyses of the politics of masculinity are not merely academic exercises—they matter in the real world. In a society where masculinity permeates both the realm of elections and the realm of governance, understanding these relationships is indispensable to understanding politics itself.

Given the importance of masculinity in American politics, the goal of this specific chapter has been to help make sense of and give order to some of the concepts and measures of masculinity that are used more frequently. In addition, it hopefully serves as an introduction to the multiple methods and measures used by the contributors to this volume. We find that while there is some overlap among different measures, there are also distinct, underlying differences. Specifically, the MRNI (masculinity ideology), most of the BSRI traits, and the measures of gendered identity each form their own factor, largely independent from (although somewhat correlated with) one another. The concept of toxic masculinity, as formulated in the existing literature, proves the most problematic, as heterosexism, believed to be a part of toxicity clearly is its own factor. The rest of this volume and the analyses presented will help bring to light the ways in which these measures matter substantively in the study and practice of American politics.

NOTES

1 Spence, Helmreich, and Stapp (1974) adopted a similar approach of measuring personality traits, although their measure is less reliable on measurement grounds (for a summary, see McDermott 2016, 41–44).

2 Although it should be noted that the original PAQ included a bipolar M-F scale in addition to its separate M (masculine) and F (feminine) scales. We choose to use the BSRI rather than the PAQ in this chapter for other methodological reasons noted by McDermott (2016, 41–44).

3 It was also at this point that Thompson and Bennett first used the term "hegemonic masculinities" to describe masculine ideology. It must be noted, however, that the measures still largely did not include Connell and Messerschmidt's (2005) central ideas of male domination over women, or of multiple masculinities, making the label one that Connell and Messerschmidt likely would have disputed.

4 The original concept behind the role strain model comes from Pleck (1981). He later (1995) argued for the correlate of masculinity ideology as part of this model.

5 We chose not to discuss the CMNI in depth in this chapter both because it has been shown to correlate highly, 0.66, with the MRNI (Levant et al., 2009), and its usage is not as widespread as traditional masculine ideology (TMI) measures. Additionally, there are concerns about its conceptual ability to capture women's views, as discussed in the section on toxic masculinity below.

6 The point here is not merely that a person's gendered identity can include additional facets beyond their personality traits (on the multifaceted nature of gender identity, see Wood and Eagly 2009). Rather, the point is whether an individual gets to say for themselves whether and how much the term "masculine" (or "feminine") applies to them.

7 We ascertain this relative preference using two separate questions in the same survey. Specifically, we ask respondents how important it is that others see them as masculine, and how important it is that others see them as feminine. Respondents who rate "masculine" with higher importance than they rate "feminine" are coded as "preferring to be seen as masculine."

8 We used exploratory factor analysis with varimax rotation. We chose not to use confirmatory factor analysis, as we did not want to limit the resulting options, even with assumptions from the existing literature in mind. We did not impose a minimum factor loading for inclusion. While some of the primary loadings in our models (here and in the appendix) might be small by some standards (as low as 0.4), all h^2 levels are well above acceptable.

9 Race and ethnicity were measured with a single question in our survey ("Do you consider yourself primarily as . . ."), making these categories mutually exclusive.

2

Masculinity and Children's Political Socialization

ZOE M. OXLEY, JILL S. GREENLEE, MIRYA R. HOLMAN,
ANGELA L. BOS, AND J. CELESTE LAY

A masculine ethos permeates US politics. National political institutions—most notably, the presidency—are gendered such that masculine traits and ways of acting are clearly valued over feminine ones (Duerst-Lahti and Kelly 1996). Masculinity is entrenched in elections, from campaign strategy and recruitment (Dittmar 2015; Oliver and Conroy 2020) to media coverage (Conroy 2015; Duerst-Lahti and Oakley 2018) to gender stereotyping of the Democratic and Republican parties (Winter 2010). Voters have long preferred masculine over feminine characteristics when evaluating candidates for political office (Holman, Merolla, and Zechmeister 2016; Huddy and Terkildsen 1993b; Schneider and Bos 2014), while beliefs that the United States should be a more masculine nation contributed to Donald Trump's election in 2016 (Deckman and Cassese 2021).

Through the processes of political socialization, children are exposed to images and information that depict politics as a masculine domain and political leaders as holding primarily masculine traits (Lay et al. 2021; Schocker and Woyshner 2013). Through the process of gender socialization, children internalize messages that gender-matched traits are those that are most desirable to hold. Together, in a process we call "gendered political socialization," the perception that political leaders are predominantly male and commonly have masculine traits coupled with the belief that girls should not have masculine traits, makes politics seem to be an unwelcoming domain for girls (Bos et al. 2022). These socialization processes contribute to girls' lower levels of political interest and ambition as compared to boys.

In this chapter, we expand upon our prior work regarding how gender shapes children's perceptions of the political world (Bos et al. 2022).

Specifically, we conduct a more nuanced content analysis of children's drawings of political leaders to explore how those drawings express masculinity and which masculine traits dominate children's perceptions of political leadership. Our coding scheme is derived from three different gendered trait categorization scales: 1) the masculine, feminine, and nontyped personality traits in Sandra Bem's (1974) Sex Role Inventory, or BSRI; 2) communal and agentic traits examined in studies of gendered leadership stereotypes, and 3) the dominance and technical expertise masculinities of R. W. Connell's (2005) theory of hegemonic masculinity. We explore variation in the types of masculinities that appear in the children's drawings. We also examine how descriptions of political leaders' masculine traits vary across characteristics of the children (sex, race, and age) as well as the leaders whom they drew (sex, race, and level of office held). We conclude by analyzing the relationship between children's depictions of masculinity and their interest in politics.

Gendered Traits

Some of the earliest work in political science on gendered traits examined how women in politics navigated sex stereotypes that led voters to value masculine traits in political leaders while demanding that women embody feminine traits (Kahn 1996). More recently, the exploration of how masculine and feminine traits operate has shifted to examine male candidates as well (Banwart and Winfrey 2013; Conroy 2015; Dittmar 2015) and to understand how the gendered personalities of voters shape their political choices (McDermott 2016). Across all this scholarship, sex stereotypes and gendered traits are central concepts.

Sex stereotypes are generalized beliefs about the strengths, abilities, and behaviors of women and men (Diekman and Eagly 2000). Within the political realm, sex stereotypes lead to associations that women are more liberal than men (Koch 2000; Rosenwasser and Seale 1988), that women and men have different areas of policy expertise (Huddy and Terkildsen 1993a; Lawless 2004), and that women and men possess different traits (Alexander and Andersen 1993; Sanbonmatsu 2002). Gendered traits are traits that are associated with femininity and masculinity and are often tied to sex stereotypes, but this relationship has weakened over time, as there is greater overlap among the roles that men and women take on in society (Diekman and Eagly 2000; McDermott 2016). Furthermore, a recent study suggests increased alignment of stereotypes of women politicians with the traits desired in political leaders (van der Pas, Aaldering, and Bos 2023).

Over the years, scholarship has featured different measures for gendered traits. Specifically, the traits highlighted in scholars' conceptions of masculinity and femininity vary. In this chapter, we use three different measures of gendered traits—the Bem Sex Role Inventory, agentic and communal traits, and Connell's concept of hegemonic masculinity—to evaluate how children portray masculinity in their descriptions of political leaders. Below is a brief discussion of each of these approaches.

Sandra Bem's Sex Role Inventory

The Bem Sex Role Inventory conceptualizes masculinity and femininity as two independent personality dimensions, any individual (regardless of sex) can score high or low on the dimensions (Bem 1974, 1978). As discussed more thoroughly in chapter 1 of this volume, the inventory classifies traits as either more desirable for a man (masculine, such as assertive and individualistic); a woman (feminine, such as yielding or compassionate); or neither (nontyped, such as conscientious or adaptable).[1] The traits in each category reflect societal-wide expectations regarding which characteristics men and women should possess.

While studies reexamining the validity of the Bem inventory have produced mixed results (Auster and Ohm 2000; Donnelly and Twenge 2017; Holt and Ellis 1998), scholars continue to employ it in work that explores the political relevance of gendered personality traits (McDermott 2016) as well as the ways in which gender roles and traits are communicated to children. For example, Diekman and Murnen (2004) examine gendered personality traits in children's literature by employing Bem's sex roles inventory to evaluate the presence of ten masculine personality and ten feminine personality traits. Evans and Davies (2000) used a similar approach in their analysis of elementary school textbooks. We use the original, long Bem inventory to capture how children express gendered personality traits in the political leaders that they draw.

Agentic and Communal Traits

Which personality traits are connected to political leadership? Early research argued that voters value competence (Funk 1996, 1997; Kinder 1986) and warmth (Markus 1982) as traits in would-be leaders (Lausten and Bor 2017). These two traits not only map neatly onto sex stereotypes (Huddy and Terkilsen 1993a), but also serve as examples from a broader set of gendered traits. Specifically, psychologists and political scientists who study leadership have categorized a large number of traits as either male- (agentic) or female- (communal) typical (see Schneider and Bos 2014). Further work has demonstrated that leadership roles are typically associated with agentic traits across a variety of occupations (Koenig et al. 2011), including politics (Bauer 2020; Holman, Merolla and Zechmeister 2022; Schneider and Bos 2014).

In a comprehensive analysis, Schneider and Bos (2014) identify over one hundred traits that have been used by scholars studying gender and leader stereotypes (Diekman and Eagly 2000; Eagly and Karau 2002; Funk 1999; Heilman et al. 1995; Huddy and Terkildsen 1993a; Kinder 1986) and document the overlap between stereotypes of men and stereotypes of male politicians.[2] We adapt the list created by Schneider and Bos (2014) to capture a full array of agentic and communal traits that emerge from work on sex stereotypes, leadership stereotypes, and gendered leadership stereotypes.

R. W. Connell's Hegemonic Masculinity

The concept of hegemonic masculinity, as articulated by R. W. Connell and summarized in chapter 1, is rooted in sociological analyses of gender and power. It is "the masculinity that occupies the hegemonic position in a given pattern of gender relations, a position always contestable" (Connell 2005, 76). What makes a specific mode of masculinity hegemonic is the societal understanding of it as superior over other masculinities and over femininity. While the concept has its share of critics, Connell's insights regarding multiple masculinities that exist within a hierarchy have been well documented, empirically, over many decades (Connell and Messerschmidt 2005).

Among the masculinities that vie for hegemonic status in the United States are dominance and technical expertise masculinities, on which we focus here. Authority, power, command, aggression, and physicality are characteristics of dominance masculinity. Technical expertise masculinity is characterized by knowledge, intellectual talent, technical prowess, and domain-specific mastery. In the arena of electoral politics, Georgia Duerst-Lahti (2006) argues that presidential elections are often contests between which of these two forms of masculinity will prevail, therefore influencing which candidates can successfully vie for the presidency and which cannot. Further, by examining media coverage of recent presidential candidates, Duerst-Lahti and colleagues demonstrate that dominance masculinity is hegemonic in this domain (e.g., Duerst-Lahti and Oakley 2018). They drew the conclusion that dominance masculinity is societally preferred even in years when the presidential contest features two candidates who project technical expertise masculinity (Barack Obama and Mitt Romney in 2012) and for presidential candidates whose campaigns emphasize traits consistent with technical expertise (Al Gore in 2000 and Hillary Clinton in 2016). In this study we explore whether children perceive political leaders as possessing traits consistent with dominance or technical expertise masculinity and use the lists of traits that Duerst-Lahti employed.

Children's Perceptions of Political Leadership

In prior work, we demonstrated that children observe politics as a male-dominated domain, and, with age, increasingly envision leaders as men and as having masculine traits (Bos et al. 2022). Here, we expand upon those findings in a number of ways. First, we explore what types of masculine traits children associate with political leaders, specifically comparing the prevalence of Bem's personality-linked masculine traits, agentic traits associated with leadership, and two cultural hegemonic masculinities (dominance and technical expertise). We expect that the agentic traits will be most common in children's images, given that these traits embody gendered leadership stereotypes, and we explicitly asked children to draw political leaders (hypothesis 1a). Further, we might also see frequent use of dominance masculinity among children's depictions of political leaders, given the documented pervasiveness of this type of masculinity in presidential politics (hypothesis 1b).

Second, we consider both the characteristics of children (sex, race, and age) and the characteristics of the specific leaders they imagined (sex, race, and type of office held) as predictors of whether masculinity is depicted in children's perceptions of political leaders. Among the children's characteristics, we predict that as children become older and learn more about the masculine domain of politics, they will be more likely to use masculine traits in their descriptions of their leaders (hypothesis 2a). We anticipate that this age effect will be particularly strong for girls who are internalizing the communal gendered expectations conveyed to them through traditional gender socialization processes and learning that the political world is dominated by men (hypothesis 2b). We do not, however, have a priori expectations regarding whether children's use of masculine traits to describe political leaders will vary by the children's race or ethnicity.

We next examine whether certain characteristics of the children's imagined leaders are associated with depictions of masculine traits. We hypothesize that children who perceive political leaders to be male or to be white will be more likely to describe their leader in masculine terms than those who see political leaders as, respectively, women or people of color (hypothesis 3a). Further, we anticipate that leaders at higher levels of office, particularly the presidency, will elicit more masculine trait descriptors from children (hypothesis 3b).

Finally, we explore whether imagining political leaders as masculine is associated with children's own levels of political engagement. We hypothesize that greater use of masculine traits to describe a political leader will predict lower levels of political interest among girls (hypothesis 4a). Through the process of gendered political socialization, girls increasingly internalize gender norms with age while simultaneously developing a sharper awareness of politics as a masculine space (Bos et al. 2022). Thus, girls who imagine political leaders are masculine should be especially likely to disengage from the political world. We might also envision a similar relationship between depicting leaders as masculine and diminished political interest among Black children, given the greater attention given to communal (versus agentic) characteristics in Black political culture (Dawson 1994, 2001) (hypothesis 4b).

Method

To examine childhood political socialization, we collected data from over 1,600 children in grades 1–6. We received permission to conduct our study from superintendents or principals at 18 different schools (14 public and 4 private), each school located in one of the following areas: greater Boston; upstate New York; northeastern Ohio; and New Orleans. Parental informed consent was granted for the children to participate. On the day of data collection at their schools, the children themselves provided verbal assent to take part in our study. It was necessary for us to use a mixed methods approach, given the reading and writing abilities of children across the elementary grades. In particular, the older children (grades 4–6) wrote their own answers on a paper survey, as a researcher read the questions aloud. The youngest children (grades 1–2) were interviewed, typically in pairs. Most of the third graders completed surveys, while approximately one-third were interviewed. More details about our methodology are contained in Bos et al. (2022) and Oxley et al. (2020).

The first item each child completed was the Draw a Political Leader (DAPL) task. This task, modeled after the Draw a Scientist task long used in STEM fields (Chambers 1983; Miller et al. 2018), began with the following prompt:

> Close your eyes and imagine a political leader at work. A political leader is a person who wins an election and then has the job of helping people and solving problems in the community and the country. In the space below, draw what you imagined. Some examples of political leaders are people like: the mayor, the governor, people who work in Congress.

The children were given a few minutes to draw the political leader they imagined, using the white paper with a blank box and bag of crayons that we provided. There were sixteen crayons in each bag: eight classic Crayola colors and eight multicultural crayons including skin tone colors such as tan, apricot, and burnt sienna. After drawing their picture, students responded to these three open-ended questions or prompts about their drawn leader:

1. Describe what the political leader is doing in the picture.
2. List three words that come to mind when you think of this political leader.
3. What kinds of things do you think this leader does on a typical day? List at least three things.

We employed multiple approaches to coding the DAPL drawings and responses to the accompanying open-ended questions. The first was automated coding of the open-ends, conducted via STATA using seven data dictionaries we created. The first three dictionaries include all traits from Bem's (1974) original inventory of masculine, feminine, and nontyped characteristics. To create dictionaries for communal and agentic traits, we relied on the trait checklist that Schneider and Bos (2014) developed for their study of female politician stereotypes. Their list includes over one hundred traits, which they compiled from prior research, in both political science and psychology, on the following topics: characteristics of male and female politicians; male and female stereotypes; leadership stereotypes; and traits of politicians generally. We retained ninety-four characteristics from their master list, categorizing male-linked traits as agentic and female-linked ones as communal.[3] The words in the dominance masculinity and technical expertise masculinity dictionaries are those that Duerst-Lahti and Oakley (2018) identified for their media content analyses of presidential election media coverage. Across all the dictionaries, we searched for either the full word or a word stem, as the latter allows us to capture different uses of the trait (e.g., "confiden" captures both "confident" and "confidence"); the online appendix contains the complete lists of words as well as our specific search terms for our four masculinity data dictionaries. Furthermore, we coded the students' DAPL images separately for each set of traits. Put another way, if a student used any trait from the agentic list and any trait from the dominance masculinity list, that student would be coded as having agentic and dominance masculinity traits present for their DAPL task.

Second, after the automated coding, we reviewed the responses to ensure that all flagged words actually captured the children's use of a trait rather than another use of the same word. For example, we corrected the coding of "drive" when a child was describing a leader driving a vehicle (e.g., "take a drive" or "drive his car to work") rather than being a driven person. Another example was when a child used the word "big" in their DAPL open-ended responses but were describing something other than their leader ("living in a big house" or speaking "to a big crowd"). However, a large majority of these corrections dealt with one specific word: "leader." Because our prompt asked the children to draw and describe a political leader, it is perhaps not surprising that many used the word "leader" in their DAPL responses. Many of these appearances referred to the fact that the child drew a leader, such as "My leader is doing a speech," "The leader is Martin Luther King Jr," "Leader is a policeman," and so on. Because such instances of "leader" do not indicate that the child considers their drawn figure to possess the trait of leadership, we manually adjusted the coding. We retained only those instances where a child used leader as a trait descriptor ("great leader," "leads the US," or "giving a speech about his leadership") or when they explicitly replied "leader," "leads," or "leading" when asked which three words come to mind when they think about the person they drew or what things the person does on a typical day.[4]

Third, trained research assistants coded other elements of the DAPL drawings. The coders identified if the leader drawn was a known contemporary political leader or a historical figure. We used the identities of such known individuals to determine the sex and race of leaders drawn during the DAPL task. Otherwise, the coders relied upon the pronouns that appeared in a child's written responses, and the color of the crayon used on the outline of the leaders' faces to identify, respectively, the sex and race of the leaders that the children drew. Coders also recorded whether the child indicated a specific type or level of political office held by their leader, such as president, mayor, or judge.[5]

Finally, in the analyses that follow, we draw upon responses to a few questions that appeared after the DAPL activity in the questionnaire. These include some demographic measures and a set of items tapping students' interest in politics. The interest questions are adaptations of those from the Noyce Enthusiasm for Science scale (Fraser 1978). They assess whether children find politics and government exciting, whether they are curious to learn about politics and government and whether they would like a political job in the future.

Results

We begin our analyses by looking descriptively at the data to understand the prevalence of masculine traits in children's descriptions of their political leaders and to understand if and how often children engage with the four types of masculinity we measure here. We find evidence of masculine traits in nearly one-third of the 1,300+ DAPL images and descriptions; 29 percent of children use at least one trait from the four masculinity measures that we employ.[6] Of the four types of masculinity, as we expected (hypothesis 1a) agentic traits are used most frequently (28 percent). Children use traits from the Bem masculinity (8 percent), dominance masculinity (5 percent) and technical expertise masculinity (6 percent) categories much less frequently. Thus, we did not find support for our assumption in hypothesis 1b that dominance masculine traits would commonly appear in the children's drawings, because of the salience of these traits in the presidency. Of note, Bem nontyped traits are mentioned often (30 percent), as are communal traits (21 percent). Children very rarely use Bem feminine traits (1 percent) to describe their political leaders. These descriptive results show that among children who see political leaders as possessing masculine traits, they employ traits from all four types of masculinity. Yet, children use traits from the agentic measure much more often than they employ traits from the three other masculinity categories.

When we explore which specific traits the children depict for each of the four modes of masculinity, a few traits stand out. For instance, of the 57 agentic traits we included, 22 (39 percent) appear in the children's responses. The following are used the most often: "leader" (nearly 100 DAPLs), "hard-working" (71), "smart" (67), "strong" (32), and "powerful" (25). Seventeen other traits are mentioned, albeit each by 12 or fewer children. Those are: "active," "aggressive," "commands respect," "confident," "daring," "determined," "dictatorial," "greedy," "independent," "inspiring," "intelligent," "knowledgeable," "power hungry," "problem solver," "rich," and "tough." Five of the twenty traits (10 percent) in the Bem masculine category appear among the children's responses. Traits associated with leadership overwhelm the other four Bem masculine traits that the children use ("decisive," "independent," "defends oneself," and "aggressive"). Of the thirteen distinct traits in our dominance masculinity categories, nine (69 percent) emerge in children's DAPLs. Most common are "strong" and "powerful," followed by "in charge," "commanding," "best," "big," "attack," "control," and "aggressive." There are nine traits in our technical expertise masculinity category; four (44 percent) were used by the children. Among these, "smart" is by far the most commonly used trait, followed by "rich," "intelligent," and "knowledgeable."

Despite some overlap in the traits that comprise each of the four categories of masculinity, the masculinity measures do not form one scale of masculinity (alpha = .54). Put another way, these measures capture different conceptualizations of masculinity. In the results that follow, we do present an "overall masculinity" measure. This represents whether a student used any masculine trait descriptors in their political leader drawings. Furthermore, because of the low alpha, we conduct all of our analyses for the overall masculinity, as well as the four separate masculinity categories, noting whether any differences emerged in findings across these measures.

Masculine Depictions and Children's Characteristics

Having established that students engage with each of the masculine trait types, we next investigate if their distribution varies with the sex, race, and age of the children who wrote these descriptors. We find that girls are more likely than boys to use masculine traits, that students of color are generally less likely than white students to use masculine traits, and that, with increased age, children use masculine traits much more often to describe political leaders.

Looking more carefully at sex (see table 2.1), we find that girls use masculine traits more often than boys (34 percent compared to 27 percent). Among the four masculinity measures, sex differences exist for agentic traits, again with these traits more common in girls' than boys' images of political leaders. The prevalence of traits from the Bem masculinity, dominance masculinity, and technical expertise masculinity scales are not statistically different between boys and girls.

In addition, we find differences by racial group in the use of these four masculinity scales, with significant differences emerging for three of the scales. Fewer masculine traits appear overall in the leader draw-

TABLE 2.1: Presence of masculine traits in political leader drawings, by children's sex and race

	Overall masculinity	Bem masculinity	Agentic traits	Dominance masculinity	Tech. expertise masculinity	N
All children	29%	8%	28%	5%	6%	1368
Sex						
Girls	34*	9	33*	6	6	626
Boys	27	8	26	5	7	692
Race						
Asian	29*	7	26*	10^	6*	94
Black	17	5	16	4	3	184
Latino/a	25	8	25	3	2	144
White	37	9	35	6	10	526

Note: Table entries are the percentage of DAPL drawings that contain each type of masculinity.
Significance tests for differences within groups (such as comparing girls to boys or across racial groups) for types of masculinities: *$p < .05$; ^$p <.10$

ings of Black and Latino/a children compared to white and Asian children. White children and Asian children use agentic traits and dominance masculine traits more frequently than Black children and Latino/a children; the differences between white and Asian children are not statistically significant, nor are the differences between Black and Latino/a children. Technical expertise masculinity traits were also used more often by white and Asian children as compared to Black and Latino/a children, with white children's use statistically larger than Black or Latino/a children.

Finally, fitting with our predictions (hypothesis 2a), we find that overall use of masculine traits increases steadily across the age range. Among children who are six years old, 15 percent use at least one masculine trait to describe their leader. By age twelve, 45 percent depict masculinity (a difference that is significant at the .01 level). As seen in figure 2.1, the trend of older children being more likely to envision that political leaders are masculine exists for all four modes of masculinity. The increase is particularly notable for agentic traits and technical expertise masculinity.

Given past findings regarding gendered political socialization shaping girls' perceptions of the political world, we also predicted, in

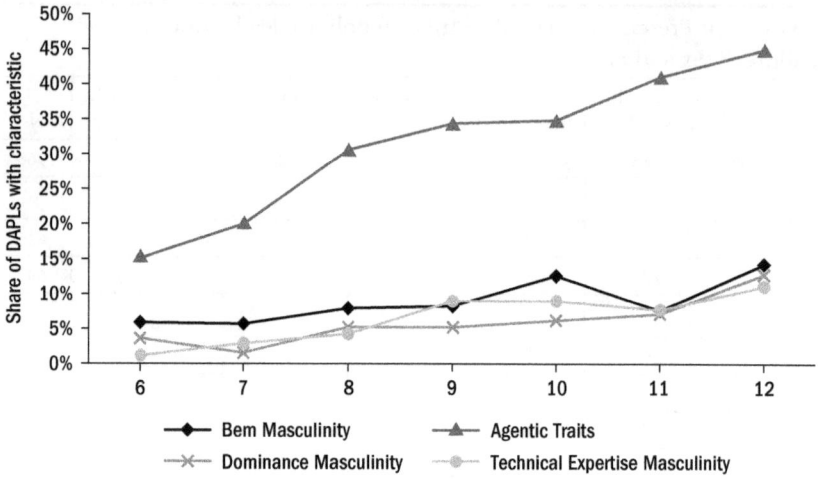

Figure 2.1: Presence of masculine traits by children's age

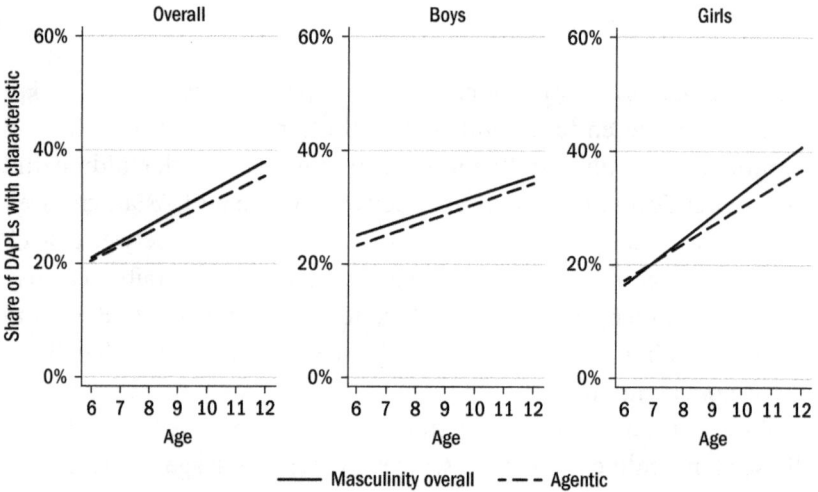

Figure 2.2: Presence of masculine traits by children's age and sex.
Note: Lines represent linear predictions from regressing masculinity overall (solid) or agentic (dashed) onto age (see table A2.1 for full data).

hypothesis 2b, that the increased use of masculine terms with age will be stronger for girls than it will be for boys. We find evidence that this is the case for some modes of masculinity. Specifically, when we explore age as a predictor of the use of masculine traits (e.g., overall masculinity) to describe political leaders, we see that the increased use of any masculine descriptors between ages six and twelve is much greater for girls as compared to boys. As demonstrated in figure 2.2, this same pattern exists for agentic traits. Girls also are more likely to use Bem masculinity and dominance masculinity trait predictors as they get older, whereas boys are not. On the other hand, boys show a marked increase in describing political leaders as technical expert masculine (from 0 percent at six to 21 percent at twelve). Girls' use of technical expert masculinity traits does not change over this age range.

Masculinity across Characteristics of Imagined Leaders

Next, we look at the relationship between the characteristics of the specific leaders described in the DAPL task (sex, race, and type of office held) and the use of masculine traits to describe those leaders. In hypothesis 3a, we predicted that children who perceive political leaders to be male or white will be more likely to describe their leader in masculine terms than those who see political leaders as, respectively, women or people of color. We do find evidence to support these expectations. Masculine traits were used to describe men leaders 33 percent of the time and women leaders 26 percent of the time. Among leaders that had no clear sex, 20 percent of these were described with masculine traits. Differences in the prevalence of specific types of masculinity by the sex of the drawn leader were significant for two (agentic and dominant masculine) of the four modes of masculinity. For agentic traits, men leaders were more likely to be described possessing these traits than women leaders (31 percent v. 26 percent). However, children used dominance masculinity traits to describe their women and men leaders nearly equally as often (8 percent and 6 percent) compared to leaders without a clear sex (1 percent). Considering the race of the leaders drawn, the use of masculine traits is lower for leaders of color (30 percent) compared to white leaders (34 percent), a difference that emerges from the rate of agentic traits applied to white (33 percent) compared to leaders of color (27 percent). Children also differed in their use of technical expertise and dominance masculinity by the race of their drawn leaders, although for these two types of masculinity, usage was higher when the race of the leader was clear versus unclear rather than between white leaders and leaders of color.

Given the research on the gendered nature of different political offices, we anticipated that leaders at higher levels of office, and particularly the presidency, would be described with more masculine traits than other offices (hypothesis 3b). To assess this, we use three categories of political offices that the children depicted in their drawings: the president, another type of office, or no office specified. We find that masculine traits are used most often in images that depict the president (34 percent) compared to images that depict other types of office holders (18 percent), or political leaders with whom they did not associate a specific political office (29 percent). This pattern is also seen when looking specifically at the use of agentic and technical expertise masculinity traits. From these findings, we conclude that children do associate masculinity with the presidency more than other elected offices.

Depicting Masculinity and Children's Political Interest

For our final set of analyses, we examine whether the use of masculine descriptors in the DAPL task is related to levels of political interest among children. To do so, we first compare levels of political interest for those children whose DAPL image depicted at least one masculine trait versus those who included no masculine traits. For Bem masculinity, agentic traits, and technical expertise masculinity, the mean level of political interest was significantly, albeit only slightly, higher for those

TABLE 2.2: Relationship between depicting masculinity and political interest

	Political interest		
	Children who did not depict masculinity	Children who did depict masculinity	p-value
Overall masculinity	2.57	2.63	0.13
Bem masculinity	2.58	2.70	0.06
Agentic traits	2.57	2.64	0.06
Dominance masculinity	2.59	2.53	0.62
Technical masculinity	2.58	2.75	0.02

Note: Results for political interest represent the average response to four items, each assessed on a four-point scale from strongly disagree (1) to strongly agree (4): Politics, government, and history is something I get excited about; I am curious to learn more about politics, government, history, and current events; I would like to have a job in government or politics in the future; learning about history and how the government works is boring (reverse coded).

children who used these traits versus those who did not (see table 2.2). No differences emerge for dominance masculinity or for our overall measure of masculinity.

Perhaps more importantly than whether interest is linked to envisioning political leaders in masculine terms for all is whether this relationship varies by characteristics of the students. We anticipated that among girls and Black students, the use of masculine traits would predict lower levels of political interest (respectively, hypothesis 4a and 4b). Put another way, we assumed that for these children envisioning political leaders as masculine is a deterrent to wanting to know more about and participate more in politics. To examine this, we run a series of OLS regressions that examine interactions between sex and masculinity type as well as race and masculinity type on levels of political interest. The only significant interactions that emerge across these models are the impact of the overall masculinity (b = −.156, se = .08) and agentic (b = −.189, se = .08) traits by sex on levels of political interest. These interaction effects suggest that among girls, using masculine or agentic traits to describe their political leaders has a negative effect on levels of political interest. This relationship is depicted in figure 2.3, which

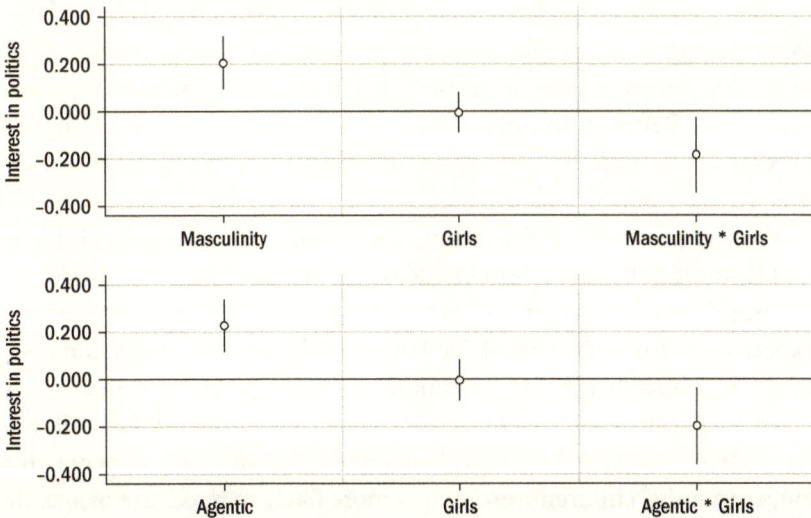

Figure 2.3: Masculinity and political interest among boys and girls
Note: Dependent variable is interest in politics. OLS regression model. See table A2.2 for full results.

provides a coefficient plot of a model estimating interest in politics by whether a child drew a masculine or an agentic masculine leader or not (the *masculinity* and *agentic* coefficients), whether the child was a girl (the *girls* coefficient) or was a girl who drew a masculine or an agentic masculine leader (the *masculinity x girls* and *agentic x girls* coefficients). The figure shows that among boys (our baseline category), drawing leaders with any masculine traits or with agentic traits are associated with increased political interest, but interest declines among girls who draw masculine or agentic leaders.

Discussion and Conclusion

To explore whether children envision political leaders as possessing masculine traits, we employed a broad approach, one that incorporates multiple conceptualizations of masculinity. While we uncover evidence that children use traits from all four measures of masculinity that we explore, agentic traits appear most frequently. The prevalence of agentic traits maps onto existing findings in the literature; these types of traits have long been associated with leadership among adults (Koenig et al. 2011; Schneider and Bos 2014). Our results suggest that children have also internalized stereotypical expectations regarding what types of traits leaders are likely to possess, and they are more likely to do so as they progress through the elementary school years. On the other hand, depictions of masculine traits that are linked to personality characteristics (Bem's conceptualization) or to cultural understandings of hegemonic masculinity appear less frequently than agentic traits in children's images of political leaders.

Why might agentic traits dominate children's view of political leaders, despite the highly visible demonstration of dominant masculinity (Messerschmidt 2019, 2021) and—less prevalent but still present—technical expertise masculinity (Duerst-Lahti and Oakley 2018) in American politics? One possibility is that the trait list for our agentic traits measure is much longer than the other trait lists. Thus, it may not be that children see masculinity overwhelmingly in agentic trait terms, but, rather, with a longer trait list, children were simply more likely to make use of agentic traits. Though children only used twenty-two of the fifty-seven agentic traits measured, even this partially utilized list of agentic traits is larger than the number of traits associated with dominant masculinity (thirteen) and technical expertise masculinity (nine) in our measures.

A second possible reason for the prevalence of agentic terms is that stereotypes of men and stereotypes of male political leaders overlap and encompass agentic traits (Schneider and Bos 2014; van der Pas, Aaldering, and Bos 2023). Thus, while children may observe demonstrations of masculinity in the news or in television ads that embody other types of masculinity, it is agentic traits that they are most likely to learn as they internalize gender and political stereotypes.

As for variation in the appearance of masculine descriptors in children's drawings of political leaders, we conclude that characteristics of the leaders and of the children are meaningful. Children's use of masculine traits were more common for male versus female leaders, and for white leaders versus leaders of color. As for the political office that the drawn leader holds, masculinity cropped up more for the presidency than other specific offices. We find it noteworthy that masculine trait descriptors were second most common for leaders who were not clearly associated with a specific office. In other words, children envision non-office-specific political leaders as possessing masculine traits more so than leaders who hold specific offices (other than the presidency). Because these leaders do not serve in a specific office, children do not have particular real-life political leaders in mind. Instead, they are imagining a generic political leader and endowing that generic leader with masculine traits.

Among the children's characteristics, the clearest trends emerge for age and sex, separately as well as in combination. Older children are more likely to imagine political leaders as masculine than their younger peers. Girls are more likely to describe political leaders as possessing masculine traits compared to boys, especially as girls grow older. Further, sex is the only individual characteristic that meaningfully impacts the relationship between depicting masculinity and children's interest in the political world. In particular, boys who envision that political leaders possess masculine traits display more interest in politics, whereas girls' interest declines as they depict political leaders as masculine. These patterns are all consistent with the dynamics of gendered political socialization, during which children learn about both the realities of the political world (notably, that it is male and masculine) and societal gender role expectations (Bos et al. 2022). This new finding enhances our knowledge in two ways. First, we understand that it is the use of agentic traits (and not other measures of masculinity) that drive this emerging sex gap in political interest. Second, it is among children who most heavily use these agentic traits to describe these leaders who have divergent levels of interest.

NOTES

1 Initially a sixty-trait inventory (Bem 1974), scholars have adapted the measure to use a short inventory of twenty traits—ten masculine and ten feminine (Bem 1978, 1979; see also Auster and Ohm 2000; McDermott 2016).

2 Schneider and Bos (2014) find no such overlap for stereotypes of women and female politicians.

3 The eliminated traits fell into two categories: those that prior research identified as characteristic of politicians generally (rather than male or female politicians specifically) and those appearing in work on female leaders in domains other than politics.

4 In addition, our manual review uncovered some uses of "hard-working" (an agentic trait) that the STATA coding missed. The automated coding was searching for "hard work," but some children expressed this trait in other ways, such as "hardworking" or "working hard."

5 After the initial set of coders coded all the DAPLs, a second set of coders recoded a randomly selected set of 15 percent of the images, with a Cohen's Kappa of 0.68.

6 While we collect data from over 1,600 children, in this analysis we drop cases where there is no DAPL drawing or where the DAPL drawing has no political content.

3

Tough and Aggressive

How Women of Color Strategically Emphasize Masculine Stereotypes in Campaign Messages

NICHOLE M. BAUER, EUGENE B. LEE-JOHNSON, AND DAN QI

Women's representation is at its height. The current women serving in elected political office after the 2022 midterm elections in the United States include a record sixty Black, Latina, Asian, Muslim, and Native American women holding a seat in the US Congress.[1] Of course, Kamala Harris serves as not only the first woman vice president but also as a Black, South Asian woman holding the second-highest office in the country. Cori Bush (D-MO), the first Black woman to serve as congresswoman from Missouri, talked about "Fighting for $15." Sharice Davids (D-KS), a Native American woman, has framed herself as a "fighter," presenting a masculine image in a campaign ad where she boxed and talked about fighting in mixed martial arts matches.[2] When Alexandria Ocasio-Cortez (D-NY) ran for congress, she reiterated the importance of "courage" and "fighting for New York."[3] These women's use of "fighting" language positions them in a stereotypically masculine role—not just on issues such as the minimum wage and jobs, but they are positioning themselves as the political actor with the agency and power to advocate for this issue. Indeed, masculinity was a common campaign theme among many Black, Latina, Asian, Muslim, and Native American women who ran for office in recent election cycles.

Current research on the campaign strategies deployed by women belonging to a racial or ethnic minority group deploy centers on how these candidates emphasize their racial and ethnic backgrounds, their personal identities, and different types of political issues (Cargile 2023; Gonzalez and Bauer 2020; Santia and Bauer 2022; Brown and Lemi 2021; Gershon et al. 2019; Bejarano 2013). Scholars on gender and race in politics argue that the intersectional nature of gender and racial stereotypes could lead individuals to perceive women of color as having positive masculine traits, such as strength, courage, and fortitude (Brown and Lemi 2021; Bejarano 2013). Masculine traits, such as being strong, tough, and aggressive, align with the traits most strongly associated with political leadership (Huddy and Terkildsen 1993; Rosenwasser and Seale 1988; Rosenwasser and Dean 1989; Conroy and Oliver 2020). Masculine traits also align with the traits that fit into racial stereotypes (but see Cargile (2021)).[4]

Our chapter makes two central arguments about masculine stereotypes and the strategic messages of women of color candidates. First, we argue that women of color candidates have different incentives relative to white women candidates to highlight masculine coded traits in their strategic campaign messages, driven by the overlap between traits that are considered masculine and desirable in political leadership, and stereotypes about racial and ethnic minority women. Second, we contend that there are sure to be differences in how minority women of different racial and ethnic backgrounds emphasize masculine stereotypes. The qualities highlighted by Black women are likely to differ from the qualities highlighted by Latinas or Asian American women.

We investigate the use of masculinity through the traits candidates used to describe themselves and the visual components of campaign messages of women running in House, Senate, or gubernatorial races between 2010 and 2018. We deploy a unique dataset that combines data on the televised campaign ads that candidates aired, from the Wesleyan Media Project, and we use these ads to conduct an original and exhaustive content analysis of the masculine traits candidates attribute to themselves in political ads and the masculine stereotypical imagery embedded in the televised ads.[5] Our research finds that, regardless of candidate race, masculine stereotypes are dominant strategies in the campaign messages of both women and men. These results refine our understanding about differences among women in their strategic political messages. Our findings on the prominence of masculinity in campaign messages reinforce that masculinity is a dominant—if not the dominant—perceptual lens through which candidates view political leadership.

Women, Masculinity and Political Leadership

Feminine stereotypes characterize women as caring, compassionate, beautiful, and intuitive (Diekman and Eagly 2000), while masculine stereotypes characterize men as tough, competitive, assertive, and rational (Vinkenburg et al. 2011). Masculine stereotypes align most closely with political leadership stereotypes while feminine stereotypes are incongruent with political leadership (Lombard, Azpeitia, and Cheryan 2021; Schneider and Bos 2019). Voters generally prefer candidates that display masculine over feminine qualities (Bauer 2015, 2017). Conroy and Oliver (2020) find that candidates who see themselves as having more masculine traits are more likely to be recruited to run for office, and that people with masculine traits are those most likely to participate in politics through activities such as voting or protesting (McDermott 2016).

The alignment between masculinity and political leadership can put female candidates at a disadvantage (Bauer 2020). Schneider and Bos (2014) show that voters see female politicians as lacking both stereotypical feminine strengths and lacking the stereotypical masculine traits most strongly associated with political leadership. Voters express doubts about the experience, competencies, and qualifications of female candidates (Ditonto, Hamilton, and Redlawsk 2014; Ditonto 2017; Fulton 2012; Bauer 2020; Holman et al. 2019; Holman, Merolla, and Zechmeister 2011)—all qualities that align with masculinity in the context of political leadership. Female candidates often emphasize masculine traits in their campaign messages to overcome perceived trait deficits (Bauer and Santia 2021; Dittmar 2015; Jungblut and Haim 2021). But the extent to which these strategies are successful in improving the evaluations of female candidates is not entirely clear in the existing scholarship (Bauer 2017; Bauer and Carpinella 2018; Krupnikov and Bauer 2014). More pertinently for our research, this scholarship largely focuses on how masculine campaign strategies operate for female candidates with the race unspecified (see e.g., Bauer 2017) or where candidate sex is manipulated with a photo of a white woman (see e.g., Krupnikov and Bauer 2014). We focus on how women of color political candidates employ masculinity in their campaign strategies.

Masculinity and Intersectional Stereotypes

There are two branches of thought on the role of masculinity in the stereotypes individuals hold about women of color. First, the double-advantage hypothesis argues that the combination of gender and racial stereotypes leads voters to associate women of color with positive feminine and positive masculine stereotypes (Smooth 2006; Ford Dowe 2020; Brown 2014). This hypothesis contends that voters attribute a unique set of stereotypical traits to women of color candidates that combines both feminine and masculine qualities. Under this model, voters see women of color as *both* strong and assertive and as caring and compassionate. This dual trait perception comes from the unique roles that women of color have held in working to provide for their families financially and emotionally (Reynolds-Dobbs, Thomas, and Harrison 2008). These traits differ from those attributed to white women which encompass largely feminine qualities (Schneider and Bos 2014) and come from a concept of white motherhood that emphasizes women's roles in the home (Deason, Greenlee, and Langer 2015). For example, Bejarano (2013) argues that Latina candidates can have a distinct advantage over Latino men when running for political office, as voters see these women as leaders of their homes and their communities. Under this approach, women of color candidates should be able to leverage masculine traits to their advantage without facing a trade-off in feminine qualities.

The double-disadvantage argument asserts that the stereotypical traits attributed to women of color encompass negative masculine qualities, that come from racial stereotypes, and as lacking positive feminine qualities that come from gender stereotypes (Brown and Lemi 2021; Johnson Carew 2016; Cargile 2021). The trope of the "angry Black woman" exemplifies the double disadvantage approach where anger is associated with being threatening and not having feminine qualities like compassion and warmth. Latina candidates face similar challenges where voters attribute fewer masculine traits to them, relative to a Latino male candidate (Cargile 2021; Cargile 2016). Under the double disadvantage approach, race and gender stereotypes combine so that women of color are seen as lacking positive masculine qualities, as possibly having negative masculine qualities, and as not having positive feminine qualities. From this perspective, women of color have a motivation to emphasize positive masculine traits to fill in the gaps in their qualifications that come from the dual sources of gender and racial prejudice. The double-advantage and double-disadvantage approaches both contend that masculinity factors into the perceptions that voters have of women of color candidates.

Women of Color and Masculinity in Campaign Messages

We argue that women of color have unique incentives to strategically highlight masculinity in their campaign messages, and that these strategic incentives differ from those of nonminority women. There are two components to our theoretical argument: first, the stereotypical impressions that are held of women of color can motivate the use of masculine traits in political messaging; and, second, the motivations of women of color to run for political office will create a special opportunity to capitalize on masculine traits.

Women belonging to a racial or ethnic minority group (i.e., Black women, Latinas, Asian American women) experience their race and gender simultaneously (Crenshaw 1991; Collins 1990). The intersectionality of race and gender stereotypes positions women of color in such a way that they may be able to emphasize masculine traits without facing the same kinds of trade-offs that nonminority women face when highlighting masculinity. Past work finds that voters, at a baseline level, often ascribe to women of color a mix of feminine and masculine traits (Johnson Carew 2016; Cargile, Merolla, and Schroedel 2016; Gershon and Monforti 2021), though there is ambiguity about whether these trait evaluations are entirely positive or negative. At the same time, Latino respondents evaluate Latinas as highly skilled on feminine issues but not on masculine issues (Cargile 2016). Black female candidates are perceived as more compassionate and hardworking than white female candidates, and Black female candidates are viewed as more trustworthy than white candidates (Johnson Carew 2016). These findings suggest that voters are unlikely to hold women of color to the norms of femininity shaped by white women (Holder, Jackson, and Poterotto 2015).

Past work is not clear on whether voters attribute positive masculine stereotypes to women of color but the association between masculinity and stereotypes about women of color gives these candidates a motivation to rely on masculine traits. If masculine stereotypes fit into the stereotypical strengths of women of color, then these candidates can capitalize on masculine traits without fear of facing the same type of counterstereotypical backlash that white women must contend with (see e.g., Krupnikov and Bauer (2014)). If, in this case of women of color, masculine traits are seen as a weakness, we argue that this still provides women of color with an incentive to emphasize positive masculine traits to fill in potential perceived deficits.

The stereotypical perceptions held about women of color are just one part of our argument about why women of color will make reference to masculine traits. Women of color run for political office to achieve policy goals, affect change in political office, and to increase the representation of underrepresented groups (Holman and Schneider 2018). This last goal of increasing the descriptive and substantive representation of women and men from racial and ethnic minority backgrounds, is a particularly unique goal for women of color candidates (Bejarano and Smooth 2022; Scott et al. 2021). Women of color are motivated by socioeconomic conditions, linked fate, education and income levels, church attendance, and history of employment outside of the home (Alex-Assensoh and Assensoh 2003; Simien 2006; Burns, Scholzman, and Verba 2001; Dawson 2001). Intersecting gender and ethnic identities also mobilize Latinas into political activism when they perceive a threat to their communities (Jaramillo 2010; Pardo 1990; García Bedolla 2005). Women of color, unlike men of color and men in general, are less motivated by the pursuit of power or building their political careers, but by advocating for meaningful and tangible change (Holman and Schneider 2018). These motivations to pursue change will, we argue, provide a further motivation for women of color to use masculine trait language in their strategic messages.

In sum, women of color have two motivations for drawing upon masculine stereotypes. First, the way that masculinity factors into the impressions that voters hold about women of color creates an opportunity for these candidates to capitalize on masculine traits without facing a backlash. Second, the policy change that women of color pursue in political office creates a natural opportunity for these candidates to capitalize on masculinity. As such, *we expect women of color to be more likely than white women to emphasize masculinity in campaign messages.*

Differences among Women of Color

Next, we turn to outlining why there might be differences in the use of masculine traits across a woman's race or ethnicity (Crenshaw 1991; Smooth 2006; Jordan-Zachary 2007). Clayton and Stallings (2000) indicate that Black women need to strike an appropriate balance by not being seen as too masculine while having the ability to accentuate certain feminine traits. Latinas historically have been held to Latino male "machismo standards." Machismo reflects patriarchy, and machismo attitudes can suppress Latinas in politics in Latin America and the United States. Machismo is ingrained in Latino men, but Latina women also perpetuate this form of masculinity. When women enter into male-dominated fields like politics, they believe that they have to show machismo or masculine traits to be elected and successful (Prado 2004).

We expect differences in the strategic use of masculinity based on the race and/or ethnicity of the woman of color. Black women may not highlight masculinity as much as other women of color, given that masculine stereotypes can stray into negative stereotypes about Black women. Latina women may feel pressured to emphasize masculine traits to overcome perceptions that they lack these qualities, while we expect Asian American women to be less likely to emphasize masculine traits.

Data and Method

We turn to campaign advertising data across nearly a decade of congressional and gubernatorial elections from 2010 to 2018 to identify how women of color employ masculinity in campaign messages. Our campaign messages dataset comes from the Wesleyan Media Project (WMP), which records the characteristics of ads aired by political candidates in the major media markets in the United States, such as the name and party of the candidate, the media market where the ad was aired, the media outlet used by the candidate, the level of the race, the sponsor of the ad, and the tone of the ad.

Our dataset combines House, Senate, and gubernatorial candidates not only to maximize the number of women of color candidates we can analyze but also to examine the strategic masculine messaging choices women of color use at different levels of political office. There

TABLE 3.1: Number of campaign ads aired by women of color in 2010–2018

Election year	Black women	Latinas	Asian women	Other minority women
2010	5	4	3	0
2012	5	1	7	3
2014	3	3	3	0
2016	4	8	8	2
2018	15	10	9	5

is a perception that higher or more executive levels of political office are perceived as more masculine relative to legislative or lower levels of political office (Dunaway et al. 2013), though there is also research that supports the contention that all political offices are strongly associated with masculinity (Sweet-Cushman 2022). Table 3.1 breaks down the number of women of color who aired televised political ads for each year in our dataset. We include more information about the candidates and the levels of office for which they ran in the online appendix 3.2.

We investigate how women of color use masculinity through the traits used in the ad to describe candidates verbally and to present them visually. For our trait coding scheme, we relied on a large body of social psychology research, work on gendered language in politics, and pretests to develop a method for coding the masculine traits in campaign ads (Prentice and Carranza 2002; Roberts and Utych 2019). Masculine ads used the following traits to describe the candidate sponsoring the ads: tough, strong, hardworking, independent, innovative, someone who stands up to others, a fighter, or a leader. We identified these traits based on work identifying the qualities that are used to describe a person as masculine (Bem 1981; McDermott 2016; Conroy and Oliver 2020). We conducted a pretest of our trait codebook that asked respondents to indicate if a woman or a man was more likely to display a specific trait (see online appendix A3.1). We use a 60 percent threshold, borrowing this threshold from the partisan stereotype ownership literature (Petrocik 1996) to determine whether a trait fits into masculine stereotypes. If 60 percent or more of respondents indicated that men were more likely to display a trait such as strength, we classified that trait as masculine. Examples of masculine trait ads from candidates include an ad from

Michelle Lujan Grisham's 2018 gubernatorial campaign where she repeatedly described herself as a fighter:

Hi, I'm Michelle Lujan Grisham and we know the challenges we face in New Mexico. I've known adversity in my own life, raising two daughters after my husband passed away. But my life's work is never backing down. At the Department of Aging I fought for nursing home reform. As secretary of health we doubled the number of school-based health centers, and then, in Congress, I secured millions of dollars for more police training. As governor, I'll never stop fighting and I never give up.

Another example is from Joyce Beatty, a Black woman representing Ohio's Third House district who aired the following ad in 2012:

We need change, we need a voice, we need Joyce. We need Joyce Beatty in Congress. Joyce Beatty. I'll fight for a new law to make sure American companies get the first crack at all government contracts, so our tax dollars create jobs here. A new voice, Joyce, Joyce Beatty. I will stand up to anyone to make sure we create new jobs right here in Ohio. I'm Joyce Beatty, and I approve this message.

Beatty, like Grisham, spoke about being a fighter while evoking an assertive image of her standing up to a power or force that might prevent progress or benefits from coming to her district. The phrase "stand up to" and the use of "fighting" language are two of the most common masculine qualities evoked in the campaign ads, and they are both qualities that align with political leadership traits. A feminine message, in contrast, would describe the candidate through more communal, care-giving-oriented language, such as an ad in support of Lauren Underwood, the 2018 House candidate in Illinois's Fourteenth House district, where the ads often described her as "someone who cares for us." This language places Underwood into the stereotypically feminine role of being a caregiver as opposed to a masculine, agentic role that might focus more on her power and agency.

We coded the traits in campaign ads using ad transcripts, and we recorded the use of masculine traits to describe a political candidate. However, if a trait was used to describe an issue or the state of the economy (e.g., "These are tough times"), we did not code the trait. Our trait coding scheme required making some subjective judgments, but we achieved a threshold for a sufficiently high level of intercoder reliability using Cohen's Kappa and Krippendorf's alpha for nearly every year in our data set (O'Connor and Joffe 2020).[6] We combined our masculine trait variables to make a masculine trait message variable coded as 1 if a message displayed at least one masculine trait.

We also coded the ads for how their visual representation of the candidate may reflect masculinity. For our masculine visual coding scheme, we relied on Carpinella and Bauer (2021). We focused our coding scheme on the clothing candidates wear in campaign ads, displays of agency or power by a candidate, interactions between candidates and other people, and the setting of the campaign ad. Our first masculine coding metric recorded whether the candidate wore business clothes, such as a suit, which reinforces the masculine norms of a political "uniform." The clothing considered acceptable for legislators to wear in office and for candidates on the campaign trail is one defined by the stereotypical professional dress of men. Next, we recorded displays of agency or power by candidates which includes visuals, such as the candidate standing over a crowd while delivering a speech. We recorded a candidate's interactions with other people as masculine if an interaction involved no physical contact beyond handshaking: a mark of business interactions between men, between the candidate and other people. Finally, we recorded whether the ad location reinforced masculinity—for example, in spaces that tend to be dominated by men such as construction sites, the floor of a legislature or inside a business office or political office. A second coder analyzed 10 percent of the campaign ads, and the intercoder reliability reached a rate that indicated substantial agreement between the two coders. With these four items, we created a measure that records whether a candidate used at least one of the masculine visual displays of the candidate that ranges from 0 to 1.

We include several other variables to test our hypotheses, starting of course with candidate sex, coded 1 for a female candidate relying on the Center for American Women in Politics (CAWP 2022) for this information. We include variables for whether the candidate identified as Black/African American, Latino, Asian/Pacific Islander, or another racial or ethnic minority group, including Native American. We found data on candidate race and ethnicity by searching for candidates through their congressional biographies, archived campaign websites, the organization Who Leads America, minority caucus memberships, and other publicly available biographies. We also added data on incumbency, competitive races, open-seat elections, and the gender of a candidate's opponent.

We cataloged the proportion of individuals in each district and state identifying as Black/African American, Latino, Asian American, Hawaiian or Pacific Islander, and/or Native American. Using these data, we recorded whether a district was a majority-minority district based on whether the racial/ethnic population was 0.40 of the total district population or higher. Our data on district race/ethnicity allow us to trace patterns of how women's strategies shift based on whether they are running in a majority-minority district or a state with a high percentage of racial and/or ethnic minorities or a majority white state.

Our final set of variables record characteristics of campaign ads including whether the candidate physically appeared in an ad, the logged cost of advertising in a media market (though this variable is not available in 2010), the tone of the ad (positive, attack, contrast), and the length of an ad as measured in seconds. For the ads from 2010 through 2018, we also include a variable for whether the candidate sponsored the ad or whether another organization or group sponsored it, and we control for whether the ad was a general or a primary election ad.

Analytical Plan and Results

We examine two ways that masculinity can emerge in campaign ads. First, we investigate how women of color use masculine traits and visuals in political messages. We focus on understanding the differences in women of color's use of masculine traits and visuals relative to white women. Our argument here rests in the unique intersection of race and gender stereotypes to shape the way that individuals think about women of color, and how women of color emphasize masculine traits they may benefit from more than white women. Second, we turn to parsing out differences among women of color to understand how Black women, Latinas, Asian American women, Muslim women, and Native American women differ from one another in their strategic employment of masculinity.[7] We divide our analyses of masculinity into two sections, first examining the use of masculine traits, and then examining the use of masculine imagery. We argue that the unique experiences of women based on their sex and their specific race/ethnicity can lead women of different racial and ethnic backgrounds to have different incentives for highlighting masculine traits.

Masculine Traits in Political Messages

Across all the candidates, 40 percent of televised campaign ads, or 11,341, relied on masculine traits in some form. We estimated a logistic regression model predicting whether a candidate aired a masculine trait ad. We include an interaction between whether a candidate belonged to a racial or ethnic minority group, coded for these initial analyses as 1 or 0, and candidate sex. We also included our full set of control variables for electoral context, ad characteristics, and office characteristics. We calculated the predicted probability for airing a masculine trait ad based on a candidate's sex and race/ethnicity. We find that women of color's predicted probability for airing a masculine trait ad is 0.43 (SE = 0.04) while white women's predicted probability is 0.47 (SE = 0.02). These rates of reliance are not statistically distinct from one another, $p = 0.571$. Where we see a difference in the use of masculinity is between women and men, with women, regardless of their race or ethnicity, being more likely to use masculine traits relative to men, regardless of race or ethnicity, $p < 0.001$. These patterns suggest that women, overall, emphasize masculine traits in their campaign messages. We argue, however, that the motivations behind women of color's use of masculinity and the way white women use masculinity likely differ. White women most likely use masculinity to fill in gaps in their qualifications (Bauer 2020) while women of color, we argue, use masculinity to play up perceived strengths in their qualifications.

As a next step, we estimated models isolated to *just women minority candidates* to better detect differences between Latinas, Black women, Asian American women, and Native American/Middle Eastern/Muslim women (who make up our other minority group category). We graphed these predicted probabilities in figure 3.1 (see online appendix 3.3, table A3.5, for the full models). We also include the predicted probabilities for white women and white men in this figure for comparison purposes,

Masculine Traits in Ads based on Candidate Gender and Race/Ethnicity

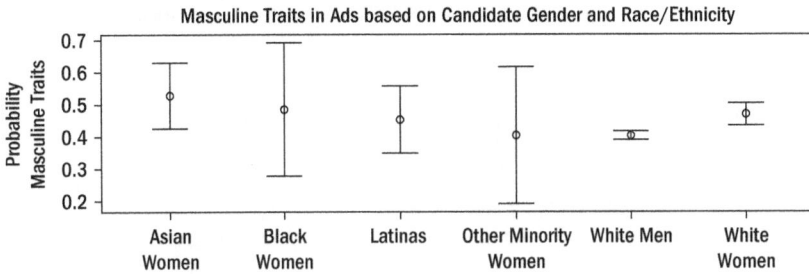

Figure 3.1: Predicted probability of masculine trait ads for women of color
Note: 95% confidence intervals included.

though we derived these probabilities from the candidate sex by minority candidate interaction models. We find that Asian American women are slightly more likely than women of other racial and ethnic backgrounds to air masculine traits in their campaign ads with a predicted probability of approximately 0.53 (SE = 0.05). There are more similarities among Black women and Latinas. The predicted probability of a Black woman airing a masculine trait ad is 0.48 (SE = 0.10) and the predicted probability of a Latina airing a masculine trait ad is 0.45 (SE = 0.05); these are nearly identical values. For Native American or Middle Eastern women, the predicted probability of airing masculine trait ads is 0.40 (SE = 0.10). Overall, these differences based on a woman's minority status largely do not reach statistical significance. We find that, generally, women of color embrace the same types of masculine trait strategies that dominate political campaign messages for women and men, regardless of their race.

Masculine Visuals in Political Messages

We estimated logit models predicting differences in masculine visual use based on a woman's race or ethnicity. We include a dichotomous variable recording whether a woman identified as Latina, Black, Asian American, or of another minority group status (Muslim or Native American women) and we leave white women as the excluded category in our analysis. We incorporated the full set of controls from our previous analyses. Figure 3.2 displays the predicted probability for women's use of masculine visuals based on their race and ethnicity (see online

Masculine Visuals in Ads based on Race/Ethnicity for Women

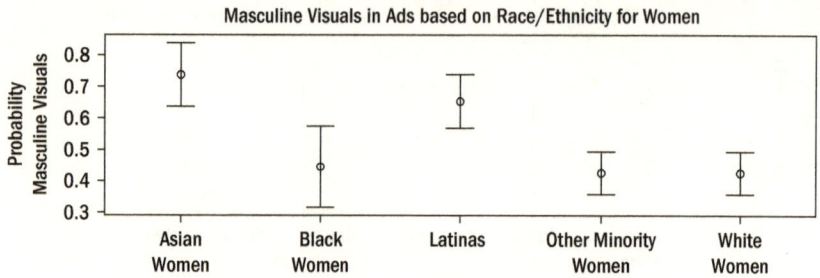

Figure 3.2: Predicted probability of masculine visual ads for women of color

appendix, table A3.5, for the full model). We find that Black women do not differ from other women in their use of masculine visuals, while Latinas and Asian American women are more likely to incorporate masculine visuals into their campaign messages. The predicted probability for Black women using masculine visuals is 0.45 (SE = 0.07), and this rate of masculine visual use is like white women's predicted probability of 0.43 (SE = 0.03). Latinas and Asian American women have significantly higher rates of masculine visual reliance. Latinas' predicted probability of masculine visual use is 0.65 (SE = 0.04), and for Asian American women the predicted probability is 0.74 (SE = 0.05). These differences between Black women and other minority women fit our theoretical expectation that Black women would not face as much pressure to highlight masculine stereotypes because the intersection of gender and racial stereotypes is likely to attribute these candidates with some masculine qualities. Thus, Black women might not have as much of a need to establish their masculine credentials compared to other women of color.

Combined Use of Masculine Traits and Masculine Visuals

Our main analyses separate the use of masculine traits and masculine visuals as past research indicates that these elements of a message are not likely to be used together (Carpinella and Bauer 2021). In this final section, we undertake an exploratory analysis to see how frequently women of color combine the use of masculine traits and masculine visuals. Of the 1,000 ads included in both our trait and visual analysis just 291, or

29 percent, use both masculine traits and masculine visuals. About 27 percent of ads use no masculine elements, 19 percent use only masculine traits and no masculine visuals, and 27 percent use just masculine visuals and no masculine traits. We created a dichotomous variable indicating whether a candidate used both masculine traits and masculine visuals. With this variable, we estimated a logit model predicting the joint use of masculine traits and visuals with variables to indicate candidate race/ethnicity and controls for candidate, campaign, and ad characteristics. We include the full model in the online appendix in table A3.6, but we summarize our main findings here.

We find that Asian American women are the most likely to use both masculine traits and masculine visuals in their campaign ads, $p = 0.004$, while the other variables for candidate race/ethnicity are insignificant. The use of masculinity through both trait and visual channels by Asian American women suggests two possibilities. First, it may be that Asian American women are seeking to overcome stereotypes of passivity about this particular group of minority women (Kawahara 2007). Second, it may be that masculine stereotypes of Asian American women, such as the "tiger mom" stereotype, creates an opportunity for these women to leverage masculinity in a way unique to the stereotypes about Asian American women (Hau 2015).

Discussion and Conclusion

In this chapter, we identified how women of color use masculine stereotypes in campaign messages through masculine traits and masculine visuals. Our results suggest that minority women and white women highlight masculine traits at similar rates. Our second set of analyses examined differences among women of color. Here, again, we find similar patterns of masculine trait reliance. Our results show the strong and prevailing pressures that candidates face to air messages that highlight masculine personal traits in campaign messages. Our analyses of masculine visuals show somewhat different patterns, with significantly more variation in how women of color incorporate masculine imagery into their campaign ads. The use of masculine visuals suggests that candidates feel pressured to highlight masculinity in campaign messages but might be hesitant to do so in an overt way (i.e., through masculine traits) and instead choose to use visual representations of masculinity, which is a more covert strategy.

Our dataset comes with limitations. We examined masculine stereotype use in just televised campaign ads. It is not clear if the patterns we uncovered here would map onto other communication mediums such as Twitter, YouTube ads, or campaign websites (Borah, Fowler, and Ridout 2018; Beltran et al. 2020; Brown and Gershon 2016). Expanding analyses of women of color's communication patterns on other platforms can offer additional insights into whether and how these women engage with masculine norms in their campaign messages. Our masculine visual analysis only included a small sample of the total ads in our dataset. Future work should not only expand our analyses to include the ads from men, especially men of color, but to also develop more expansive ways for identifying the use of masculine visual elements in campaign ads.

Our results have implications for the stereotypical perceptions individuals hold of political leaders, and the ways in which feminine stereotypes are valued or devalued on the campaign trail. Nearly 50 percent of messages from the candidates in our sample relied on masculine traits in some form. While we did not extend our analyses to how candidates used feminine traits or made trade-offs between feminine and masculine traits, past work suggests that candidates do, in fact, make trade-offs between masculinity and femininity with the balance in messaging tilted toward masculine qualities (Bauer and Santia 2021). This leads to an implicit undervaluing of feminine traits in political leaders. Feminine traits, such as being honest, promoting compromise, or exhibiting compassion, *should* be valued in political leadership, such as honesty and compassion, but are not because so much of candidate messaging is devoted to masculine traits. A next step for this scholarship is to see whether women of color use feminine traits to redefine the expectations held for political leaders so that feminine traits hold more value and weight in how we view who makes a good leader.

NOTES

1 "Women Officeholders by Name and Ethnicity," Center for American Women and Politics (CAWP), https://cawp.rutgers.edu/facts/women-officeholders-race-and-ethnicity.

2 "Sharice Davids Fighting for Progress," YouTube Video, 1:05, May 29, 2018, https://www.youtube.com/watch?v=vGa5qQsYY-g&ab_channel=ShariceforCongress.

3 "The Courage to Change, Alexandria Ocasio-Cortez," 2:07, May 30, 2018, https:// www.youtube.com/watch?v=rq3QXIVRobs&ab_channel=AlexandriaOcasio-Cortez

4 Research is split on whether people associate women of color with positive masculine qualities, such as strength, or negative masculine qualities, such as anger (Skevrin 2015; Smooth 2006; Ford Dowe 2020; Gershon and Monforti 2021).

5 For more information on the Wesleyan Media Project data, see Fowler et al. (2020); Fowler et al. (2019); and Fowler, Franz, and Ridout (2017, 2015, 2014).

6 The one outlier was 2018 House races that had an alpha coefficient below the 0.67 level threshold necessary. But, overall, the other years and levels of office had ratings at about 0.72 or higher for intercoder reliability.

7 Our data offer us the ability to include Native American and Muslim women, as several women belonging to these groups won elections in 2018. While existing literature and our theory draws more on the research about Black, Latina, and, to a lesser extent, Asian American women, we include these categories to better understand differences across women of color of different racial and ethnic backgrounds.

4

Masculinity and Ableism

The Electoral Effects of Candidate Mental and Physical Illness and Voters' Evaluations

MONIKA L. MCDERMOTT AND JACOB F. H. SMITH

Introduction

As previous chapters have demonstrated, politics is a masculine game in the United States. The stereotypes, and thereby the expectations, attached to potential leaders in most occupations are that they should be masculine (Koenig et al. 2011). Politics is no different. Those who are not sufficiently masculine may have trouble getting elected to power positions, as voters expect masculine, (i.e., "agentic" or "instrumental"; see chapter 1 in this volume) traits from candidates (Eagly and Karau 2002). These include, among others, independence, aggressiveness, strength, and self-reliance (see McDermott 2016). Most of the work on this topic has focused almost exclusively on the way these expectations affect women candidates' chances of being elected to public office (see, e.g., Dolan and Sanbonmatsu 2011).

Women candidates, however, may not be the *only* ones at a disadvantage due to the stereotype that leaders should be masculine or agentic.[1] Research shows that male candidates who lack masculine traits, or, more importantly, who hold feminine traits, are also at a disadvantage (Huddy and Terkildsen 1993); and existing literature demonstrates that many men, presumably some of whom aspire to political office, hold feminine traits (McDermott 2016). Additionally, while work on candidate masculinity has typically revolved around candidate sex, there is no need to limit it to that single aspect.

In this chapter we examine a group of potential candidates who, similarly, may not be seen as masculine "enough": disabled candidates.

Specifically, we examine voters' ableist stereotypes surrounding disabilities and the role that a candidate's mental and physical health may have on their chances of being elected. Stereotypes about mental and some types of physical illness include that those who suffer from them are unauthoritative, even helpless, characteristics that run counter to stereotypically masculine or agentic traits. As a result, it is likely that candidates who admit to such ailments will be viewed as less masculine than they would otherwise be, and possibly even insufficiently masculine for political office.

Using original experimental data, we simulate the case of US senator John Fetterman of Pennsylvania who suffered a stroke while on the campaign trail in 2022 and who, once in office, was hospitalized for six weeks due to clinical depression. While Fetterman was in fact elected despite his medical emergency, opponents openly questioned whether he was "fit" to hold office, both during the campaign (McDuffie 2022) and subsequently during his hospitalization (Roche 2023).[2] One detractor went so far as to accuse Fetterman of "hiding in his basement" after his stroke, and his opponent's campaign painted his reluctance to debate as "dodging" (McDuffie 2022). Both claims could arguably be seen as attacks on his masculinity.

While Fetterman is far from the only politician to suffer either a physical or mental health crisis, on or off the campaign trail, he provides a unique, realistic, and timely opportunity to test voters' reactions to both. Fetterman is especially interesting given his public persona—he is a tall, imposing, and nontraditional candidate. As one reporter put it: "In Pennsylvania, John Fetterman rose to prominence as the biggest, beefiest lieutenant governor the land had ever seen. His size; his plainspoken affect; his hoodies and tattoos; and the working-class appeal of his policies on marijuana, guns, and unions—they all screamed masculinity in a way that was rare for a popular Democrat" (Maxon 2022). If any candidate could overcome the nonmasculine stigma associated with mental and physical health ailments, it would be Fetterman. While Fetterman is not named in the experiment—to avoid direct partisan cues and name cues—we expect that his experience and image could linger with voters, providing a particularly stringent test case.

Research on any disabilities or illnesses of political leaders is sparse, at best, and research into the potential *reasons* for any ableist sentiments on the part of voters is simply nonexistent. This chapter takes a rare look into the intersection of masculine expectations and politicians' health to begin a conversation on—and, hopefully, spark further research interest into—candidates' and politicians' disabilities. Not only is this an important topic currently, but it is also likely to become increasingly so as the median age of candidates for national office rises (Potts 2023).

Information Cues and Public Views of Mental and Physical Health

While there is a lack of direct research linking politicians' health to public opinions of them, more general research into positive or negative reactions to health conditions can provide a guide for how voters may react. From the outset, however, we must define what we mean by "disability." Definitions of what constitutes disability vary widely across multiple scholarly fields—and there is even disagreement over definitions *within* fields.

Given that the purpose of this chapter is not to debate the merits of any particular definition of disability, we make use of our own definition, which is appropriate for a political study. For voters to judge a candidate based on any impairment or disability, they must first know about it. Therefore, we define disability as any physical or mental impairment on the part of a politician that is *knowable* to a voter. This includes any visible impairment, such as senator Tammy Duckworth's (D-IL) double leg amputations, or something invisible but that a politician (or another source) acknowledges publicly, such as Fetterman's depression, as well as conditions that may lie in-between the two.[3] Such knowable cues are available to voters, who may choose to use them when forming an impression of a politician or deciding whether to vote for them. This definition is consistent with other more commonly studied types of low-information and stereotypical cues, as discussed in the following section.

Low-Information Voting

If there is one aspect of practical politics upon which political scientists agree, it is the relatively uninformed and uninterested nature of the

American citizen when it comes to politics (Campbell et al. 1960; Lau and Redlawsk 2006). Extensive research in political psychology demonstrates how voters deal with this lack of information or knowledge: through mental heuristics—or, more simply put, information shortcuts (e.g., Popkin 1991). Voters can take cues from who a candidate is, or what a candidate does, to infer a type of "information" about the candidate that aids them in forming opinions of that candidate. These cues usually involve the application of cultural and political stereotypes, or schema, that are relevant to the cue provided.

One important element of which cues voters use is what Taylor (1981) calls "solo status." When an obvious trait makes an individual stand out in a crowd, that trait becomes a likely target for stereotyping. What this means for voting cues is that distinctive, or relatively rare, scenarios are attended to more than commonplace ones, making illness (mental or physical) a prime target for stereotyping as disabled or ill candidates are relatively rare. As of 2022, only 12 of the 535 members of the US Congress were listed as having disabilities according to the National Council on Independent Living (NCIL). This 2 percent is a far cry from the estimated 25 percent of Americans living with disabilities. As a result, it is reasonable to expect that seeing a candidate with a disability draws voters' attention and generates disability stereotyping.

Reher's (2021) study of physical disabilities in hypothetical candidates in the UK lends support to the argument that a candidate's disability can act as an information cue to potential voters. Reher finds that candidates who are described as either blind or deaf or who use a wheelchair are viewed as more honest and more caring—notably feminine, or communal, traits (see Dolan 2014)—than similar nondisabled candidates, presumably because of the experiences disabled candidates have been through and the barriers they have overcome. She finds no significant differences in the evaluation of physically disabled candidates on the more masculine traits of competence and strength.[4]

Like Reher, we believe that stereotypes about disabilities can affect opinions about candidates. However, we are interested in how disabilities can affect perceptions of candidates as appropriate leaders, given what we know about voters' preferences for *masculine* traits in their political leaders.

Leader Schema: Think Politics, Think Masculine

When we choose leaders in American politics, research demonstrates that we are looking for masculine types (Eagly and Karau 2002). Masculinity has long been a feature of US politics (see, e.g., Testi 1995), and there is even evidence that the importance of masculinity in political leaders may have increased over time (Lawless 2004). Even political offices themselves take on masculine aspects, with masculine traits being found more desirable at almost all levels of political office than feminine traits (Rosenwasser and Dean 1989).[5]

Miller and colleagues' (1986) seminal study of open-ended responses to voters' likes and dislikes regarding presidential candidates finds two significant patterns in voters' evaluations of politicians, both of which are important to our hypotheses. The first is that personal aspects of candidates far outweigh issue and party aspects, a finding that is now taken as a political science "given" (see, more recently, McAllister 2007), and, importantly, one that even holds in our era of increased partisan polarization (Christenson and Weisberg 2019), making personal factors like health important considerations. The second finding is that there are five general factors of personal information US voters consider important in their politicians: competence, integrity, reliability, charisma, and individual personal elements. Competence is the quality of being sensible, well informed, intelligent, and efficient. Integrity indicates honesty and associated elements. Reliability consists of being dependable, cautious, and stable. Charisma is the state of being a dignified leader who inspires confidence. Finally, individual personal elements are comprised largely of demographic considerations; notably, candidate health is one of them.[6]

Many, if not most, of these traits found important by Miller and colleagues (1986) are, not coincidentally, included in the classic stereotype of masculinity. Competence, leadership (i.e., charisma), and reliability are all masculine traits (again, see chapter 1 in this volume, as well as Spence, Helmreich, and Stapp 1975; Bem 1974). As stated previously, they also tend to be the same traits seen as desirable in politics. Sapiro (1991, 178) notes that masculine characteristics are "normal and healthy" in politics. Some of the specific masculine characteristics that voters find politically attractive include being assertive, tough, aggressive, self-confident, active, and rational, along with being "masculine" (Huddy and Terkildsen 1993, 523), echoing elements of Miller's broad factors.

None of this is to say that feminine traits are not also attractive at times. For example, voters can value compassion and empathy in a political leader, though less so than masculine traits (Huddy and Terkildsen 1993). And as long as masculine traits dominate, it is this standard to which political candidates will be held (Schneider and Bos 2019). This, in turn, may damage the prospects of candidates with mental or physical health concerns.

Mental Health and Stereotyping

To our knowledge, one of the only studies that investigates voting for candidates with mental illness is by Loewen and Rheault (2021). Theirs is an experimental study that compares the effects of candidate depression to the effects of physical impairments, such as cancer, high blood pressure, and the flu, among others. Overall, they find that voters "punish" candidates with depression, voting for them by an average of ten points less than candidates with physical ailments, an effect found even among their co-partisans (for Republican candidates specifically). They also find that candidates with depression are viewed as having less character and as being less prepared than candidates with physical illnesses. While this finding is consistent with our contention that candidates with mental illness may suffer at the hands of voters, it does not address masculinity, our chosen topic. The literature on mental health stereotypes, however, provides specific, applicable fodder for our hypothesis.

There are three central stereotypes discussed in the literature about people with mental illness (hereafter PWMI, a term regularly used in the existing literature).[7] The most frequent is that PWMI are dangerous, unpredictable, and sometimes even violent (Kobau et al. 2010). Perhaps surprisingly, this belief has increased over time in the United States (Parcasepe and Cabassa 2013). As a result of these expectations, individuals frequently have negative associations with mental illness and those who suffer from it. This stereotype presents a challenge to the ideal agentic or masculine political image. Desirable masculine traits include being analytical (Bem 1974), or rational (Huddy and Terkildsen 1993), which the qualities of unpredictability and dangerousness seem to directly undermine. Additionally, as chapter 1 of this volume demonstrates, the more violent and aggressive traits frequently included in agency are not a part of the traditional masculine prototype, but rather of a "toxic masculinity."

Another common stereotype of PWMI is the perception of incompetence: questioning whether they can be trusted with decisions regarding, for example, their own treatment, finances, and other day-to-day matters. Studies demonstrate that the public sees PWMI as less able to handle responsibility (Pescosolido et al. 1999) than people with other conditions, such as those with health concerns or those who are described as generally "troubled" (Pescosolido et al. 2011). Self-sufficiency and self-reliance have long been part of the masculine prototype (see Bem 1974); judgment of an individual as unable to handle their own affairs directly undermines this prototype.

The final relevant stereotype of PWMI is that they have bad or weak characters (see Corrigan and Watson 2002): they may lack the strength of will to overcome their illness, or, still more damaging, they brought the illness upon themselves. Kobau and colleagues (2010) find strong statistical support for including the public attitudes of both "I believe a person with mental illness could pull himself or herself together if he or she wanted," and "I believe a person with mental illness has only himself/herself to blame for his/her condition" as elements of negative stereotyping. Here, again, self-reliance would be cast in doubt, as would the masculine traits of independence, competitiveness, and ambition (Bem 1974).

Each of these stereotypes, as part of the overall stigma of mental illness, has the potential to impact voters' views of a candidate with a mental illness. More specifically—and relevant to the research in this chapter—these stereotypes may impact voters' views of candidates as sufficiently masculine for political office. Being seen as dangerous, unpredictable, incompetent, or weak-willed are all contenders for lowering one's masculine image.

Physical Health and Stereotyping

While research into physical disabilities and their associated stereotypes is relatively deep (see, e.g., Louvet 2007), there exists little research into stereotypes (or even general stigmas) associated with physical disabilities like strokes—a central focus of the research in this chapter. What limited research does exist on these less obvious forms of physical disability tends to focus on the locus of responsibility for the condition. In relatively early examinations, Weiner (1995) looks at how the attribution of responsibility—whether the person themselves is to blame for a situation—as a key factor in assessing social reactions to illness.

The causes of strokes, our subject here, are myriad, making causal attribution difficult. Genetics are a contributing factor, but so are some lifestyle choices that indirectly contribute to stroke risk, such as cardiovascular disease (Boehme, Esenwa, and Elkind 2017). While the public generally lacks knowledge of stroke risk factors (Pancioli et al. 1998), they could conceivably understand or believe that some individual health choices are contributors. In other words, some voters may blame a candidate who has a stroke for their overall health condition.[8]

There also remains the possibility that voters could be leery of a candidate who has suffered a stroke for reasons largely separate from attribution—namely, the possibility of ill health and incapacitation.[9] Studies show that public knowledge about brain injuries such as strokes is low (Ralph and Derbyshire 2013). At the same time, however, the public does overwhelmingly (85 percent) understand that strokes are related to the brain (Budin-Ljøsne et al. 2022).

The literature on brain injuries touches on the stigma that *could* accompany a stroke. A literature review by Ralph and Derbyshire (2013) shows that the public tends to hold negative views of those who have suffered but survived brain injuries (stroke is but one possibility of an acquired brain injury, or ABI) in terms of avoiding interacting with them, like the public's reactions to PWMI. Additionally, while those who are labeled as suffering from ABI are viewed sympathetically by the public, they are also seen as less competent than other groups, such as homemakers, professionals, and even criminals (Fresson et al. 2017). In fact, those with ABI are seen as equally competent as individuals who suffer from mental illness. In multiple studies, ABI is treated by the public in much the same way as mental illness. It can lead to stereotypes of incompetence and behaviors of public avoidance.

It is important to note that while a stroke does not automatically result in brain damage, by any means, the possibility remains and may occur to the public, especially if the candidate publicly suffers from temporary, associated difficulties, as Fetterman did. As a result, we expect to find that, in our experimental scenarios, a candidate who has suffered a stroke with some temporary resulting difficulties will be treated similarly to a candidate who has suffered from depression: voters should rate them as lower on measures related to masculinity.

Masculine Traits and Illness: Theory and Hypotheses

Gender intersects, writ large, with disability. As Asch and Fine (1988, 3) note: "Having a disability [is] seen as synonymous with being dependent, childlike and helpless—an image fundamentally challenging all that is embodied in the ideal male: virility, autonomy and independence." More specifically, it also intersects with depression and, potentially, physical illness. As discussed above, the stereotypes surrounding depression and brain injuries lend credence to the idea that those who suffer from either or both of these ailments may be seen as less masculine than they otherwise would be. For politicians, regardless of sex—though we only examine a male candidate here—this could pose an electoral problem.

McDermott and Jones's chapter in this volume (chapter 1) reviews how the definition and measurement of masculinity has changed over time. One thing that virtually all definitions (be it the BSRI, hegemonic masculinity, or masculinity ideology, to name just a few) have in common, however, is that masculinity means strength—if not necessarily physical, then at least emotional and performative. The masculine ideal is expected to be leader-like, self-sufficient, and dominating, among other things. Voters may judge that mental and physical illnesses impair someone's ability to live up to the masculine standard that society and culture—or, even more importantly, politics—set.

Research into both depression and strokes indirectly supports our contention that mental and physical conditions damage the masculine image. Not only are those who are depressed seen as having a weak or bad character, but they are also seen as simply weak all-around. Sheehan, Dubke, and Corrigan (2017) find that that individuals suffering from depression are seen as being "cowardly," "weak," and "a failure" by the public. This fits with Kobau and colleagues' (2010) negative stereotype factor, in which individuals endorse the view that people who are mentally ill can pull themselves out of their illness and may be responsible for their own condition. In a political world that values, even requires, masculinity, experiencing or having experienced depression is likely to hurt a candidate's perceived masculinity. Many of the traits voters expect from their politicians could also be seen as lower than average in a candidate whose health is not top-notch or who has a potentially recurring physical issue. For those suffering a stroke, it is not uncommon to have recurring problems with strokes; roughly one-quarter will suffer at least one subsequent stroke (American Stroke Association 2023). Additionally, both PWMI and those who have suffered brain injuries are seen as less competent to handle their own affairs (Pescosolido et al. 2011). In sum, strength and competence are associated with masculinity, making each of these types of illnesses targets for stereotypes that decrease views of a candidate's potential masculinity.

Taken together, the existing literature in these areas leads us to the following hypotheses:

HMI1. Individuals will rate a candidate who suffers from depression lower on stereotypically masculine characteristics than they do a candidate who does not.

HMI2. As a result, individuals will be less likely to support a candidate who suffers from depression than for a candidate who does not.

HPH1. Individuals will rate a candidate who has suffered a stroke lower on stereotypically masculine characteristics than they do a candidate who does not.

HPH2. As a result, individuals will be less likely to support a candidate who has suffered a stroke than for a candidate who has not.

Data and Method

To test our hypotheses, we use an original, nationally representative survey conducted by Verasight.[10] Verasight is an internet survey company whose panel is recruited through a combination of both address-based probability sampling and online targeting to reach a representative national sample.[11] The survey was conducted online from August 18–23, 2023, among 1,500 US adults nationwide. The data are weighted to match the 2023 Current Population Survey on key demographics.

The survey was designed with an embedded experiment to gauge opinions about a candidate with no name or party affiliation, but with Fetterman's profile (his age, education, experience, and family) and health situations. Given that Fetterman and his condition were national news in 2022 and 2023, there is a chance that respondents may have recognized this candidate as Fetterman himself and rated the candidate using outside information about the actual person, predominately his party affiliation as a Democrat. In acknowledgment of this possibility, at the end of the traits analysis we run a party check on our results to ensure that respondents of both major parties use the predicted stereotypes. In addition, in the multivariate analysis we control for the respondent's party affiliation.

The experiment had a total of four conditions: (1) a control candidate with some of Fetterman's background but with no mental or health conditions mentioned; (2) a depression condition, which includes his hospitalization for six weeks for "clinical depression"; (3) a condition that includes information about his stroke and auditory issues following it; and (4) a condition that provides information on both the stroke and the depression. Complete wording for each scenario can be found in the online appendix, but as an example, the combined stroke and depression scenario was as follows:

> Now we would like to ask you about [a] candidate for office. He is fifty-three years old, married with three children, and he has an MBA (from the University of Connecticut) as well as a master's degree in public policy (from Harvard).[12] His political career started as mayor of a small town and then he served as his state's lieutenant governor. Now he is seeking national legislative office. This candidate recently suffered a stroke. As a result of the stroke his auditory (speaking and hearing) skills suffered some, although they have since recovered. More recently, he was hospitalized for six weeks for clinical depression. If he were running in your area, how likely would you be to support this candidate?

Each of the scenarios was accompanied by a five-point (Likert-style) measure of support, ranging from "extremely unlikely" to "extremely likely." To measure respondents' views of the experimental candidate's relevant traits, we constructed a battery of questions on a seven-point numeric scale, asking how well each trait described the candidate, from not at all well to extremely well. The traits included "competent," "fit for office," "masculine or manly," "a leader," "strong and authoritative," "helpless," and "honest." (The traits "strong and authoritative," "honest," and "competent" are also included in Reher 2021). We do not mean to imply that this list contains all traits affected by disability. But, to keep the list of traits manageable for respondents, we intentionally focused on traits related to our masculinity hypotheses, with honesty being the only non-agentic trait we tested. Including the honesty trait allows for the possibility of finding positive feminine trait associations while also presenting a contrast or control trait for the battery of otherwise masculine traits.

Results

Traits

As a first look at the data, we compare the means of the traits by experimental condition. Table 4.1 presents the results of an ANOVA post-hoc independent samples tests for each trait, identifying any significant mean differences among experimental conditions. On the traits of "competence" and "fitness for office," respondents rate the candidates in all experimental scenarios as significantly less competent and less fit for

TABLE 4.1: Mean candidate trait rating by experimental condition

	Candidate trait						
Condition	Competent	Fit for office	Masculine or manly	A leader	Strong and authoritative	Helpless	Honest
Control	5.09[b,c,d]	5.09[b,c,d]	4.68[c∧]	5.15[b,c,d]	4.97[b,c,d]	2.84[c,d]	4.65[b,c]
Depression only	4.76[a,d]	4.44[a,d]	4.53	4.72[a]	4.50[a,d∧]	3.12	5.04[a]
Stroke only	4.77[a,d]	4.50[a,d]	4.41[a∧]	4.76[a]	4.44[a]	3.23[a]	4.92[a∧]
Depression + stroke	4.40[a,b,c]	4.01[a,b,c]	4.43	4.54[a]	4.23[a,b∧]	3.43[a]	4.80
F	11.51**	26.71**	2.44∧	9.97**	14.10**	6.55**	4.44**

*p ≤ .05; **p ≤ .001; ∧p ≤ .10 (all two-tailed)
Post-hoc paired comparisons (Tukey HSD): a = diff. from control; b = diff. from depression; c = diff. from stroke; d = diff. from depression + stroke (all at p ≤ .05; except +∧at p ≤ .10 two-tailed)

office than they view the control candidate. In addition, when compared with each other, the combined stroke plus depression candidate is rated lower on these traits than all other conditions. In other words, having depression or experiencing a stroke significantly lowers the candidate's perceived competence and fitness for office, but experiencing both lowers these ratings significantly more still. Contrary to Reher's (2021) finding that disabled candidates are no less competent than a control candidate, we find that when the disability is mental or physical illness the situation changes substantially. This finding accords with research on mental and physical illness stigmas.

We see similar but less consistent effects for the traits of being "a leader" and being "strong and authoritative." The candidate in each illness condition receives significantly lower ratings on these two traits than does the control candidate, as expected. But the combination condition of stroke plus depression is not significantly different from either of the other treatment conditions, although it is marginally lower (p = 0.09) than depression on the trait of being "strong and authoritative." It is possible that any one of these conditions in and of itself is sufficient to lower voters' opinions on these candidate's traits. Importantly, each of these traits is one that has traditionally been linked to the politically masculine ideal, indicating that a candidate in any one of these situations could be seen as less agentic than other candidates.

Perhaps surprisingly, while the experimental candidates are rated significantly lower on these specific traits, all of which are traditionally associated with masculinity, they are not viewed as lower on the *specific* measure of "masculinity or manly." Only the stroke condition is marginally lower (p = 0.07) than the control condition on the masculine trait. While this finding deserves further study, it is beyond the purview of this chapter. We can speculate, however, that the label "masculine" has far more complex meaning to respondents than the other traits; certainly, the label has multifaceted meanings to researchers (see chapter 1 of this volume).

The result for the trait "helpless" is only significantly lower for the candidates who experienced a stroke—either alone or in combination with depression. The depression candidate is rated statistically equal on this measure to the control candidate. This reinforces previous findings that some in the public may view those with depression as *not* helpless in that they could, conceivably, pull themselves out of it (Kobau et al. 2010).

As Reher (2021) found among candidates with disabilities, we also see that the experimental candidates are seen as more honest than the control candidate. The difference is statistically significant for both the depression alone and stroke alone conditions. The combination candidate is also rated higher than the control candidate on honesty, although the difference is not statistically reliable. Together, the finding of higher ratings on honesty indirectly supports our hypotheses by demonstrating that it is solely on masculine or agentic traits that voters view our experimental candidates as "less than."

Potential Party Effects

To ensure that these findings are not merely due to recognition of Fetterman's profile and resulting partisan preferences, we run the key masculine traits by respondent party affiliation as well as candidate condition. While we do not name our candidate or provide his geographic context, it is possible that in the experimental conditions individuals begin to recognize the similarity to Fetterman, especially in the stroke and depression condition given the unique combination of the two experiences. If indeed the experiment is capturing only recognition effects, then we would expect to find that only Republicans respond negatively in the illness conditions as they become likely to recognize Fetterman and use party cues. Democrats, on the other hand, should, if anything, rate the candidate more positively on these traits as they are increasingly likely to recognize one of their own.

We present the party results for the three main masculine-associated traits—"competent," "fit for office," and "strong and authoritative"—in the online appendix, table A4.1. We focus on Democratic and Republican respondents as they form the bulk of the expected effect. The data demonstrate that while effects are stronger among Republicans than Democrats, overall, there is the same pattern of significant differences among experimental conditions, regardless of respondent party. For example, on the trait of fit for office, the control candidate is rated an average of 5.2 and 5.24 from Democrats and Republicans respectively. And, just as we see in table 4.1, these ratings drop in the treatment conditions, resulting in a low of 4.48 among Democrats and 3.49 among Republicans for the stroke and depression combined candidate. In both cases, this candidate is significantly lower than all other conditions. On all three of these important and agentic traits, Democrats' ratings of the candidate are significantly lower in the experimental conditions than the control condition, as are Republicans.

Rather than undermining the experiment and results, the partisan results bolster the hypothesis findings. The fact that effects are found among Democrats (his fellow partisans) as well as Republicans strongly supports the overall hypotheses that these conditions and the health information they provide can supply voters with informational cues they to use when making candidate judgments.

Overall, the trait results strongly support our hypotheses HMI1 and HPH1. Candidates who suffer from depression (HMI1) and those who have had a stroke (HPH1) are rated lower than a "healthy" candidate on a host of politically meaningful masculine characteristics. While "masculinity" itself may not reflect expectations, the component parts of masculinity, according to existing research and measurement, do reflect the expectation that candidates with mental or physical illness are seen as less masculine or agentic than a candidate without these illnesses. In a world of politically masculine standards, these traits could harm disabled candidates' chances of being elected.

Candidate Support

To examine candidate support, we first look at simple bivariate effects among experimental conditions. Table 4.2 presents these results.

The results offer initial support for our voting hypotheses HMI2 and HPH2. We tested for differences between each condition and the control condition with a gamma coefficient, expecting that support would be lower for the candidates suffering from mental or physical illness. In each case, as expected, support is significantly lower than for the nondisabled candidate.[13] The largest difference, not surprisingly, is between the control condition and the combined depression and stroke candidate condition.

The bivariate results are strong evidence, but they still leave open a further question: Are the affected traits—particularly the masculine

TABLE 4.2: Candidate support by experimental condition

Support	Control	Depression only	Stroke only	Depression + stroke
		Condition		
Extremely unlikely	4%	9%	8%	15%
Somewhat unlikely	9	16	12	20
Neither likely nor unlikely	41	36	37	34
Somewhat likely	34	28	30	23
Extremely likely	13	10	12	9
γ		0.20**	0.11*	0.35**
(s.e.)		(0.06)	(0.05)	(0.05)

γ (gamma) = symmetrical difference from control condition.
*$p \leq .05$; **$p \leq .001$; ^$p \leq .10$ (all two-tailed)

traits—contributing to this reduction in support? It seems a reasonable assumption that these traits matter to the vote, given extensive findings from existing research (as noted above), but we can also directly test it here. We conduct an ordinal logistic regression of candidate support on all the measured traits, also controlling for party affiliation (a five-point variable ranging from Democratic, to Republican, with party leaners and independents/nonpartisans as separate categories) and ideology (a seven-point scale ranging from extremely liberal to extremely conservative), as well as a respondent sex variable (a dummy variable for male). We control for ideology to capture possible effects of conservatives being less sympathetic to individuals with depression (see, e.g., Watson et al., 2005), we accordingly also include an interactive variable for the depression condition and respondent ideology since that is the one condition where we have reason to expect that it may have a differential effect.

The complete results of the regression analysis are included in the online appendix (table A4.2) for this chapter. In brief, they demonstrate that the important influences on the vote, overall, are "competence," "fitness for office," being "strong and authoritative," and "honesty." "Fitness for office" is the most substantive (and significant) influence on the vote in all conditions together, and in each separately (in separate regressions for each condition, including the control condition).[14]

Importantly, the three agentic traits that are determinative in the candidate support regression are precisely the same traits on which our three experimental candidates are rated significantly lower than the control candidate (table 4.1). It bears emphasizing that this again supports our contention in this chapter that candidates with mental and/or physical illnesses are seen as less politically masculine than an average candidate. We can conclude that voters judge candidates suffering from depression or having a stroke as less appealing for political office *because* they do not measure up to expectations for certain masculine traits, in comparison to candidates with no such publicly known ailments, in support our hypotheses HMI2 and HPH2.

Discussion and Conclusion

Our results provide strong support for our expectations regarding the effects of candidate mental and physical illness on perceptions of candidates' masculine-related traits and on vote choice. Voters use candidate disability stereotypes to form impressions and preferences about candidates who suffer from a mental or physical illness, or both. As a result, these candidates are seen as less agentic or masculine than candidates who do not have these conditions. In turn, these masculine-associated traits are of vital importance to voter support for political candidates, resulting in lower vote shares for candidates who have mental or physical ailments. In summary, candidates who admit to a mental illness, even depression, and who have potentially debilitating heath concerns, such as a stroke, are disadvantaged by the masculine expectations of our political culture.

These findings are important and unique as they extend research on disability stigmas into the political realm specifically regarding the role masculinity has long played in politics. Our findings also extend research on candidate masculinity beyond its traditional focus on candidate sex, specifically on women, and broaden it into how masculine expectations affect other individuals who may not automatically meet agentic expectations. The research in this chapter is only a first step, we hope, in what could be much more comprehensive considerations of nontraditional candidates of all types and how they are affected by our traditionally masculine-focused system.

Our study also has limitations, however, which we should mention. First, and most notably, we focus solely on a male candidate for office, so our results cannot be directly translated to a female or nonbinary candidate. As just one example, John Fetterman noted, following his stroke, that the experience had made him a more empathetic person. Renstrom and Ottati (2020) find that voters rate female candidates who demonstrate empathy more favorably than they rate male candidates who do the same. Also, the intersection of candidate sex and gender for women or the nonbinary, combined with a disability, is likely to make for a much more complicated set of effects (e.g., Schneider and Bos 2019). The inclusion of candidate party would add still more inter-activity, especially given that the parties themselves have feminine and masculine images (Winter 2010).

Second, our study carries the limitations of any experimental study. In the 2022 Pennsylvania Senate election, as in most statewide elections, voters also saw other features of the candidate's identity. As noted, Fet-terman is a tall, large, bald man who voters may have perceived as physi-cally masculine. Additionally, voters—at least in Pennsylvania—knew Fetterman's party affiliation and may have known that the election could potentially determine party control of the Senate. Using an experiment has the benefit of allowing us to look at the role of specific factors (here, illness and masculinity) in isolation from these other factors, but, in a real Senate election, many features of a candidate (alongside the national political environment) go into voting decisions.

Third, and finally (though not necessarily exhaustively), our study leaves some questions unanswered while bringing to light new ones. While we find that a candidate suffering from depression, a stroke, or both is rated lower on several traits associated with masculinity and is also likely to get less support from voters, future studies could more closely examine factors that may reduce such stigmas. One possibility, consistent with the contact hypothesis (Allport 1954, and supported by many later studies) is that voters who know somebody from a differ-ent group are less likely to hold prejudice against them. Discrimination against a candidate with a stroke or depression may be relatively higher or lower than prejudice against a candidate with a different condition based upon its prevalence. Additionally, as more elected officials—particularly those who, like Fetterman, hold other traits or features as-sociated with masculinity—are willing to speak about their physical or mental disabilities and Americans see them succeed in office, they may be willing to support other candidates with disabilities in future elections. Additionally, those voters who share a disability with a candidate may also be more likely to support that candidate for office.[15] In other words, there are potential mitigating factors that could come into play and that warrant further research.

NOTES

1 We use the terms "masculine" and "agentic" interchangeably. While there may be some differences in measurement strategies, the traits in question are the same.

2 This is not to say that all reactions to Fetterman's health issues were negative. As Roche (2023) notes, the public was largely supportive of Fetterman taking time off to recover. In addition, Democratic leaders were largely united in praise for his honesty and courage. Such effects also show up in the data presented here.

3 Senate minority leader Mitch McConnell's (R-KY) recent (as of this writing in October 2023) freeze-ups in front of the press have raised questions about his health and cognitive abilities, though his staff report that he is fine (Karni 2023).

4 We, not Reher, have categorized these traits as "feminine" or "masculine." These distinctions become important for crafting our hypotheses.

5 This is especially noteworthy in the highest offices of government, as demonstrated in the styles of women like Hillary Clinton in the United States, Margaret Thatcher of the UK, and Angela Merkel of Germany (Jones 2016).

6 Further research has found slightly different factor solutions, but in large part they do not deviate from this basic model (e.g., Pancer, Brown, and Barr 1999).

7 While depression may seem like a mild form of mental illness, especially when compared to more stigmatized illnesses such as schizophrenia, research has repeatedly found that the stereotypes surrounding mental illness apply to depression (Parcasepe and Cabassa 2013).

8 In the particular case of Fetterman, the campaign of his opponent, celebrity heart surgeon Dr. Mehmet Oz, made at least one well-publicized attempt to blame Fetterman for his stroke by mentioning to reporters that if Fetterman "had ever eaten a vegetable in his life, then maybe he wouldn't have had a major stroke" (CBS News 2022).

9 In general, it is highly unlikely that most of the public knows the replacement process for a politician in their state or locality (Galston 2001), making the fear of losing someone popularly elected a real one. In Fetterman's case, the Democratic governor would (almost certainly) have appointed a Democrat to serve out Fetterman's term had he needed to step down. Not knowing this, the public may have feared a loss of representation in the event of another stroke.

10 Funding for the survey was generously provided through a grant from Fordham University's Research Consortium on Disability.

11 All respondents are verified, and Verasight never outsources any data collection. They are a member of the American Association for Public Opinion Research's Transparency Initiative and archive nonproprietary data with the Roper Center.

12 Fetterman himself turned fifty-four years old three days before the survey was fielded.

13 We also tested the differences between each experimental condition. The depression and stroke conditions had statistically similar results, but support in the stroke and depression combined condition was significantly lower than in both the depression and stroke only conditions.

14 Given that these traits are all part of the leader profile that the US electorate desires, there is little reason to believe that they *should* have differential effects across any of the conditions. The one exception would be that, based on existing findings (Watson et al. 2005), depression might have a larger than average negative effect among conservative respondents, but we do not find that to be the case (table A4.2). In addition, the helpless trait does not affect the vote in these or any of the conditions, despite being significantly lower, in our ANOVA post hoc tests, for the candidate in the stroke only condition.

15 For example, a number of stroke survivors interviewed after the Fetterman and Oz debate spoke of how they identified with Fetterman and his experiences (Ryan 2022).

PART 2

Masculinity and Individual-Level Political Views
and Preferences

5

An Introduction to Masculinity and Political Attitudes

CHRISTINA PAO AND NATE ROUNDY

Research on sex (frequently conflated with "gender") and politics in the United States has proliferated over the last several decades. Scholars have shown that sex is associated with differences in political views and behaviors. However, much of what has been identified by political science as a "gender gap" (hereafter more appropriately dubbed the "sex gap"), might be better understood as a gap between more and less masculine individuals, rather than as a gap between men and women, as assigned by sex. In this chapter we briefly introduce the relationship between gender and politics, with a focus on masculinity, and discuss developments in these subfields of gender and politics—namely, the gendering of politics and political attitudes and behaviors, and an associated gendered backlash. Through this, we provide a brief overview of the literature that currently exists on individual attitudes and gendered identities, primarily masculinity, as an introduction to the empirical chapters that follow in this section of the volume.

Sex, Gender, and Politics

In political science and in colloquial language, discussions of politics often center on issue of gender. Often, these discussions are most centered on a binary division between men and women, frequently defined by sex assigned at birth. As discussed at length in the introduction to and chapter 1 of this volume, however, gendered aspects of an individual (e.g., masculinity and femininity) have more explanatory and potentially causal value to politics than does biological sex (see also McDermott 2016).

Theorists have shown the manifold ways in which gender is socially and interactionally constructed through day-to-day acts and constrained by social sanctioning (Butler 2020; West and Zimmerman 1987). Gender has both been articulated as a structure (Ridgeway and Correll 2004) and as an embodied place of power and control (Bordo 2004). Nonetheless, gender itself has many underlying components—all of which can differentially affect social and political beliefs and experiences. For instance, gender beliefs and expression, even among people within the same sex, can affect political positionality. For example, a study of the 2016 election shows how gendered *beliefs* drive electoral outcomes, concluding that "gender differences in candidate support were largely driven by gender differences in beliefs that the United States has grown too soft and feminine" (Deckman and Cassese 2021, 277). Also, gendered *identity* (e.g., one's own relationship with femininity and masculinity) has become associated with many foundational political constructs; the norms of gender govern how individuals behave and how they are treated by institutions and others, and are an omnipresent source of socialization pressure that affects behavior and attitudes (Butler 2020).

Masculinities, Attitudes, and Political Behavior

In recent years, researchers have begun to focus on *masculinity* as a driver of sociopolitical views. Given how much masculinity has been shown to drive a wide range of behaviors and attitudes, such as binge drinking (Peralta et al. 2010), paranormal beliefs (Silva 2023), and sexual preferences (Moskowitz and Hart 2011), it would be surprising if masculinity were not a driver of social and political attitudes and behaviors.

The most significant barrier to observing this relationship has been the persistence of measuring the gender gap by looking at differences between men and women, without looking holistically at gender. Many foundational studies in the field outlined baseline differences in political behavior and attitudes of voters by sex (specifically those within a conflated sex/gender binary), even while talking about the "gender" gap in voting/participation (Caughell 2016; Whitaker et al. 2008). It is common for research to conflate sex with gender, as Butler (1990) observes (and as noted in the Introduction and in chapter 1). But the "gender gap" in which men and women differ in political opinion and behavior emerges not from their sexed characteristics, but from cultural norms about gender performance and appropriateness. Women's and men's gender identities differ inasmuch as they are expected to perform different sets of gendered norms, leading to significant, albeit subtle, differences in political socialization and its corresponding effect on behavior, attitudes, and prioritizations. For example, literature from the late twentieth century indicated that women were "less politically interested, informed, and efficacious than men and that this gender gap in political engagement has consequences for political participation" (Verba, Burns, and Schlozman 1997), or that women and men have different motivations for political activation (Klein 1984).

But, just as theory would lead us to believe, what is seen as a gap between men and women is better explained by differences in masculinity. McDermott (2016) shows that while there is a substantial gap between men and women on measures of political engagement—a category that includes traits like interest in the news, knowledge about politics, and the frequency of political discussions—sex matters much less than masculinity (as measured using the Bem Sex Role Inventory, or BSRI). While not as important in shaping political engagement as education, masculinity is more predictive than traits that seem like they should matter a lot, like partisanship or ideology. People who are more masculine pay more attention to politics and are better able to answer questions about it (though measurement error may be an issue; see Dolan 2011 and Lizotte and Sidman 2009).[1] The fact that McDermott's data come from before the candidacy of Donald Trump made masculinity a central issue of concern highlights the long-standing nature of this truly gendered gap.

It seems likely that this gap in political interest and participation is driven by masculinity, but this alone does not tell us why that might be. Wolak (2022) and McDermott (2016) point to a relationship between masculinity and greater tolerance for disagreement and conflict. If politics is viewed as contentious, and masculinity leads people to be more likely to embrace conflict, it makes sense that more masculine individuals would more often engage in politics (especially on measures involving actions like having discussions about political issues).

Masculinity is a driver of issue and partisan preferences as well. Studies have continually shown a growing gap of 1) men being more likely to favor Republican candidates and women being more likely to support Democratic candidates; and 2) men being more likely to declare themselves as Republicans and political independents than women (Newport

2009; Norrander 1999). Recent polling has shown that 56 percent of women identify as Democrats or lean Democratic, in comparison to 42 percent of men; 50 percent of men are Republican and/or lean Republican, as opposed to 38 percent of women (Igielnik 2020). But, as with the difference between men and women in political engagement, masculinity seems to be a substantial driver of these gaps, with masculinity as much as sex leading men to be more likely to identify as Republicans and vote for Republican candidates. The difference between masculinity driving votes and sex driving votes is of vital importance to the future of US politics: a durable sex gap, in which women are more likely to support Democrats, is likely to benefit Democrats. But in a world in which women are becoming more likely to assert masculinity (or are at least expected to according to Diekman and Eagly 2000), a gender gap could well benefit Republican candidates (McDermott 2016).

Data from from USC's 2020 preelection Understanding America Survey (UAS) has shown that there are also descriptive differences in masculinity and femininity among men and women, particularly by party affiliation (see tables 5.1–5.3). Using a single-item, first-person masculinity-femininity scale, respondents were asked to place themselves on a six-point scale, ranging from "completely masculine" to "completely feminine," with intermediate categories of "mostly" and "slightly" masculine or feminine (as described by Cassino 2020). As UAS is a panel survey, the answers of respondents to the masculinity/femininity item were matched with their responses on other waves of the survey as needed (the UAS, during this period, was fielding multiple times per month).

On the whole, men were more conservative than women, and women were more likely to be Democrats than men. Further, descriptively, more masculine men were more likely to be Republicans than Democrats, and women who were *less* feminine were more likely to be Democrats than Republicans (though, across all femininity categories, women were still more likely to be Democrats than Republicans). In table 5.3, with the full sample, we see that the most extremes of gender expression (i.e., completely masculine or completely feminine) have the highest mean conservatism. Altogether, these data suggest that gender expressions of femininity and masculinity are highly correlated with ideology, both between and within gender identity categories, and that the greatest

TABLE 5.1: Differences in political attitudes and affiliations gender identity, men

Gender	Mean self-placement on liberal (= 0) to conservative (= 100) scale	% Democrat*	% Republican*
Completely masculine	64.1	30.6	45.8
Mostly masculine	47.8	48.7	22.2
All other	41.2	51.8	21.5
Overall	58.3	36.5	38.1

TABLE 5.2: Differences in political attitudes and affiliations gender identity, women

Gender	Mean self-placement on liberal (= 0) to conservative (= 100) scale	% Democrat*	% Republican*
Completely feminine	60.0	40.1	39.3
Mostly feminine	46.3	48.6	24.1
All other	45.2	48.8	19.5
Overall	53.93	43.6	32.5

TABLE 5.3: Differences in political attitudes and affiliations gender identity, all

Gender	Mean self-placement on liberal (= 0) to conservative (= 100) scale	% Democrat*	% Republican*
Completely masculine	63.9	30.8	45.6
Mostly masculine	47.3	49.0	21.9
Slightly masculine	45.8	48.6	20.5
Slightly feminine	42.8	50.0	17.8
Mostly feminine	46.6	48.7	24.1
Completely feminine	60.0	40.3	38.8
Overall	55.8	40.6	34.9

*Percentages exclude partisan leaners.

likelihood of identifying as a Republican comes from the most masculine respondents, rather than from biological sex.

Some studies have shown that these gaps could be explained by sex differences in attitudes toward "cultural issues," such as gay rights and reproductive rights; women are said to be more influenced by issues and policy priorities when deciding their political alignment than men are—specifically as it relates to issues dealing with equality and social marginalization (Kaufmann 2002). Studies such as this emphasize the gendered differences in sociocultural issues reflect our earlier observation that norms surrounding gender eventually affect political socialization and subsequent behavior, highlighting again that masculinity and femininity associated with gender norms have significant political implications that have traditionally been attributed to sex.

In part, gender gaps, like those found in the USC survey data regarding partisanship and ideology, as well as potential issue differences, have also driven some of the images around the parties themselves. Evidence from American National Election Studies data reveal that "Americans have come to view the parties increasingly in gendered terms of masculinity and femininity," with the Republican Party seen as more masculine and the Democratic Party as more feminine (Winter 2010, 587). This argues for a gendered, rather than sexed approach, to politics, at least in terms of parties, and supports a gendered approach to issue differences among individuals.

Also supporting the gendered approach is the fact that men and women are not monolithic. The sexed approach to politics masks considerable heterogeneity *within* each sex. We know from existing research that there is "considerable heterogeneity in political identity and behavior among women based on race, class, and other key sociodemographic characteristics"—a tendency especially evident in the 2020 US presidential election, in which a majority of white women voted for Trump (Cassese and Barnes 2019, 677). The same differences have been found among men (see, e.g., Bedolla and Scola 2006), demonstrating that men are no more of a bloc than are women. The literature, particularly in recent years, has underscored that the sex gap in preferences cannot be understood as detached from other identity-based gaps (Junn and Masuoka 2020).

Sex gaps in attitudes and behaviors are particularly stark in light of the issue-driven approaches that are taken by parties to maintain and recruit their base. While women have historically been thought to be more engaged with "compassion" issues (e.g., those which support social well-being through welfare services or safety/regulation policies; Shapiro and Mahajan 1986), and sex gaps stayed somewhat consistent over time with policies relating to violence or the use of force (Eichenberg 2003; Hansen, Clemens, and Dolan 2022), more recent literature has also revealed greater heterogeneity in policy preferences. Overall, there is still an indication that there are differences between the sexes toward issues like gun control and torture in "expected" ways pertaining to compassion issues (Lizotte 2019; Thomas, Miller, and Murphy 2008), but there is also more evidence of heterogeneity in preferences within parties—for example, intraparty differences in ideology (Norrander 2003) or beliefs about the role of the government (Lizotte 2020). Further, there is an indication that the mechanisms of differences in policy support are not necessarily driven only by preferences, but also by expectations regarding risks and other exogenous factors (Ranehill and Weber 2022). All of these point to gendered—that is, socialized—differences rather than biological ones.

The sex gap literature in political attitudes and behavior has revealed both long-standing and changing differences in the US political landscape and, more importantly, has shown 1) the underlying heterogeneity that exists even within these gender divides; and 2) how these divides are socially constructed, upheld, and reinforced by gendered expectations of men and women (e.g., the association of women and caring qualities, like empathy).

Threatened Masculinity and Backlash

An important part of the politics of gender, especially in structuring the politics of masculinity in the United States, has been the effects of the feminist movement on gendered roles (Gelb 1989; Phillips 1998). With the incremental mainstreaming of feminism, there has been ongoing backlash: as feminism has continued to accumulate an even broader audience for the advancement of women and gender minorities in society, there has also been a set of countermovements that have been established to uphold patriarchal norms (Messner 1998), fueled by a perceived threat to masculinity's dominance in American culture. The rise of LGBTQ+ rights and racialized civil rights have also contributed to this perceived threat by the traditionally hegemonic white masculine structure.

Even though our society is nowhere near social and economic parity between men and women, the mean relative advantage of men over women in areas like income and education has decreased over time, a trend that might be expected to fuel countermovements like meninists, masculinists, and the men's rights movements. Pro-masculinity movements such as these argue that women have gone too far in their pursuit of liberation and are now oppressing men, whom they see as the victims of the rise in the relative power of women (Carian, DiBranco, and Ebin 2022). Importantly, men's opposition to feminist politics has been an important socialization agent that affects how masculinity and femininity are structured in US politics. In first-wave feminism, men's opposition to suffrage stemmed from norms around men's role as a head of household. In contemporary feminist politics, many anti-feminist men see feminist organizing as an assault on masculinity itself.

Evidence for this role of threatened masculinity in shaping political views comes from experiments that induce state-based gender identity threat among men, leading them to believe that their masculinity is in question. Mansell and colleagues (2022) show that men who receive negative feedback about their performance on a task makes men—especially masculine men—much more likely to endorse sexist views. Harrison and Michelson (2019) find that threatened masculinity among men is a substantial predictor of opposition for transgender rights. In the run-up to the 2016 US presidential election, Cassino and Besen-Cassino (2021) found that gender role threat primes made men more likely to support Trump rather than a female (Hillary Clinton), but not a male (Bernie Sanders), opponent.

While we normally think about a backlash against feminist movements and the relative progress of women in society as being driven by men, studies like these show that, once again, gender differences are being occluded by sex differences. It may be the case that—on average—threat to men's status in society leads them to be more likely to hold certain countervailing political views, but it seems that this is likely driven by the fact that men are more likely to hold masculine gender identities, and, here again, it is gender, not sex, driving the response.

Conclusions

While the study of gender and political behavior has centered on gaps between men and women, many of these differences are better understood as being driven not by sex, but by gender, and, in particular, by masculinity. Much of the observed gaps between men and women in areas like political engagement and partisan preferences are driven not by differences between men and women, but by differences between more and less masculine individuals. This gendering of politics extends to views of the parties, which are seen as masculine and feminine, and even indicated in issue positions within areas like foreign policy and social welfare.

Masculinity has also been shown to have political implications when men experience gender identity threat. This threat can arise in multiple ways: as a state-based threat (temporarily induced by researchers), as a trait-based threat (a lasting mismatch between their perceptions of their own masculinity and their beliefs about idealized masculinities), or even by a perception that men are losing status relative to women. This type of threat seems to lead men to adopt political attitudes and behaviors that might be perceived as masculine, but the effect of such threat on women who identify as masculine has not been fully developed in the literature.

The chapters that follow are all new investigations into the relevance and effects of masculinity and politics among individuals and their attitudes and beliefs. They build on the existing literature in this chapter's review, as scant as this literature is to date, and demonstrate empirically the importance of masculinity in politics.

NOTE

1 Several studies have shown that much of our understanding of gender and politics has been skewed by the measures of gender themselves. See chapter 1 of this volume for in-depth measurement discussion. We also discuss this point further in our conclusion.

6

Masculinities and Political Ideology in the United States

CATHERINE BOLZENDAHL, CANTON WINER, AND
TARA WARNER

Men and masculinity dominate political power, a finding well established over decades of research (Paxton, Hughes, and Barnes 2020; Alexander, Bolzendahl, and Jalalzai 2018; Duverger 1955; Pateman 1989; Schlozman, Burns, and Verba 1994). Yet this finding obscures a great deal of complexity regarding how the average person understands and relates to masculinity, as well as how political ideologies are linked to masculine ideologies. Thus, this chapter asks: How are divergent constructions of masculine ideology tied to a person's political ideology?

Why are masculinities so complex? In large part, this is because the dominance of men/masculinity is not maintained solely via men as a *categorical group* monopolizing access to and use of political power, but also through the broader *social constructions* of hegemonic masculinity (Connell and Messerschmidt 2005; Connell 1995). Specifically, although hegemonic masculinity is sometimes treated as a specific set of static traits—violence and aggression, physical strength, athleticism, emotional stoicism, competitiveness, professional/monetary achievement, and heterosexuality (Donaldson 1993)—Connell and Messerschmidt (2005) have clarified that the concept refers to a *process* that produces various expressions of masculinity (and femininity). Core to this process is the fact that hegemonic masculinity "legitimates hierarchical gender relations between men and women, between masculinity and femininity, and among men" (Messerschmidt 2012, 58). Hegemonic masculinity thus produces a variety of masculinities, which are often categorized as dominant, marginalized, or subordinate (Messerschmidt 2018; Chen 1999; Silva 2017). This underscores why understanding the relationship between masculine and political ideologies is best served through a multidimensional approach to measuring masculinity, one that allows for multiple masculinities rather than assuming a simple masculinity/femininity dichotomy.

After reviewing the main findings regarding masculinity and politics, we explain the relevance of hegemonic masculine social norms as another dimension of gendered political engagement. Using data from a unique online dataset of American adults that is not nationally representative but is balanced equally by respondents' political and gender identities, we examine descriptive and inferential patterns in masculinity and political ideology.

Our findings show that respondents hold multidimensional views of masculinity. In general, there is a strong relationship between the most traditional views of masculinity and political conservatism. However, most respondents—including political conservatives—value a more moderate framing of masculinity. Political liberals indicate less agreement with the most traditional tenets of normative masculinity, as well as reject the larger system of masculine expectations. Gender and racial cleavages matter above and beyond political ideology, however, and suggest opportunities for conservative operatives to make inroads toward nonwhite voters.

Masculinities and Political Ideologies

There is a robust set of research identifying differences between men and women in their political identities and ideologies, from the gender voting gap (Kaufmann 2006; Manza and Brooks 1998) to gender differences in issue preferences (Shapiro and Mahajan 1986; Barnes and Cassese 2017). More recently, nonbinary measures of gender identity have allowed for more nuanced assessments of these differences (Westbrook and Saperstein 2015; Alexander, Bolzendahl, and Wängnerud 2021). For example, some researchers have allowed respondents to identify along a continuum of masculinity, extrapolating from personality surveys to create scales of typical masculine traits (McDermott 2016). Much of this work suggests that there is a strong relationship between how an individual views themself as a gendered person and their political beliefs and behaviors. In general, it suggests that the stronger a person's polarized gender self-conceptualization—men as mainly masculine and women as mainly feminine—the more likely they are to be politically conservative (Alexander, Bolzendahl, and Öhberg 2021). For both men and women, self-assessed masculine traits may also drive greater conservatism and higher engagement in political activism (Coffé and Bolzendahl 2021; McDermott 2016).

Yet being held accountable to gendered social expectations is one of the cornerstones of gender theory. We are not "free agents" in a relentlessly gendered world; thus, measures that rely solely on self-assessed gendered characteristics miss the socially prescriptive role of gender in shaping how individuals see/treat and are seen/treated by others (West and Zimmerman 1987; Ridgeway 2011). It is this contextual interaction between the individual and the social that makes gender a particularly reified social structure (Galea and Gaweda 2018). Research on political ideology and identity in this vein has largely focused on the constraints experienced by women, due to constructions of femininity, from early childhood socialization (e.g., Bos et al. 2021; Lay et al. 2021) to the denigration of feminized traits and constructs (e.g., Childs 2004; Schneider and Bos 2014). Typically, the association of effective political leadership, participation, and efficacy are framed as strongly tied to stereotypical masculine traits (Lovenduski 2005; but see Johnson and Williams 2020).

Beyond the general association, however, research finds that hegemonic and dominant masculinity themes are particularly strongly associated with right-wing and conservative ideologies and identities. In a paper associating efficacious and agentic traits with masculinity and empathetic and communal traits as feminine, Winter (2010) finds that Americans view the Republican Party as "masculine" and the Democratic Party as "feminine." Although US conservatives have previously embraced a "tough but compassionate" ethos (e.g., Messner 2007), US conservative politics has long found it difficult to fully embrace gender egalitarianism (Klatch 1987; Freeman 1993), and more recent studies have explored connections between hegemonic and even neofascist masculinities and politically conservative identities (Deckman and Cassese 2021; Marx Ferree 2020; DiMuccio and Knowles 2020; Agius, Rosamond, and Kinnvall 2020). Based on a convenience sample of young American adults through Qualtrics, McDermott et al. (2021) found that men and women who hold a conservative political ideology also endorse traditional masculine ideologies. As a whole, this literature highlights the utility of understanding masculinity as linked to political ideology, especially right-wing ideologies/identities, but it is less helpful in identifying a nuanced understanding of variations within masculinity.

Measuring Masculine Ideology

Masculine ideology, or what it means to be a man, can only be understood through its relation to the larger gender structure, which is maintained through the social construction of gender at the individual, interactional, and institutional levels (Acker 1990; Risman 2004; Ridgeway 2011; Britton 2000; Pateman 1989). Masculinity scholars emphasize the need to recognize hierarchies of masculinities wherein hegemonic masculinity can be understood as presenting exemplar masculinities that legitimize the subordination of women (as a group) to men (as a group) while selectively incorporating elements of subordinated masculinities and femininities and enlisting the participation of women and girls (Connell and Messerschmidt 2005).

This presents several important implications. The first is that persons subordinated by processes of hegemonic masculinity can still support and (re)produce it. In other words, although men (as a group) are the primary beneficiaries of hegemonic masculinity, even those disadvantaged by it (such as women) may support it. Through this understanding of hegemony, we see hegemonic masculinity as a process in which individuals can act as accomplices to their own subjugation (and to the subjugation of others) (Chen 1999). Second, although hegemonic masculinity often produces culturally exalted forms of masculinity (i.e., dominant masculinities), they may not be the most commonly experienced forms of masculinity. Thus, there can be many levels and types of masculine dominance constructions, and the embrace or embodiment of hegemonic or dominating masculinities is not limited to men/males (Bridges and Pascoe 2014; Rubin 2003; Schilt 2006; Warner et al. 2022).

Psychological researchers have long demonstrated that men inconsistently identify with the most stereotypical notions of masculinity (McDermott et al. 2019; Thompson and Pleck 1986; Levant 1992). Identifying areas of contestation and change, scholars emphasize that, as a social construct, hegemonic masculinity can be contested, allowing for the emergence of equality masculinities centered on legitimating egalitarian relations between men and women and among men (Messerschmidt

2012; Connell and Messerschmidt 2005; Anderson 2012). Scholars have also noted the rise of hybrid masculinities, which incorporate elements of dominant and subordinate masculinities and even of femininities (Bridges and Pascoe 2014; Winer 2022)

Furthermore, research has shown that social constructions of masculine ideology vary by other major social cleavages, such as gender and race/ethnicity. As Messerschmidt (2012) notes, the process of constructing hegemonic masculinity is about gender relations and coconstructs women within its logic (Winer 2021). Men and women are both socialized to value traditional aspects of masculinity, and men and women are often complicit in constructing and maintaining hegemonic constructions of masculinity (see also McDermott et al. 2021). Yet, some of the traits associated with traditional masculinity, such as violence, control, or hypersexuality, have been tied to negative outcomes for women, such as domestic abuse or sexual assault (Murnen, Wright, and Kaluzny 2002), suggesting that women may be more critical of some aspects of masculinity as compared to men (Levant 2011).

In creating hierarchal gender relations, hegemonic masculine ideologies typically also marginalize men of color. Although Black men are sometimes framed as hypermasculine in domains of toughness and sexuality, they are often barred by anti-Black racism from conventional masculine frames of success, power, and respect (Wingfield 2009; Rogers, Sperry and Levan 2015; Collins 2004). Asian American men, in contrast are often framed as feminine/nonmasculine and desexualized, even as they are stereotyped as hewing to traditional notions of masculine success, such as education, career, or income (Chen 1999; Feliciano et al. 2009). Yet immigration from patriarchal systems and negotiating a marginalized masculinity may increase some Asians Americans' investment in traditional masculine ideology (Phua 2007; Chen 1999; Lu and Wong 2013).

For these reasons, it is important to measure masculinity beyond a person's identity as a man and their identity as masculine and to consider how people may have differing or competing notions of idealized or dominant masculinities. Referring to the literature on political identities, measures of masculinity fall short if they present only one version of stereotypical or toxic masculinity as a linear construct, de facto associate leadership/agentic traits as generically masculine, ignore social cleavages in masculinity constructions, or do not directly measure masculinity itself. In this chapter, we take on the question of how divergent beliefs about masculinity are linked to political affiliations and ideologies.

Data

Data were collected from a survey administered in March 2019 to a nationwide, crowdsourced sample of adults (eighteen and older) in the United States. The study designs and protocols secured Institutional Review Board approval for human subjects' research prior to data collection. Participants were recruited from Amazon's Mechanical Turk (Mturk) platform via the TurkPrime (now CloudResearch) online platform, where "workers" sign up to participate in "human intelligence tasks," or HITs (e.g., surveys, cognitive tests), for money. The study HIT included a link to an anonymous Qualtrics survey with the title "Answer a Survey about Public Policy" that was described as a "twenty-minute survey about your community, the economy, personal values, and public policy." Workers were offered a three-dollar compensation for participation. The use of Mturk in the social sciences has increased significantly since 2010, and although the data are not nationally representative, comparison studies have found Mturk samples to be more representative than college student samples, college town community samples, and other online sources (Chandler and Shapiro 2016). The study followed best practices of other Mturk research (Warner and Ratcliff 2021) in securing the participant panel, recruiting equal numbers of men/women and Republicans/Democrats. The rate of missing data for the survey—from survey breakoff and item nonresponse—was low: 898 workers began the survey; 879 (98 percent) completed it. Missing values were dropped list-wise, bringing the final sample size to 861.[1]

Measures and Method
Masculinity Items
Respondents were asked how much they agreed with twelve statements regarding appropriate behavior and treatment for men. All items are listed in table 6.1. Responses range on a scale from Strongly Disagree (0)

TABLE 6.1: Masculine ideology items

#	Item Wording	Mean	SD
1	A man has the right to act with physical aggression toward another man who insults him.	1.39	0.91
2	A real man doesn't let other people push him around.	0.79	0.80
3	A man has the right to act with physical aggression toward another man who insults or mistreats his family.	1.28	0.85
4	A real man can always take care of himself.	1.17	0.91
5	A man has the right to act with physical aggression toward another man who openly flirts with his wife/partner.	1.11	1.02
6	A real man can "pull himself up by his bootstraps" when the going gets tough.	1.59	0.90
7	A real man will never back down from a fight.	0.89	0.87
8	A man always deserves the respect of his wife and children.	1.63	0.98
9	It bothers me when a guy acts like a girl.	0.52	0.72
10	I don't think a husband should have to do housework.	0.76	0.76
11	Men are always ready for sex.	1.04	0.89
12	It is important for a young man to have a reputation as someone who is tough and not to be messed with.	0.90	0.81

to Strongly Agree (3). Conceptually, these items tap into core aspects of stereotypical constructions of traditional masculinity. The items were developed as a part of two psychological masculinity scales. Items 1–7 and 12 are from the Masculine Honor Ideology scale (Barnes, Brown, and Osterman 2012), and items 8–11 are from the anti-femininity component of the MRAS (Pleck, Sonenstein, and Ku 1994). Linking this to broader social constructions, per Messerschmidt's (2012) clarification that the core of hegemonic masculinity is the legitimation of a patriarchal gender hierarchy, items 5, 8, 9 and 10 are most clearly reflective of hegemonic masculinity, while the others fall more loosely into what he terms dominant or dominating masculinities. These items reflect respondents' embrace of characteristics such as aggression, toughness, control, independence, competitiveness, and success that are widely recognized as comprising the most exalted forms of traditional manhood (Brannon 1976; Smith et al. 2007; Pascoe 2005; Lay et al. 2021).

Political Ideology and Control Variables

Respondents were deliberately recruited to ensure a balance of self-identified Republicans and Democrats. Given that balance, we focus on one political measure: ideology. The political ideology measure asks for self-placement from very liberal (0) to very conservative (4).

Full models control for whether the respondent identifies as a man (ref: woman),[2] age measured in years, level of education, marital status, employment status, region of the country, income, and race/ethnicity (Hispanic/Latinx, Black, Asian American, other race, white).[3] Table A6.1 in the online appendix lists descriptive information for all variables.[4]

Methods

We first explore patterns within the masculinity items. Standard scaling approaches are used: intercorrelation measures and factor analysis before turning to a latent class analysis (LCA). Where the previous approaches are variable centered, latent class analysis is person centered, identifying major patterns among individual responses. Using these classes as comparison groups, we present predicted probabilities from a multinomial logistic regression. Results based on an OLS regression of the scaled items are not presented, but they are discussed as a further robustness check and are available upon request.

Patterns in Masculinity Beliefs

Looking at the means for the items in table 6.1, it is notable that, on average, respondents disagree with most of these items. The most agreement is with item 8: "A man always deserves the respect of his wife and children." To the extent that this positions a man as superior to (dependent) women and children, it corresponds to notions of hegemonic masculinity. The second most popular item, "A real man can 'pull himself up by his bootstraps' when the going gets tough," is a core stereotypical manhood belief (Brannon 1976), but in this case it positions a man relative to the wider world and potentially other men who fail to be "real men" when they must ask for assistance from others. Yet there are a number of historically dominant beliefs that respondents largely reject: that it bothers them when a "guy acts like a girl," or that men should not have to do housework. Already, descriptive patterns suggest variation in how respondents view these aspects of masculinity.

As we are most interested in how and whether respondents differ in their values around masculinity, we have chosen to focus on a person-centered approach to understanding variation: Latent Class Analysis, or LCA (Nylund-Gibson and Choi 2018). This method allows us to explore the existence of "hidden" patterns of responses (classes) based on individuals' responses to a set of items. With LCA we explore evidence for differing numbers of classes in the data and use model fit statistics and theoretical insight to determine which number of classes best represent variation in respondents' patterns of choices. As is common in LCA, we recode all items into binary indicators (0) Disagree and (1) Agree, but results are similar when treated as ordinal logistic outcomes. An analysis in Stata determined that the three-class solution had the best fit (AIC and BIC) and strongest theoretical relevance. Class sizes and items are listed in table 6.2.

Many respondents (38 percent) reject all the items as comprising their view of masculinity (hereafter "Rejectors"). A plurality of respondents tends to agree with four items centered on men's role as protectors and their need to defend their dignity vis-à-vis other men and within their families (hereafter "Protectors"). The final, smallest group agrees with all of these items but one. This reflects support of both hegemonic and dominance constructions of masculinity, but for the sake of shorthand these will be referred to as "Hegemonics."[5] Overall, these results confirm expectations that traditional masculinity traits are contested and that variations in individuals' perceptions of masculinity are theoretically and empirically meaningful.

Masculinity Classes and Political Ideology

Looking among each class from the latent class analysis, we can see how political ideology differentially relates in figure 6.1. Those who tend to disagree with all of the masculinity items are highly likely to be politically liberal. Those in the Protector class are most likely to be conservatives, though ideology is somewhat more evenly distributed and this class has the highest percent of moderates. Among those who fit the Hegemonic

TABLE 6.2: Latent class sizes and item loadings for a three-class solution

# Item wording	Class 1 "Rejectors" 38%	Class 2 "Protectors" 48%	Class 3 "Hegemonics" 13%
1 A man has the right to act with physical aggression toward another man who insults him.	–	+	+
2 A real man doesn't let other people push him around.	–	–	+
3 A man has the right to act with physical aggression toward another man who insults or mistreats his family.	–	+	+
4 A real man can always take care of himself.	–	–	+
5 A man has the right to act with physical aggression toward another man who openly flirts with his wife/partner.	–	–	+
6 A real man can "pull himself up by his bootstraps" when the going gets tough.	–	+	+
7 A real man will never back down from a fight.	–	–	+
8 A man always deserves the respect of his wife and children.	–	+	+
9 It bothers me when a guy acts like a girl.	–	–	–
10 I don't think a husband should have to do housework.	–	–	+
11 Men are always ready for sex.	–	–	+
12 It is important for a young man to have a reputation as someone who is tough and not to be messed with.	–	–	+

class, there is a strong conservative association where nearly 67 percent of those in the Hegemonic class are conservatives. Descriptively, there is strong support for an association between political conservatism and traditional hegemonic views of masculinity.

Masculine Ideology and Political Ideology: Inferential Results

Descriptively, these patterns are compelling; however, gender and political ideology are both highly interrelated with other social identities. For these reasons we ran full multinomial logistic regressions with all controls discussed earlier. In figure 6.2 we illustrate the marginal predicted probabilities for the relationship between political conservatism and

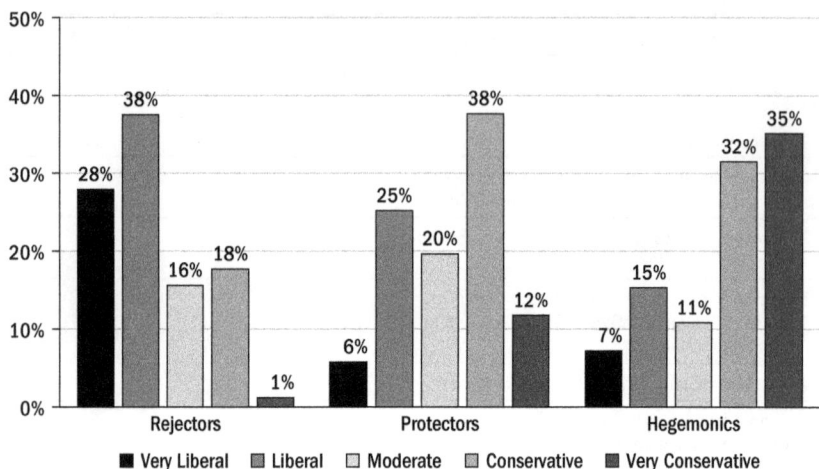

Figure 6.1: Relationship between masculinity class membership and political ideology

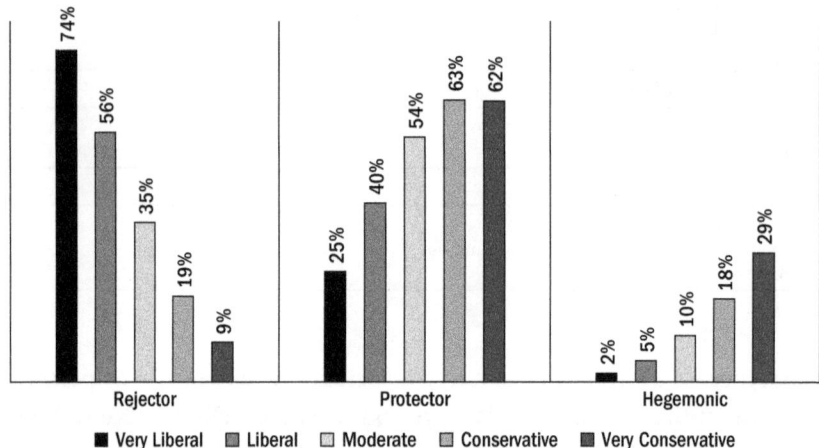

Figure 6.2: Marginal predicted probabilities for class membership and political ideology

masculine class membership. All other control variables were held at their means.

The patterns starkly illustrate the linkages between political values and masculinity beliefs. Nearly 75 percent of very liberal respondents completely reject traditional masculinity, and only 2 percent endorse a hegemonic view. To be fair, the hegemonic view is broadly unpopular, but nearly 30 percent of very conservative respondents endorsed this class. For the most part, moderates and conservatives are predicted to endorse the items comprising the Protector class. These probabilities suggest that a majority of respondents expected men to live up to expectations of physical protection and respect/honor from those around them.

What about findings regarding the control variables? Do our sociodemographic measures relate to masculine class membership? Again, using predicted probabilities to interpret the regression findings (online appendix, table A6.2), a few cleavages emerge. The most consistent are by gender and race. First, men are much more likely than women to fall in the Hegemonic class (15 percent versus 6 percent). Second, as illustrated in figure 6.3, Black and Asian Americans are more likely than whites to be both Protectors and Hegemonics—meaning a more traditional masculine ideology. Recall, however, that all of these patterns are holding political ideology constant. In fact, Black Americans are significantly more politically liberal than whites. Without controlling for political ideology, the Black/white difference disappears. Without political ideology Asian Americans are more likely still to be Hegemonic than whites.

Given that political conservatism is so strongly associated with masculine ideology, we wanted to explore whether holding a more

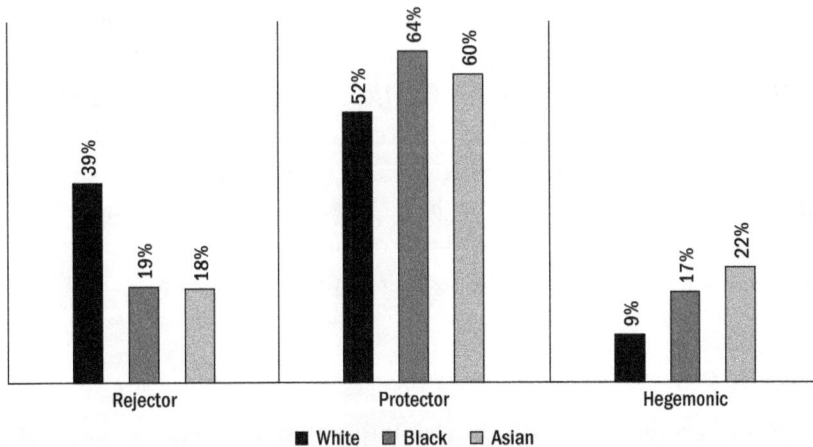

Figure 6.3: Marginal predicted probabilities for class membership and political ideology

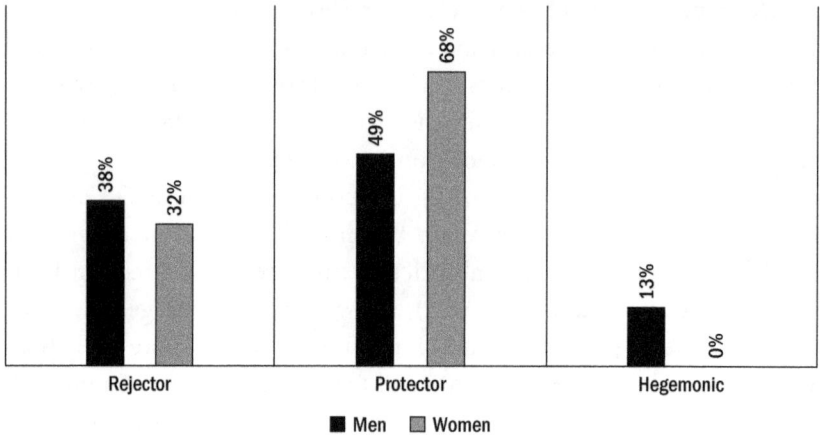

Figure 6.4: Marginal predicted probabilities for masculinity class membership among politically moderate men and women

conservative ideology mattered more for some groups rather than others. Explorations of these interaction effects for political ideology indicate some significant group differences by gender and race. The main effect by gender appears to be among political moderates. As shown in figure 6.4, politically moderate women are much more likely to belong to the Protector class, with virtually no probability (less than a .01 percent chance) of being in the Hegemonic class. In comparison, moderate men have a much higher probability of being Hegemonic, though they still prefer the Protector or Rejector class.

For race, in general the effect of conservatism is significantly stronger among whites than among Blacks in terms of supporting the Hegemonic class. On average, greater political conservatism led to a 7 percent increase in white identification with the Hegemonic class and did not affect Blacks. Because of the small size of the nonwhite racial categories, however, such research should be interpreted with caution.[6]

Discussion

Examining a series of items that tap into traditional stereotypical characterizations of masculinity quickly shows that not all respondents endorse all of these beliefs. Most only endorse a few, and 21 percent overall would strongly disagree or disagree with all of these items. Yet variation in responses reflected the theoretical and conceptual expectations developed in previous masculinity scholarship, and a latent class analysis provided strong evidence for three distinct classes of masculinity definers.

As expected descriptively, many respondents reject the idea of these traditional notions of masculinity entirely, but a sizeable group (the plurality) maintain that men should be characterized by their ability to physically protect and defend their honor, independence, and family. A smaller but distinct group tended to agree with the majority of the items, representing a fuller embrace of hegemonic and dominant forms of masculinity. Translating this to political values and identities, descriptive statistics indicated a strong relationship between conservatism and a stronger endorsement of traditional masculinity. This is regardless of a person's own binary gender identity or other sociodemographic characteristics.

The other sociodemographic characteristics provide important controls while revealing some interesting patterns. Men and women differ most with regard to the Hegemonic class, where women are much less likely to fall. Interaction effects show that being a political moderate drives more women to the Protector class than men, but more men to the Hegemonic class. Somewhat surprising was the effect of race, particularly among Black and Asian American respondents; however, most racial differences emerge only with controls for political ideology. If Black Americans were as conservative as whites, they would tend to hold more traditional or hegemonic views of masculinity.

It is difficult to speculate on how these findings may differ in a nationally representative sample. The greater representation of middle-aged, middle-class, and white respondents may have had a moderating effect on responses. From aging research, the youngest persons are generally more gender egalitarian and older persons are more gender traditional. Lower-income persons in very rural and very urban settings may also relate differently to masculinity. However, having a balanced representation of Democratic- and Repulican-identifying persons bolsters conclusions about the more politically identified but cannot speak well to the masculinity ideologies of politically uninterested/unaffiliated. To further explore these cleavages, as well as the tentative racial group different findings, we strongly suggest further research with a broad national panel.

Conclusion

Politically, men and social constructions of traditional masculinity have dominated. Even as women have increasingly gained political power, they have often had to do so by accepting and working within dominant masculine frameworks (Galea and Gaweda 2018). However, in recent years, a variety of social, political, economic, and cultural factors have demanded change in the status quo regarding men and masculinity. For example, a spotlight has been cast on the concept of "toxic masculinity" (Harrington 2021). The rise in popularity of this controversial term overlaps with scholars' previous work on patriarchy, homonegativity, sexism, and hegemonic masculine social constructs. Further, a number of high-profile figures have come out publicly as transgender, nonbinary, or genderqueer, giving more Americans than ever the opportunity to question basic assumptions around gender as binary, biological, and/or essential.

In the current highly polarized political climate, gender has often been pulled into political ideological battles. Heated debates over nongendered bathrooms, transgender healthcare rights, and gender education in the classroom blare from political talk shows across various media platforms (Schilt and Westbrook 2015; Castle 2019). Similarly, these results suggest that clear *political* lines are being drawn around what it means to be a "real man." Essentialized, traditional norms of appropriate behavior are most strongly held among political ideological conservatives and Republicans, but largely rejected by Democrats and political ideological liberals (Deckman and Cassese 2021; Strolovitch, Wong, and Proctor 2017).[7]

Nevertheless, as the latent class analysis shows there is a substantial group—particularly among those who are politically conservative—that only wants to keep some "protective" tenets of traditional masculinity. This emphasizes work showing the ongoing role of *benevolent sexism*, a form of gender ideology that lacks the more repressive and hostile forms of rigid gendered expectations, such as women needing to focus primarily on home and family, but it continues to uphold sexism by failing to challenge the underlying logic of who women and children need protection from: other men.

In this way, benevolent sexism perpetuates the larger gender system and continues to undermine the precepts of women's self-determination and right to unconditional personal safety. Benevolent sexism may therefore produce hybrid masculinities (Bridges and Pascoe 2014), which allow individuals to symbolically distance themselves from hegemonic masculinity while simultaneously buttressing sexist structures, ideologies, and systems (Jackman 1994). Furthermore, it is this class that we find politically moderate women most drawn toward supporting. As noted earlier, women are complicit in constructing masculine ideologies, but our work suggests that this is so primarily among women who want men to act as protectors and providers for their families. Women are much less likely than men to endorse a more hegemonic view of masculinity. In constructing masculinity as part of gender relations, politically moderate or conservative (white) women may view this form of masculinity as directly supporting their own more traditional views of femininity as vulnerable to outside threats and economically dependent on men's work (Schippers 2007; Budgeon 2014).

In analyses of the 2016 election of Donald Trump to the office of US president, scholars note that white women have cast a majority of votes for Republican presidential candidates in all but two elections since 1952 (Strolovitch, Wong, and Proctor 2017; Junn 2017). Although Republican Party identifiers hold substantially more conservative positions on gender equality, voters in both parties have come to normalize women as workers and political figures, blunting the movement toward extreme patriarchy (Sharrow et al. 2016). Nevertheless, white women link their fate to the privilege accorded white men and the ways that their roles as wives and mothers protect that (Junn and Masuoka 2020; Campi and Junn 2019; Campi 2021).

Outside of politics, some sociodemographic patterns are compelling and worthy of further study. Men are least likely to reject the themes traditional masculinity. Socialized in a system that both punishes and rewards men for their compliance to masculine norms, it is much more difficult for men to opt out of these expectations (Chen 1999; Winer 2022). Finally, Black and Asian American respondents, as compared to whites, are significantly more likely to hold more Protector and Hegemonic masculine views. Previous research has illustrated the importance of maintaining these traits in a pervasive system of racism that discriminates against and devalues Black and Asian American men. Black feminists have discussed the importance of respect, toughness, and the "cool pose" for Black men (Majors and Billson 1993; Ferguson 2020; Collins 1990), and scholars of Asian American studies note that Asian American men must navigate feminizing and desexualizing stereotypes (Chen 1999; Feliciano, Robnett, and Komaie 2009). Further, many Asian Americans have more recent ties to their immigrant background based in more traditional cultures of gender norms, which may also drive an emphasis on more rigid concepts of masculinity (Lu and Wong 2013). The sample is small, however, and further research should test to see if these relationships hold more broadly. If they do, it could suggest that Democrats/liberals focus on gender nonconformity conflicts with the views of some Black and Asian American constituents and could drive further schisms in electoral outcomes.

Overall, the findings from this study are not nationally representative, but they provide an important insight into the patterns of association between various manifestations of idealized masculinity and political identities. Previous research indicates that party stereotypes matter more than gender stereotypes (Hayes 2011), but conservatives and Republicans in particular may infuse their political beliefs and behaviors with a simultaneous belief in the need to protect and preserve traditional forms of masculinity, making efforts to attain greater gender equality a zero-sum game (English, Pearson, and Strolovitch 2019; Campi 2021; Junn and Masuoka 2020; Junn 2017). Yet, even among the most conservative, relatively few embrace the most traditional and rigid views of masculinity. Most respondents feel that there is value in expecting men to "protect and defend," and nearly all reject a view that would devalue a guy for "acting like a girl." Psychological researchers have offered a variety of approaches to measuring individuals' conceptualization of masculine ideology. Our chapter shows that by tying these fine-grained approaches into our broader understanding of hegemonic masculinity and the social construction of gender relations we can better understand how and why masculinity matters for political identities and ideologies.

NOTES

1 Although MTurk draws participants from across the United States, it is not meant to be nationally representative. Deviations are in the expected directions for an internet convenience sample, with our MTurk sample containing slightly more middle-aged persons (30–49), more whites, and more middle-income persons (US$30,000–US$74,000). Given the study sample selection design, our MTurk

sample also includes more self-identified Republicans and Democrats (and fewer Independents) than would be captured in nationally-representative designs.

2 Nonbinary measures of gender identity were not available through the MTurk platform.

3 All racial/ethnic groups were coded as dummy variables, but, given the weak overlap across categories, white is treated as the de facto reference category but should be understood as also containing multiracial respondents who do not belong to a particular category (e.g., Blacks versus whites/multiracial non-Blacks). Findings remain the same when entering race/ethnicity one group at a time.

4 Further analysis indicates that partisanship and political ideology measures are moderately correlated ($r = .42$). Models using only partisanship produce results similar to those using ideology.

5 Patterns of responses vary marginally when examining LCA among men and among women. More women tend to disagree with all items (41 percent of women versus 35 percent of men); a second class for women had item 5 loading more strongly than for men, but 49 percent of women and 45 percent of men would fall in this class. The largest difference was in the third class, which is constructed the same for women and men: 21 percent of men fall in this class and only 10 percent of women. Controlling for gender in the models below will account for these variations.

6 Only eleven Black respondents identified as politically conservative or very conservative and were placed in the hegemonic class based on their answers.

7 These results cannot disentangle potential biases in what respondents think they are "expected" to say regarding masculinity norms, but the strong association of the responses to the self-assessed political ideology suggest that these normative differences are meaningful to them. In fact, if social desirability bias is a concern, our results may offer a conservative estimate of the variation in masculinity ideologies. Future surveys would benefit from utilizing techniques to measure possible social desirability biases (Krumpal 2013).

7

The Unique Role of Masculine Ideology in Political Attitudes and Behaviors

NATHANIEL E. C. SCHERMERHORN AND THERESA K. VESCIO

Presidential candidates in the United State have long relied on embodiments of masculinity to appeal to voters. For example, Ronald Reagan was regularly photographed wearing cowboy hats atop his horse, embodying the rugged "cowboy masculinity" that represented the All-American virtues of hard work and ruggedness (Katz 2016). Similarly, George W. Bush was often photographed wearing blue jeans, doing physical labor on his ranch, and driving around in his pickup truck (Katz 2016). Many other US presidents and presidential candidates have positioned themselves as sporting figures, as in Theodore Roosevelt's persona as a rugged outdoorsman or John F. Kennedy's appearance on the cover of *Sports Illustrated* alongside an article warning about the feminization of America (Moore and Dewberry 2012). Masculinity has also been weaponized in American politics by attempting to reduce support for opponents by feminizing them. For example, George W. Bush's 2004 campaign painted John Kerry as feminine by comparing him to the "effete" French who had recently disapproved of the United States' military entry into Iraq (Fahey 2007). In fact, presidential elections in the United States have often been about candidates proving who is masculine enough for the job (Ducat 2005; Katz 2016).

Given the success that candidates have had capitalizing on masculinity in their presidential campaigns, it may not be surprising that Donald Trump sought to employ the same rhetorical strategies in his 2016 bid for the US presidency. Donald Trump, a political outsider and reality television star, weaponized masculinity first to win the Republican primary and, eventually, the presidency (Kurtzleben 2016). In the primaries, Trump emasculated his male primary opponents with names such as "Low Energy Jeb" (Jeb Bush) and "Liddle Marco" (Marco Rubio), and imputations of femininity (e.g., implying that Rick Perry was not tough enough to be on debate stages; see Relman 2019). Trump continued his campaign with frequent sexist and misogynistic remarks against opponent Hillary Clinton, such as saying she was playing the "woman card," alongside assertions of his own health, strength, and virility (Kurtzleben 2016). Research shows that Trump's campaign rhetoric and actions successfully led voters to see him as masculine and, therefore, right for the job (e.g., Carian and Sobotka 2018; Powell, Butterfield, and Jiang 2018).

The purpose of this chapter is to better understand the unique role that masculine ideology plays in people's political attitudes and behaviors. More specifically, using data collected during and between the 2016 and 2020 US presidential elections, we examine how voters' endorsement of masculine ideology influenced their evaluations of key candidates and their voting intentions. First, we briefly review two existing bodies of research: research on masculine ideology and research on the election of Donald Trump. Second, we summarize our key findings that connect masculine ideology to support for Trump. Finally, we ask two additional and important questions that extend these findings: Does masculine ideology influence people to support candidates across political party lines, and does masculine ideology influence political attitudes and behaviors in distinct ways from other legitimating ideologies (i.e., social dominance orientation, system justification, and right-wing authoritarianism)? We end by discussing the political arena as an area in which we can better understand the ways in which a culturally idealized form of masculinity that privileges certain men is upheld.

Masculine Ideology

"Masculine ideology" here refers to a constellation of beliefs that uphold and legitimate the culturally idealized form of masculinity, or hegemonic masculinity (see McDermott and Jones in this volume). Thus, masculine ideology refers to the form of masculinity that is exalted above other masculinities and femininities, even though most men will not meet the stringent standards and expectations of this form of masculinity (Connell 1995; Vandello et al. 2008). The form of masculinity considered hegemonic varies across time and cultures, as well as within cultures (Connell 1995; Connell and Messerschmidt

2005). In the United States, the construction of hegemonic masculinity is based upon white, heterosexual, able-bodied, middle-to-upper-class, conservative, and Protestant ideals (e.g., Brannon 1976; Carter 2007; Connell 1995; Connell 2000; Kimmel 1994; Ward 2015). With slight deviations of labels, hegemonic masculinity in the United States has been relatively stable since the 1950s (Deikman and Eagly 2000) and prescribes that men should be high in power, status, and dominance; mentally, emotionally, and physically tough; and nothing like women or gay men (Brannon 1976; Courtenay 2000; Fischer et al. 1998; Thompson and Pleck 1986; see also Pascoe 2007; Vescio, Schlenker, and Lenes 2010).

Hegemonic masculinity is constructed through its relation to other forms of masculinity and femininity (Connell 1995). Therefore, maintaining a hegemonic construction of masculinity leads to the marginalization of racial minorities, disabled men, working-class men, religious minorities, and gay and effeminate men, as well as women (Connell 1995). In support of this, research shows a correlation between masculine ideologies that uphold hegemonic masculinity with sexism (e.g., Leaper and Van 2008; Vescio and Schermerhorn 2021; Whitley 2001), sexual harassment and violence (e.g., Gale 1996; Jakupcak, Lisak, and Roemer 2002; Wade and Brittan-Powell 2001), racism (Liu 2002; Vescio and Schermerhorn 2021; Wade and Brittan-Powell 2001), anti-gay attitudes (Adams 2014; Juge 2013; McCusker and Galupo 2011; Vescio and Schermerhorn 2021; Whitley, 2001), and xenophobia (Vescio and Schermerhorn 2021). In other words, those who strongly endorse masculine ideologies also endorse a host of attitudes that subordinate women and various subgroups of men.

Understanding Trump's Successful 2016 Presidential Campaign

Many researchers have sought to understand how Donald Trump, a political outsider, successfully won the 2016 presidential election over Hillary Clinton, a woman whose life has been devoted to public service and who had a proven record in politics. Findings focus on three areas for understanding Trump support: demographics, prejudicial attitudes, and legitimating ideologies.

Demographics

Perhaps at the most basic level, the 2016 presidential election seemed to inspire a strict partisan divide, with Republicans supporting and voting for Trump, and Democrats supporting and voting for Clinton (e.g., Bartels 2020). In addition, exit polling found demographic differences between Trump and Clinton supporters with men more than women, white people more than people of color, and less (versus more) educated voters all being more likely to vote for Trump over Clinton (Pew Research Center 2018).

Prejudicial Attitudes

Beyond political party affiliation and voter demographics, research has found that support for Trump has also been linked to various prejudices held by voters. For example, Trump support has been associated with voters' sexism (e.g., Blair 2017; Bock, Byrd-Craven, and Burkley 2017; Bracic, Israel-Trummond, and Shortle 2019; Monteith and Hildebrand 2020; Ratliff et al. 2019; Rothwell, Hodson, and Prusacyz 2019; Setzler and Yanus 2018), racism (e.g., Bobo 2017; Swain 2019; Shook et al. 2019), homophobia (e.g., Blair 2017), xenophobia (e.g., Blair 2017; Shook et al. 2020), as well as populism, including anti-establishment and anti-elitist attitudes (e.g., Oliver and Rahn 2016).

Legitimating Ideologies

Research has also found associations between Trump support and various legitimating ideologies—namely, social dominance orientation (SDO), system justifying beliefs, and right-wing authoritarianism. "SDO" refers to the ideological belief that some groups deserve to be at the top of a social hierarchy, and the desire to maintain these social hierarchies (Pratto, Sidanius, and Levin 2006). Research has shown that people with a stronger SDO reported more favorable attitudes toward Trump and a greater likelihood of voting for him (e.g., Choma and Hanoch 2016; Crowson and Brandes 2017; Womick et al. 2019; Wright and Esses 2018). Research has also shown that system-justifying beliefs, or the belief that existing institutions and authorities are fair and legitimate (Jost and Banaji 1994), predicted support for Trump and a greater likelihood of voting for him (e.g., Azevedo, Jost, and Rothmund 2017; Miller and Borgida 2019). Finally, right-wing authoritarianism, or the ideological belief that people should obey and respect authorities and tradition (Duckitt 2001), was also found to be associated with more positive evaluations of Trump and a greater likelihood of voting for him (e.g., Choma and Hanoch 2016; Crowson and Brandes 2017; Womick et al. 2019).

There are some inconsistencies in the existing research connecting system-justifying beliefs to support for Trump, and these help to illuminate the ways in which Trump supporters navigate and support the status quo. First, people's motives to justify the existing political system did not influence their support for Trump (Weinschenk and Dawes 2019). Second, some findings reveal that motives to justify systems of gender inequities and economic inequities were predictive of support for Trump. However, the endorsement of general system-justifying beliefs predicted support for Clinton (Azevedo, Jost, and Rothmund 2017; Jost et al. 2017). These findings lend support to the rhetoric that Clinton was an "establishment candidate," but that maintaining gender and class hierarchies were reflective of Trump supporters' values. Similarly, those who more strongly justified gendered inequalities were less supportive of Clinton, whose rhetoric and policies may have posed a threat to existing gender hierarchies, and their support for her continued to wane over time (Miller and Borgida 2019). Taken together, it is possible that Trump supporters do not necessarily justify existing systems in general (e.g., "Society is fair"). Rather, Trump supporters may fear change in specific systems in which inequalities are apparent (e.g., gender, class) and were persuaded by Trump's reactionary appeals to uphold these inequalities (see Liekefett and Becker 2022).

Examining Masculine Ideology in the 2016 and 2020 US Presidential Elections

As previously noted, men were more supportive of Trump than were women and more likely to vote for him. This may have been particularly true for men who felt that a Hillary Clinton presidency would have threatened their higher social status as men (e.g., Mutz 2018).

In fact, research has found that men experiencing a threat to their masculinity—operationalized as a threat to their employment status—were more supportive of Trump versus Clinton (Carian and Sobotka 2018; see also Cassino and Besen-Cassino 2022). However, Trump's success could not have relied on male voters alone. In fact, white (versus nonwhite) women were more likely to vote for Trump in 2016—a trend that was even stronger in the 2020 election (Igielnik, Keeter, and Hartig 2021). In addition, those who more strongly supported systems of gender inequality were more supportive of Trump. Therefore, our research asks if masculine ideology was a unique legitimating ideology that influenced both men *and* women's candidate support in the 2016 and 2020 US presidential elections.

Between the days immediately following the 2016 election (November 10, 2016), to the weeks immediately preceding the 2020 election (September 14, 2020), we conducted seven studies ($N = 2007$), which measured participants' endorsement of masculine ideology, their evaluations of the candidates, their 2016 vote, their 2020 voting intentions, and a host of prejudicial attitudes (Vescio and Schermerhorn 2021). In addition to these seven studies, we also continued to measure participants' endorsement of masculine ideology and, in six additional studies, their evaluations of Trump (Schermerhorn, Vescio, and Lewis 2022, studies 2 and 3; Schermerhorn and Vescio, in preparation, studies 1, 2, and 3; 1 unpublished dataset).

To measure masculine ideology, we used the Male Role Norms Scale (Thompson and Pleck 1986), which measures endorsement of the hegemonic ideals of masculinity: power/status, toughness, and anti-femininity. Consisting of twenty-six items, the Male Role Norms Scale measures the prescription that men should be high in power and status through the belief that men should strive for employment success (e.g., "Success in his work has to be a man's central goal in this life") and be his family's breadwinner (e.g., "A man owes it to his family to work at the best-paying job he can get"). The scale also measures the prescription that men should be physically tough (e.g., "I think a young man should try to become physically tough, even if he's not big") and emotionally tough (e.g., "Nobody respects a man very much who frequently talks about his worries, fears, and problems"). Finally, the scale measures masculinity in relation to femininity—namely, the prescription that men should reject femininity (e.g., "It bothers me when a man does something that I consider 'feminine'") and avoid feminine hobbies and occupations (e.g., "It is a bit embarrassing for a man to have a job that is usually filled by a woman").

The first seven studies tested if the endorsement of masculine ideology influenced participants' political attitudes and behaviors, and whether this effect held when controlling for one's political party affiliation (Democratic, Republican), demographic variables (i.e., sex, race, and level of education), and prejudicial attitudes known to drive Trump support (i.e., sexism, racism, homophobia, xenophobia, and Islamophobia). Individually, at the study level, men and women who more strongly endorsed masculine ideology more positively evaluated Trump and reported a greater likelihood to vote for him. Importantly, masculine ideology was associated with men and women's support for Trump regardless of one's political party affiliation, race, or level of education (Vescio and Schermerhorn 2021). In addition, although stronger prejudicial attitudes (sexism, racism, homophobia, xenophobia, and Islamophobia) were associated with support for Trump, replicating previous research, masculine ideology uniquely predicted men's and women's support for him as the presidential candidate (Vescio and Schermerhorn 2021). Therefore, it is important to include masculine ideology alongside demographics and prejudicial attitudes when seeking to understand support for political candidates.

We also conducted a series of meta-analyses across the seven studies described above and the additional data collected in the six subsequent studies. The meta-analyses were undertaken to examine the overall effect of masculine ideology on political attitudes and behaviors in the 2016 and 2020 elections by aggregating across studies. These meta-analyses helped to more clearly examine the unique influence of masculine ideology separate from political party affiliation. As shown in table 7.1, political party affiliation was the strongest predictor of voting and candidate evaluations, with participants identifying as Republican reporting a greater likelihood of voting for Trump, more positively evaluating Trump, and more negatively evaluating Clinton or Biden. In addition, our meta-analyses reveal that the endorsement of masculine ideology was significantly related to a greater likelihood of voting for Trump, more positively evaluating Trump, and, although much less robustly, more negatively evaluating Clinton/Biden.

TABLE 7.1: Results of meta-analyses on voting and candidate evaluations

	Vote Trump	Trump evaluations	Clinton/Biden evaluations
Political party	1.56***	.57***	−.67***
	(.08)	(.04)	(.03)
Masculine ideology	.71***	.27***	−.08**
	(.10)	(.02)	(.03)

Note. Effect sizes represent the meta-analytic effect of unstandardized coefficients and the standard error of the coefficient. Ninety-five percent confidence intervals are included as is the calculated standard error. Meta-analyses for Vote Trump and Clinton/Biden evaluations were conducted across seven studies. Meta-analyses for Trump evaluations were conducted across thirteen studies.
*** p < 0.001, ** p < .01, * p < .05

Masculine Ideology and Democratic Voters

Although each of the original seven studies as well as the meta-analyses provide robust evidence for the role of masculine ideology in the 2016 and 2020 presidential elections, several interesting questions remain to be answered. First, and of particular importance, does masculine ideology predict voting behavior and candidate evaluations for Democrats and Independents as well as Republicans? The results of our hierarchical regression analyses across the studies suggested that masculine ideology predicted voting behavior and candidate evaluations regardless of one's political party affiliation as (1) masculine ideology was a unique predictor when controlling for political party, and (2) there was not consistent evidence that the effect of masculine ideology was moderated by political party (i.e., lack of consistent masculinity X political party interactions). However, no single study contained enough Democrats or Independents who reported voting for Trump to contain meaningful analyses that isolated participants by their political party affiliation. Given the partisan divide in both the 2016 and 2020 elections, it is important to examine motivating factors that may have led Independents to choose Trump over Clinton and Democrats to unexpectedly support Trump.

To more thoroughly examine whether masculine ideology predicts over and above political party affiliation, sex, race, and level of education among Democrats and Independents, we aggregated data across the original seven studies (Vescio and Schermerhorn 2021). In other words, we created a larger sample of "unlikely Trump voters" (i.e., Democrats/

Independents who reported voting for him) to conduct exploratory analyses.

We first conducted a binary logistic regression on voting for Trump like those in the original seven studies with one exception: we only included Democratic and Independent participants ($N = 1360$; 177 Trump voters). Therefore, political party was not included in the model. Controlling for participant sex, race, and level of education, an increase in masculine ideology increases the probability of Democrats/Independents having voted for Trump by sixty-eight points.[1]

We also conducted an analysis of variance (ANOVA) examining the mean differences of the endorsement of masculine ideology between Democratic/Independent participants who voted for Trump and Democratic/Independent participants who did not vote for Trump. The analysis revealed a small, but statistically significant, difference. Democrats/Independents who reported voting for Trump had higher scores on masculine ideology ($M = 3.85$) than those who voted for another candidate ($M = 3.32$).[2]

Finally, we conducted a mediation analysis examining the indirect effect of the endorsement of masculine ideology on voting behavior via candidate evaluations for Democrats/Independents. As shown in figure 7.1, stronger endorsement of masculine ideology predicted more positive evaluations of Trump. In turn, the more positively one evaluated Trump, the more likely they were to vote for him.[3]

Together, the series of three analyses provide evidence that, despite strong opposition to Donald Trump by Democrats and mixed support of Donald Trump by Independents, masculine ideology may have influenced how individuals from these two groups behaved. Although

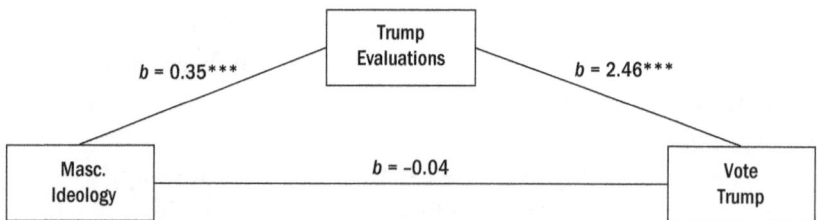

*** $p < 0.001$, ** $p < 0.01$, * $p < 0.05$

Figure 7.1: Results of mediation analyses for Democratic and independent Trump voters

these analyses were exploratory, and larger samples of "unlikely voters" are still needed to draw more robust conclusions, these initial findings are significant for two reasons. First, although overt prejudicial
attitudes are often examined in political behavior, masculine ideology
may mask more overt forms of sexism, racism, and homophobia. Thus,
masculine ideology may be one intrinsic factor in understanding how
"well-intentioned" people who are publicly against prejudice and discrimination behave in ways (i.e., supporting Trump) that reinforce the
existing status quo. Second, these three analyses further lend support
to the differentiation of masculinity and conservatism. In other words,
masculine ideology is an ideology that can be, and is, endorsed by people regardless of their political party affiliation and may lead them to
behave in ways unaligned with the principles of their political party. In
the final section, we turn to examining if masculine ideology is unique
from other legitimating ideologies.

Is Masculine Ideology a Unique Legitimating Ideology?

A second, remaining question is whether masculine ideology is a unique
legitimating ideology or if it simply captures elements of other legitimating ideologies—namely, SDO, system justification, or right-wing
authoritarianism. We conducted three studies using convenience samples of undergraduates that examined masculine ideology alongside that
of SDO ($N = 292$), system-justifying beliefs ($N = 260$), and right-wing
authoritarianism ($N = 171$) in predicting evaluations of Trump and the
likelihood of voting for him in the 2020 Presidential election.

As shown in table 7.2, political party affiliation and masculine ideology were both correlated with the various legitimating ideologies. Identifying as Republican and more strongly endorsing masculine ideology
were both associated with greater SDO, stronger system-justifying beliefs, and greater authoritarianism.

We analyzed the predictive utility of political party affiliation and
legitimating ideologies (i.e., SDO, system-justifying beliefs, right-wing
authoritarianism) using hierarchical regressions while also controlling
for additional demographics (i.e., gender, race, level of education). Consistent with our previous findings and shown in table 7.3, political party
affiliation continued to be the strongest predictor of Trump evaluations

TABLE 7.2: Correlations among political party affiliation and legitimating ideologies

	Political party	Masculine ideology
Social dominance orientation	.40***	.45***
System justification	.54***	.49***
Right-wing authoritarianism	.38***	.48***

Note. Political party was measured on a 1–5 scale, with higher numbers indicating greater identification with the Republican Party.
*** p < 0.001, ** p < .01, * p < .05

TABLE 7.3: Results of hierarchical regressions across legitimating ideologies

Independent variables	System-justifying beliefs		Social dominance orientation		Right-wing authoritarianism	
	Trump evaluation	Trump 2020	Trump evaluation	Trump 2020	Trump evaluation	Trump 2020
	β (SE)	β (SE)	β (SE)	β (SE)	β (SE)	β (SE)
Political party	.92*** (.08)	1.42*** (.10)	.85*** (.05)	1.16*** (.07)	.78*** (.05)	1.03*** (.07)
Ideology	.47*** (.11)	.31* (.14)	.23*** (.07)	.26* (.10)	.27* (.11)	.45** (.15)
Masculine ideology	.34** (.12)	.22 (.15)	.26** (.09)	.47*** (.12)	.14 (.10)	.30* (.13)

Note. Ideology = System-justifying beliefs in the two left-most columns, social dominance orientation in the middle columns, and right-wing authoritarianism in the right-most columns. Unstandardized beta coefficients and standard errors are presented.
*** p < 0.001, ** p < .01, * p < .05

across analyses as well as in predicting the likelihood of voting for him in the 2020 election. Replicating the research findings described above, SDO and right-wing authoritarianism predicted more positive evaluations of Trump and a greater likelihood of voting for him in the 2020 election. In addition, our results found a significant relationship between general system justifying beliefs and support for Trump with stronger system-justifying beliefs predicting more positive evaluations and a greater likelihood of voting for him in 2020.

A stronger endorsement of masculine ideology continued to be a unique predictor of support for Trump when controlling for political party affiliation, sex, race, education, and each individual ideology in four of the six analyses. Thus, masculine ideology seems to function separately from other legitimating ideologies in predicting political attitudes and behavior, with some potential exceptions. For instance, masculine ideology predicted evaluations of Trump, but not intent to vote for him, over and above system-justifying beliefs. On the other hand, masculine ideology predicted a greater intent to vote for Trump in the 2020 election, but not evaluations of him, over and above right-wing authoritarianism.

Although additional research is necessary to fully understand these nuances, we offer a potential explanation. Data from the three studies presented here were collected between December 2018 and March 2019, at the beginning of the second year of Trump's term, whereas the existing research on legitimating ideologies and support for Trump described above was conducted either before or directly after the 2016 election (i.e., before Trump's term began). At the time of collecting the present data, the Trump administration had already implemented regulations and policies that undermined the rights of women and perpetuated gender inequality (Ahmed, Phadke, and Boesch 2020) and set the groundwork for his eventual ban on training that addressed gender and racial discrimination (Hinger and Hauss 2020). Thus, contrary to preelection data that found general system justification to predict support for Clinton (Azevedo, Jost, and Rothmund 2017; Jost et al. 2017), system-justifying beliefs may have predicted continued voting intentions for Trump in the present data because his administration perpetuated a system that reinforced the social stratification that his supporters felt Clinton threatened (Miller and Borgida 2019). Similarly, right-wing authoritarianism, but not masculine ideology, may have predicted evaluations of Trump during his presidency (on characteristics such as fair, moral, leader-like, respectable) because his leadership paralleled authoritarian qualities and his policies upheld authoritarian tenets (Ben-Ghiat, 2021).

As evidenced by both the correlational and hierarchical regression analyses, masculine ideology is a legitimating ideology that is related to, but distinct from, SDO, system justification, and right-wing authoritarianism. In addition, these preliminary findings suggest that, like the other legitimating ideologies, masculine ideology has unique predictive power in understanding political attitudes and behaviors. However, additional research is necessary to understand the nuances of the similarities and differences between the endorsement of masculine ideology and other legitimating ideologies. One possibility is that these four legitimating ideologies are related but may be relevant to different contexts and function in different ways. Another possibility is that different ideologies are particularly influential among distinct populations of people. Future research is needed to understand the interrelations and unique predictive utility of the various ideologies and our research points to the importance of including masculine ideology in studies of political attitudes and behaviors.

Masculine Ideology as a Foundation for Maintaining Hegemonic Masculinity

Masculine ideology functionally legitimizes idealized forms of masculinity that privilege certain men over others and over women. However, for a particular form of masculinity to remain hegemonic within a given society, it must be endorsed even by those who are marginalized and subordinated by it. In other words, people may act against their own interests if those actions align with an ideology they strongly endorse. Importantly, contemporary scholars of hegemony note that the consensual basis of an existing political system is built upon a shared ideology that has been constructed and popularized by the ruling class (Bocock 1986). A successful ideology ensures the reproduction of existing social structures (Althusser 1990); thus, ideology is the intrinsic mechanism (i.e., internalized belief system) that produces extrinsic practices (i.e., behaviors) that maintains hegemony. Applying the concept of hegemony to gender, R. W. Connell argues that hegemonic masculinity can help us to understand the persistence of patriarchy by examining gendered practices that reinforce male dominance (1995). Masculine ideologies are the internalized belief systems that inspire these behaviors.

Our findings confirm that further explorations of how hegemonic masculinity is reinforced within the political arena are warranted. First, women who more strongly endorsed masculine ideology were also more likely to support and vote for Trump. This is despite repeated examples of Trump's sexism in his tweets and speeches, sexual assault allegations against him, and his strong anti-abortion rhetoric. Thus, masculine ideology appears to influence certain women to go against their own interests by voting for a candidate who clearly sought to maintain—and perhaps strengthen—existing gendered inequalities (see also Glick and Fiske 1996; Hammond, Sibley, and Overall 2014). Second, although our findings are initial and exploratory, masculine ideology also seems to have influenced certain Democrats and Independents to vote for Trump. Existing research shows a strong relationship between conservativism and masculine ideology (see Bolzendahl, Winer, and Warner in this volume). However, it is possible that, for certain voters in the center and on the left, beliefs about masculinity and gender relations may lead them to unexpectedly support more conservative politicians. Finally, our data suggest that masculine ideology is a unique predictor of candidate support from other legitimating ideologies and may function separately from SDO, system-justifying beliefs, and authoritarianism.

The form of masculinity considered hegemonic in our society has remained relatively stable over the years, despite the emergence of alternative masculinities that aim to challenge the status quo. Understanding why requires not only examining the people it privileges most (i.e., straight, white men) but, perhaps even more importantly, examining the conditions under which those who are subjugated by hegemonic masculinity may continue to endorse it and contribute to its legitimization. Including measures of masculine ideology in studies of political attitudes and behaviors is one avenue of better understanding hegemonic masculinity and the perpetuation of the status quo.

NOTES

1 Results of the binary logistic regressions revealed that those who more strongly endorsed masculine ideology were more likely to report voting for Trump ($b = .75$, OR = 2.11, $p < .001$). No significant interactions emerged between masculine ideology and sex, race, or education.

2 Results of the ANOVA showed a higher endorsement of masculine ideology for Trump voters ($M = 3.85$, SD = 0.79) than non-Trump voters ($M = 3.32$, SD = 0.89), $F(1, 1289) = 54.06$, $p < .001$.

3 Mediation analyses were conducted using the process Macro for SPSS (Hayes, 2018). The indirect effect of endorsement of masculine ideology on voting for Trump via evaluations of Trump was significant [indirect effect = .8745, SE = .1003, 95% CI [.7068, 1.0987].

8

Understanding the Role of Precarious Manhood in Politics

SARAH H. DIMUCCIO AND ERIC D. KNOWLES

Introduction

In this chapter, we discuss a gender phenomenon—*precarious manhood*—that is related to, but distinct from, the constructs of masculinity explored elsewhere in this volume. Drawing from our own research, we argue that precarious manhood helps explain the role of masculinity in men's political attitudes and behavior. After defining "precarious manhood," we articulate its relationship to hegemonic masculinity, describe its known consequences, and trace out its relevance to politics. Second, we present correlational evidence that precarious manhood predicts support for aggressive policies and politicians (Donald Trump and Republicans). Third, we describe three experimental studies that evidence the causal effects of manhood threats on politically aggressive policies and suggest that liberal men may be particularly susceptible to such threats. Finally, we will discuss the implications of this research for understanding real-world political dynamics.

Precarious Manhood

Research over the last several decades has examined masculinity and the prevailing societal norms and expectations to which men are expected to conform (Brannon 1976; Connell 1995). Only more recently, however, have scholars begun to examine the fraught nature of these expectations and the psychological and behavioral consequences for men who fail to live up to strict masculine standards (Vandello et al. 2008). In particular, a fast-growing body of research demonstrates that American men are expected to actively achieve their (socially constructed) manhood and readily defend this high-status title (e.g., act like a "real man"), or else risk losing the status altogether (i.e., not be considered a real man; Vandello et al. 2008). Indeed, research shows that men and women alike view manhood as a status that is *elusive* (achieved rather than ascribed) and *tenuous* (not guaranteed once earned; Vandello and Bosson 2013).

The precarious manhood thesis, while connected to the other theories of masculinity and manhood discussed in this volume, is distinct in important ways. It uniquely focuses on the concept of manhood itself as an inherently fragile societal status. While other theories, such as the gender role strain paradigm (Pleck 1995), explore the challenges and stresses that men may face in conforming to traditional masculine norms, the precarious manhood thesis emphasizes that manhood itself is hard earned and easily lost (Bosson and Vandello 2013). Other theories focus on the consequences of adhering to or deviating from these gender norms without highlighting the underlying vulnerability of manhood as a social status.

In all societies, there are gender-specific prescriptions and proscriptions specifying how men and women ought to behave. Manhood, however, is distinctive in two ways: (1) deviations are more likely, given manhood's precarious nature; and (2) the punishment for deviations is greater (i.e., loss of access to a high-status identity). While there is no doubt that women are expected to conform to strict standards of femininity or risk social penalties, they do not stand to lose their status *as women*, presumably because womanhood is undervalued by society. Research supports this distinction, such that both men and women agree that men must *do* something in order to be considered real men, whereas women become women through biological maturation (Bosson, Vandello, and Caswell 2013; Vandello and Bosson 2013).

The expectation that men must constantly work to embody prevailing norms of masculinity and thus earn and retain membership in the privileged gender status is likely to trigger anxiety in many men. Regardless of the masculine criteria to which they are exposed, which vary between cultures and over time, men in almost all cultures must confront the real possibility that they will fail to convincingly perform prevailing masculine norms and thus cease to be real men. Indeed, this risk is only heightened by the fact that gendered proscriptions and prescriptions have been and continue to be much more restrictive for men than for women (Koenig 2018), making the rules for achieving and maintaining manhood narrower and easier to violate. Thus, while the *content* of what it means to be a man (specific qualities, behaviors, preferences, and traits) varies with cultural and historical context, the *structure* of manhood as an elusive and tenuous social status that must be earned and maintained persists (Kimmel 2006; Vandello and Bosson 2013).

Hegemonic Masculinity

Though manhood is precarious irrespective of the specific characteristics assumed to define it, making predictions about the consequences of precarious manhood in a particular culture requires consideration of that culture's construction of masculinity. *Hegemonic masculinity* refers to the idealized form of masculinity in a given society at a given time. While what constitutes hegemonic masculinity varies depending historical and cultural context, researchers highlight that it usually enforces the dominant position of men and the subordinate position of women and effeminate men and is largely characterized by traits associated with agency and action (Bird 1996; Brannon 1976; Donaldson 1993; Fahey 2007; Gallagher and Parrott 2011; Pascoe 2003; Pfeffer et al. 2016; Talbot and Quayle 2010; Zurbriggen 2010). More specifically, research from the past fifty years has identified several key traits and behaviors that characterize hegemonic masculinity, and therefore "real" manhood, across a wide range of cultures. These include status-seeking, work achievement, athleticism, independence, confidence, competitiveness, eschewal of femininity and homosexuality, risk-taking, aggression, and the subjugation of women (Brannon 1976; Connell 1995). Possessing some or all of these idealized masculine traits helps men achieve and maintain the coveted status of manhood. But what happens when men do not convincingly evince these traits? Relatedly, what happens when men's manhood is directly challenged or threatened?

Consequences of Precarious Manhood

Research shows that precarious manhood can trigger a range of behavioral, cognitive, and attitudinal processes. Threats to men's manhood often trigger psychological anxiety and distress, which may in turn motivate compensatory behaviors or beliefs meant to reaffirm manhood and reduce this anxiety. These compensatory behaviors and beliefs most often involve engaging in masculine activity (e.g., status-seeking, risk-taking, or aggression) as these are the ones that constitute hegemonic masculinity in many cultures. For example, research has found that threats to manhood cause men to take greater financial risks (Weaver et al. 2013), express more homophobic attitudes (Willer et al. 2013), and even display higher pain tolerance—presumably because men are expected to be strong (Berke et al. 2017). In this chapter, we limit our review to research on the aggressive consequences and correlates of precariousness, since these are the ones most relevant to political outcomes.

Precarious manhood has typically been studied using correlational or experimental methodologies. In correlational research, men's *trait* precariousness or masculine anxiety is measured and used to predict outcomes. In experimental research, men's *state* precariousness is manipulated, and masculine anxiety is induced to assess the causal influence on outcomes.

Trait precariousness is typically measured using scales that assess men's *gender role discrepancy stress* (Eisler and Skidmore 1987; Reidy et al. 2014, 2015). This construct reflects the extent to which men feel stress about failing to live up their society's masculinity ideals: "Simply put, discrepancy stress arises when a man believes that he *is*, or believes he *is perceived* to be insufficiently masculine" (Reidy et al. 2014). Research shows that higher levels of discrepancy stress predict risky and aggressive behavior in men, including risky sexual behavior (Reidy et al. 2016), risky health behaviors (Eisler et al. 1988), intimate partner and sexual violence (Copenhaver et al. 2000; Jakupcak et al. 2002; Reidy et al. 2009, 2014, 2015), and more anger and aggression toward gay men (Parrott 2009). Correlational research cannot, however, establish the direction of this effect, and it is also possible that precariousness and behavioral outcomes are confounded with a third variable (e.g., trait anxiety or aggression). Experimental research can help establish the causal path between precariousness and its potential consequences.

State precariousness is brought about by challenging manhood experimentally. Typically, masculine anxiety is induced by threatening men's self-perceived adherence to masculine gender roles. While it is conceivable that a threat to any component of masculinity would produce similar outcomes, the most common paradigms involve the implication of femininity. One type of threat paradigm has men engage in a stereotypically feminine task such as hair braiding (Bosson and Vandello 2011) or using a fragrant, feminine hand lotion (Weaver et al. 2013). Another popular paradigm provides participants with false feedback on a "gender knowledge test" implying that they are high in feminine knowledge compared to other men (Berke et al. 2017; Stanaland and Gaither 2021; Vandello et al. 2008; Willer et al. 2013). In another example, men testing a grip strength meter were told that their strength was more similar to the average woman's than to the average man's (Cheryan et al. 2015). These threat paradigms, as well as others, have shown that threatened men react with increased anxiety (Bosson et al. 2009; Caswell et al. 2014; Vandello et al. 2008); more hostility toward women (Maass et al. 2003); more aggressive cognitions (Berke et al. 2017; Stanaland and Gaither 2021); more public discomfort, anger, shame, and guilt (Vescio et al. 2021); harder punches to a punching bag (Bosson et al. 2009); the administration of more shocks to a confederate (Cohn et al. 2009); and more aggression toward gay men (Bosson et al. 2012).

Taken together, both correlational and experimental work shows that threats to manhood can result in cognitions and behaviors that are likely to affirm one masculine trait in particular—namely, physical aggression. Our research asks whether these psychological and physical responses extend to the political realm—specifically, to political attitudes and behavior.

The Role of Precarious Manhood in Politics

Although the research outlined above clearly shows that precarious manhood is related to cognitive and behavioral aggression, much less work has examined the link between precarious manhood and *political* aggression. We feel that the political realm is a particularly appealing arena for men to both prove and reaffirm their status as "real men." Not only are politics highly consequential and a domain in which voters' can extend their sense of social efficacy; politics also allow men to signal their masculinity by supporting parties, politicians, policies, and ideologies that convey masculine traits such as aggression, risk-taking, and toughness. In addition, supporting aggressive pursuits via political decision-making and behavior might present a more socially accept-able alternative to raw physical aggression. As such, we theorized that precarious manhood is a unique driver of men's political attitudes and behavior—and one distinct from the role of masculine ideologies per se in such outcomes (DiMuccio and Knowles 2019).

Because other chapters in this volume describe in detail research on masculinity's importance to politics, we limit our review to *precarious* masculinity. Relatively little work has been done in this area. In a pioneering experimental study, sociologist Robb Willer and colleagues found that threatening men's manhood led them to express more sup-port for the decision to invade Iraq and for the Bush administration's handling of the Iraq war (Willer et al. 2013). More recently, research shows that manhood threats increased support for Donald Trump in 2018 by increasing the desire for a more masculine president (Car-ian and Sobotka 2018). Despite this work, more research is needed to understand how precarious manhood influences men's broad political views—especially those that can be considered aggressive, as these are the ones that men are prone to support more than women (Lizotte 2018). In the following sections, we review our own research, which demonstrates the significance of precarious manhood to men's politi-cal beliefs and voting behavior (DiMuccio and Knowles 2020; DiMuc-cio and Knowles 2022).

Precarious Manhood Predicts Support for Aggressive Policies and Politicians

We first set out to explore the relationship between precarious manhood and support for aggressive political policies and candidates using a cor-relational approach (DiMuccio and Knowles 2020). Our first challenge was to identify policies that met our conceptual definition of *aggressive*: those that signal "strength, toughness, or forcefulness" (1171). We did this by looking for policies that both garner support from men scoring high on dispositional aggression (Buss and Perry 1992) and are judged by male and female raters to be "aggressive" (using our definition of the term). Policies that failed one or both of these criteria were catego-rized as "nonaggressive." This procedure allowed us to generate a list of aggressive policies (e.g., the death penalty, torture, increase military spending) and nonaggressive policies (e.g., marijuana legalization, vaccine mandates, and Obamacare).

Having generated a list of relevant policies, we required a measure of masculine anxiety—that is, the worry that one is failing to live up to culturally prescribed masculine norms. We found this in Dennis Reidy and colleagues' Gender Role Discrepancy Stress Scale (GRDS; Reidy et al. 2014), which measures the degree to which men chronically worry that others view them as insufficiently masculine (e.g., trait precariousness). In keeping with the idea that men seek to shore up their manhood by supporting aggressive policies, we hypothesized that discrepancy stress would be positively associated with support for aggressive (but not nonaggressive) policies. This is exactly what we found: men high in masculine discrepancy stress were more likely to support aggressive policies, such as the death penalty and torture, and *less* likely to support nonaggressive policies, such as marijuana legalization and Obamacare. We were also fascinated by another finding in this study: gender role discrepancy stress was positively associated with support for Donald Trump. This result inspired our next study, which examined the relationship between precarious manhood and voting behavior.

In thinking about how precarious manhood might affect voting behavior, we realized that political aggression is disproportionately the province of one major political party in the United States: the Republican Party (indeed, our list of "aggressive" policies overlaps closely with the GOP platform). Numerous observers have linked political aggression (e.g., support for torture and tough-on-crime policies) to right-wing politics in general (e.g., Ducat 2004; Katz 2016; Winter 2010). The rise of Trumpism, of course, makes this connection even starker, with its explicit invocations of aggressive masculinity (Krieg 2016; Kurtzleben 2016). Thus, it stands to reason that precious manhood might predict support for Republican political candidates—perhaps especially when that candidate is Donald Trump.

Focusing on voting behavior as a dependent variable presents a special challenge, as voting records are private, and people do not always honestly or correctly report for whom they voted (Himmelweit et al. 1978; van Elsas et al. 2016). Researchers do, however, have access to voting results aggregated to the level of the US county. Hence, we gathered data on the percentage of people who voted for the Republican and Democrat candidate in several recent presidential and congressional elections across every county in the United States (DiMuccio and Knowles 2020).

Locating our analysis of voting at the county level required us to develop a corresponding county-level measure of precarious manhood. Because no comprehensive national polling data provided the information we needed, we constructed a county-level index of precarious masculinity based on Americans' use of the Google search engine. Rates of particular Internet searches, as revealed by the Google Trends service (http://trends.google.com), are particularly useful for studying people's level of concern regarding sensitive topics, as they tend to regard their search behavior as private (Stephens-Davidowitz 2017). As such, we identified search terms that we reasoned would be highest among men concerned about their adherence to masculine norms of strength and virility (Courtenay 2000; Hunt et al. 2013). We validated our final set of terms by retaining only those that male survey participants high in masculine anxiety (as assessed using the GRDS; Reidy et al. 2014) reported having searched for in the past or being likely to search for in the future. These terms were: "erectile dysfunction," "hair loss," "how to get girls," "penis enlargement," "human penis size," "anabolic steroid," "testosterone," and "Sildenafil" (Viagra). (Note that, with the exemption of "how to get girls," these were Google Trends "topics" that included sets of synonymous search terms.) We extracted the rates at which these search terms were used in clusters of US counties in the year preceding the 2016, 2012, and 2008 presidential elections and the 2018, 2016, and 2014 congressional elections.

Armed with indices of both voting and precarious masculinity, we proceeded to examine the relationship between masculine anxiety and voting for Republican candidates. As we predicted, precarious masculinity strongly and positively predicted the Trump vote across regions. Interestingly, however, we observed no such relationship when the Republican candidate was Mitt Romney (2012) or John McCain (2008). As for the congressional elections, we observed a significant and positive relationship between precarious masculinity and support for Republican candidates in 2018—but not in 2016 or 2014. This presents evidence that, despite the historical affinity of the Republican party for political aggression, the GOP has recently become a stronger source of affirmation for men concerned about their manhood. We suspect that it is not a coincidence that we only began to detect a relationship between precarious manhood and voting behavior once Donald Trump—whose performance of masculinity is hard to overlook—became the standard-bearer of the Republican Party.

Manhood Threats Increase Political Aggression among Liberal Men

Given our previous work showing the link between men's precarious manhood and their propensity to vote for aggressive politicians such as Donald Trump (DiMuccio and Knowles 2020), we wanted to ascertain whether this link was causal—that is, to determine whether situational threats to manhood cause men to become more aggressive in their political attitudes (DiMuccio and Knowles 2022). In three experiments, we tested the effects of manhood threats on men's support for aggressive (versus nonaggressive) political stances. In the first experiment, we induced masculinity threat by giving men false feedback suggesting that they possessed feminine traits; participants then indicated their support for a range of political policies deemed aggressive and nonaggressive. In the second experiment, we induced masculinity threat by having men participate in a feminine activity (nail painting); participants then responded to a fictional foreign-policy scenario with either an aggressive or nonaggressive approach. Finally, in the third experiment, we induced masculinity threat by leading men to believe that their hand grip was only as strong as that of the average woman; participants then responded to the policy questions from experiment 1 and the foreign-policy scenario from experiment 2.

In our experimental research, we also sought to examine *for whom*—liberal or conservative men—the effect of masculinity threat on political attitudes is strongest. Reasoning that conservative men may have internalized hegemonic masculine norms to a greater extent than liberal men, we originally predicted that conservative men would display a stronger politically aggressive response to manhood threats. As we will discuss, this expectation proved incorrect: it was liberal, not conservative, men who adopted more aggressive political positions after exposure to manhood threats.

Manhood Threat Manipulations

The first challenge in conducting these experiments was to decide *how* to threaten men's manhood. As discussed in the beginning of this chapter, there are many ways in which masculinity can be challenged experimentally, most of which involve the insinuation of femininity (e.g., hair braiding, false feedback on a personality test, or applying scented lotion; Bosson and Vandello 2011; Stanaland and Gaither 2021; Weaver et al. 2013). We ultimately decided to threaten manhood with the use of three different paradigms.

In experiment 1, we threatened manhood by falsely insinuating that the male participants were less masculine in their personality traits than the average man. This was accomplished via an online experiment in which participants were asked to complete the Bem Sex Role Inventory (BSRI; Bem 1974). The BSRI has participants rate themselves on sixty common personality characteristics, one-third of which are considered stereotypically masculine, one-third stereotypically feminine, and one-third gender neutral. All traits were positive in valence and participants indicated their agreement on a scale from 1 ("never true of you") to 7 ("always true of you"). A score from 0 to 100 was then calculated for each participant, whereby higher scores indicate more agreement with masculine traits and lower scores meant more agreement with feminine traits (with neutral traits excluded). Manhood threat was induced by subtracting thirty points from their actual score, thereby artificially placing them closer to the score of the "average woman." Half of the participants received the threat feedback, while the other half received no feedback at all following the BSRI.

In experiment 2, we threatened manhood by having men complete a stereotypically feminine task: painting their nails pink. This was a novel threat paradigm whereby participants came to the lab and were told that they were participating in a "usability test" for a marketing class at NYU: they would be testing a novel product on camera and asked to rate its ease of use. Participants in the threat condition were led to believe that they randomly chose "nail polish" as their product and were asked to carefully apply the pink nail polish to all ten fingernails while being videotaped. Participants in the no-threat condition were instead asked to paint ten circles on a sheet of paper with white nail polish.

Finally, in experiment 3, we threatened manhood by leading men to believe that they were physically weak. We used a modified version of Cheryan and colleagues' (2015) hand-grip paradigm. Participants in various parks and on the streets of New York City were given a hand dynamometer and asked to grip it as hard as they could for several seconds. In the threat condition, the unit of measurement was displayed in kilograms but told the number was in pounds, thus showing a smaller number than if it were set to pounds. In the no-threat condition, the unit of measurement was in pounds. Participants were then asked to announce their score so that the researcher could record it on an iPad. The researcher next showed participants a chart with overlapping distributions ostensibly depicting the scores of previous male and female participants. In the threat condition, the researcher pointed to the chart and showed the men that their hand grip was closest to the average woman (the kilogram reading). In the no-threat condition, the researcher pointed to the chart to show the men that their hand grip resembled the average man's (the pound reading).

Measuring Aggressive versus Nonaggressive Policy Support

The second challenge was to measure participants' policy support in a way that captures the many varied and complex beliefs that people have about politics. In experiment 1, we assessed participants' support of seventeen different foreign and domestic policies. These were split into aggressive and nonaggressive groupings, based on our own and others' previous research (DiMuccio and Knowles 2020; Lizotte 2017). Participants rated their agreement with each policy on a scale from 1 ("strongly oppose") to 7 ("strongly support"). There were nine aggressive policies (e.g., banning Muslim immigration and the death penalty) and eight nonaggressive policies (e.g., marriage equality and climate regulation).

In experiment 2, we measured political aggression using a novel "warring countries" vignette. The participants read a 260-word scenario describing an unstable political situation involving two fictional countries. Participants were asked to imagine that they were the president of one of the countries and were then asked a series of questions about how they would handle the mounting tensions. One set of questions assessed participants' inclination toward a politically aggressive approach to the foreign-policy dilemma (e.g., deploying troops, dropping bombs on enemy territory) and three of the items were meant to assess non-aggressive or more diplomatic approaches (e.g., imposing sanctions, offering a peace deal). In experiment 3, participants were given both of these measures: the same policy questions from experiment 1, and an abridged version of the scenario from experiment 2 followed by the same questions.

For brevity, we discuss the results of an integrative data analysis (IDA; Curran and Hussong 2009) combining the data from all of our experiments (specific details about the participants, methods, measures, and data from each individual study can be found at https://psyarxiv.com/qnpw4). Combining datasets yielded a total sample of 445 men. For both measurement types (policy attitudes and vignette responses), we averaged all aggressive and nonaggressive items together to form overall aggressive and nonaggressive composites. Results of the IDA indicated that, contrary to our initial predictions, *liberal* men consistently reacted with greater political aggression following a threat; manhood threat did not change conservative men's (already high) levels of politically aggressive policy endorsement. Consistent with expectations, men in the no-threat condition remained unchanged in their beliefs, regardless of ideology, and the threat manipulations had no effect on men's nonaggressive policy support and political approaches. Table 1 summarizes the sizes of the effects of threat on liberal and conservative men's political judgments in DiMuccio and Knowles (2023).

We were particularly intrigued by the findings regarding male participants' preexisting political ideology. Why did only relatively liberal men

TABLE 8.1: Size of threat effect for liberal and conservative men across three experiments

	Experiment 1 (N = 341) [Trait feedback]	Experiment 2 (N = 235) [Nail painting]	Experiment 3 (N = 64) [Grip strength]		Combined dataset (N = 445)
	Policies	Vignette	Policies	Vignette	
Liberals	0.582	0.382	0.813	1.310	0.566
Conservatives	−0.060	0.006	0.313	0.510	0.050

Note. Values are effect sizes (Glass's Δ). Bold type indicates effects significant at p < .05.

become more politically aggressive under threat? We see a few possible answers. First, it may be that our dependent measures of political aggression (e.g., support for military intervention and the death penalty) failed to allow sufficient room for movement among conservative participants, who already strongly endorsed such positions. If this is true, then more extreme outcome measures might reveal comparable threat effects for conservatives—that is, when threatened, conservative men may to venture outside the range of socially sanctioned political aggression (e.g., military intervention) into the realm of violent extremism (as exemplified the 2021 Capitol insurrection).

Yet it may be that liberal men are genuinely more vulnerable to masculinity threat in political contexts. We know that liberals tend to be stereotyped as feminine and conservatives as masculine (Katz 2016; Rudman et al. 2013; Winter 2010). Thus, liberal men may have experienced a political form of *stereotype threat* (Spencer et al. 1999), reacting to threat with heightened political aggression in order to avoid confirming a negative stereotype of their ideological group. Suggesting that this stereotype is, in fact, negative, accusations of femininity constitute a recurring attack line against liberal politicians, presidents, and laypeople—from both the Left (Dowd 2006; Prabhu 2016) and the Right (Fahey 2007; French 2015). Future research should further examine the possibility that liberal men experience a form of gendered stereotype threat in the realm of politics.

Discussion

We have discussed two lines of research, one correlational and the other experimental, that bear on the question of how masculine anxiety—a symptom of precarious manhood—affects men's political behavior. Our correlational work suggests that *trait* anxiety is associated with politically aggressive policy views and candidate preferences. Our experiments imply that *state* anxiety shifts liberal men's views in a politically aggressive direction.

It is worth asking how these sets of findings fit together. It may be that our correlational findings represent a "macrolevel" snapshot of outcomes created by "microlevel" threat processes. In other words, it may be that repeated experiences of state masculinity anxiety ossify into high levels of trait anxiety over time—and thus that our experimental scenarios model how people in cultural contexts where hegemonic masculinity is salient acquire high levels of concerns about their adherence to male gender roles. Moreover, against the backdrop of our finding that liberal men are especially sensitive to information that threatens masculinity, it may be that the individuals driving our correlational findings are liberal men (or *formerly* liberal men) who were subject to sustained levels of pressure derived from hegemonic masculinity over extended periods of time. It may in fact be that many men who eventually come to evince the politically aggressive dimensions of modern conservatism are formerly left-leaning, and perhaps politically moderate, men. This possibility implies that politically aggressive political ideologies and movements may garner a portion of their support by "peeling off" relatively liberal males who were subject to masculinity pressures over the long haul. Although this interpretation is highly tentative, we propose that the longitudinal dynamics of precarious and hegemonic masculinity are ripe areas for future study.

Our findings regarding the connection between masculine anxiety and political aggression carry important implications for the future of US politics. Critically, our results imply that right-wing elites can effectively garner votes by positioning themselves as paragons or protectors of masculinity while simultaneously stoking gender-based anxiety among male voters. Unfortunately, conservative political consultants appear to have already realized this—as right-wing stars such as Tucker Carlson and Sen. Josh Hawley promulgate the notion of a culture-wide "attack on men" (Brownstein 2021; Capehart 2022; Malloy 2022), and GOP politicians continue to broadcast their masculine bona fides.

At the same time, understanding the link between precarious masculinity and right-wing political behavior may be the first step toward short-circuiting it. Although the necessary empirical work has yet to be done, we believe that our and others' work on this topic supports the development of an effective countermessage. Because precarious masculinity has its origins in unyielding masculine norms ("hegemonic masculinity"), the first element of such a countermessage is *flexibility*: men should feel free to adopt any version of masculinity that feels right to them—traditional or otherwise. For men compelled to adopt a form of hegemonic masculinity that feels disingenuous or inauthentic, communicating flexibility promises to relieve anxiety and thus reduce the need to engage in masculinity-affirming behaviors. A second, and related, element of effective countermessaging is *complexity*. While traditional American manhood may be inherently associated with certain "aggressive" traits, such as competitiveness, we suspect that what fuels right-wing movements is the insecurity and need for validation that can accompany this (or any) type of masculine identity. Reconstructing even traditional masculinity as complex enough to allow for moments of vulnerability and counterstereotypical emotions (e.g., sadness and compassion) may alleviate some of the pressure to prove one's masculine bona fides through hyper-aggressive personal or political behavior.

9

Masculinity, Race, Ethnicity, and Political Efficacy

Neighborhoods and the Use of Politics to Assert Masculinity in Newark, New Jersey

DAN CASSINO AND IVELISSE CUEVAS-MOLINA

Introduction

This chapter connects the study of political efficacy to masculinity and racial/ethnic groups. We explore how the racial and ethnic context in men's zip codes in the City of Newark, New Jersey, is associated with their self-reported levels of masculinity, and how masculinity and the racial and ethnic context is related to men's belief that voting is an effective political activity.

Political Efficacy

Political efficacy is one the most continuously measured and studied political attitudes in political science (Converse 1972; Lane 1959; Balch 1974; Craig and Maggiotto 1982; Abramson 1983; Finkel 1985; Craig, Niemi, and Silver 1990; Morell 2003; Niemi, Craig, and Mattei 1991). In 1954, Campbell, Gurin, and Miller first defined political efficacy as the "feeling that individual political action does have, or can have, an impact upon the political process, i.e., that it is worthwhile to perform one's civic duties" (187). Initially, measures of political efficacy were used as a fundamental explanatory variable for individuals' propensity to participate in elections. Eventually, social scientists became more concerned with understanding which factors are associated with having a greater sense of political efficacy, and how to help develop a sense of political efficacy among individuals.

The construct is typically measured by using a series of questions that assess two types of political efficacy: internal and external. Internal efficacy is reflective of how individuals feel about their personal ability to effectively participate in political processes, while external efficacy is reflective of whether or not individuals see governmental institutions as responsive to political action (Craig, Niemi and Silver 1990; Morell 2003). Additionally, some studies have assessed political efficacy by measuring two attitudes: first, by measuring how individuals feel about the effectiveness of a particular type of political action, and, second, by measuring a group's ability to elect representatives who are also members of their group (Mangum 2003; Ananat and Williams 2009). Consequently, a great many studies have examined the role that a sense of political efficacy plays in a person's likelihood to participate in politics.

Research has found that people who express a strong belief that their participation in politics can make a difference in the outcome of both elections and the policy-making process are more likely to engage in political action (Abramson 1983; Clarke and Acock 1989; Rudolph, Gangl, and Stevens 2000; Verba, Burns, and Schlozman 1997; Verba, Brady, and Schlozman 1995; Rosenstone and Hansen 1993; Pollock 1983). Findings consistently show that individuals who score highly on political efficacy measures are more likely to engage in all manner of political activity, and particularly more likely to exercise their right to vote (Finkel 1985; Verba, Brady and Schlozman 1995; Rosenstone and Hansen 1993). More importantly, there is a reciprocal relationship between political efficacy and participation. Participation in politics makes individuals more efficacious generally, and more politically efficacious individuals have higher levels of participation across modes (Finkel 1985).

Feelings of political efficacy are not equally distributed among the population, and a variety of individual and contextual factors can affect whether a person believes that their individual action can impact politics. Early studies of the construct found that demographics can be associated with feelings of political efficacy; factors like socioeconomic status, race, and gender are related to differences in this political attitude. Specifically, individuals with low socioeconomic status were more likely to feel less efficacious, and, conversely, those with high socioeconomic status were likely to feel more efficacious (Form and Huber 1971; Lane 1969; Almond and Verba 1963; Wu 2003). This relationship

between political efficacy, class, and political participation is clearly illustrated by resource models of participation and voter turnout where
individuals with higher incomes are consistently found to be more likely
to participate in politics and elections and so were those who felt more
efficacious (Verba, Brady, and Schlozman 1995; Rosenstone and Hansen
1993). With regard to gender, studies have shown that men express high
levels of political efficacy while women express lower levels, even though
gender difference in voter turnout no longer exists (Almond and Verba
1963; Abramson 1983; Bennett and Bennett 1989; Banducci et al.1999;
Chanley et al. 2000; Verba et al. 1997; Coffé and Bolzendahl 2010; Fraile
and De Miguel Moyer 2021).

While differences in political efficacy are associated with race (Form
and Huber 1971; Rogers 1974; Klieman 1976; Carmines et al. 1986;
Abramson 1972, 1983; Niemi and Junn 1998) and ethnicity (Michelson
2000; Stokes-Brown 2009), the race and politics literature finds that
there are certain conditions under which members of minority racial
groups feel more efficacious. In 1990, Bobo and Gilliam described what
they define as "Black empowerment," which is the link between having control of local political office by African Americans and having a
greater sense of political efficacy, trust in government, and increased
participation in politics among Black Americans. For Latinos, the link
between political efficacy, descriptive representation at the local level,
and political participation also exists (Michelson 2000). This relationship between descriptive representation and political efficacy has been
further identified when Black Americans have viable Black candidates
to vote for (Merolla, Sellers, and Fowler 2013; West 2017). Additionally,
both Black Americans and Latinos have more positive views of government (i.e., external efficacy) when they have a descriptive representative
in Congress (Sanchez and Morin 2011; Fowler, Merolla, and Sellers 2014;
Stout, Tate, and Wilson 2021).

It is important to note that descriptive representation, which is
linked to a greater sense of political efficacy, often results from majority-
minority electoral jurisdictions. Majority-minority districts are effective at increasing descriptive representation in both Congress and state
legislatures for both Black Americans (Lublin 1999; Hicks et al. 2018),
and Latinos (Preuhs and Gonzalez Juenke) by enhancing their opportunities for success in determining the outcome of elections. Based on

this evidence, scholars like Mangum (2003) and Ananat and Washington (2009) measure political efficacy as group political efficacy, which they define as a social group's ability to elect a candidate from their own group, particularly racial and ethnic minorities. In their view, when studying political efficacy among racial and ethnic minorities, academics should account for groups' higher propensity toward having a strong sense of linked fate (Dawson 1994; Gay, Hoschchild, and White 2016) and group consciousness (McClain et al. 2009). Mangum (2003, 41), in particular, argues that "perceived group efficacy may serve as a proxy for personal efficacy."

Masculinity, Race/Ethnicity and Political Efficacy

While the voting turnout gap between men and women has closed in recent years, there are still substantial gaps between men and women in other forms of political behavior, such as contacting politicians or attending political meetings (Coffé and Bolzendahl 2010). Some of this could be caused by mean differences in resources, such as money and time (Stolle et al. 2005), but some of the difference is also due to gendered traits, like assertiveness, aggression, and dominance (McDermott 2016; Schrock and Schwalbe 2009). McDermott's results, based on the BSRI, show a strong correlation between political participation and masculine-coded gender traits, while Coffé and Bolzendahl (2021) demonstrate that masculine traits in a Dutch sample are related to political participation (with a stronger relationship for more conflict-based forms of participation).

Essentially, the prior research argues that the traits men see as part of a masculine gender identity are the same traits that lead individuals to be more likely to engage in political actions and hold higher levels of political efficacy. But the work on race, ethnicity, and political efficacy suggests that political efficacy is highly contextual, with efficacy being linked to racial/ethnic representation in a particular residential area or political locality. But if these are stable, long-term traits, why should context matter? The key comes from social identity theory, which holds that individuals hold many different identities, but, depending on context, some of those identities are more important than others at a given point in time.

Schneider and Bos (2019) argue that social role theory provides a link between political efficacy and demographic factors like race and ethnicity. Applied to politics, social role theory in general holds that differences in observed behaviors between groups is driven by the application of normally diffuse identities to particular social stimuli (e.g., Diekman and Schneider 2010). For instance, in an election in which gender was a major issue, individual level attitudes and behaviors might be more structured by gender, rather than other roles (e.g., race, ethnicity, or religion) that might otherwise be applied.

Rather than look at differences in elections as being the drivers of differences in political efficacy, it makes sense, then, to look at the context in which men are asserting, or attempting to assert, their masculinities. In contexts where political activism is likely to be fruitful—that is, in which men are more likely to be able to have an influence on politics—they should be likely to use political participation as a way to assert a masculine gender identity. In areas where they are less likely to be able to influence political outcomes, they should be less likely to do so.

Measurement of Gender

Masculinity is a complex, multidimensional construct, but quantitative analysis requires that we operationalize it, creating a variable that does a reasonable job of measuring gender identity in a form that we can easily include in surveys. We recognize, of course, that any such operationalization is a massive simplification—but, as discussed in chapter 2, that doesn't mean that it can't be useful.

Here, we make use of a unidimensional self-report scale, in which respondents are asked to place themselves on a scale that runs from "completely masculine" to "completely feminine" (Cassino 2020). In order to try and elicit more responses toward the middle, the introduction to the question notes that gender is a continuum and is socially determined, rather than being innate or synonymous with sex. The question read:

The traits that we see as being masculine or feminine are largely determined by society, and have changed dramatically over time. As a result, everyone has some combination of masculine and feminine traits, which may or may not correspond with whether they are male or female. How do you see yourself? Would you say that you see yourself as Completely Masculine, Mostly Masculine, Slightly Masculine, Slightly Feminine, Mostly Feminine, or Completely Feminine?

One potential issue with this scale is that it presents masculinity and femininity as being somewhat incompatible, when, from a theoretical perspective, it would be better to represent them as entirely separate scales (i.e., BSRI; Bem 1974). However, when US respondents are allowed to independently place themselves on masculinity and femininity scales, the correlation between their responses is greater than −0.9, meaning that they're defining masculinity and femininity in opposition to each other, even when they don't have to, and the instructions tell them so (Cassino and Besen-Cassino 2021). As such, asking about masculinity and femininity separately in general population surveys adds to respondent burden without substantially increasing data quality.

Also, responses to masculinity-femininity scale questions like this have been shown to capture important variance in political and social views. Bittner and Goodyear-Grant (2017), for instance, find that variance in gender identity (measured using a similar 100-point scale) within sex categories is an important predictor of voting preferences in Canadian elections.

The responses that individuals give to this, and related, self-report scales are rather different than the results of indirect scales, like the Bem Sex Role Inventory (Bem 1974), which has been applied to political attitudes and behaviors by McDermott (2016). In her analyses, individuals are much more likely to show traits traditionally associated with a different sex in the BSRI than they are in the self-report scales used here.

It seems likely that the difference comes down to a difference between the gendered traits an individual holds, and gendered traits that an individual wants to assert as part of their performance of gender. An individual might have feminine traits but feel the need to assert an unequivocal masculinity, and the self-report might well be picking up on the desired assertion, rather than the underlying traits. However, for our purposes, that assertion is itself interesting. The fact that men might feel the need to assert a "completely masculine" gender identity, despite the question telling them that most people have a mixture of gender traits, tells us about the importance of that gender identity to the individual, and their perceived need to express it in a certain way.

Data

The data in this study come from a mixed-mode survey of residents of Newark, New Jersey, carried out between July 9 and August 11, 2021. The sample was drawn from a list of certified city residents. Voters were randomly chosen from the list and contacted in one of two ways. Three-quarters of the respondents (827) received an invitation through SMS (text) to fill out the survey online, via a provided link. The other quarter of respondents (273) were contacted via telephone, using the same registered voter list. The survey covers 1,100 Newark residents, ages eighteen and older, and was conducted mostly in English (1039), with the remainder in Spanish (57) and Portuguese (4). The survey was carried out by Braun Research Inc, of Princeton, New Jersey. Of the interviews, 146 were conducted over landlines, the remainder via cell phones. The survey included a significant oversample (300) of African American and Black voters in Newark, meaning that the unweighted figures do not accurately represent population characteristics of the city.

The mixed SMS and live caller telephone modality (what we refer to as "SMS with a live caller chaser") is used primarily to increase the representativeness of the sample. Generally, live caller surveys have higher response rates among older and white respondents, while SMS-based surveys have higher response rates among younger and nonwhite respondents (Soszynski and Bliss 2023). The relatively young and non-white sample found in Newark meant that an SMS-based strategy was desirable, while reaching older cohorts made live caller sampling necessary as well. In the analyses presented, we did not find any significant differences in the variables of interest based on modality, once demographic characteristics were included as controls.

The overall weighted sample was 50 percent women, 59 percent Democratic (or leaning), 49 percent African American or Black, and 36 percent Hispanic or Latino/a/x. The age distribution was much flatter than in most general population surveys, with 35 percent of respondents under thirty-five, and only 13 percent over sixty-five (all of these figures are in line with census estimates of Newark's population at the time).

We isolate neighborhoods within Newark by looking at the zip codes of respondents. There are nine standard zip codes within the city (there are a total of twenty, but eleven are unique zip codes referring to, for instance, PO boxes or specific buildings or organizations), and we analyzed the racial and ethnic makeup of each, based on 2020 estimates. Because the number of respondents within each zip code varies widely (as low as 33, to as many as 176, with a mean of 121), they are aggregated based on their racial and ethnic makeup. Six of the zip codes are majority Black or African American, and three are more than 80 percent (the values range between 13 percent and 95 percent). Similarly, three of the zip codes are majority Hispanic or Latino (the lowest is 7 percent, and the highest is 66 percent). Note that these percentages are based on the known composition of the zip codes, rather than the sample gathered from within each, though the samples generally correspond.

Overall, white men in the sample are less likely to assert a "completely masculine" gender identity than Black or Hispanic/Latino men in Newark. Sixty-three percent of white men said that they were "completely masculine," compared to 75 percent of African American or Black men and 75 percent of Hispanic or Latino men. The white men in the sample are, on average, younger and have higher levels of education than the other men in the sample, and both factors tend to drive down the proportion of men asserting traditional gender roles. White men's assertions of masculinity might also be driven by local context: to the extent that men in Newark are more likely to assert a "completely masculine" identity when they live in neighborhoods dominated by their own racial or ethnic group, we'd expect white men to be less likely to do so, as there are no mostly white residential zip codes in Newark.

However, these results differ substantially from national samples using the same question, in which about 55 percent of men overall rate themselves as "completely masculine." In national samples, as in this one, African American or Black and Hispanic/Latino men are more likely than white men to assert a "completely masculine" gender identity. While a national sample of men is not directly comparable to a sample of men in one particular city—especially a city as unique as Newark—this does suggest that expressions of gender in Newark, and perhaps in other cities as well, may be different than the ways in which gender is expressed in other places.

The City of Newark was selected for the survey chiefly because it is both New Jersey's largest city, and an understudied population as attention in New Jersey politics typically turns to suburban areas considered to have the potential to swing between political parties. Because Newark is solidly Democratic, it is considered less interesting. Newark also has the advantage of having various neighborhoods with very different ethnic and racial mixtures. There are neighborhoods that have a relatively even mix of African American or Black and Hispanic or Latino residents, as well as neighborhoods in which one of these groups is a large majority. The combination of racial and ethnic diversity with neighborhood diversity, difficult or impossible to achieve outside of an urban context like Newark, allows us to separate out the effects of race and ethnicity from the effects of neighborhood, or context.

Newark also makes for an interesting test case for political efficacy as it still exists in the shadow of the massive uprisings of 1967, which have shaped it and the surrounding towns ever since (Foerster 2019). In particular, the uprising, and the reactions to it, led to a durable "Don't riot" ethos that has largely prevented violent demonstrations in the years since—an outcome made more possible by the cooperation of city leadership and local police.

Gentrification, which had been on the rise, seems to have stalled out. Given the general prosperity of the New York City metro area and the pro-growth policies of city leadership, this has presented a puzzle for researchers (Morel et al. 2021), but it means that Newark remains one of the few cities in the area that has maintained a majority nonwhite population and has a long tradition of nonwhite leadership in city offices (though county offices are dominated by white representatives).

Hypotheses

The fact that we have sufficient data to look at samples on the zip code level means that we can look at how the link between assertions of masculine gender identity among men and their political efficacy differs based on local context—a potentially important interactive effect, as noted. Prior work leads us to believe that the link between asserted masculine gender identity and political efficacy should be stronger in areas in which men's racial or ethnic group is in the majority. For instance, in areas where African American or Black men are in the majority, political participation is more likely to be effective, as they will be more influential in choosing or influencing their representatives. As such, men seeking to assert a masculine gender identity should be more likely to assert the efficacy of their political participation than they would in areas in which they are a minority.

Findings

While there are no significant differences in assertions of masculine gender identity based solely on the race or ethnicity of respondents within a particular zip code, there are significant differences among the various zip codes. For instance, in majority African American or Black zip codes, 73 percent of African American or Black men assert a "completely masculine" gender identity, no different than the 74 percent of other residents of those zip codes. However, that 73 percent is significantly higher than the 63 percent of African American or Black

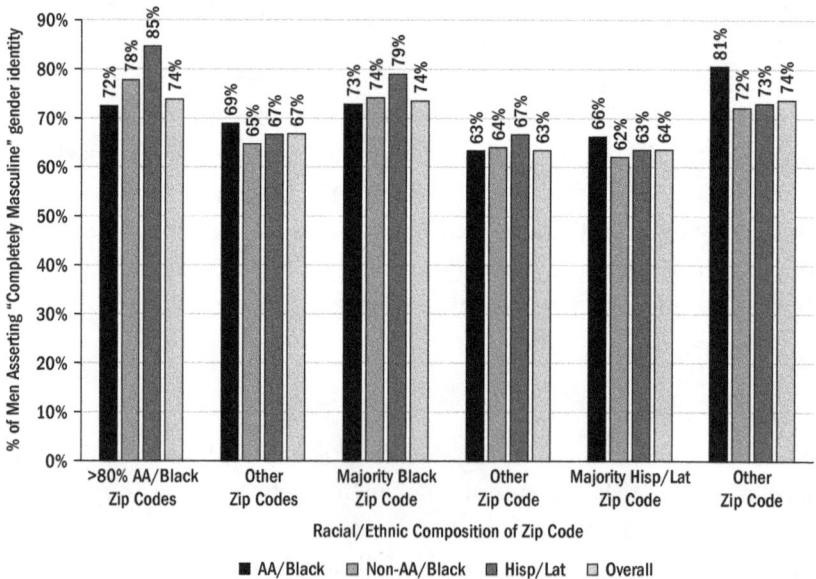

Figure 9.1: Percent of men asserting a "completely masculine" gender identity, by race/ethnicity and zip code

respondents living in other zip codes who assert that gender identity. The same holds true if we instead look at zip codes that are 80 percent African American or Black.

Nor is this effect limited to areas dominated by African American or Black populations. Similarly, in zip codes where the majority of the population is Hispanic or Latino, there is no difference between members of the majority group and other residents—but there is a significant gap between individuals living in those zip codes, and individuals with the same racial or ethnic background living in other zip codes. Note that the category of "non–African American or Black" in the graphs includes all white and Hispanic/Latino men, so there is significant overlap with the Hispanic/Latino group.

In sum, while it may seem that there are substantial racial and ethnic differences between individual men's asserted gender identities, what we're really seeing is differences between neighborhoods. This makes sense: gender identities aren't inborn, but are, at least in part, learned social behaviors that arise from a particular context, and they can be used to display an identity within that context. If the context—operationalized here through the racial and ethnic composition of the zip code—changes, so, too, does the display of gender identity. If we see large scale differences between racial and ethnic groups, that's mostly a sign of segregation, which places those men within different contexts than members of other groups.

There is a suggestive difference between Hispanic or Latino men living in African American–dominated zip codes, and those living in zip codes where their own ethnic group is in the majority. Hispanic or Latino men living in parts of Newark where they are not the majority group are marginally more likely to assert a "completely masculine" gender identity than other residents of those areas. While survey-based analysis of these groups is necessarily difficult, because they are definitionally in small numbers, this suggests the existence of complicated racial and ethnic dynamics such that men from some minority ethnic or racial groups within an area might assert their masculinity differently, perhaps more stridently, then they would in areas where their racial group was in the majority. Again, though, this is not a difference based on a main effect of racial or ethnic group, but, rather, one based on the context in which members of a group live.

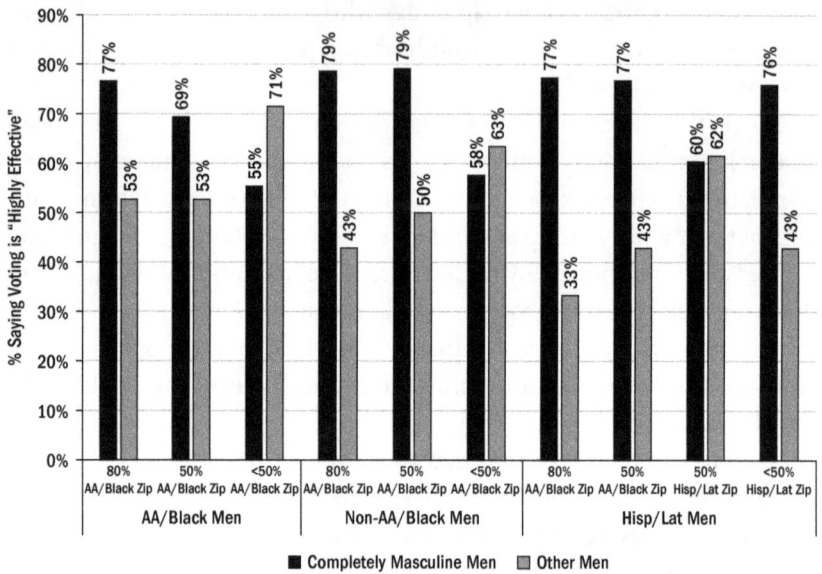

Figure 9.2: Percent of men saying that voting is "highly effective" by gender identity, race/ethnicity, and neighborhood composition

We see the same pattern if we look at expressions of political efficacy by racial/ethnic group and zip code. Within a particular racial/ethnic group and zip code, there are significant differences in men's political efficacy between those men who assert a "completely masculine" gender identity and other men. But the extent and nature of those differences varies widely *between* zip codes.

For instance, in zip codes that are more than 80 percent African American or Black, "completely masculine" African American or Black men are 24 points more likely than other men to say that voting is a "very effective" way of effecting political change (p<.01). But in neighborhoods where they are a minority, African American or Black men who assert a "completely masculine" gender identity are 16 points *less* likely than other men to say the same (p<.02). Hispanic or Latino men show a very similar pattern in zip codes where they are in the majority. Indeed, within zip codes that have the same racial and ethnic composition, there are no significant differences between men of different racial and ethnic groups. The difference is not between different men, but between different neighborhoods.

We can carry out a type of robustness check on the results by running the model backwards: interacting zip code and political efficacy as a predictor of asserted gender identity among men (with the same controls). When we run the model this way, there is indeed a positive effect, such that men living in Black–dominated zip codes who believe that voting is "very" effective are more likely to say that they're "completely" masculine.

For men not living in Black neighborhoods, the voting efficacy measure doesn't significantly change the likelihood of being "completely masculine" (it goes from 70 percent among those who say "very" effective to 77 percent for those that say "not at all"). But it does have an impact on those in Black neighborhoods: 81 percent among those men who say that voting is very effective, down to 46 percent among those who say that it's not at all effective.

As with the assertion of a masculine gender identity, the ways in which men choose to express their gender identity is dependent on context. Displays of masculinity, therefore, vary by the context in which the man is making the display, with some displays being more appreciated or recognized and therefore being a more effective way of presenting gender than others. These results imply not only that political efficacy is a way in which men can display their gender identities—hence the link between asserted masculinity and statements of political efficacy—but also that the propensity to make this link (and thus the magnitude of the difference between "completely masculine" and other men) varies by context.

Discussion

The results of the survey support our expectations about the link between local context, race/ethnicity, and political efficacy. Political efficacy is strongly linked with assertions of masculine gender identity—but only in the contexts in which political action is likely to be effective. So, in areas in which a man's racial group is dominant, they're more likely to use political efficacy as a way of asserting masculinity, simply because it's more likely to work. In areas in which political action is perceived to be less likely to be effective—in this case, areas in which their racial or ethnic group is in the minority—men are likely finding other ways to assert their gender identities.

This dovetails nicely with other findings on the conditionality of actions seeking to assert a masculine gender identity. Masculinity is a remarkably broad concept, so men are able to pick and choose which means of asserting their gender identity are likely to be most effective in their local context. For instance, Cassino and Besen-Cassino (2020) show that gender identity threat among men is linked with higher gun sales, but the relationship is mediated by the existing prevalence of guns within an area. Having a gun—or asserting masculinity in any particular way—is likely to be more effective in an area where that particular assertion is meaningful to the intended audience of other men. As such, behaviors meant to demonstrate an asserted masculine gender identity are as fluid as masculinity itself, changing based on what behaviors are likely to be effective and recognized in a given context, even one as small as a particular zip code.

The results also suggest a link between expressions of masculinity among Latino or Hispanic men and political efficacy. Much of the research about gender identities among Latino, Hispanic, and Chicano men has centered on the concept of machismo (e.g., Saez, Casado and Wade 2010; Hurtado and Sinha 2016), but our results suggest that the relationship between gender identity and political efficacy among Latino and Hispanic men may be moderated by local context. This could help to explain some results showing depressed political efficacy among Latino men in other cities (Michelson 2000), but, given the complexity of the issue, and the multidimensional nature of machismo as a concept (Walters and Valenzuela 2020), more detailed data is probably needed to explore the relationship.

This work also helps us to understand the role that politics might play in helping men from racial and ethnic minority groups express a masculine gender identity. Political efficacy is a potentially potent way for men to express their gender identities, especially among communities that might be otherwise marginalized. The nature of hegemonic masculinity (Connell and Messerschmidt 2005) excludes either directly, or indirectly, through structural barriers, men from historical underprivileged groups like racial and ethnic minorities. Therefore, men in these groups have to find alternative ways to assert a masculine gender identity, and our work here supports the argument that politics—potentially even local and hyperlocal politics—may be an important way for them to do so. Of course, the link between masculinity and politics has been problematized in the past, to the extent that it marginalizes women's political participation, but in an era in which toxic forms of asserting masculinity (e.g., those involving homophobia, sexism or violence) are a concern, an assertion that's at least *potentially* socially desirable is worth further exploration.

10

Masculinity, Knowledge, and the Gender Gap

Using Masculinity and Femininity as Predictors of Political Knowledge

CARL L. PALMER AND ROLFE DAUS PETERSON

Introduction

Political knowledge and its uneven distribution among American voters occupies a central place in American political behavior. Perhaps no finding has been replicated and debated more frequently than the dearth of political knowledge by the average adult citizen. As opinion scholar John Zaller states, "It is easy to underestimate how little typical Americans know about even the most prominent political events—and also how quickly they forget what for a time they do understand" (1992, 16). Although some scholars push back on the empirical findings of an ignorant populace by critiquing instruments and survey items (Lupia 2015; Achen 1975), the general consensus is that knowledge in the population is low. As noted by Converse (1990, 372), "The two simplest truths I [Converse] know about the distribution of political information in modern electorates are that the mean is low and the variance high" (see also Dalton 2000; Grönlund and Milner 2006; Fraile 2013), and the distribution of knowledge varies by age, race, and socioeconomics (Fortin-Rittberger 2016).

Among the many extensions of research on knowledge, numerous articles study the gender—for our purposes here, the "sex"—gap in political knowledge men consistently appear to hold higher levels of political knowledge than women (Baldega 2014; Dolan and Hansen 2020; Ihme and Tausendpfund 2018; Jerit and Barabas 2017; Lizotte and Sidman 2009). While a sizable portion of the difference in knowledge is attributed to propensity of men to guess rather than answer "Don't know," (Frazer and Macdonald 2003; Kenski and Jamieson 2000), a durable gap in political knowledge by sex is present, even accounting for differences in guessing, as previous research finds women to be more likely to give "Don't know" responses (Atkeson and Rapoport 2003; Frazer and Macdonald 2003; Kenski and Jamieson 2000; Lizotte and Sidman 2009; Mondak and Anderson 2003, 2004; Mondak and Canache 2004). The sex gap is troubling, due to the multifaceted relationship of knowledge to other aspects of political engagement and participation, and political knowledge has long been treated as a key factor in a citizen's ability to effectively advocate for themselves politically. Furthermore, lower levels of knowledge among women is correlated with depressed participation (Ondercin and Jones-White 2011).

In this chapter, we build upon research on the sex gap in knowledge by incorporating more refined and robust measures of gendered personality. McDermott (2016) argues that the preponderance of research in political science employs an underdeveloped conception and measurement of gender. Rather than using the simple dichotomous measure of sex, gender is better treated as multifaceted, with feminine, masculine, and androgynous components making up an individual's gendered personality (Bem 1974). This conception provides an opportunity to reexamine the sex gap in knowledge using an enriched and updated understanding of gender. Leveraging data from two original surveys with gendered personality measures drawn from Bem (1974, 1981), we explore how masculinity and femininity relate to the expression of political knowledge. With a knowledge battery adapted from prior scholarship and the American National Election Study (ANES), we find that femininity and masculinity have unique, and somewhat contradictory, effects on political knowledge. This chapter presents novel empirical research on an important question of political knowledge and gender. Does gendered personality (masculinity and femininity) help us better understand the expression of political knowledge rather than simply relying on sex?

Gendered Knowledge and Gendered Personality

The sex gap in political knowledge is the focus of numerous articles in political science (Fortin-Rittberger 2016; Ihme and Tausendpfund 2018;

Jerit and Barabas 2017; Lizotte and Sidman 2009; Miller 2019). The predominant explanations offered for the existence of this gap include life situations, resources, and socialization, as well as methodological critiques of the measurement of knowledge. The life cycle and resource explanation suggests that inequality in time spent on family may affect this observed gap in information simply due to time constraints brought on by family responsibilities and socialization (Burns and Schlozman 2001; Verba et al. 1995). However, subsequent work has found very little evidence that life circumstances are correlated with knowledge (Dow 2009; Fortin-Rittberger 2016; Verba et al. 1997). There is evidence that the knowledge gap may be mitigated when evaluating gendered knowledge items (Dolan and Hansen 2020).

All of these studies consider gender in the traditional measurement in political behavior—a dichotomous variable. In our analytical approach, we consider the dichotomous self-reported measure as sex, not gender. Scholars in psychology and gender studies have long considered different aspects and granular measures of gender. In particular, the Bem scale of gendered personality opens up the possibility of measuring the masculinity and femininity of individuals regardless of their gender identity or sex (Bem 1974). When considering types of individuals, Bem (1974) used four categorizations (masculine, feminine, androgynous, and undifferentiated) to describe groups by gendered personality. Recent research by McDermott (2016) makes a compelling case for understanding gender and gendered personality beyond the binary.[1] In a book-length treatment of masculinity and femininity in political behavior, McDermott (2016) transfers Bem's conception of gender to questions of political science. The result is a shift in how scholars conceive of gender and its applications to political behavior. By differentiating between gender and sex and utilizing rich tools of measurement developed in psychology, McDermott explores the relationship between political identity and attitudes toward sex roles and partisanship through the lens of gendered personality (2016). Following McDermott, we consider the standard two-category survey item as a measure of sex, while gender is measured by the degree of expressed femininity and masculinity.

Empirically, McDermott (2016, 70–74) applied her framework to explore the connection between gendered personality and political identity and voting. Among the notable findings, higher masculinity is associated with identification with the Republican Party and the propensity to vote for Republican candidates, while higher femininity is significantly related to identifying with the Democratic Party. Notably, biological sex does not significantly influence partisanship once gendered personality is accounted for in the models. Thus, the oft-discussed sex gap in candidate support and party identification is more thoroughly explained by the gendered personality than sex alone.

While separating sex and gendered personality allows researchers to analytically delineate between biological sex and gender effects, McDermott (2016) also explores the interaction between the two by incorporating gender conformity. Gender conforming refers to an alignment between reported sex and gendered personality or the extent to which an individual's gendered personality aligns or diverges from their biological sex (146). The more masculine the man or the more feminine the woman, this factor may affect how they interact with the world and their attitudes. McDermott finds that conformity significantly influences attitudes toward sex roles in society with gender conforming individuals most strongly holding traditional sex role beliefs (150). We believe that conformity might have far-reaching effects on political behavior as well.

This chapter's focus is to extend and transfer gendered personality to an exploration of the sex gap in political knowledge. Broadening the conceptual understanding of gender provides a richer tool kit to theorize the determinants of political knowledge and engagement. For example, one might propose that masculine personality is the key element in the attainment and expression of political knowledge rather than sex. If politics via socialization and cultural framing is considered a masculine endeavor, perhaps men and women who are more masculine will hold more political knowledge, regardless of sex. In this scenario, sex would be less important to our understanding of imbalances between men and women than the gendered personalities of the individual. Would more masculine women, for example, be more likely to hold higher political knowledge commensurate with their male counterparts?

Conversely, gender conformity may play a key role in political engagement and knowledge, with divergent effects. We might expect that gender nonconforming individuals might be less engaged with and connected to conventional political and social life and might even experience alienation. A masculine woman or feminine man might be less likely to be fully welcomed in politics and feel less connected in what scholars consider traditional pillars of political knowledge, like recalling names of figures or following the majority shifts in national legislatures (Bauer and Santina 2022; Winter 2010). According to this line of thinking, gender nonconformity may have powerful inhibiting effects on the expression of political knowledge and engagement. However, there is substantial heterogeneity of masculine and feminine traits across sexes; men and women can display varying levels of masculinity and femininity. In fact, we should expect that men will report higher femininity and women more masculinity today than the 1970s, given the shifting societal conceptions of gender and roles.

Prominent extensions of the sex gap research are also ripe for analysis through this new lens. The propensity for women to respond "Don't know" to survey knowledge items is a particularly rich vein for researchers (Dolan and Hansen 2020; Jerit and Barabas 2017; Mondak and Anderson 2003, 2004). Because women are more likely to respond "Don't know" and register fewer correct guesses than men, knowledge batteries and the reported gap is inflated between men and women. Men simply guess more and are hesitant to say that they do not know. Reconsidered through gendered personality, a likely expectation is that masculinity more than sex might underpin the refusal to acknowledge not knowing political figures and procedures.

This leads us to tantalizing questions: How does the knowledge gap play out when we measure gender beyond the limitations of a dummy variable? Is the expression of political knowledge captured better through understanding masculinity and femininity rather than simply

TABLE 10.1: Summary of included studies

Study	Sample	Personality measure	Knowledge measure	Study dates
Study 1	Amazon MTurk convenience sample; N=994	Bem {~?~EJS: AU: ("BEM" here and below?)//}Sex Role Inventory-short (10-items per)—see Bem 1981	2-item additive index: recognition of control of Houses of Congress	10/4/2016
Study 2	Amazon MTurk convenience sample; N=807	Bem Sex Role Inventory (20 items per)	10-item additive index	2/14/2022

sex? Do individuals who conform with their sex in their gendered personality behave differently in regard to political knowledge and propensity to respond "Don't know" to survey items? To answer these questions, we present analyses from two online studies to tease out the nuances of gendered personality on knowledge. A quick guide to the data sets and their relevant characteristics appears in table 10.1.

Study 1: MTurk 2016

Study 1 is an Amazon Mechanical Turk (Mturk) study of 994 respondents collected by McDermott and Jones in the fall of 2016.[2] The partisan breakdown of the sample is approximately 45 percent Democratic (including leaners), and 20 percent Republican (including leaners). The racial composition of the sample is 77 percent white, 9 percent African American, 6 percent Latino, 8 percent Asian American, and 1 percent other race, and our sample sex composition is 47 percent women and 53 percent men. The survey contained items on gender personality, knowledge of majority control of the US House and Senate, trust in government, political discussion and engagement, ideology, partisanship, education, age, race, and, of particular importance, self-reported sex.

The study 1 design uses the short BSRI, consisting of a ten-item scale to capture femininity and a ten-item scale to capture masculinity (Bem 1981); full wording for the short BSRI can be found in the online appendix. In terms of scale reliability, the brief Bem items scale together quite well, with femininity items obtaining an alpha of 0.90 and the masculinity items 0.89. These scores are comparable to other applications (Choi et al. 2009; Huddy and McDonnell in this volume). We also include common correlates of knowledge as control variables in our models. In the 2016 study, these controls include political engagement and discussion, race (nonwhite vs. white), age, and education level.

We use the brief knowledge battery—recognition of a "current events" item and knowledge of majority control of the House and Senate—to create our measure of political knowledge. We generate two additive indexes. The first item is the frequency of correct responses, coded from 0–2, where 0 indicates no correct response and 2 indicates correct knowledge of control of the House and Senate prior to the 2016 election. Our knowledge variable has a mean of 1.32. To capture the propensity to say "Don't know," we simply code a "Don't know: response as 1 for each knowledge time. This "Don't know" index is, therefore, also coded from 0–2. "Don't know" responses are relatively rare, with a mean of 0.39.

Our modeling strategy is to estimate base regression models including the Bem items for feminine and masculine personalities, sex, and our demographic and political control variables. Thus, the base model tests our initial question on the added value of gendered personality beyond sex. We then incorporate gender conformity concerns by splitting the sample by sex and running separate models for women and men. By running the model for both men and women, we can tease out further implications on whether masculinity and femininity behave differently based on sex. For simplicity and clarity, we present figures that plot the marginal effects for feminine and masculine personality traits from our three models (full sample, men only, and women only). Although we present figures in text, full statistical models for all findings are found in the appendix. Figure 10.1 presents the coefficient estimate plots for our initial regression models exploring the influence of gendered personalities on correct knowledge items in 2016.

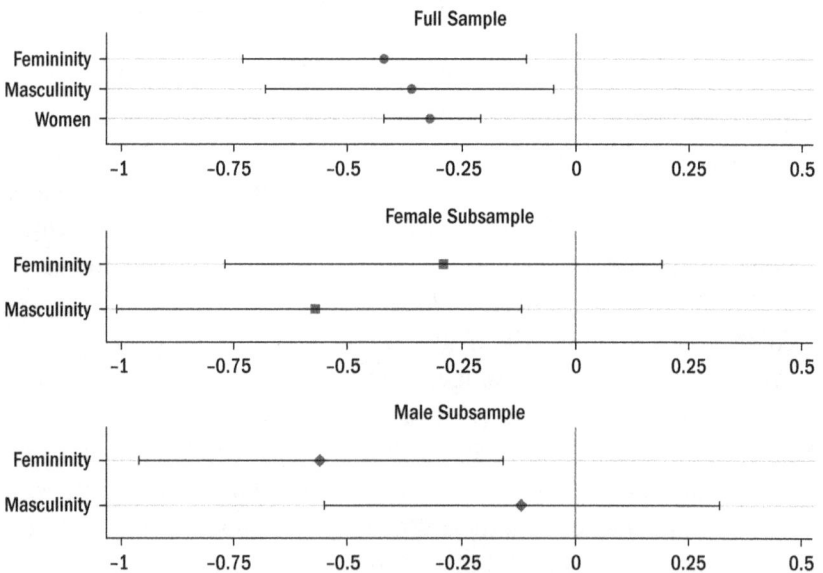

Figure 10.1: Effect of gendered personality on number of correct responses (2016)

Figure 10.1 displays the effect of femininity and masculinity on knowledge for the full sample as well as split by sex from the 2016 data. The key findings are that femininity and masculinity have a negative influence on correct answers in the full sample. However, once separated by sex, the data shows that masculinity has a negative effect for women and femininity has a negative effect for men. These are estimated from an OLS regression model and plotted with 95 percent confidence intervals.

The effects in our base model, as shown in the first panel of figure 10.1, presents us with findings consistent with our expectation that gendered personality influences political knowledge beyond sex. The Bem measure of femininity is negative and statistically significant; higher femininity corresponds to less expressed political knowledge. Further, sex is consistent with previous research, as women respondents are associated as having a lower level of political knowledge. The unexpected finding comes from the Bem masculinity measure. Rather than the expected positive effect, the effect is both negative and statistically significant, though the masculinity effect is smaller than that of femininity. Our control variables behave as we would expect, with political engagement, age, and education all statistically significant and in the positive direction. The consistent behavior of our control variables with older, more educated respondents expresses higher knowledge lends some validity to our knowledge measure.

We next consider whether gender conformity beyond gendered personality affects political knowledge. To test this conceptualization, we reestimate the base model splitting the sample by sex and creating subsamples for men and women. These results also appear in table A10.2 of the online appendix, and for simplicity are plotted in the second and third panels of figure 10.1.

The influence of gendered personality is less clear when including the notion of conformity. There is a significant and negative effect for masculinity in the female subsample, suggesting that nonconforming women express lower levels of political knowledge. However, this is also true in the opposite circumstance, as more feminine men also demonstrate significantly lower levels of political knowledge. This is a potentially important finding, because it speaks to the notion that masculinity does not have unidirectional effects on political knowledge (i.e., more masculinity for men or women should increase the expression of knowledge). By finding that higher masculinity for women and higher femininity for men hinders the expression of knowledge, it opens the theoretical door for a more nuanced understanding of how nonconformity might influence the acquisition and expression of knowledge.

Our second analysis from the 2016 study focuses on predicting the propensity to say "Don't know." These analyses follow the same modeling strategy as the knowledge models; each model includes our gendered personality measures, sex, and control variables. The difference is that our dependent variable is the likelihood of responding "Don't know" to knowledge items on the survey. As mentioned previously, research finds that women are more likely to respond "Don't know" to knowledge questions, which inflates the reported gap in knowledge. Our statistical models are reported in full in table A10.3 in the appendix, and the results for masculinity, femininity, and sex are plotted in figure 10.2.

Figure 10.2 displays the effect of femininity and masculinity on the likelihood of "Don't know" responses for the full sample as well as split by sex from the 2016 data. The key findings are that femininity increases

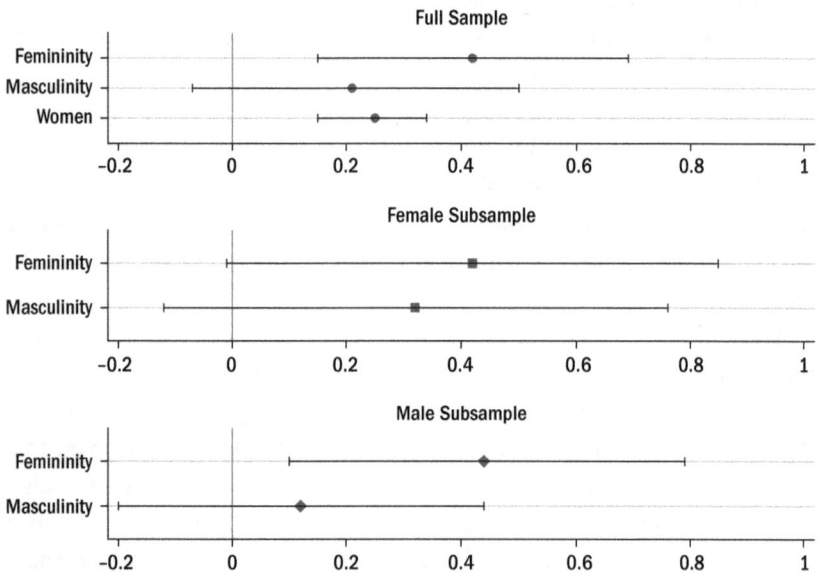

Figure 10.2: Effect of gendered personality on number of "Don't know" responses (2016)

the likelihood of responding "Don't know" to knowledge items, even controlling for sex. This effect is present for both men and women. Once again the plotted effects are estimated from an OLS regression model and shown with 95 percent confidence intervals.

Our analyses of "Don't know" responses yield several significant effects. Women are significantly more likely to respond "Don't know," which fits with the scholarship in political knowledge. However, sex does not solely affect this propensity, as femininity is positive and significant. Individuals who score higher in femininity are more likely to respond "Don't know," rather than engage in guessing, regardless of sex. This result again bolsters the contribution of this chapter and the added value of exploring gendered personality. Our control variables behave as expected, with more educated, older individuals expressing fewer "Don't know" responses.

As with our examination of correct responses to the knowledge battery items, we can explore the interplay between sex and gender personality on the proclivity to respond "Don't know." We split the sample by sex and ran separate models for those who identify as women and those who identify as men. For women respondents, as shown in panel 2, masculinity and femininity are not significant predictors of the likelihood of responding "Don't know." Though both variables are in the positive direction, neither reaches conventional levels of significance. Our model for men tells an intriguingly different story. For men, as shown in panel 3, femininity is significant and positive in the likelihood of responding "Don't know." This is particularly interesting, because it implies that a possible factor driving the femininity effect observed in our full sample comes from non–gender conforming men. Sex and gendered personality are working in conjunction to affect behavior, but, in this case, non–gender conforming men (those expressing high levels of feminine personality traits) are more likely to respond "Don't know."

Study 2: MTurk 2022

To both supplement and build upon the 2016 analysis, we conducted a second survey containing more detailed gendered personality and political knowledge measures. Study 2 consists of 807 respondents recruited from MTurk in the winter of 2022. The partisan breakdown of the sample is approximately 61 percent Democratic (including leaners), and 33 percent Republican (including leaners). The racial composition of the sample is 81 percent white, 7 percent African American, 3 percent Latino, 4 percent Asian American, 2 percent Native American, and 1 percent other race, and our sample sex composition is 56 percent men and 43 percent women. with less than 1 percent nonidentifying. While the survey contains similar items like political interest, race, partisanship, age, and sex, the 2022 MTurk study employs two key measurement changes from the 2016 data. First, it utilizes the full BSRI, consisting of twenty items to femininity and twenty items to measure masculinity. The Bem scales were randomized within dimensions and presented in random order.[3] As with the brief version, the femininity and masculinity items scale together quite well, with the femininity items obtaining an alpha of 0.91, and the masculinity items 0.93.

Additionally, the study included a more robust knowledge battery, consisting of ten items drawn from a combination of standard knowledge items used in the ANES as well as supplemental items used by Luskin and Bullock (2011). For example, who has the final responsibility to determine whether a law is constitutional or not, and which party is more conservative at the national level? We also included standard "current events" items, asking respondents who was currently serving as vice president, and what leadership position was held by Nancy Pelosi. The questions are a mixture of procedural knowledge and current political environment questions; all questions appear in the online appendix. From these items we generate two additive indexes: the first, a sum of the correct responses, running from 0–10. The average correct response score was a 6.54. The second is a sum of "Don't know" responses, also running from 0–10. As with our other sample, "Don't know" responses are much less frequent as compared to correct responses, with a mean of 0.55. In addition to these key items, our models also include measures of political engagement (measured with self-reported political interest), age, education, race, and self-reported sex.

The results for political knowledge in the 2022 study are plotted in figure 10.3, and full statistical results are in table A10.4 in the appendix. With our enhanced measures of the full BSRI and political knowledge, our base model results resemble the results from the 2016 study. Notably, femininity is negative and significant; higher femininity is associated with lower political knowledge.

Figure 10.3 displays the effect of femininity and masculinity on correct answers to knowledge survey items for the full sample as well as split by sex from the 2022 data. The key findings are that femininity is negatively related to political knowledge, and the negative effect is especially pronounced for men in our subsample model. Effects are estimated from an OLS regression model and plotted with 95 percent confidence intervals.

However, contrary to our expectations, respondents higher in masculinity do not exhibit higher political knowledge, as the coefficient is not statistically significant and is in the opposite direction (similar to the 2016 survey).[4] Our subsequent analyses displayed in the center and bottom panels of Figure 10.3 consider the effects of gender conformity on the frequency of correct responses. For our subsample of women, we see that more masculine women express significantly less political knowledge, as evidenced by fewer correct responses to the knowledge battery items on average. Women expressing more feminine personalities appear to express slightly higher correct responses on average, but the effect is not statistically significant.

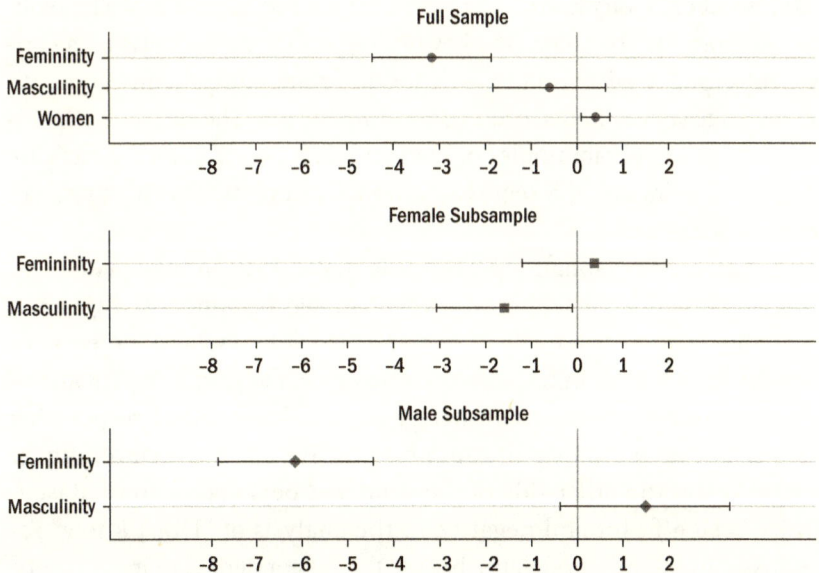

Figure 10.3: Effect of gendered personality on number of correct responses (2022)

For male respondents, the opposite story is depicted in figure 10.3. While masculine men again appear to express slightly higher political knowledge, the effect is not significant. On the other hand, men who express more feminine personality traits score lower on the knowledge scale. Femininity is significant and negative for men. Together, these results suggest that gender nonconformity is an influential predictor of political knowledge, in addition to biological sex. We will return to these key findings in comparison to the 2016 study in the discussion section.

In our final set of analyses, we replicate the models on the likelihood of responding "Don't know" to knowledge items using our 2022 data. As with our previous analysis, the models include femininity, masculinity, sex, and our control variables. The dependent variable is the number of "Don't know" responses to our ten-item knowledge battery. As noted above, the propensity for women to respond with "Don't know" compared to men is one driver of the measured sex gap in knowledge. Because men are more likely to guess, they tend to score higher on knowledge batteries on average. The results are plotted in figure 10.4, and full statistical results appear in table A10.5 of the appendix.

Figure 10.4 displays the effect of femininity and masculinity on the likelihood of "Don't know" responses for the full sample as well as split by sex from the 2022 data. The key finding is that masculinity has a consistent negative effect on the likelihood of responding "Don't know" to knowledge survey items, even controlling for sex. The negative effect is consistent across subsamples of men and women. As before, effects are estimated from an OLS regression model and plotted with 95 percent confidence intervals.

If gendered personality plays a role beyond sex in how people express political knowledge, we expect to see respondents higher in masculinity to be less likely to respond "Don't know," and, potentially, respondents higher in femininity to be more likely. In our 2016 analysis, femininity was the main driver of the likelihood of responding "Don't know," with a significant and positive effect. However, figure 10.4 displays the other side of the gendered personality coin. Masculinity is significant and negative in the analysis of "Don't know" responses. In the full model, the higher the respondent is in masculinity, the less likely they are to respond "Don't know." This effect is present

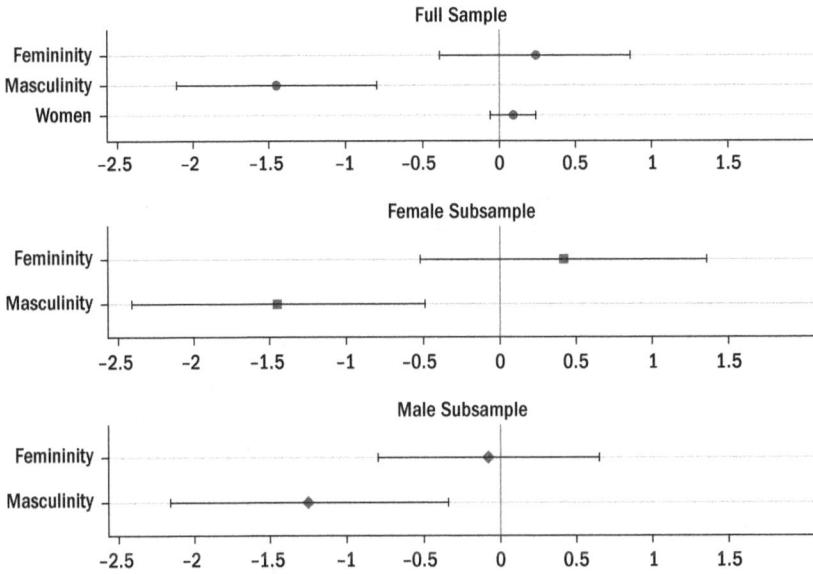

Figure 10.4: Effect of gendered personality on number of "Don't know" responses (2022)

even when controlling for sex and even when looking at subsamples of men and women. Femininity and sex are not significant in the base model. Our control variables largely perform as expected. Older respondents with more political interest and higher education levels are less likely to respond "Don't know."

When looking at the subsample models, men higher in masculinity are significantly less likely to respond "Don't know," But so, too, are the women in the sample. This finding speaks to the sizable literature in political behavior on estimating political knowledge and sex gaps. The results also yield novel evidence into how gendered personality might drive the expression of political knowledge. Despite differences in knowledge batteries and the time when the studies were conducted, it is interesting to contrast the findings in the 2016 analysis where femininity was the more significant influence on "Don't know" responses than masculinity. Theoretically, femininity and masculinity could independently affect the propensity to say, "Don't know." In the 2022 data, however, masculinity is the personality trait that has a consistent and significant effect. Overall, the "Don't know" response analysis collectively provide evidence that this propensity may have more to do with gendered personality than sex.

Discussion

What have we learned? In our analysis of gendered personality and the gap in political knowledge, we have ample evidence to speak to the questions that motivated this chapter. First, there is certainly merit in moving beyond the binary measurement of gender and avoiding the conflation with sex. Masculinity and femininity have significant, though sometimes contradictory, effects, on knowledge that are distinct from sex. When it comes to expressing political knowledge, masculinity and femininity and, to a lesser extent, gender conformity matter in our models. Even with limited measurement of knowledge in the 2016 study, we find that femininity, even controlling for sex, had a negative effect on expressed political knowledge. Masculinity was significant and negative as well, which contradicts the conjecture that masculinity is the key driver of political knowledge. We still find these effects even when controlling for traditional predictors of knowledge like education, age, political interest, and, most importantly, sex.

When extending the analysis to gender conformity, we find that femininity is particularly important for low knowledge among men. In the 2022 study, the results and frequency of knowledge are similar yet different. Women reported higher political knowledge in the sample. However, femininity remains significant and negatively associated with knowledge as with the previous study. Moreover, in the subsample models, feminine men are less likely to express political knowledge. Intriguingly, gender conforming women (i.e., women with higher femininity) have a positive effect in our female subsample model.

When exploring "Don't know" responses, we find consistently that a portion of the propensity to offer "Don't know" is driven by masculinity and femininity not sex. In study 1, higher femininity corresponds to more "Don't know" responses. On the other hand, in the 2022 study, masculinity was significant and negative; the higher the masculinity, the less likely the individual was to respond "Don't know." Whether consistent, expected, or contradictory, all of these results are novel contributions that point to further research and incorporation of refined measures of gendered personality.

While the findings are promising, our analysis is not without notable limitations that can be ameliorated in future research. For example, some of our findings may be contingent on the nature of our convenience samples or the divergence of MTurk samples from the general population. For example, in our 2022 sample, women expressed more political knowledge than men. While this is empirically traditionally rare, it is a phenomenon that will likely increase in its frequency as women become more politically activated, engaged, and even more educated than their male counterparts. The sample limitation makes us cautious in overinterpreting our novel results, but it also provides impetus for researchers to continue studying gender *beyond sex*. Going forward, our hope is that more representative, national sample surveys will include items like the BSRI to measure gendered personality and not simply sex. Then, researchers will be able to test, corroborate, and refine the findings presented in this chapter. Political behavior has a good way to go in properly articulating and measuring gender and understanding the complex ways gender interacts with political life.

NOTES

1 See Bittner and Goodyear-Grant (2017) for an excellent article-length treatment of the argument for an improved conception of gender in political behavior.

2 While there have been questions about the validity and generalizability of MTurk samples, scholarship has demonstrated that, while demographically the samples may skew younger and vary on other factors, findings from studies have closely mirrored those from previous studies (Berinsky et al. 2012; Clifford et al. 2015; Goodman et al. 2013).

3 Our survey also collected the twenty "neutral" Bem items. These items are not considered in our analyses.

4 Our control variables generally behave as expected: age, political interest, and education have a positive and statistically significant effect on correct responses to the knowledge scale. This consistency is juxtaposed by an interesting inconsistency for the effects of sex. Contrary to previous findings, the effect for the sex dummy variable is positive and statistically significant—in this sample, self-identified women give more correct answers to the knowledge battery items than men.

11

Men Care, Too

Gender, Empathy, and Political Compassion

LEONIE HUDDY AND MAGGIE K. MARTIN

Introduction

Sex is a common variable in political science research, and numerous studies have examined differences in men and women's political behavior (Huddy, Cassese, and Lizotte 2008). There is increased research interest, however, in moving away from a singular focus on men and women to understand the political implications of gender identity (Schneider and Bos 2023). McDermott (2016) is at the forefront of this shift, advocating for the use of gendered self-conceptions to explain men and women's political behavior. From this vantage point, it is far more important to know whether a woman or a man sees themselves in terms of stereotypically masculine traits, such as competence, or stereotypically feminine traits, such as compassion, than their female or male sex. Not all men endorse traditional masculine gender roles, and not all women embrace traditional feminine roles, resulting in greater diversity among men and women than is currently reflected in much political research (Cassino 2020). This diversity helps to explain why political differences between men and women are often meager in size. By focusing on gender identities, political science researchers hope to gain deeper insight into the complex ways in which sex conditions political behavior.

In this chapter, we define gender identity as the internalization of feminine and/or masculine gender-linked personality traits (Cassino 2020; Westbrook and Saperstein 2015). Feminine gender identities can be described as communal, focusing on traits and behaviors such as nurturance, emotional expressiveness, compassion, warmth, tenderness, and benevolence (Barbee et al. 1993; Diekman and Schneider 2010; Eagly and Wood 2012; Laurent and Hodges 2009). In contrast, masculine gender identity is characterized by agency, including traits such as achievement, autonomy, emotional control, assertiveness, and power (Barbee et al. 1993; Diekman and Schneider 2010; Eagly and Wood 2012; Laurent and Hodges 2009).

In this chapter, we largely focus on the feminine-linked trait of empathy to better understand the gendered nature of political compassion. We demonstrate that self-reported empathy is more powerful than sex in explaining support for compassionate public policies. We show that, despite expectations, men and women do not differ greatly in terms of empathy and are thus equally likely to embrace a key facet of a feminine identity. Moreover, there is no evidence that highly empathic men and women differ in their willingness to respond with compassion to relevant political issues. The powerful political effects of empathy underscore why it is important to focus on masculine and feminine identities and their component traits to understand political behavior. In essence, there are empathetic men and women who translate empathy into support for compassionate policies. Likewise, there are men and women who are indifferent to human suffering and feel no compunction to support policies that alleviate it.

Social role theory provides an important foundation for the study of masculine and feminine gender roles (Eagly, Wood, and Diekman 2000). Traditionally, women and men were seen as better suited to different social roles, such as working in a caring occupation or engaging in hard physical labor, based on their underlying physical and biological differences. According to social role theory, such differences interact with society's culture to generate gender-stereotyped behaviors in which women are associated with caring activities and men associated with greater agency (Eagly and Wood 2012; Barbee et al. 1993; Vonk, Mayhew and Zeigler-Hill 20162016). In addition to gender-stereotyped traits, gender-stereotyped behaviors are an important part of the gender role self-concept for both men and women (Athenstaedt 2003). Within this framework, empathy is clearly associated with the communal feminine stereotype and is absent from the agentic masculine stereotype. However, members of both genders can exhibit empathy, and empathy is linked, in turn, to compassionate policy support. Viewing gender roles in terms of stereotypical masculine and feminine traits helps researchers to move away from a focus on sex and toward a deeper and more complex understanding of gendered politics.

Gender Gap or Gender-Identity Gap?

This shift in focus away from the political effects of sex toward gender identity has important implications for the study of the gender gap. There are persistent but small gender gaps in Democratic partisanship, support for social welfare policies, and other issues that have attracted considerable research interest (Huddy, Cassese, and Lizotte 2008). In the United States, women are somewhat more likely than men to identify with the Democratic Party, to support spending on social welfare policies including education and assistance to the elderly, to favor greater racial equality, and to back overseas humanitarian interventions (Eagly et al. 2004; Lizotte 2017; Schlesinger and Heldman 2001; Shapiro and Mahajan 1986; Howell and Day 2000). The political gender gap has led various researchers to suggest that women's greater empathy and compassion, and, by implication, men's lack of these qualities, is one possible explanation for such gender gaps (Costa, Terracciano, and McCrae 2001; Huddy, Cassese, and Lizotte 2008). From this vantage point, women's greater and men's diminished capacity for empathy translates into a gender gap in support for compassionate government policy both domestically and internationally.

But the gender gap is dwarfed in size by political differences linked to gender identity (McDermott 2016; Winter 2010). For example, describing oneself in terms of masculine traits such as logic and rationality is associated with support for the Republican Party and conservative ideology, whereas feminine traits such as caring and compassion are associated with the Democratic Party and liberal ideology (Hayes 2005; Roberts and Utych 2020; Winter 2010). McDermott (2016) finds that women and men who score highly on a feminine identity scale are far more likely to support the Democratic Party than those low in femininity. She also finds that women and men who score highly on masculine identity are far more engaged in politics than those who are low in masculinity. In other words, the gender gap on many facets of political behavior is far smaller in size than the gender-identity gap.

We extend the focus on the gender-identity gap to concentrate on the empathy gap and its implications for support of compassionate policies. We examine the difference in political attitudes between those who do and do not embrace aspects of a caring, feminine self-conception rather than a simple gap between men and women. The existence of an empathy gap among both men and women is of considerable political importance because factors such as climate change and pandemics ravage vulnerable populations. In such contexts, the ability and willingness to empathize with others plays an important role in driving support for compassionate public policies and governmental actions (Feldman and Steenbergen 2001; Newman et al. 2015).

It is important to point out that there is only a modest link between sex and gender identity. McDermott (2016) included the short-form of the Bem Sex Role Inventory, or BSRI (Bem 1974), in a national survey and found that women scored more highly than men on feminine traits (e.g., sympathetic, compassionate) and lower on masculine traits (e.g., aggressive, independent). Somewhat surprisingly, men scored more highly on feminine than masculine traits overall, suggesting that many men endorse aspects of a feminine identity. Moreover, both men and women scored well above the midpoint on both scales in McDermott's research. In a similar vein, women score slightly higher than men on self-report empathy scales (as they do on feminine identity), but women and men's scores also overlap extensively. In addition, sex differences are smaller and at times nonexistent in studies that examine helping behavior or physiological reactions that potentially indicate an empathic response. For example, women report higher levels of empathy and concern for others than do men on scales such as the Davis empathic concern subscale, but do not exhibit more supportive, nonverbal responses to those in distress in observational studies and are typically less likely to help those in distress in real-world helping situations (Beutel and Marini 1995; Blinder and Rolfe 2018; Eisenberg and Lennon 1983; Eagly and Crowley 1986).

This chapter unfolds in the following way. First, we review the existence and magnitude of sex differences in empathy, examining men and women's scores on various self-reported empathy scales and a behavioral measure of empathic ability, the Mind-in-the-Eyes (MIE) test. We document slightly larger sex differences in self-reported empathy than empathic ability. Second, we examine the degree to which self-reported empathy shapes men and women's support for a specific individual in need of assistance: a child refugee at the US border and a man who lost his job following the 2008 recession. We also draw on MIE scores to examine the degree to which men and women are unwilling to empathize (downregulate) with an individual when it conflicts with a relevant political belief. Third, we examine the degree to which masculine and feminine roles (the measure of the latter is akin to self-reported empathy) influence men and women's support for a compassionate political candidate.

Sex Differences in Empathy

We begin with an overview of sex differences in various measures of empathy, defining empathy as something that "allows one to quickly and automatically relate to the emotional states of others" (de Waal 2008, 282). There is widespread research consensus that empathy involves a complex mix of affect and cognition (Blair 2005; de Waal 2008; Decety 2011; Hodges and Wegner 1997; Singer and Lamm 2009; Zaki and Ochsner 2013). Empathy scales include a cognitive facet called "perspective taking" and an affective component referred to as "empathic concern" (Davis 1980; Baron-Cohen and Wheelwright 2004). Both cognitive and affective components of empathy predict who is most likely to share another's emotional state, help a person in need, and support humanitarian values (Batson et al. 2002; Barr and Higgins-D'Alessandro 2007; Feldman and Steenbergen 2001; Laurent and Hodges 2009).[1] We examine measures of empathy grounded in self-report survey data and behavioral indicators of empathic ability to attain a robust assessment of the magnitude of sex differences in empathy.

Self-Reported Empathy

In general, women score modestly higher than men on self-report empathy measures (Eisenberg and Lennon 1983; Karniol et al. 1998; Michalska, Kinzler, and Decety 2013; Christov-Moore et al. 2014; Pelligra 2011; Rueckert, Branch, and Doan 2011; Blinder and Rolfe 2018).

Differences are small in size, however, and reflect substantial similarity in the range of empathy among men and women. There are several key measures of self-reported empathy.

Davis Interpersonal Reactivity Index

The Davis (1980) Interpersonal Reactivity Index (IRI), one of the most popular measures of empathy, is divided into cognitive perspective taking, empathic concern, and affective personal distress subscales. The empathic concern subscale has been linked to compassionate assistance and helping behaviors (Smith 2006; Bar and Higgings-D'Alessandro 2007), physiological responses to another's distress (Rodrigues et al. 2009), and prosocial behavior in economic games (Kamas and Preston 2019). It contains twenty-eight items and includes questions such as whether respondents have "tender, concerned feelings for people less fortunate," or describe themselves as "pretty soft-hearted." Women typically score somewhat more highly than men on the scale, especially on the empathic concern subscale (Blinder and Rolfe 2018; Eagly and Crowley 1986; Laurent and Hodges 2009; Rueckert, Branch, and Doan 2011).

Empathy Quotient

The Empathy Quotient (EQ) Scale (Baron-Cohen and Wheelwright 2004) is a more recently developed empathy measure designed for clinical applications that was originally validated on a sample of individuals with Asperger's Syndrome. The scale contains sixty items divided into three types of statements concerning cognitive empathy, emotional reactivity, and social skills. Sample items ask respondents whether they "are good at predicting how someone will feel," "find it difficult to judge if something is rude or polite," or if others often find them "insensitive" and they "don't always see why." Women typically score higher than men on this scale, especially on the cognitive empathy and emotional reactivity measures (Baron-Cohen and Wheelwright 2004; Lawrence et al. 2004; Pelligra 2011). In a study of mental health professionals, Lawrence and colleagues (2004) observed a score of .52 for women and .59 for men when the scale was standardized to range from 0 to 1.

Empathic Ability

Self-reported empathy measures are close to items used to measure feminine gender identity; respondents are typically asked to report how caring or concerned they are about others. There is some criticism, however, that such measures exaggerate sex differences in self-reported empathy because some of the words used to assess empathy have feminine connotations, resulting in their weaker endorsement by men than women. There are other ways to measure empathy that evade potential social desirability pressures inherent in asking individuals about their ability and willingness to feel the pain of others (Laurent and Hodges 2009).

Reading Mind in the Eyes (MIE)

The MIE scale was developed by Baron-Cohen and colleagues (2001) to assess empathic accuracy or ability and successfully differentiates those with and without Autism spectrum disorders (ASD). The test measures an individual's ability to correctly understand the emotion felt by another person by looking at an image of their facial expression and choosing the expressed emotion (Feldman et al. 2020). While the test does not indicate an empathic desire to help, to feel what another is feeling, or to take someone else's perspective, it does identify differences in basic empathic ability. As other researchers have noted, it is very difficult to react with empathy to someone if you cannot decipher what they are feeling (de Waal 2008).

The MIE scale is less subject to social desirability than self-report measures of empathy and provides a way to examine sex differences in the capacity for empathy and the willingness to translate empathy into compassion (Lawrence et al. 2004). In general, facial emotion recognition tests elicit smaller differences between women and men than self-reported empathy scales (Baron-Cohen and Wheelwright 2004; Eisenberg and Lennon 1983; Vellante et al. 2013). Women score slightly higher than men on MIE (Baron-Cohen et al. 2001; Declerck and Bogaert 2008; Engel et al. 2014; Hallerback et al. 2009; Khorashad et al. 2015; Kirkland et al. 2013). These differences do not always exist, however, suggesting that, at best, men and women are very similar in their empathic ability (Ainley, Maister, and Tsakiris 2015; Guariglia et al. 2015; Olderbak et al. 2015).

The MIE test of empathic ability provides a way to assess empathy regulation. Acting on empathy can be costly, and it is often downregulated (Preston and de Waal 2002; Zaki 2014). In a political context, this occurs when empathic ability conflicts with other political beliefs, such as individualism (Feldman et al. 2020; Petersen et al. 2012). The pervasive regulation of empathy allows us to examine whether women are less likely than men to downregulate empathy. In other words, are men who score highly on the MIE test more likely than highly scoring women to show decreased compassion and support for someone in need? We think of empathy down regulation as linked to a chronic tendency to avoid compassion (and thus a rejection of one aspect of a feminine gender role) and its up regulation as the chronic tendency to enact compassion. In that sense, empathy regulation provides another test of the competing importance of sex and gender identity in driving political compassion.

Measures of Self-Reported Empathy and Empathic Ability

We present data on the political effects of empathy drawn from several studies. We begin with an assessment of sex differences in several measures of empathy (Feldman et al. 2020; Huddy et al. 2022). The studies are described in table 1 and labeled according to data source, date of data collection, and topic. Two studies include eight items from the Empathy Quotient (EQ; Baron-Cohen and Wheelwright 2004), and one of those studies also includes eight items from the Toronto Empathy Questionnaire (TEQ; Spreng et al. 2009). Sample items taken from the EQ scale include "I am good at predicting how someone will feel" and "Other people often say that I am insensitive, though I don't always see why." Sample items from the TEQ include "I find that I am 'in tune' with other people's moods" and "I remain unaffected when someone close to me is happy." All studies include eighteen items drawn from the MIE empathic ability scale described in Feldman et al (2020). The 2021 MTurk Compassionate Candidate study also includes twelve gender-identity items from the BSRI.[2]

TABLE 11.1: Empathy studies

Study name	Topic	Sample	N	# Waves	Measures
Mturk 2014	Social welfare	non-Hispanic, non-Asian whites	400	1	MIE
YouGov 2014	Social welfare	non-Hispanic, non-Asian whites	400	1	MIE, EQ
YouGov 2014/15	Immigration	non-Hispanic whites	1,000 (W) 400 (B)	2	MIE, EQ, TEQ
Bovitz 2021	Immigration	non-Hispanic whites	1,477 (W1) 1,218 (W2)	2	MIE
MTurk 2021	Compassionate political candidate	—	382	1	MIE, BSRI

MIE = Mind-in-the-Eyes test
EQ = empathy quotient
TEQ = Toronto Empathy Questionnaire*; W1 = wave 1; W2 = wave 2; W = white; B = black
*Note. The Toronto Empathy Quotient (Spreng, McKinnon, Mar and Levine 2009) is a lesser-known scale developed as a parsimonious compilation of multiple self-report empathy scales. This scale consists of sixteen items such as "I remain unaffected when someone close to me is happy" and "I can tell when others are sad even when they do not say anything." There are modest gender differences on the TEQ scale with women, on average, scoring more highly than men (Spreng et al. 2009).

All scales were standardized to range from 0–1 to facilitate the comparison of sex differences across measures; mean differences between men and women are reported in table 2. As seen in that table, the average empathy score for all measures is well above the midpoint, indicating that respondents score reasonably highly on an empathic ability test (MIE) and self-reported empathy. Women score significantly higher than men on almost all measures (based on a series of t-tests), although the gender gap in empathic ability is smaller than for self-reported empathy. There are also modest sex differences in feminine and masculine identities, with women scoring more highly than men on feminine traits but scoring equally on masculine traits.

In tandem with modest sex differences in empathy, there is considerable variation in empathy among men and women. Data from the YouGov 2014/15 immigration study demonstrate considerable overlap between men and women in their empathic ability and self-reported empathy. Figure 1 plots the kernel density of MIE, EQ, and TEQ by gender. As seen in figure 1, there are modest differences between men and women on the EQ and TEQ self-report scales and far greater overlap between the sexes, especially on the EQ scale. The difference in MIE by sex is even smaller, reflecting even greater overlap in empathic ability between men and women. The two self-report measures are more highly correlated with each other (r = .61, p < .01) than with MIE (MIE and EQ, r = .16, p < .01 and MIE and TEQ = .12, p < .01). This suggests a difference between self-reported empathy and the inherent ability to read emotion in the face of others; some who are capable of empathy do not translate that into compassion. Nonetheless, there is vast overlap and modest differences between men and women on these measures, reinforcing our interest in the political effects of the gender-linked trait of empathy.

There is considerable overlap between men and women in the distribution of the feminine and masculine scales in the BSRI (fig. 2). As seen in figure 2, women are more likely than men to score highly on the feminine scale, but the distribution of masculine traits is far more similar among women and men (see also Twenge 1997). Feminine traits are more strongly endorsed than masculine traits among both men and women in the 2021 MTurk Study, as seen in table 2. In other words, there are many men who are high in feminine traits and many women who are high in masculine traits, just as there are men low in masculine traits

TABLE 11.2: Gender differences in empathy and gender identity

	Men	Women	Sig	N
Empathy quotient				
YouGov 2014, social welfare	0.64	0.70	p < .01	399
YouGov 2014/15, immigration	0.63	0.67	p < .01	1,399
Toronto Empathy Questionnaire				
YouGov 2014/15, immigration	0.66	0.73	p < .01	1,400
Mind-in-the-Eyes				
YouGov 2014, social welfare	0.71	0.74	p < .05	387
MTurk 2014, social welfare	0.72	0.76	p < .01	414
YouGov 2014/15, Immigration	0.69	0.70	p < .05	1,400
Bovitz 2021, Immigration	0.64	0.68	p < .01	1,477
MTurk 2021, empathic candidate	0.69	0.69	n.s.	379
BSRI (MTurk 2021)				
Feminine traits	0.62	0.80	p < .01	379
Masculine traits	0.56	0.52	n.s.	379

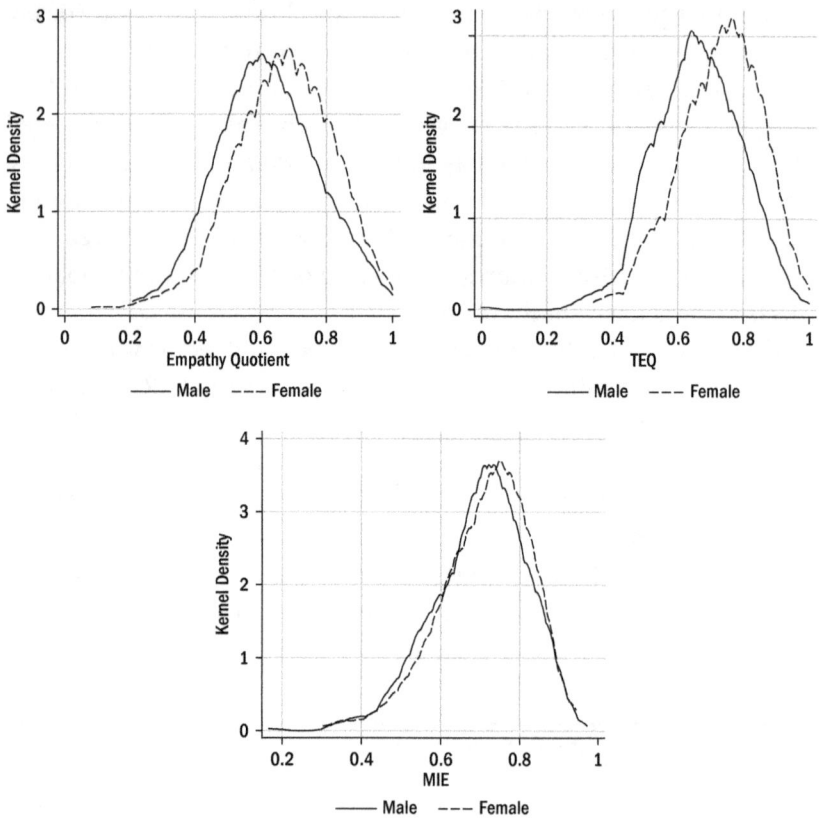

Figure 11.1: Kernel density plot for empathy scales by gender. Source: YouGov 2014/15 Immigration Study.

and women who are low in feminine traits. These distributions reflect greater in-sex than between-sex variation in gender-linked traits.

The Political Consequences of Empathy

We turn to the political consequences of sex- and gender-linked traits such as empathy to better understand the gendered nature of policy attitudes. Past research has documented a modest gender gap in support of social welfare policies, with women expressing greater support than men for government assistance (Huddy, Cassese, and Lizotte 2008). There is also evidence that empathy and compassion drive support for welfare policies. Feldman and Steenbergen (2001) find greater support for social welfare

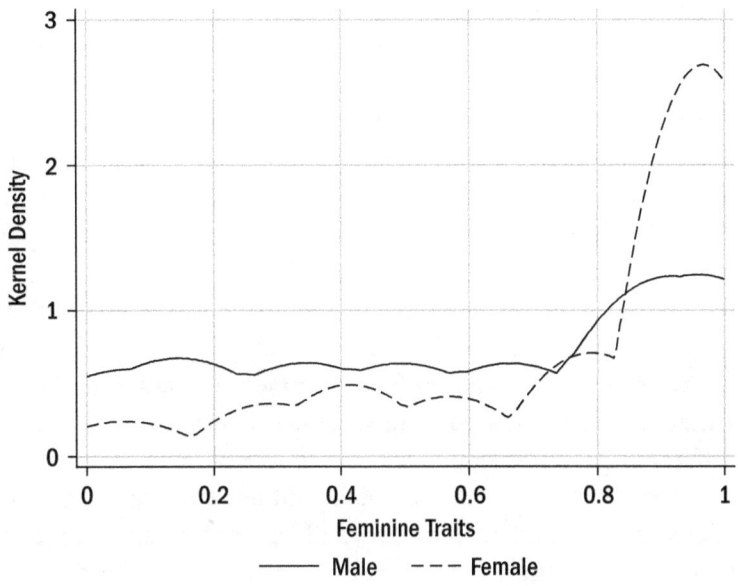

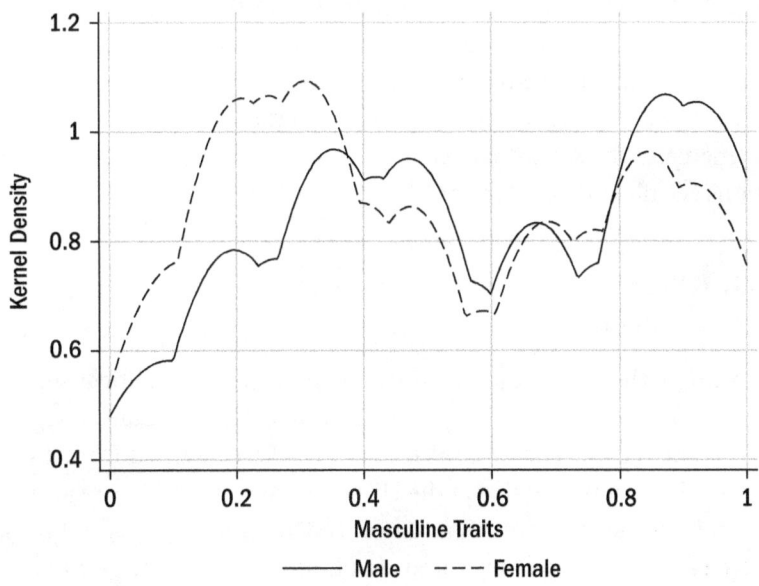

Figure 11.2: Kernel density plot for MIE and EQ by gender. Source: MTurk 2021, Empathic Candidate Study

spending, assistance to the poor, Medicare expansion, and direct assistance to the elderly among Americans who scored highly on a humanitarianism scale. Moreover, a measure of empathy predicted the humanitarian scale in this research. In another study, empathy boosted opposition to restrictions on immigration when such restrictions were presented as at odds with humanitarian values (Newman et al. 2015). Others have also uncovered evidence that humanitarianism and the principle of care boost support for government welfare policies (Willhelm and Bekkers 2010).

This brings us back to our original focus on gendered political behavior: Is it driven by sex or gender identity? More specifically, does empathy better explain support for government assistance than sex? Past research has yielded mixed results. Blinder and Rolfe (2018) analyzed the effects of the Davis empathic concern subscale and sex on partisanship in the United States, but empathy did not erase the effects of sex. Similarly, empathy did not remove sex differences in partisanship, ideology, or vote choice in research by McCue and Gopoian (2000). In contrast, Bäckström and Björklund (2007) found that empathy mediated the gender gap in generalized prejudice in Sweden. Kamas and Preston (2019) found that empathy explained the gender gap in support of social welfare policy and government spending in the United States. Empathy also mediates the sex difference in preference for victim support policy actions (Gault and Sabini 2000).

Study 1: Empathy and Support for a Teenaged Central American Refugee

To examine the effects of empathy on compassionate political support, we turn to the YouGov Immigration data. The study included a vignette concerning a teenaged Central American refugee named Daniel Ortiz who had been apprehended at the US southern border. After reading the vignette, respondents were asked how much sympathy they felt for the refugee and how much they cared about him, items that were combined to create a measure of "compassion towards Daniel" ($r = .79$). Respondents were asked how strongly they supported granting Daniel asylum, providing government assistance, and sending him back to El Salvador (reversed) to create a reliable scale of "willingness to assist Daniel" (mean inter-item $r = .85$). Four items also tapped respondents support

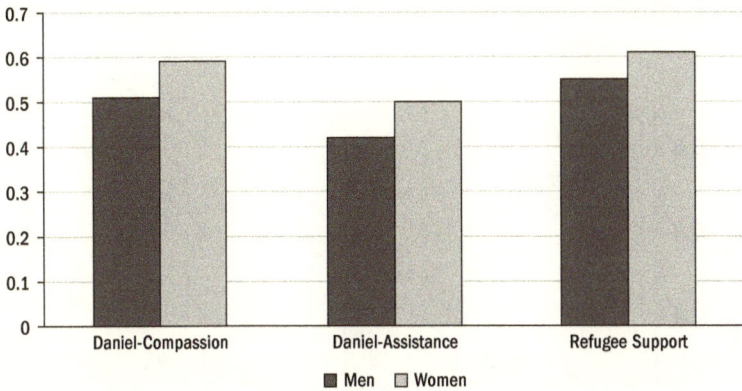

Figure 11.3: Gender differences in support for Central American child refugee

for Central American child refugees which were combined to form a reliable scale of pro-child "refugee support" (mean inter-item r = .76).

There are significant sex differences in compassion and support for Daniel and Central American child refugees, as seen in figure 3. Women are more compassionate, more supportive of Daniel's entry, and more supportive of Central American refugees than men. These effects of sex on compassion and assistance to Daniel persist in multivariate analyses that include empathy (the TEQ scale), negative Latino stereotypes, partisanship, and ideology. But the effects of sex are reduced in size with the inclusion of the empathy scale. More importantly, the effects of empathy are significant and far larger in size than the effects of sex. Empathetic respondents are more compassionate and supportive of Daniel and of child refugees more generally. Not surprisingly, negative Latino stereotypes and conservative ideology also have sizable and negative effects on all three dependent variables (table A2). Moreover, empathy had similar effects on refugee support among men and women.

The small effect of sex and the far more pronounced effects of empathy on support for Daniel can be seen in figure 4 (based on analyses in table A2). In this figure, women express slightly more compassion for Daniel than men (panel A) but are only barely more inclined to express support for his entry to the United States (panel B). In contrast, individual differences in self-reported empathy have far greater effects on refugee support among both men and women. Individuals at the low

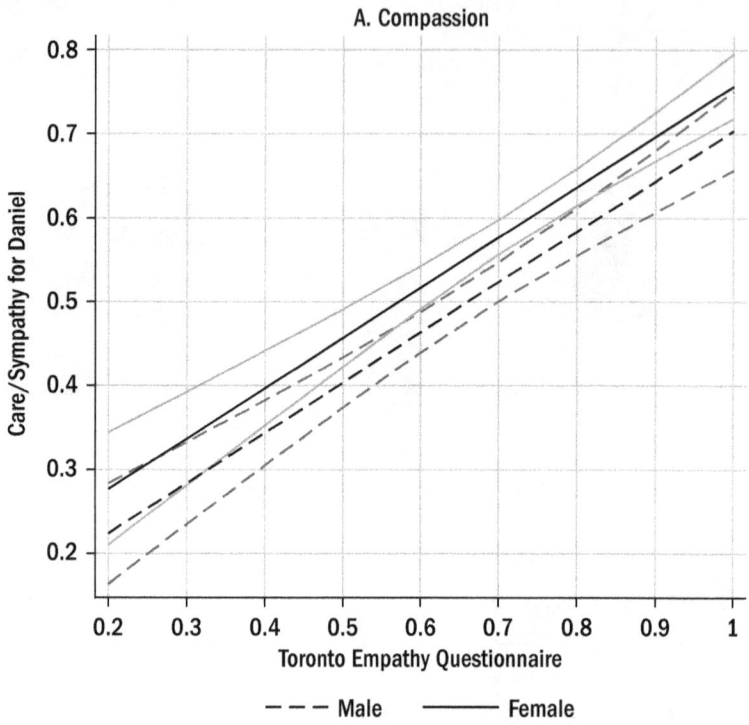

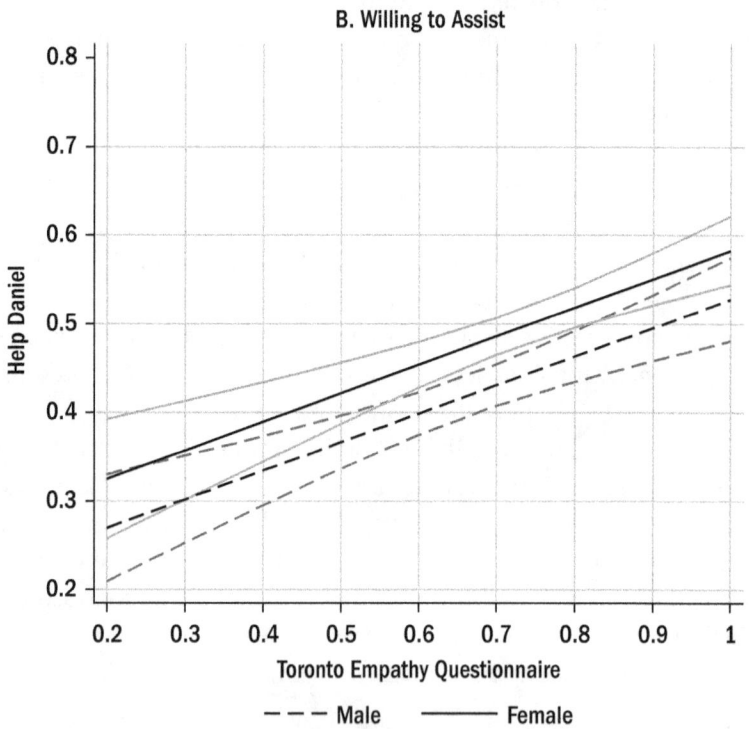

Figure 11.4: Sympathy and assistance for child refugee by empathy

end of the empathy scale express little compassion or willingness to assist Daniel, whereas those at the high end of the scale are far more compassionate and supportive.

Self-reported empathy is essentially a chronic up regulation of empathy into compassion. As noted earlier, we can capture the process of empathy regulation by observing the reactions of those high in empathic ability to a situation in which they have reason to suppress compassion. To assess the political effects of empathy and empathy regulation among men and women, we examine whether men high in MIE are more likely than comparable women to downregulate empathy for Daniel when empathy clashes with negative Latino stereotypes. We regress compassion and support for government assistance on empathic ability, negative Latino stereotypes, and their interaction, along with partisanship and ideology. The findings of this analysis (table A3) are depicted in figure 5, separately for men and women.

As expected, there is a pronounced and significant negative backlash toward Daniel among those highest in MIE, who also hold the most negative Latino stereotypes. The down regulation of empathy is equally common among men and women. If anything, the graphs in figure 5 suggest that women are more likely than men to downregulate empathy. Those who reject negative Latino stereotypes and are high in empathic ability are most compassionate toward Daniel, demonstrating the up regulation of empathy. The important point is that there is little sex-based difference in the tendency to downregulate empathy for a Central American teenager. In sum, information about someone's empathic ability provides greater insight than their sex into compassionate support for a teen refugee. If the up regulation of empathy is a feminine trait it is equally common among men and women.

Study 2: Empathy and Government Support for an Unemployed Male

We conducted a second study involving support for a male who had lost his job in the 2008 recession. This vignette, which was embedded in the 2014 YouGov Immigration study, included a photo of a dejected-looking man in his late thirties named Mark Sperling, his wife, and two sons. Sperling was described in deserving terms as a civil engineer who

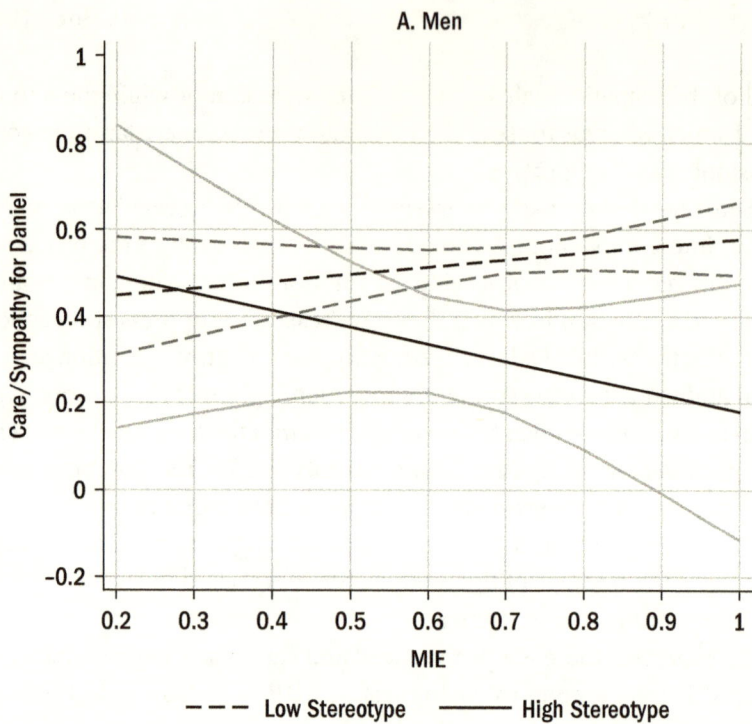

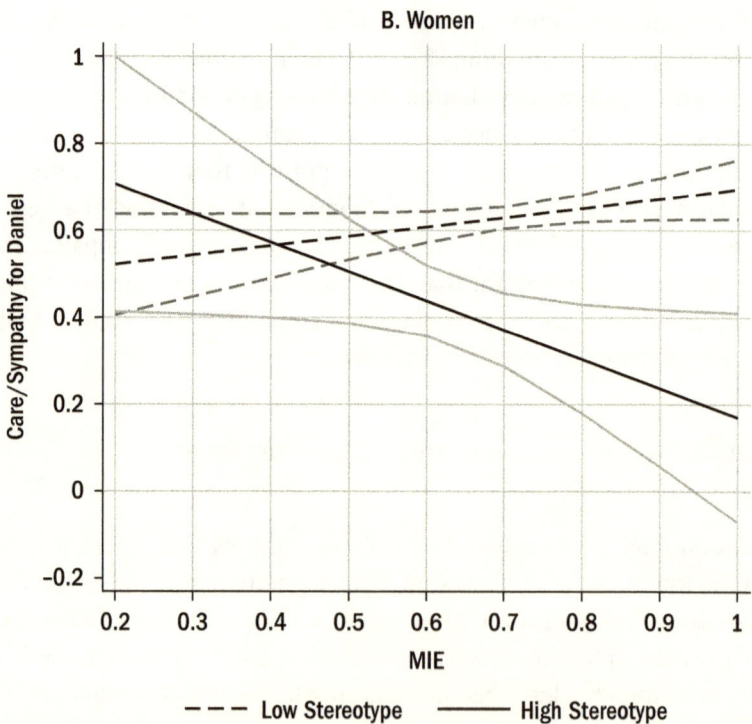

Figure 11.5: Compassionate support for the Central American Teen refugee: empathic ability clashes with negative stereotypes

had lost his job in 2011, taken occasional part-time work, actively looked for work, and updated his skills. Respondents were asked how much they cared about Sperling, whether they supported his receipt of unemployment benefits, and how much he deserved government assistance. The last two items were combined to form a single scale. There was no simple sex difference in concern about Sperling, but men were significantly less supportive than women of giving him government assistance (0.65 vs. 0.70).

When analyzed in multivariate models that included controls for political attitudes (i.e., partisanship, ideology, individualism), there was no sex difference in caring about Sperling or support for his receipt of government assistance. In this instance, empathy had mixed and weak effects. It significantly increased levels of caring about Sperling but only modestly (and non-significantly) increased support for government assistance (table A4). The findings provide a clear reminder that not all policy attitudes are driven by gendered traits. In the context of unemployment and the 2008 recession, reactions are highly political in nature. The major drivers of caring and support for assistance to Sperling are Democratic partisanship and a disavowal of individualism. The absence of sex differences and the meager effects of empathy on support for government assistance to Sperling can be seen in the right-hand panel of figure 6.

The YouGov Social Welfare survey also included a question about whether the government should pay for the cost of prescription drugs for all low-income seniors. Women were more supportive than men of government provided prescription drugs for low-income seniors (0.80 vs. 0.71). In additional analyses, women and those high in empathy expressed strongest support for the program, as seen in table A5, and the effects of empathy were substantially larger in driving support for the program than the effects of sex. The coefficient for empathy was roughly three times larger than that for sex in the regression equation. Moreover, there was no interaction between sex and empathy (based on analyses in table A5), indicating that men and women who scored more highly on empathy were far more supportive of the program than those low in empathy.

There was also evidence that men and women engaged equally in empathy regulation when it came to support for the prescription drug

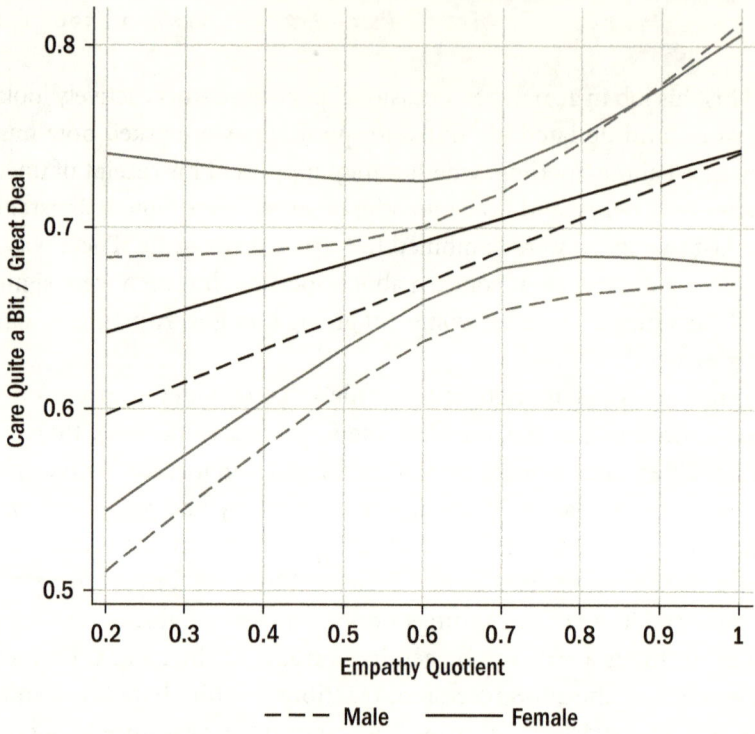

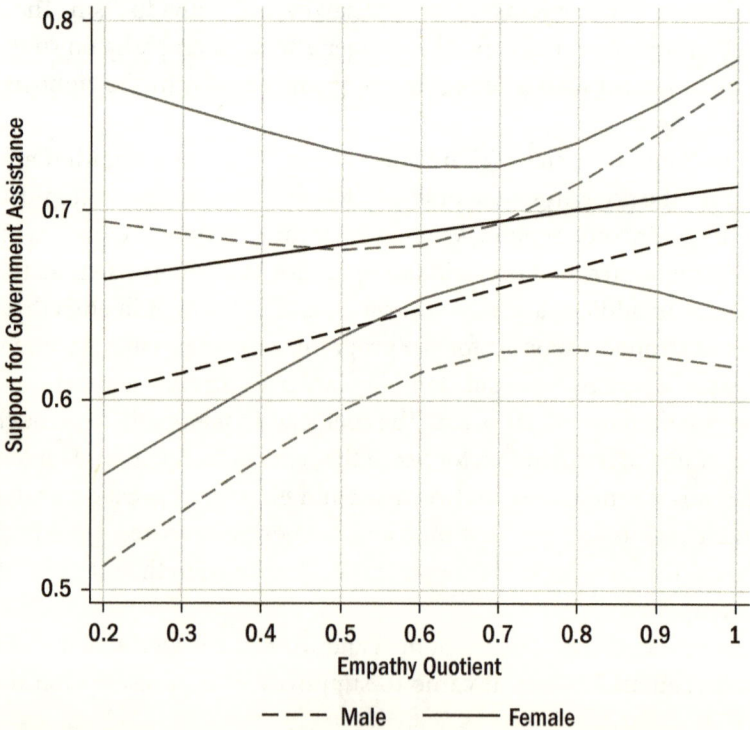

Figure 11.6: Effect of empathy on compassion and assistance to unemployed male by gender

program. Men and women who were high in empathic ability and scored highly on individualism downregulated empathy to the same degree, resulting in their marked opposition to government-funded drugs for seniors. Support for prescription drugs declines dramatically across the range of empathic ability for men and women high in empathic ability. Moreover, there is little sex difference in the tendency to downregulate empathy for those high in individualism. This suggests more uniformity than difference in the way women and men respond to those in need when it conflicts with their existing beliefs.

Study 3: Gender Roles and Compassionate Candidates

Finally, we examine the effects of sex and gender identity on support of compassionate political candidates. In this analysis, we focus squarely on feminine traits that are closely tied to measures of self-reported empathy. It is not surprising that individuals who score highly on feminine traits also report higher levels of empathy, given the considerable overlap in items used to assess the two concepts (Karniol et al. 1998).

Respondents in a 2021 MTurk Study read about two candidates running in a nonpartisan mayoral election in the US Southwest. One male candidate was described in masculine terms as "rational" and "logical," whereas the other male candidate was described in feminine terms as "compassionate" and "thoughtful." After reading the profile of both candidates, respondents indicated their vote choice and rated each candidate's competence (how well they would perform in office and handle different types of issues; $\alpha = .85$).

Women were slightly more likely to vote for the compassionate candidate (52 percent of women vs. 43 percent of men; see fig. 7) and significantly more likely to rate the compassionate candidate as competent (fig. 8). Both men and women rated the instrumental candidate as more competent than the compassionate candidate, but women rated the compassionate candidate as significantly more competent than did men (0.74 vs. 0.69).

These sex differences disappear, however, once we account for gender identity. When masculine and feminine traits are included in multivariate analyses, the gender gap in rated candidate competence is no longer significant. Feminine traits significantly boosted the compassionate candidate's rated competence, but sex did not (fig. 9). Feminine traits

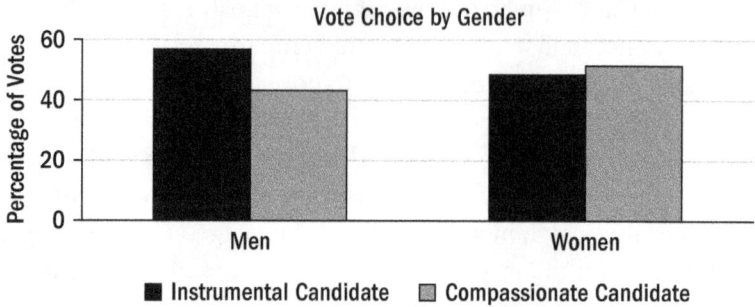

Figure 11.7: Gender differences in candidate support

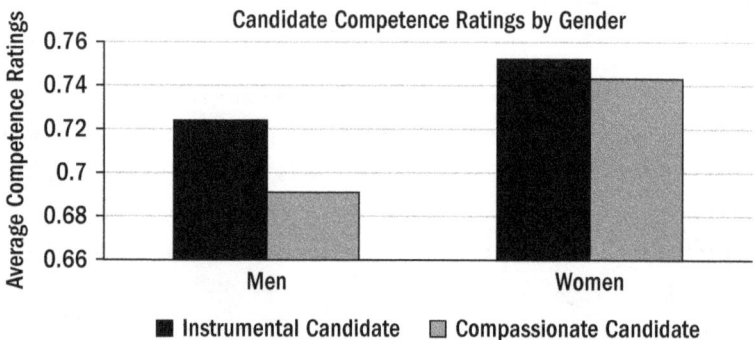

Figure 11.8: Gender differences in rated candidate competence

also slightly increased voting for the candidate, although this was not statistically significant (table A6). Moreover, there is no interaction effect between sex and either masculine or feminine traits. In other words, individuals scoring highly on feminine traits perceive the compassionate candidate as more competent. Feminine gender traits did not translate into greater electoral support for the compassionate candidate, however. Overall, it was difficult to predict respondents' vote choice in this nonpartisan election. Vote choice was not affected by sex, gender traits, partisanship, or ideology.

Conclusion

Overall, we uncovered small sex differences in compassionate political responses and larger differences grounded in gender identity and

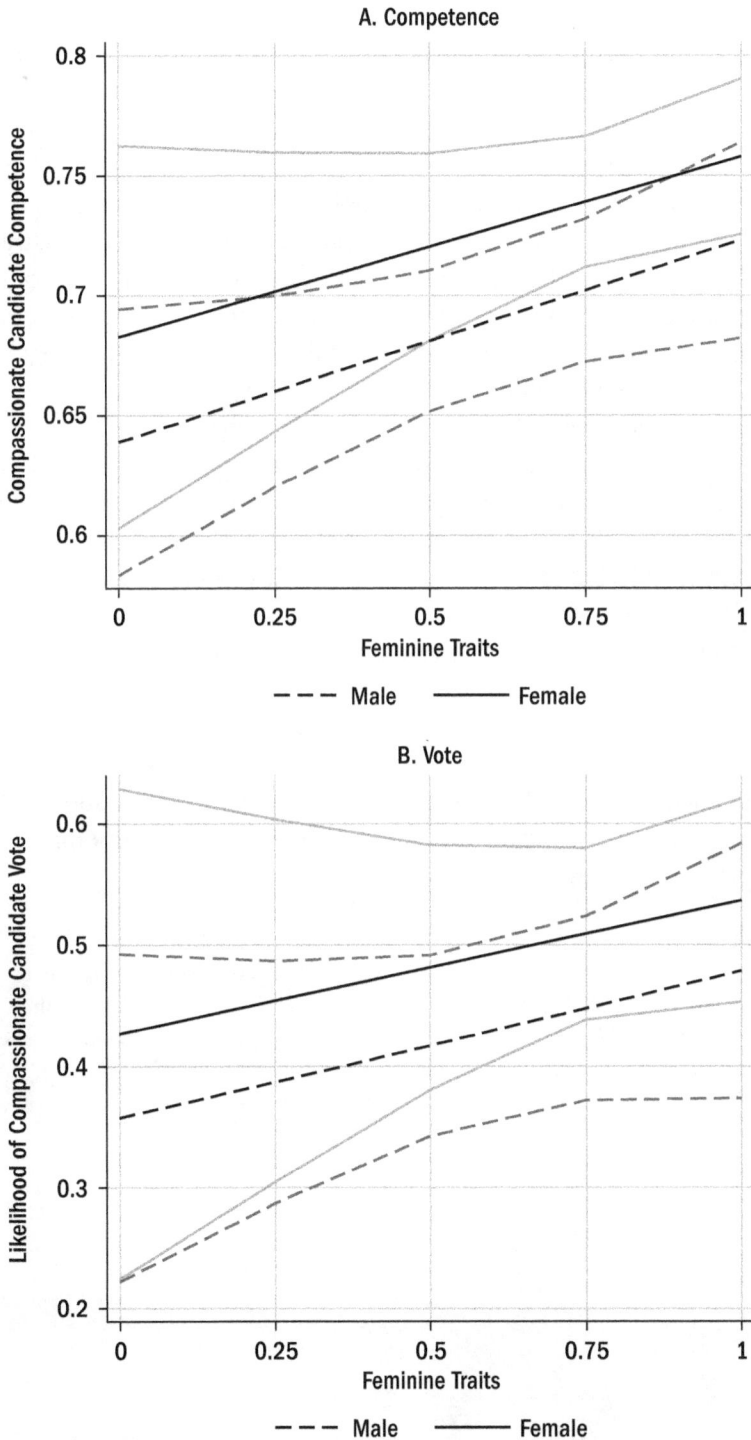

Figure 11.9: Feminine traits and support for compassionate candidate by gender

feminine personality traits such as sympathy, warmth, and compassion. As we note, feminine traits and empathy are linked, and both go further than sex to explain political compassion. Despite common assumptions about a male rejection of feminine traits, men are entirely capable of empathy and readily translate it into political compassion. In these data, there is far greater overlap between men and women in feminine traits and empathy than there are differences. Men and women tend to rely to the same degree on empathy to shape their support for compassionate government policies, and women and men similarly downregulate empathy when it conflicts with important beliefs.

Empathy and feminine traits do not always drive support for those in need or increase electoral support for a compassionate political candidate. Empathy played a far greater role in shaping support for a child refugee and prescription drugs for seniors than an unemployed male. Feminine traits led to more positive estimates of a compassionate male candidate's competence, although that did not translate into an electoral preference. These findings help to place boundaries around the political circumstances in which sex and gender identity shape political reactions. As noted earlier, empathy is a highly controlled commodity that is readily downregulated, especially when it conflicts with partisan or ideological concerns. Nonetheless, when empathy leads to support for a compassionate policy or candidate, it does so equally among highly empathetic men and women.

NOTES

1 Feeling personally upset or distressed about the plight of another is also often included in measures of empathy but can be regarded as more self- than other-regarding and is less likely than empathic concern or perspective taking to generate compassionate assistance.

2 Item wording for all self-report scales can be found in table A1.

12

Masculinity and Public Opinion

Are Canadians and Americans Different?

AMANDA BITTNER AND ELIZABETH GOODYEAR-GRANT

Introduction

Masculinity seems to have increasingly infused politics and political orientations in recent decades (Cassino and Besen-Cassino 2021; Pascoe 2017; McDermott 2016). It has even been "weaponized" by opportunistic politicians such as Donald Trump, who invoked manliness to defend his lax approach to and securitization of the COVID-19 pandemic (Kuteleva and Clifford 2021). Promoting a narrative of masculine threat and "turning the bare face into a litmus test of Trump loyalism, his rhetoric suggested that masks threatened masculinity and functioned as a form of anti-choice bodily oppression" (Neville-Shepard n.d., 1). In Canada, similar narratives were advanced during the 2021 federal election by the fringe People's Party of Canada (PPC) and its leader, Maxime Bernier, that has all the characteristics of a populist radical right (PRR) party (Mudde 2017), as well as during the 2022 convoy protests that occupied Ottawa and closed the Ambassador Bridge between Detroit and Windsor.

On the other hand, Canada generally has less polarized politics and news media, and no comparable history of gendered nationalism on domestic or external affairs and defense issues. Masculinity is politicized everywhere, but that doesn't mean that it's politicized everywhere in the same ways. As such, we may expect different patterns in men's public opinion about social spending, group rights, and cultural questions.

Our chapter is oriented around two questions. First, is there reason to believe that Canadian politics is moving toward the masculinized populism that has shown up all over the world? And, second, how does the interplay of masculinities and politics differ in the United States and Canada, and what does that say about masculinized populism in Canada?

Gender Threat

There have been important developments in the tone and substance of political life over the past ten to twenty years: the (re)emergence of the populist radical right (Mudde 2017; 2007), growing partisan polarization (Mason 2018; Iyengar et al. 2019; Iyengar and Westwood 2015), and increasing prevalence of misinformation and disinformation in political life. These forces are intertwined with and have effects on citizens' political orientations. Our chapter focuses on men's attitudes within this changing political environment and the related emergence of culture wars. Group status threat seems to be the primary explanation for men's attitudinal shifts (Cassino and Besen-Cassino 2021). As Cassino and Besen-Cassino state (2021, 1), "Against all evidence, American men have come to believe that the world—economically, socially, politically—is tilted against them."

The PRR has often promoted a political narrative focused on alleged economic, cultural, and security threats caused by immigration, racial diversity, feminism and women's equality, and, increasingly, gender identity and trans rights. PRR parties tend to vilify immigrants, asylum seekers, and minority groups, claiming that outgroups take jobs, abuse social programs, and cause crime. In Europe, Jewish, Muslim, and Roma people are traditional targets of the PRR (Mudde 2007), but, in other locations, the scapegoated groups vary.

Trump and his allies targeted Mexicans and Central Americans, both sources of significant migration to the United States, and also regions with durable cultural and economic ties with the United States. In his 2016 campaign, a common Trump talking point was building a wall between the United States and Mexico. Trump officially launched his campaign for President in front of a "Make American Great Again" (MAGA) sign, a slogan that invoked the idea that America was much better in some unspecified past, presumably when immigration was lower or originated predominantly from Western European countries, when traditional social hierarchies were protected as a result of racial segregation and women's subjugation. In his launch speech, Trump said that "when Mexico sends its people, they're not sending their best. . . . They're sending people that have lots of problems. . . . They're bringing drugs. They're bringing crime. They're rapists."[1]

Similarly, feminism and women's equality are often framed as threats to men's primacy within established hierarchies. Language invoking fear of status loss is used to appeal to male voters, echoing or even activating feelings of group threat among (predominantly white) men (Mutz 2018; Powell, Butterfield, and Jiang 2018; Paxton and Hughes 2018; Carian and Sobotka 2018). Hostile sexism—"a set of beliefs focusing on threats to men's power over women" (Cassese and Holman 2019)—rather than benevolent sexism, which focuses on paternalist protection of women, was often central to the Trump camp's attacks on Hillary Clinton. Campaign paraphernalia encountered at Trump events provide extreme examples of the mobilization of masculinity and hostile sexism on the campaign trail: pins and T-shirts with slogans like: "Don't Be a Pussy. Vote for Trump in 2016," "Trump 2016: Finally Someone with Balls."[2] Importantly, "Trump avoided wholesale attacks on women per se (who after all, constituted a majority of the electorate). But he tossed demeaning insults at particular women who looked like easy targets" (Ferguson et al. 2020, 104). Other targets included Carly Fiorina, Elizabeth Warren, Alexandria Ocasio-Cortez, and Nancy Pelosi.

The relationship between gender and populism is not well researched (Mudde and Kaltwasser 2017; Erzeel and Rashkova 2017), including how and why gender or feminism are mobilized within populist rhetoric. In some contexts, PRR parties have defended liberal gender equality policies and LGBTQ rights as a way to advance an anti-immigrant or anti-Muslim agenda. Bans on headscarves and other (non-Christian) religious clothing or adornments fit this bill, in which minority religious practices are restricted to ostensibly advance women's equality and autonomy. In other contexts, PRR actors adopt hostile stances toward feminism and gender equality.

While the PRR in the United States uses the same nativist rhetoric as PRR abroad, a distinctive feature of American PRR is its social conservative focus, a strategy that distracts voters from the tensions inherent in its unique plutocratic populism (Hacker and Pierson 2020). As such, cultural insecurities around race, immigration, and gender helped drive Trump support in the 2016 presidential election (Ferguson et al. 2020; Hacker and Pierson 2020). Economic insecurity—of white men in rust-belt states, for example—was also an essential part of the story, especially in the ways that cultural and economic threat intertwined (Ferguson et al. 2020; Hacker and Pierson 2020).

Have Men Shifted Rightward in Canada?

While the "tendency in the literature comparing public opinion in Canada and the US has been to emphasize difference" (Kevins and Soroka 2018, 107), we might anticipate similar right-moving trends among Canadian men. Media consumption patterns are important, given Canadians' exposure to US content, which may promote the spread of American frames and talking points.[3] This is part of the reason why members of the 2022 Ottawa trucker convoy spoke so often about First Amendment rights. In a bail hearing for Tamara Lich, one of the organizers, her husband tells the judge that they thought the Emergencies Act was invoked unlawfully because the people's right to protest in Canada "was part of our first amendments."[4] The judge responded: "First amendment? What's that?" Incidentally, the first amendment to the Canadian Constitution, passed in 1870, deals with the establishment of Manitoba as a province.

Canadian viewership of US networks is also growing, as is the attention US networks pay to Canada. For example, in January 2022, former NHL player Theo Fleury appeared on Fox News speaking on the pandemic response and truckers' convoy in Canada. Fleury is a vocal critic of vaccine and other COVID mandates, and generally posts various conspiratorial, PRR-consistent views on Twitter. The Canadian intelligence community has warned about the threat to stability posed by conservative media outlets like Fox News, which are popular in Canada. Domestic right-wing media and online forums have also grown (Elmer and Burton 2022), expanding reach and domestic influence of the far-right media ecosystem.

Looking at the substance and tone of politics, it is also important that partisan polarization has increased in Canada over time (Kevins and Soroka 2018; Cochrane 2010; 2015; Johnston 2019), similar to the United

States. Polls have shown that Canadians have been open to "voting for a candidate with a Trump-like platform" (Kevins and Soroka 2018, 103), and the growing influence of the populist right can be seen in right-wing parties' leadership contests and campaigns, which increasingly emphasize "us versus them" motifs around immigration and multiculturalism, often tied to lingering post-9/11 anti-Muslim sentiment. Examples include the "snitch line" targeting "barbaric cultural practices" proposed under Conservative Party of Canada (CPC) prime minister Stephen Harper; CPC leadership candidate Kellie Leitch's proposed "Canadian values test" for potential immigrants; and Prime Minister Harper's comments about "old stock" Canadians during the 2015 federal election campaign.[5]

The CPC and others have also used gendered attacks on political rivals, particularly Prime Minister Trudeau, in an effort to feminize him (Sabin and Kirkup 2019; Goodyear-Grant 2019; Grant and MacDonald 2020). A political strategy grounded in masculinity ideology, as discussed in McDermott and Jones's chapter in this volume, traits and behaviors seen as feminine are criticized as signs of weakness or incompetence. Various political rivals called Trudeau a "lightweight" and a "pretty boy" in his first election as Liberal leader and, in the 2021 election campaign, released an ad portraying Trudeau as Veruca Salt from *Charlie and the Chocolate Factory*, a petulant and emotional girl prone to tantrums when she does not get her way. The CPC used Trudeau's hair in symbolic ways, to communicate things that cannot be said explicitly: "It was too messy, too fun, too girly, not serious enough, too fussy, too gay—and, therefore, so was the candidate."[6] Domestic and international media did the same (Sabin and Kirkup 2019), focusing on Trudeau's hair, his alleged lack of experience, and his background as a drama teacher, something various CPC politicians have sneered at over the years. There is a partisan dimension to this pattern as well, and it is mirrored in the United States and other jurisdictions where gender and party stereotypes interact, producing gendered partisan stereotypes that pair the Left with femininity and the Right with masculinity (McDermott 2016; Dolan 2014). This leads to perceptions, for example, that Democratic men in the United States are less masculine than Republican men (Hayes 2011).

The CPC has also made public appeals inching closer to "toxic masculinity": a specific subcategory of hegemonic masculinity "characterized by a drive to dominate and by endorsement of misogynistic and homophobic views" (Parent, Gobble, and Rochlen 2019, 278), as McDermott and Jones describe. For example, in October 2022, it was revealed that some of current CPC leader Pierre Pollievre's YouTube videos contained tags designed to reach out to the "male supremacy" movement. The tags were acronymns standing for "Men Going Their Own Way"—a movement that rhetorically advocates men's separation from the perceived toxicity of women—and have been used in Pollievre's videos for more than four years.[7] These misogynistic sentiments and tags are part of far-right online movements.

At the same time, the CPC and its leaders have not gone down the same path as Trump and others like him. Much of the CPC program and rhetoric reflects traditional Toryism, and CPC leaders have often been reluctant to embolden social conservatives in the party, given the limits of such appeals to the general electorate. Critically, one of the party's key limitations has been its unpopularity among women. The CPC under former prime minister Stephen Harper put a lot of effort into closing the persistent sex-vote gap with an electoral strategy that combined programmatic elements directed at rural and suburban mothers with growing the nominations of women candidates (Goodyear-Grant 2013). Interestingly, this strategy is similar to the "strategic descriptive representation" strategy adopted by various European populist right parties (Weeks et al. 2022). Since 2011, the CPC sex vote gap has again grown in every federal election, and is currently near double digits (Goodyear-Grant et al. 2021).

The founding of the People's Party of Canada (PPC) in 2018 by former Harper-era minister of foreign affairs Maxime Bernier, brought an explicitly PRR option to Canadian party politics. The PPC echoes PRR parties in Europe in style and substance and arguably puts pressure on the more moderate CPC to shift right at times to avoid vote losses. The PPC advocates for restricting immigration, screening potential immigrants in face-to-face interviews "to assess the extent to which they align with Canadian values and societal norms," as well as scrapping what the party calls "extreme multiculturalism" via an end to official multiculturalism policy.[8] The party's website claims that "the government of Canada has pursued a policy of official multiculturalism that encourages immigrants to keep the values and culture they left behind instead of integrating into Canadian society and adopting Canadian values and culture. With his cult of diversity, Justin Trudeau has pushed this ideology even further into a form of extreme multiculturalism."

On sex and gender, the PPC promotes ideas and policies consistent with other PRR parties. For example, a press release during the 2021 federal election campaign announced that "a PPC Government will Fight Radical Gender Ideology."[9] The release "pledged to change various laws and rules promoted by radical trans activists that are harmful to women, children, and gays and lesbians," claiming that "with the active support of the woke far left and Trudeau's Liberals, a minority of radical trans activists are trying to transform society in a way that curtails everyone's freedoms." The release focused on issues around pronoun use and "compelled speech," bathroom politics, and the notion that children are being encouraged to transition "when most of them would grow up to become healthy gays and lesbians," which is a wild argument. Maxime Bernier says he is not a feminist and argues that affirmative action policies aimed at increasing women's representation is discriminatory.[10] Bernier has also been criticized for using the red-pill meme popular among anti-feminists, men's rights groups, and incel chat networks, dog-whistling anti-woman and anti-feminist politics.

These shifts go far beyond the actions of individual parties and actors. The increased reach of white supremacist organizations, QAnon, and the "manosphere" are illustrative of the growth of right-wing extremism, which has trickled into party politics. Most relevant to questions about the effect of gender and gender norms on public opinion is the emergence of the "manosphere," a network of websites and other online venues such as the red-pill subreddit that is preoccupied with "men's rights" and that present themselves as a counterculture to feminism. The manosphere has been linked with growing violence toward and abuse of women (Grant and MacDonald 2020; Krook 2020; MacDonald and Dobrowolsky 2020), both in and outside politics. British MP Jo Cox was murdered in 2016 by a man with links to far-right white supremacist groups, and the 2020 plot to kidnap Michigan governor Gretchen Whitmer was planned by thirteen men with ties to a paramilitary militia group that called themselves the Wolverine Watchmen. In Canada, the abuse and harassment of Catherine Mckenna, Rachel Notley, Celina Caesar-Chavannes, and others has been encouraged and intensified by the manosphere (Grant and MacDonald 2020; MacDonald and Dobrowolsky 2020).

Data and Method

Moving to our empirics, first we describe our data and our measure of masculinity. Then, we examine how masculinity is correlated with political attitudes in Canada and the United.

Our data are from two original surveys conducted in 2019 in Canada and the United States. These pose common questions about political orientations, demographics, and social identity, and issue stances, allowing comparisons of gender opinion gaps across the two countries. Our questions are: Is the American growth in masculinized populism happening in Canada too? Related, how does the interplay of masculinity and politics differ in the United States and Canada, and what does that tell us about the possibilities for masculinized populism in Canada? Because of our questions, our focus on masculinity in the chapter is really on intensely felt more traditional masculinity—something close to hegemonic masculinity, which is one of the forms most closely associated with masculinized populism.

Data were collected in the United States in April 2019. We purchased a sample of one thousand from Dynata, seeking to closely mirror the US population. The survey tested some measures of gender, building on our previous work (Bittner and Goodyear-Grant 2017b, 2017a). In addition, we included all twenty-two questions of the ambivalent sexism battery (Glick and Fiske 1997) as well as questions related to attitudes about the role of the state, the economy, social services, and various groups. The Canadian data were obtained from a purpose-built module included in the 2019 Canadian Election Study. This module included the same measures of gender as in the US study, as well as three questions from each of the benevolent and hostile sexism batteries that make up ambivalent sexism (due to space considerations on this larger omnibus survey we could not field all twenty-two questions).

The analyses proceed as follows: first, we describe basic patterns linking sex and gender as seen in the data across both countries. We then introduce our measure of masculinity, outlining how it was created and describing it in more detail, including patterns of other identities and belonging linked to masculinity. We then assess attitudes by masculinity, presenting a series of graphs that plot average responses to various questions related to economic and social issues, groups, the two sexism batteries, and partisan attitudes.

Analyses

Patterns of Identity: Sex, Gender, and Masculinity in the US and Canada

In the United States, 45 percent of the sample identified as male.[11] Eight of these individuals (2 percent) identified as transgender. Twelve (2 percent) of female identifiers also identified as trans. Our analysis that follows does not really focus on whether an individual is male or female; instead we look at gender—specifically, masculinity and femininity. We do not differentiate between those who are cisgender versus transgender, focusing solely on individuals' gender identity at the time of interview, not their assigned sex at birth.

We asked respondents to provide us their gender identity in two different ways across both surveys, asking respondents to identify how masculine and/or feminine they felt they were on 0–100 scales.[12] In both countries, we also asked respondents how important their gender identity is to them on a 0–100 scale, where 100 reflects very important (Bittner and Goodyear-Grant 2017b; Bittner and Goodyear-Grant forthcoming).

Figure 12.1a-b presents gender identity by respondent sex in both Canada and the United States. In both countries a large majority of respondents place their gender identity close to their sex. Men in particular place themselves close to the masculine pole (0), and women place themselves close to the feminine pole of the continuum (1).[13]

In the United States, 23 percent of men were on the 100 percent masculine pole, while only 1 percent of women placed themselves there; 17 percent of women placed themselves at 100 percent feminine, while 2 percent of men placed themselves there. In Canada, 29 percent of men and 1 percent of women were at the masculine pole. Twenty-seven percent of women and no men placed themselves at the feminine pole.[14]

More men were also likely to say that they felt more masculine *and* more feminine in that version of the question in the United States. This

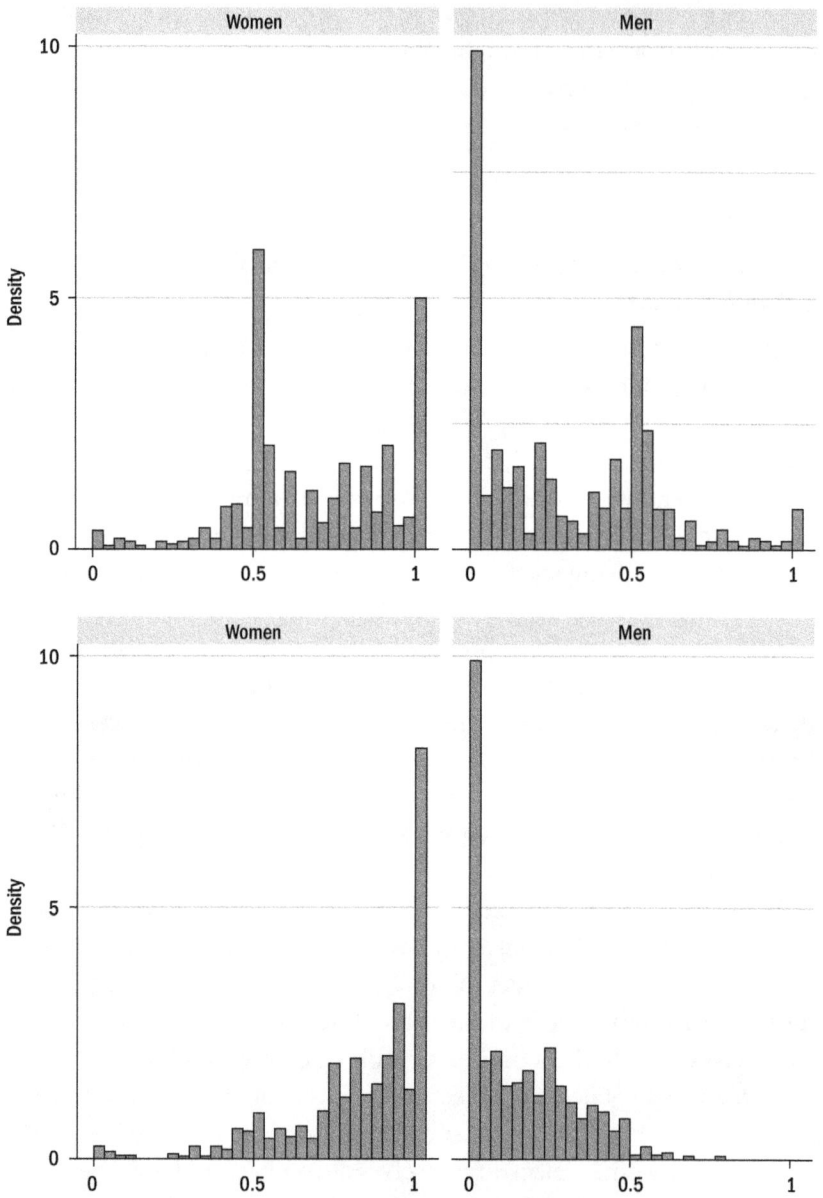

Figure 12.1a-b: Distribution of gender identity by sex in the United States and Canada (L-R)

was true in Canada, too, for responses to our two-dimensional question, but where we combined the two measures (and respondents were each asked both measures), the graph emphasizes overall patterns, in which gender identity fairly closely maps onto respondent sex.[15]

Exploring and Defining Masculinity

Our goal for this paper is to assess the role of masculinity in shaping political attitudes. In particular, we are interested in how intensely felt traditional or hegemonic masculinity affects public opinion in Canada and the United States, given the growing influence of masculinized populism in politics. Our measure of gender ranges from 0–1.

Self-placement at the masculine pole (0) when there is a 100-point range to choose from is a signal of intense masculine identity. Ten percent of Americans and 14 percent of Canadians identified as 100 percent masculine. Other factors can also be taken into consideration in terms of getting a handle on intensely felt, more traditional conceptions of masculinity. Our data include a gender salience question, measured on a 100-point scale from low to high.[16] The mean in Canada was 0.83 (SD = 0.25), while for Canadian men it was higher 0.87 (SD = 0.19) and for women it was lower, at 0.8 (SD = 0.29). In the United States, the mean score was 0.8 (SD = 0.26), while for men it was 0.78 (SD = 0.27) and for women it was slightly higher at 0.81 (SD = 0.24). Thus, for most respondents, gender is quite important.

Among those American respondents who placed themselves at the masculine pole, 71 percent also said that their gender was very important to them, choosing a score of 100 on the 0–100 scale. In Canada, 78 percent of those who placed themselves at the masculine pole of the gender identity question also placed themselves at 100 on the gender salience variable. These 78 individuals in the US and 111 individuals in Canada indicated that they are completely masculine, and that their gender is of the highest importance to them. These individuals arguably come closest to our interest in the growing importance of masculinity in politics, particularly the type of masculinity associated with masculinized populism. Thus, we created a new dichotomous variable that we simply call "hypermasculinity," where 1=hypermasculine and 0=all others. We therefore operationalize hypermasculinity as self-placement at 0

TABLE 12.1: Demographic breakdown of the hypermasculine

	United States	Canada
Male identity	99%	98%
Transgender (US)/genderdiverse (Canada)	0 people	1 person
White	77%	89%
Black	12%	2%
Racialized/minoritized* (includes Black & Indigenous)	23%	11%
Indigenous	9%	4%
Top income tercile	41%	34%
University degree	58%	51%
Working full time	46%	44%
Republican (US)/Conservative (Canada)	58%	30%

*Note. "Racialized" is a term that reflects "the process of investing skin colour with meaning, such that 'black' and 'white' come to function, not as descriptions of skin colour, but as racial identities" (Ahmed 2002). We operationalize this concept with a binary variable that groups all nonwhite respondents as racialized/minoritized. We say "minoritized" because white is racialized, too, and minoritized captures the power dynamics of racialization. As coded above, it is the inverse of "white" in this table.

(the masculine pole of the gender identity scale), combined with a gender identity salience at the highest value (100), indicating very strong association with masculinity. In the United States, 6 percent of the sample fits the hypermasculine category, and 10 percent in Canada. Table 12.1 provides additional demographic information about the individuals in the hypermasculine category, and it is important to note that, overall, many of the differences between the two national groups are indicative of differences between the demographics of Canada and the United States.[17]

Hypermasculine respondents in the United States are predominately white male university-degree-holders, 41 percent of them are in the top income tercile, nearly half are working full-time, and more than half are Republican Party identifiers. In Canada, the patterns are slightly different. There are slightly more who fit into the hypermasculine category, and, within that group, nearly 90 percent are white, 4 percent are Indigenous, 2 percent are Black,[18] 34 percent are in the top income bracket, 51 percent have a university degree, 44 percent are working full time, and 30 percent identify with the Conservative Party.[19]

The Role of Hypermasculinity in Canadian and American Attitudes

In the analyses that follow, we examine the impact of hypermasculinity on public opinion across a variety of issues and attitudes: a) taxes versus spending; b) attitudes toward groups; c) social values; d) benevolent sexism and hostile sexism; and e) partisan political attitudes. We chose these domains based on available data and their importance to political discourse and behavior. The figures illustrate differences in mean attitudes among the hypermasculine compared to all others. All attitudinal variables are coded on a 0–1 scale, where 1 = most liberal position. The appendix provides all coding details, but the higher the mean, the more liberal the position on the given issue or dimension.

To assess the impact of hypermasculinity on attitudes, we conducted a series of bivariate regression analyses in which we regressed attitudinal variables on hypermasculinity. We then plotted the coefficients and standard errors for each of these separate regression analyses into a single figure to be able to compare across issues. Figure 12.2a-b, for example, plots the coefficients for the hypermasculine variable across seven attitudinal variables related to taxes and spending, comparing Canada and the United States side by side. Negative coefficients indicate that the hypermasculine hold less progressive attitudes on the issue than other respondents (i.e., the less masculine and the feminine respondents). In figure 12.2a-b, we see that most of the coefficients do not reach traditional levels of statistical significance, and none in Canada. In the United States, the hypermasculine are less supportive of immigration spending and prefer reduced personal taxes. Thus, for these two issues, hypermasculinity leads to less progressive stances.

What is not shown, because we focus on correlations with hypermasculinity rather than overall attitudes, is that the mean attitudes in Canada are more progressive or left-leaning than in the US.

In figure 12.3a-b, we examine how hypermasculinity is correlated with attitudes toward various groups, using standard feeling thermometers. Note that the questions asked in the United States are not identical to the questions asked in Canada, impairing direct comparisons for all issues. We report as many "exact" questions across both countries as we have data for, and then we also report on single-country data where it fits the broad theme in this figure. Across both countries, where there

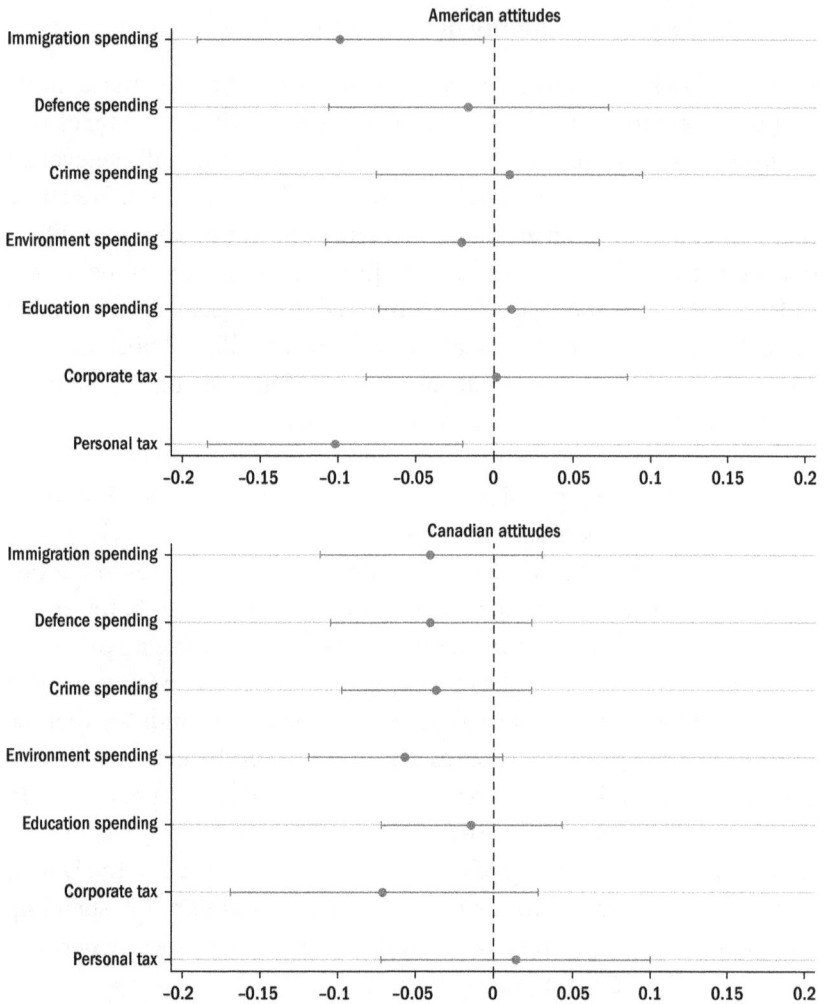

Figure 12.2a-b: Comparing attitudes on taxes and spending in the United States and Canada (L-R)

are differences, the hypermasculine have less warm feelings than other respondents toward various groups, most of them marginalized. In the United States, the hypermasculine are more hostile toward feminists, trans people, and Democrats, consistent with the literature's findings about the PRR, masculinity, and growing outgroup animosity.

In Canada, the patterns are not much different. Most of the group feeling coefficients are not statistically significant, but the hypermasculine do

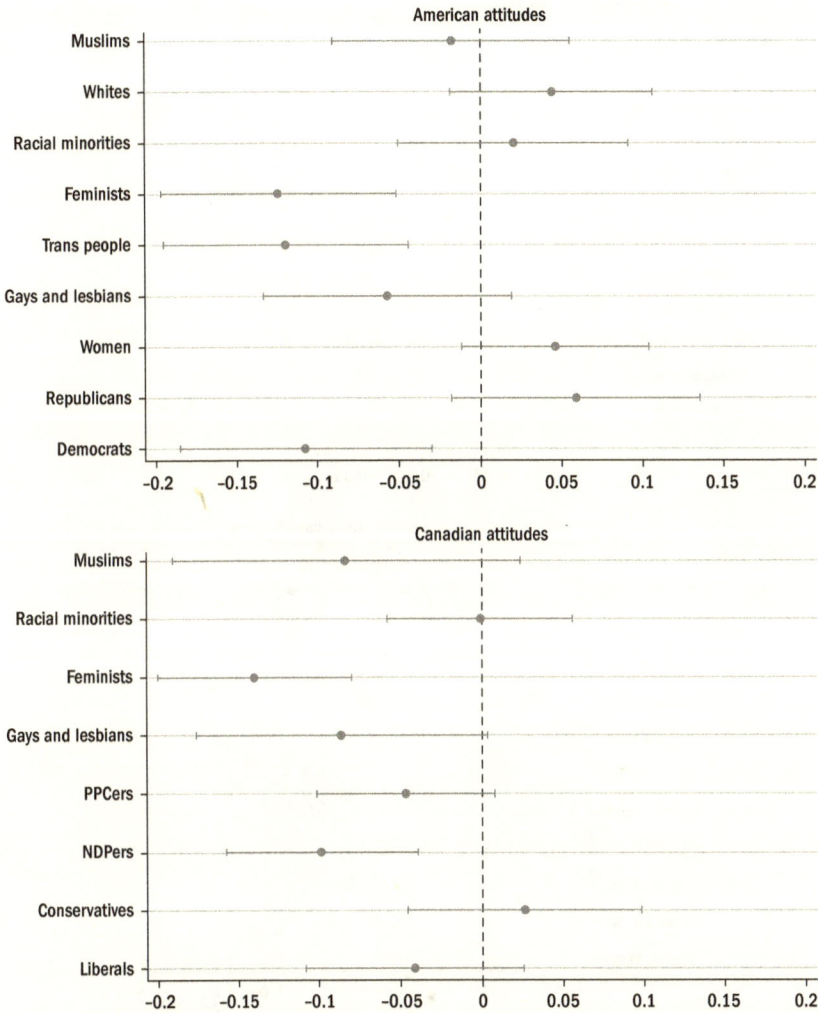

Figure 12.3a-b: Comparing feelings about groups in the United States and Canada (L-R)

view feminists less favorably, similar to American hypermasculines. They also hold less favorable attitudes toward members of the New Democrat Party, similar to American hypermasculines' lower favorability toward the Democrats. Thus, in both countries, attitudes toward feminists and more liberal parties—both explicitly political groups—are particular targets of disdain by the hypermasculine, compared to all other gender identifiers.

Figure 12.4 displays the correlation between hypermasculinity and a series of classic political issues related to equality, so-called family values,

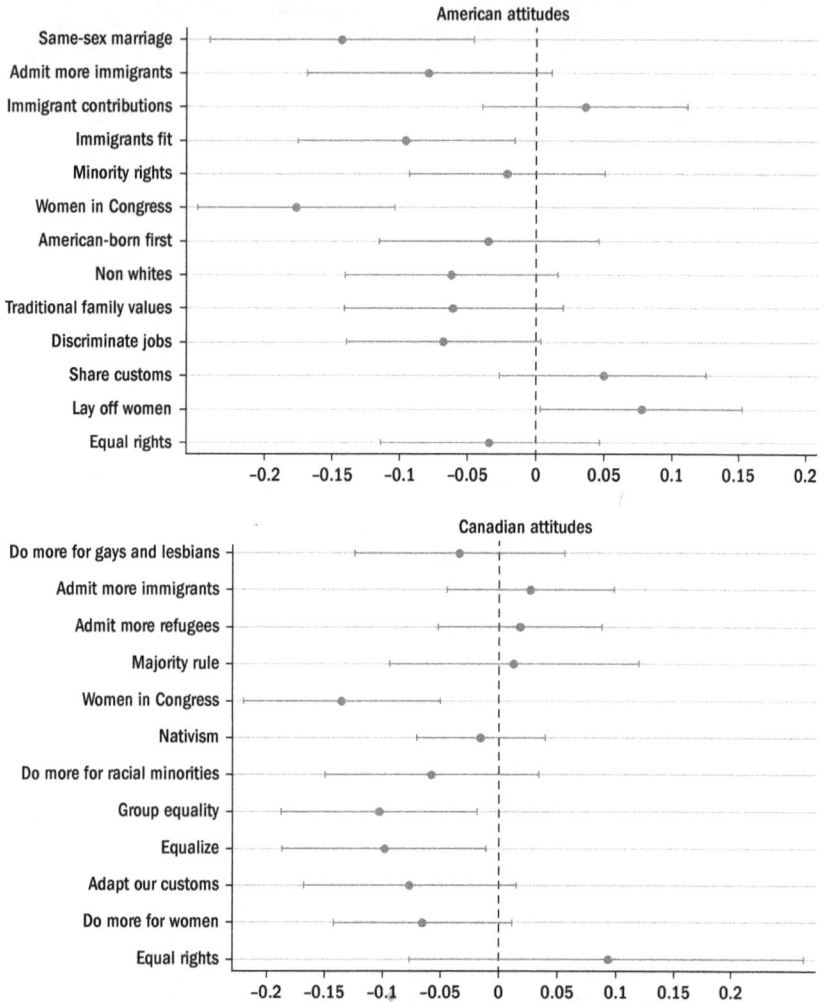

American attitudes

Same-sex marriage	
Admit more immigrants	
Immigrant contributions	
Immigrants fit	
Minority rights	
Women in Congress	
American-born first	
Non whites	
Traditional family values	
Discriminate jobs	
Share customs	
Lay off women	
Equal rights	

-0.2   -0.15   -0.1   -0.05   0   0.05   0.1   0.15   0.2

Canadian attitudes

Do more for gays and lesbians	
Admit more immigrants	
Admit more refugees	
Majority rule	
Women in Congress	
Nativism	
Do more for racial minorities	
Group equality	
Equalize	
Adapt our customs	
Do more for women	
Equal rights	

-0.2   -0.15   -0.1   -0.05   0   0.05   0.1   0.15   0.2

Figure 12.4: Comparing attitudes on classic questions about social values in the United States and Canada (L-R)

immigrants, racialized groups, and group-based state supports. All variables are coded so that values closer to 1 reflect more liberal stances.

In both countries, most coefficients do not achieve traditional levels of statistical significance. Where they do, generally the hypermasculine hold less progressive positions. In the United States, the hypermasculine are less supportive of same-sex marriage, less likely to have positive views about immigrants fitting into American society, and less likely to see women's underrepresentation in Congress as a problem. Interestingly, the hypermasculine are more progressive than others on the issue of whether or not (when layoffs are necessary) we should first lay off women whose husbands have jobs. In Canada, only a few coefficients achieve traditional levels of statistical significance: the hypermasculine are less likely see group equality as an ideal, less likely to think we should do what we can to equalize conditions for different groups, and less likely to believe that women's legislative underrepresentation is a problem.

Interestingly, issues related to immigration did not produce divergent attitudes between the hypermasculine and others. Immigration is closely tied to the health of the economy, and it is possible that respondents are looking at this issue from that perspective. Moreover, Canada does not share a border with an important immigrant- or refugee-sending country, is difficult to reach, and thus has much more control over immigration than various other OECD countries, including the United States, in principle. Canada's immigration streams are able to emphasize skills and education requirements with comparatively low migration outside legal channels. Canada also has a small population within a vast geographic space. In short, immigration is not as ripe for politicization by the populist right in Canada, especially given the electoral importance of various racialized and immigrant communities for both major parties, which are broadly pro-immigration. Still, among these, only one question led to any significant difference between the hypermasculine and others in the United States, and that is the issue of immigrants fitting into society. In figure 12.3, we see that the hypermasculine were less supportive of spending on immigration. We anticipated that in both countries, questions related to immigration, race, and ethnic diversity would be more of a hot button for the hypermasculine, and this does not appear to be broadly the case.

Scholars have spent much energy on examining the impact of sexism on political attitudes, and, in the American survey we fielded, we included the entirety of the ambivalent sexism battery developed by Glick and Fiske (1997), which incorporates eleven questions in the benevolent sexism battery and eleven questions in the hostile sexism battery. Due to space constraints in the Canadian Election Study, we asked a subset of six of these, three from each battery. The inclusion of these questions in the surveys allow us to assess the potential influence of hypermasculinity on sexist attitudes. We assess both components of the ambivalent sexism battery in figures 5 and 6. Figure 12.5a-b presents the impact of hypermasculinity on attitudes toward items in the benevolent sexism battery. All variables are coded on a 0–1 scale so that 1 reflects more progressive or less sexist attitudes.

Figure 12.5a-b presents a mixed picture. Like the figures that precede this, we do not show mean scores for each item of the battery; we show the differences between the hypermasculine and all others. Thus, we do not see overall trends in general feelings about these statements. Most of these coefficients do not reach traditional levels of statistical significance (in Canada none do), but in three cases in the United States, those in the hypermasculine category are less progressive/more sexist in their attitudes than others. These individuals are more likely to agree that "a good woman should be set on a pedestal by her man," that "every man ought to have a woman whom he adores," and that "women should be cherished and protected by men."

Figure 12.6a-b shows the impact of hypermasculinity on attitudes related to the hostile sexism battery. Negative coefficients indicate more sexist attitudes. In Canada, none of the coefficients reach traditional levels of statistical significance. In the United States, a few do, and they indicate that the hypermasculine are more sexist than others, similar to the finding for the so-called benevolent sexism scale.

The data show that the hypermasculine are less likely to believe that "feminists are making entirely reasonable demands of men," more likely to believe that "women seek to gain power by getting control over men," less likely to agree that "feminists are not seeking for women to have more power than men," more likely to believe that "most women interpret innocent remarks or acts as being sexist," and more likely to believe that "many women are actually seeking special favors, such as hiring policies that favor them over men, under the guise of asking for 'equality.'" Thus, the picture painted is one where the hypermasculine feel that social claims about sexism are overblown, and women are manipulative and greedy.

What these data do not show, because they focus on the difference between the hypermasculine and others, is that the mean scores for all are also quite low. The extent to which society as a whole has internalized

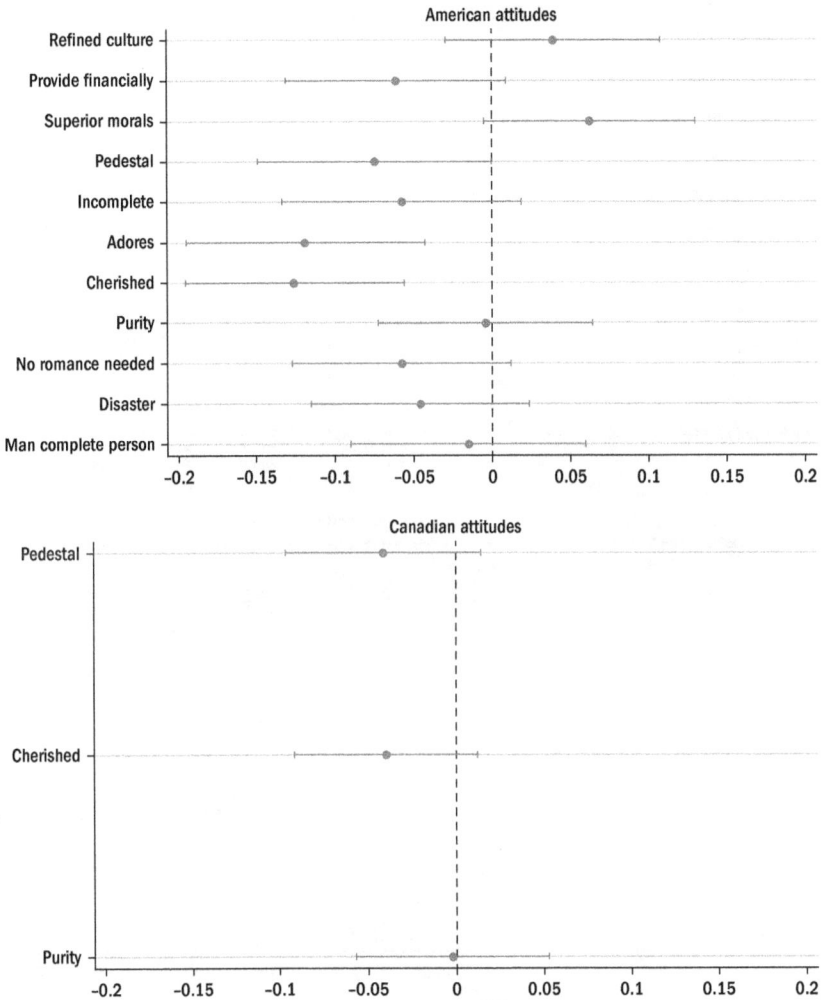

Figure 12.5a-b: Comparing attitudes on items from benevolent sexism battery

toxic patriarchal norms is remarkable, and even those who are not hypermasculine speak about women in this deeply sexist way. Two examples of statements in this battery that are particularly toxic include "There are actually very few women who get a kick out of teasing men by seeming sexually available and then refusing male advances," and "Once a woman gets a man to commit to her, she usually tries to put him on a tight leash." That the mean rating on the first statement is slightly below

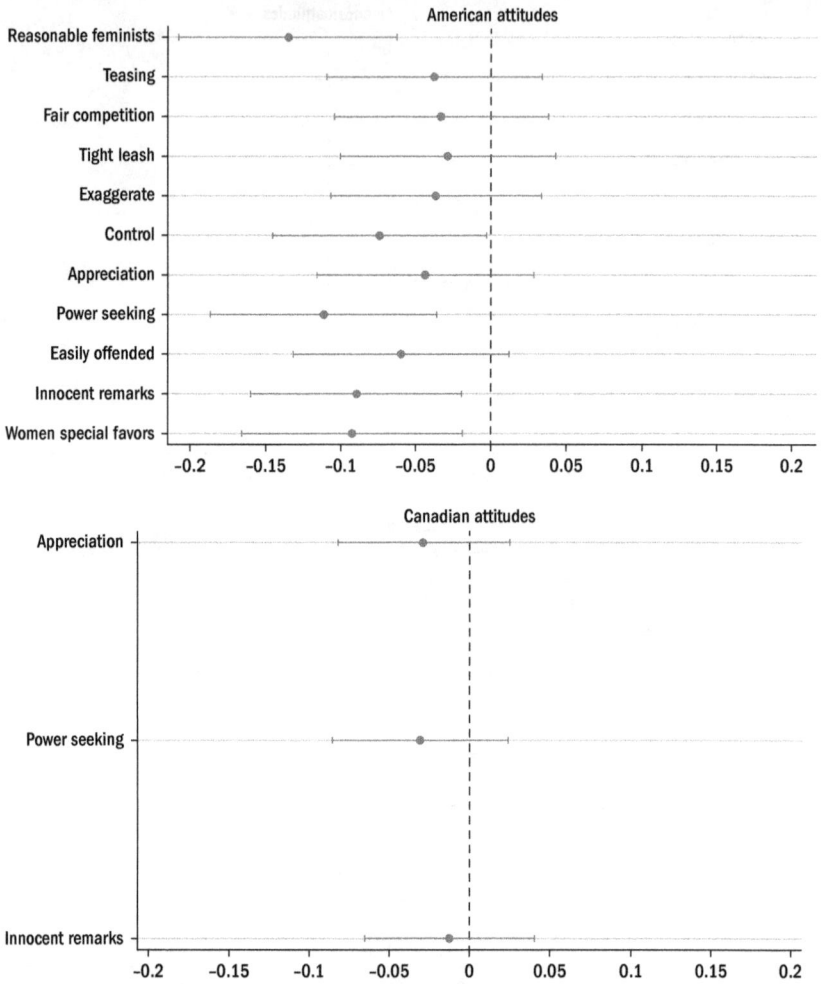

Figure 12.6: Comparing attitudes linked to hostile sexism in the United States and Canada (L-R)

.6, and slightly above .6 for the second statement for the whole sample is revealing about the pervasiveness of sexism. It is not "just men" who are hostile toward women. Overall mean scores are higher in Canada than in the United States (data not shown), suggesting that the baseline levels of hostile sexism may be slightly lower in Canada, but certainly not compelling evidence of full-chested egalitarianism or the "niceness" for which Canada is stereotyped.

Our last set of bivariate analyses looks at more explicitly political variables: partisan party identification, ideology, thermometers for prominent politicians, and vote choice. Figure 12.7a-b presents the coefficients from a series of bivariate regressions where the dependent variable is regressed on hypermasculinity, across both countries. Important to note, the ideology variable is coded in the opposite direction of most of the attitudinal variables: on a 0–1 scale where 1 reflects right-leaning folks. Positive coefficients mean that the hypermasculine are more con-

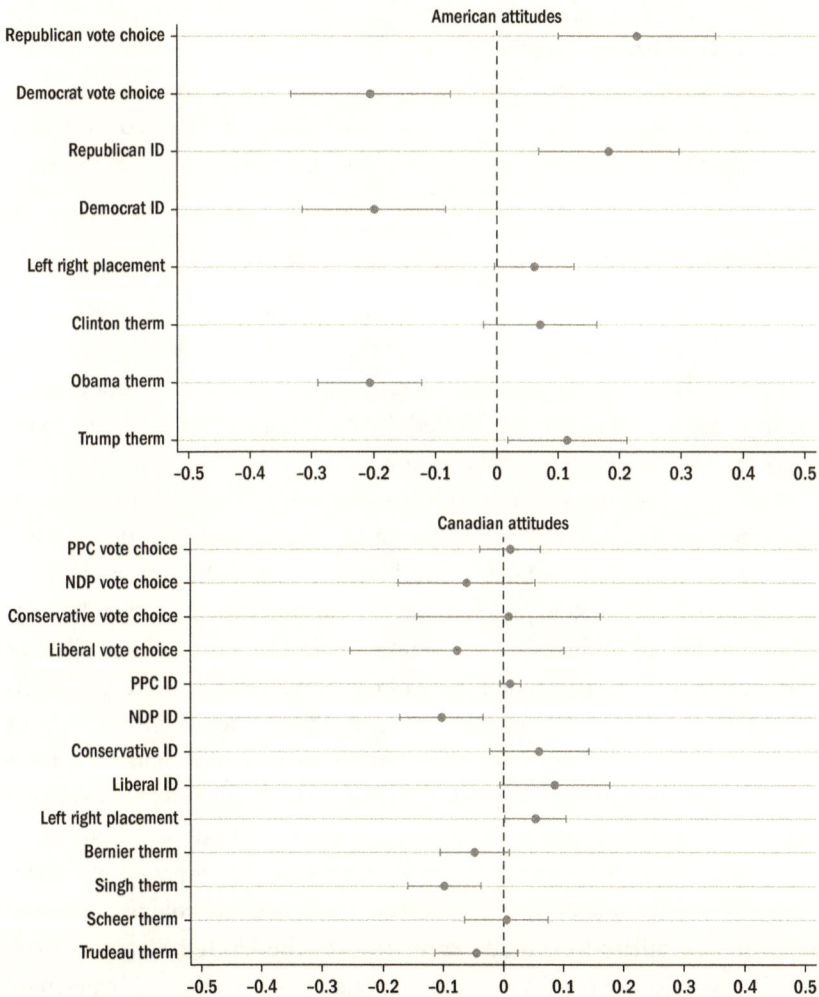

Figure 12.7a-b: Comparing partisan political attitudes

servative than others. The literature tells us to expect those who are male identified to be more to the right, more likely to be Republican, more likely to vote Republican, and more likely to have warmer feelings toward Trump. We expect this to be true of the hypermasculine as well. Indeed, these expectations all hold. In addition, the hypermasculine feel less warmly toward Obama.

In Canada, the patterns are less clear, as many of the coefficients are not statistically significant. The hypermasculine are less likely to identify with the left-leaning NDP, more likely to place themselves on the right side of the ideological spectrum, and less likely to hold positive attitudes toward NDP leader Jagmeet Singh.

Taken together, what do these data tell us? These bivariate analyses suggest that those who are hypermasculine often hold more conservative attitudes. Our findings are suggestive, but further research is needed.

Conclusions

We see patterns whereby the hypermasculine are more conservative on some attitudinal issues than the rest of the population. On the comparative front, these data suggest that masculinized populism has not gone as far in Canada as it has in the United States, at least not yet. Despite having somewhat stronger identification with hypermasculinism in Canada, this identity does not seem as strong a motivator of opposition to social spending, environmental protection, and other issues as it does in the United States, including hostile and benevolent sexism. Speculating on these outcomes, the key question is why masculinized populism has not taken hold in quite the same way politically in Canada as of now. Part of the explanation has to be the nature of the party system and regionalized competition for seats. Indeed, the CPC consistently faces a dilemma about whether to move right to appease its base or move to the center to attract votes. Unlike in the United States, the base for the major right-wing party is concentrated in a single region (Alberta and parts of Saskatchewan), with relatively little room for electoral expansion elsewhere on a socially conservative agenda, especially given the very different role of organized religion in politics in Canada compared to the United States and the relative centrism of the Canadian electorate. As such, elite-led hypermasculinization of politics is not a winning strategy in Canada.

While we do not show these data, as we focus on the differences between the hypermasculine and all others, for the most part the national means on all attitudinal questions were higher in Canada, indicating that Canadians are more progressive/left-leaning in their political views than Americans. They generally hold more egalitarian attitudes and appear to hold slightly more feminist attitudes and less sexist attitudes.

Canada also seems to have some preference for softer, less hawkish, or "strongman" leaders, in general. Canada is not a major military power compared to the United States, and Canada's role on the global stage has often been one of peacekeeper and role model on egalitarianism (deserved or not). As such, a highly masculinized style of political leadership is not as prized in Canada compared to the United States, whose president is the commander in chief of the world's strongest military. Put differently, we suspect a lot of the differences in how masculinity informs political attitudes across the two countries lies in institutional and structural characteristics that distinguish the countries, thus producing differing incentives for elites to use rhetorical or programmatic appeals to masculinized populism in politics.

More research is needed. There are a number of potential directions for future work in this area. First, it will be important in the coming years to examine and assess alternate conceptualizations and operationalizations of hypermasculinity. What do we mean when we talk about hypermasculinity, and how do we best measure this concept? Is a combination of gender identity and gender salience the best way to capture this phenomenon, or is there a better way? If we create a better measure of hypermasculinity, will we also see a corresponding nuance in the relationship between hypermasculinity and political attitudes? Second, it would also be helpful to look at the role of hypermasculinity over time, to see whether Canada and/or the United States are moving in a direction in which masculinized populism is becoming more prevalent among citizens. Third, more comparison would also be valuable: How do values in Canada and the US compare to attitudes in Europe? To Central and South America? There is lots of scope here for further research, and, while this paper provides early indications of the role hypermasculinity has in political attitudes, we still have many questions. Finally, to what extent are these patterns of attitudes and behavior "new" or related to hypermasculinity and the PRR, and to what extent are these

simply the patterns we have seen for decades in the gender gap literature, where men are to the right of women? Longitudinal research would
be compelling on this question.

NOTES

1 Amber Philips, "'They're Rapists.' President Trump's Campaign Launch Speech
Two Years Later, Annotated," *Washington Post*, June 16, 2017.

2 Peter Beinart, "Fear of a Female President," *Atlantic*, October 2016.

3 "Main Offline News Sources Used by Anglophone News Consumers in Canada as
of February 2022," Statistica.

4 Stephanie Taylor, Mike Blanchfield, and Erika Ibrahim, "Ottawa Police Push
Ahead to End Protest as Bail Hearings for Organizers Move Forward," *Toronto
Star*, February 19, 2022.

5 Tony Keller, "Kellie Leitch: Xenophobia Doesn't Have to Be a Conservative Value,"
Globe and Mail, September 7, 2016.

6 Megan MacKenzie, "What Canada's New 'Pretty Boy' Prime Minister Can Teach
Us about Hegemonic Masculinity," Duck of Minerva, October 25, 2015.

7 Stephanie Taylor, "Justin Trudeau Demands Pierre Poilievre Apologize after Misogynistic Tag Found on YouTube Videos," *Toronto Star*, October 6, 2022.

8 People's Party of Canada, https://www.peoplespartyofcanada.ca/.

9 People's Party of Canada, https://www.peoplespartyofcanada.ca/.

10 Tyler Buist and Vassy Kapelos, "Bernier Says He Doesn't Need to Be a Feminist:
'I believe in people.'" CBC News, November 7, 2018.

11 All question wordings can be found in the appendix.

12 In the United States, we conducted a split-sample experiment, where respondents were assigned to one of two gender questions: the first was a question in
which we asked respondents to place themselves on a single continuum from
0–100, 100 percent masculine to 100 percent feminine, replicating the scale
we used in our 2017 (a/b) work; the second was a question in which we asked
respondents to place themselves on two separate continuums for each of masculinity and femininity, both from 0–100, asking how masculine they feel they
are and how feminine they feel they are. The conceptual difference for the two
treatments is that in the second formulation, the question allowed individuals
to be both 100 percent masculine and 100 percent feminine, while in the first
formulation these two categories were on opposite poles of the continuum. In
order to conduct our analyses, we combine this two-dimensional gender scale
into a single continuum from masculine to feminine; thus those who indicated
they were 100 percent masculine and 100 percent feminine would be right in
the middle of the combined measure, whereas in the first formulation these two
components of gender were found on opposite poles of the continuum, and individuals had to place themselves somewhere between the two. We have a split
sample in the United States between those who answered the first question and

the second question. In Canada, we asked both questions of all respondents, so there is no split sample.

In both Canada and the United States, we combined the two types of questions together, in order to generate a gender identity variable that includes all respondents' gender self-assessments.

13 The mean for the whole US sample is 0.52 (SD = 0.32) and the mean for men is 0.3 (SD = 0.27) and women is 0.69 (0.24). Ten percent of the American sample stated that they feel 100 percent masculine, and 21 percent of the sample placed themselves between 0 and 0.2 on the 0–1 scale. In Canada, the dynamics are quite similar, although not exactly the same. The mean for the whole sample is 0.52 (SD = 0.38), the mean for men is 0.16 (SD = 0.16) and the mean for women is 0.82 (SD = 0.21). Fourteen percent of the sample placed themselves at 100 percent masculine, and 29 percent of the sample placed themselves between 0 and 0.2.

14 What is also clear from these data, which combine responses to both types of gender identity questions into a single measure, is that, in the US data, in which we had a split sample, respondents are more likely to have a wider distribution on the scale—this is the influence of the two-dimensional question, in which respondents could place themselves on the masculine scale and the feminine scale separately. For example, while many women indicated they felt very feminine and not very masculine, mirroring the bipolar scale, many also indicated they felt very masculine and very feminine, ultimately leading them to be somewhere in the middle (hence the number of women in the United States who are at the .5 in the panel of figures).

15 These patterns provide evidence in support of the two-dimensional measure, which allows for more nuance in respondent gender identity and permits respondents to diverge from a model of gender norms in which women are always feminine and men are always masculine.

16 Respondents were asked, "Using a scale from 0–100 where 0 means not at all close and 100 means extremely close, how closely do you identify with your gender group?"

17 Compare for example, demography statistics from Statistics Canada to the US Census Bureaus's population estimates. Canada's Black population is about 4 percent of the total population, while the "visible minority" population is 22 percent of the total (Statistics Canada). In the United States, the Black (or African American) population is 14 percent of the total population, while the racialized (nonwhite) population is 24 percent (US Census Bureau). Our data approach the census distribution of each population fairly closely. Our Canadian survey data include 2 percent Black respondents and 12 percent racialized respondents. The US survey data include 12 percent Black respondents and 22 percent racialized respondents. Thus, both datasets underrepresent racialized populations.

18 Coding race in the CES is challenging due to the way that the survey instrument is designed. We borrowed coding from Meghan O'Reilly's (2021) master's thesis.

She hand-coded the open-ended "other" ethnicity categories (CPS19_ethnicity_41 and 42) and generously agreed to share her code with us.

19 Interestingly, 39 percent of those Canadians in the hypermasculine category identify with the Liberal Party, while only 2 percent identify with the PPC (Canada's most right-leaning party) and the New Democrat Party (the left-leaning party). It seems that the partisan-hypermasculine dynamic may be different in the two countries.

13

Gen Z and Politics

Masculinity, Femininity, and Beyond

MELISSA DECKMAN

Introduction

While political scientists have spilled much ink analyzing how sex impacts a wide array of political behaviors, from public opinion to vote choice to political participation, it is only in more recent years that we have begun to consider how the gendered traits of individuals or their attitudes *about* gender have colored their political views. Recent scholarship is beginning to show that attitudes about gender and considerations of masculinity and femininity may be far more consequential for understanding American political behavior than knowing whether someone identifies as female or male. Considering how Americans' attitudes about gender, as well as their own perceived gendered personalities, impact political behavior is especially important, given that an increasing number of Americans are beginning to identify their gender as beyond the gender binary, particularly Gen Z Americans, defined as Americans born between 1997 and 2012 (Dimock 2019). In 2022, Gallup found that 1 in 5 Gen Z Americans identify as LGBTQ+ compared with about 7 percent of the overall US adult population, with Gen Z women being three times as likely to identify as LGBTQ+ (Doherty 2022). Although exact estimates are hard to come by, the Williams Institute at UCLA says that there are about 1.2 million nonbinary Americans currently in the United States, among their analyses of Americans aged 18 to 60, which represents about 1 in 10 LGBTQ+ Americans; the vast majority are under the age of 29 (2021).

Gen Z is also redefining notions of masculinity and femininity on both a personal and a societal level. For instance, the advertising firm Bigeye Agency found that half of Gen Zers agree that traditional gender roles and identities are outdated; most Gen Zers also believe that society will subscribe less to gender stereotypes in the future (Clifton 2021). As a result, Gen Z is more likely than older Americans to challenge notions of what some consider to be the "toxic" or negative consequences that stem from traditional depictions of masculinity. While the #MeToo Movement shed light on the pervasiveness of sexual harassment in American society writ large, it has also potentially shaped a generation of young Americans, regardless of sexual and gender identity, to further reconsider the more traditional culture of masculinity (Keller 2018). Most young Americans, according to data from PRRI, believe that young men face pressure to conform to traditional masculine stereotypes, although younger women are more likely to strongly believe this than young men (Jones et al. 2018).

This chapter takes a deeper dive into how issues regarding gender identity, self-perceptions of masculinity and femininity, and masculinity attitudes pertain to Generation Z. Using an original dataset of 2250 Gen Z Americans that I collected in July 2019, I compare the political behavior of noncisgender Gen Z Americans and cisgender Gen Zers (both straight and LGBTQ+) with respect to partisanship and political participation. Next, I ask Gen Z Americans of all genders to rate their own perceived masculinity and femininity and analyze how such self-perceptions relate to political behavior. Lastly, I tackle the issue of toxic masculinity attitudes by asking Gen Zers whether such societal pressure for men to behave a certain way leads to negative effectives on society, creating a toxic masculinity scale to determine whether views about toxic masculinity also shape partisanship and behaviors.

Among Gen Z Americans, identifying beyond the cisgender binary results in higher levels of political engagement among Gen Z as well as a greater propensity to identify as a Democrat. In contrast to other work on Americans more broadly, femininity (not masculinity) works as an agent to drive political participation rates higher among Gen Z women; gender traits do not affect the political participation rates of Gen Z men. However, attitudes about gender stereotypes influence the political choices of *both* Gen Z women and men. Scoring higher on the toxic masculinity scale, which denotes agreement that pressuring young men to behave in traditional masculine ways can lead to toxic behaviors, results in a greater propensity to identify as Democratic and to engage at higher levels of political participation for both cisgender Gen Z men and women.

Masculinity and Femininity in American Political Behavior

For decades, political scientists and pundits have examined how women and men differ when it comes to their voting behavior (Welch and Hibbing 1992; Chaney, Alveraz, and Nagler 1998; Carroll 2006; Ondercin 2017), partisanship (Kaufmann and Petrocik 1999; Kanthak and Norrander 2004), public opinion (Shapiro and Mahajan 1986; Howell and Day 2000; Schlesinger and Heldman 2001; Box-Steffensmeier, De Boef and Lin 2004; Norrander 2008, 2020), and political participation more generally (Burns, Schlozman, and Verba 2001; Burns et al. 2019). Many—though not all—such gender differences are much less important than the powerful influence of partisanship on political behavior, as women are far from politically monolithic in their political views (Deckman 2016; Barnes and Cassese 2017).

Scholars are increasingly recognizing that attitudes *about* gender may explain far more about political behavior among Americans than knowing whether someone identifies as female or male. After controlling for sex and partisanship, recent studies find that voters who held traditional views about gender roles and hostile sexist views were more likely to vote for Donald Trump in the 2016 election, controlling for party and sex (Bock and Byrd-Craven 2017; Cassese and Barnes 2017; Cassese and Holman 2019; Junn 2017; Schaffner, McWilliams, and Nteta 2018). Further, Deckman and Cassese (2021) found that attitudes regarding gendered nationalism—whether individuals believe that America has gotten too soft and feminine—drove votes for Donald Trump for president by both women and men, even after controlling for partisanship and other factors.

While studies about the impact of gender attitudes in explaining Americans' political choices are becoming more common, scholars are beginning to recognize that self-perceptions of masculinity and femininity also shape Americans' political behavior, including Monika

McDermott's (2016) important book, *Masculinity, Femininity, and American Political Behavior*. McDermott argues that "masculinity and femininity are distinct personality traits that influence individuals' social attitudes and behavior" (4). Societal changes that have allowed for men and women to have a greater diversity of career choices and to become more adept at coparenting means that not all men will primarily share masculine traits, nor will all women primarily share feminine traits. Thus, significant portions of the population have gendered personality traits that are not linked to their biological sex (McDermott, 16–17), although work by political scientists Amanda Bittner and Elizabeth Goodyear-Grant (2017) shows that about 70 percent of individuals largely match their biological identification with the more "conventional" gender traits of masculinity and femininity. For McDermott's part, she finds that citizens with higher levels of masculine traits are more likely to identify with the Republican Party, while femininity among Americans increases their propensity to identify as Democrats; Cassino and Besen-Cassino (2022) corroborate these findings. The latter's work also finds that consideration of gender traits may have a more pronounced impact on the political behavior of men; indeed, Cassino and Besen-Cassino (2021) find that merely *asking* men on surveys to express their gender identity led them to identify as Republicans, compared with men who were not asked that question in a survey experiment. Additionally, in the 2016 presidential election, Cassino (2018) finds in experimental research that male voters in New Jersey who were primed to consider gender norms were more likely to favor Donald Trump over Hillary Clinton in the election. Yet no effect of gendered priming exists among women (Cassino 2018; Cassino and Besen-Cassino 2021), which suggests that the political impact of gender identity may actually be better interpreted as involving threats to masculinity.

Scholars from various discipline for the past several decades have analyzed the negative societal effects of masculinity (see, e.g., Kimmel 2013), what sociologists and psychologists term "toxic masculinity," although its impact on political behavior remains somewhat underdeveloped, at least in the American context (but see Cassino and Besen-Cassino 2022). As McDermott and Jones note in this volume, measuring the concept of toxic masculinity, with its roots in psychology, can be challenging, but the authors point to how such earlier attempts are linked to adherence or conformity to male role norms and to behaviors such as depression. In the field of international relations, feminist scholars often consider how masculinity is linked to violence extremism and militarism (see, e.g., Zalewski and Parpart 2019; Pearson 2019); other work examines how narratives of "masculinity in crisis" have allowed far right groups internationally and in the United States to recruit followers and to perpetuate strict, heteronormative, and patriarchal norms (Grieg 2019; Kimmel 2013). Some scholars also consider how political parties use masculine tropes to build support, particularly overseas. For instance, Daddow and Hernter (2021) develop a conceptual framework that considers how toxic masculinity shapes the policy development and discourse of two popular right-wing parties, the Alternative for Germany (AfD) and the UK Independence Party (UKip). In both cases, they provide ample evidence that both parties are imbued with the ethos "that traditional masculinity is under threat" and "tolerate a culture of the abuse and harassment of women" (749).

In the American context, considering the linkage between toxic masculinity and public behavior is still less well understood, although the efforts by governments to mitigate the COVID-19 pandemic through public health measures has led to some research that links masculine views and public opinion. For instance, Palmer and Peterson (2020) found that Americans who embrace "masculine norms of toughness" are less likely to view wearing a mask positively—although such norms apply to both men and women. Increasingly, then, scholars are beginning to examine, apart from party, ideology, gender, and other factors, how toxic masculinity filters into our political choices. These questions are particularly important to consider among Gen Zers, who are entering adulthood during a time of intense critical national conversations about the #MeToo movement, women's rights, and gender identity, and who, themselves, are far more fluid in terms of their gender identity than previous generations.

Method

Data for this paper come from a survey I conducted through Qualtrics Panels in July 2019 of 2,250 Americans aged eighteen through twenty-two at the time of administration, representing Americans who are born after 1996, following the definition of "Gen Z" set forth by demographers. Qualtrics Panels draws its respondents from a national panel it recruits through a variety of websites, using incentives. Although this sampling procedure is not random, the survey was designed to be representative of the adult Gen Z population based on gender, race, and region, and the data are weighted accordingly (see appendix table A13.1 for a demographic breakdown of the survey and how Gen Z compares with older Americans).

My survey included six response options in terms of gender identity: female, male, trans female/trans woman, trans male/trans man, genderqueer/gender nonconforming or a different identity. I also asked respondents if they are straight, homosexual, bisexual or some other category in terms of their sexual orientation. With respect to self-described gender traits, respondents were asked to select, on a scale of 1 to 10, where 1 is the most masculine and 10 is the most feminine, the number that best describes their own trait. Finally, I asked respondents a series of questions, drawn from the 2018 PRRI/MTV study of young millennials and Gen Zers, concerning whether respondents believe (yes/no) that there are any negative consequences that come from society pressuring men to act in traditionally masculine ways, such as preventing them from expressing their emotions in healthy ways, limiting the type of friendships men can have with other men, leading mean to treat women as weaker and less capable, or encouraging violent or homophobic behavior. Notably, McDermott and Jones in this volume tap into similar themes in their measure, such as fears around being thought of as gay and male domination over women—though their scale also taps into how winning at all costs is linked to masculinity. These six questions are then used as the basis for a toxic masculinity scale.

Gender Identity and Political Behavior

Turning first to gender identity, 48 percent of Gen Z respondents are cisgender female (N = 1077), 47 percent are cisgender male (N = 1066), and the remaining 5 percent are noncisgender (N = 107), with 44 respondents indicating that they are transgender, 48 respondents who are genderqueer or nonconforming, and 15 choosing a different identity. With respect to sexual orientation, most respondents identify as heterosexual—74 percent—with 6 percent identifying as homosexual and 14 percent identifying as bisexual and 5 percent as something other. When both gender identity and sexual orientation are considered together, 26 percent of my sample falls into the LGBTQ+ category (N = 585). Gen Zers who are not cisgender, then, make up about 18 percent of LGBTQ+ Gen Zers overall—a higher number than the data from the Williams Institute, which reports that about 11 percent of LGBTQ+ Americans are noncisgender. It is important to remember, however, that their work examines Americans aged 18 to 60, so my data show that Gen Z Americans express more comfort in identifying outside of the gender binary.

Next, I consider how gender identity is linked to partisanship, and I include the category of LGBTQ+ Gen Zers as a point of comparison (inclusive of both cisgender and trans/binary folks; see fig. 13.1). For Gen Z men and women who are cisgender, identifying as a Democrat is the plurality category, although Gen Z women identify as Democrats at higher rates. Notably, well over half (56 percent) of Gen Z Americans who are LGBTQ+ identify as Democrats. Democratic identification jumps dramatically, however, among noncisgender Gen Zers, with almost two-thirds identifying as Democratic. While relatively few Gen Zers identify as Republicans overall, only 15 percent of LGBTQ+ Gen Z and noncisgender Gen Z Americans claim the GOP mantle. Notably, though, in all categories, Gen Z Americans identify as "pure" independents at about double the rates of older Americans (Devine 2018).

I also asked Gen Z Americans about their political participation habits. Specifically, I asked Gen Zers whether they had engaged in any of 17 different political activities in the past year, ranging from discussing politics with friends and family, using social media for political purposes, or the more retail sorts of politics, including protesting, attending meetings, or volunteering for campaigns.[1] On average, Gen Z Americans reported engaging in 3.61 political actions, with cisgender Gen Z men engaging in fewer political actions (3.31) than cisgender Gen Z women (3.81). However, both LGBTQ+ Gen Zers and those who are trans/nonbinary report significantly higher levels of engagement than other Gen Zers: LGBTQ+ Gen Zers engaged in 4.05 political actions compared with 3.46 political actions among their straight counterparts.[2]

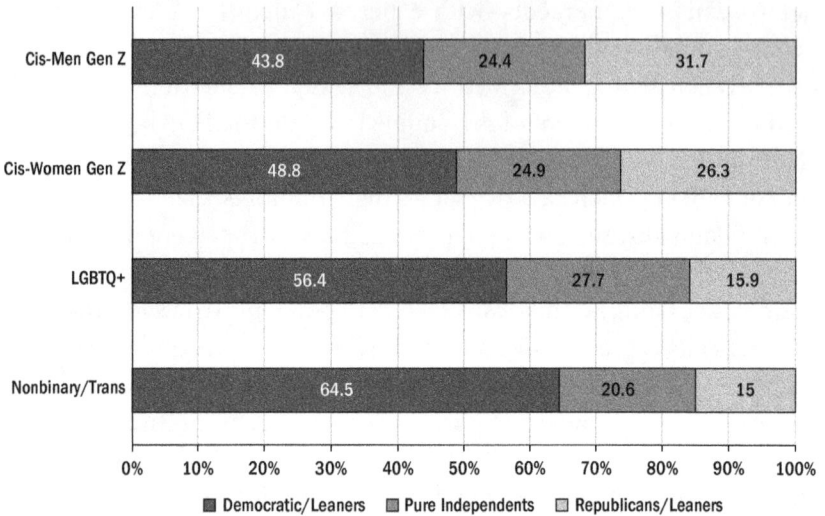

Figure 13.1: Gen Z partisanship by gender identity and sexual orientation

Gen Zers who identify as beyond the gender binary reported the highest levels of political engagement overall: 4.30 political actions.[3]

That both LGBTQ+ and transgender/nonbinary folks are the most engaged among Generation Z may be linked to their own personal experience facing discrimination in society—and their prioritization of LGBTQ+ equality as a political concern. I asked Gen Z Americans about their political priorities, specifically whether a host of issues are critically important to them personally, one among many important issues, or not that important compared to other issues. While some issues revealed few differences among Gen Z regardless of their gender identity or sexual orientation, such as infrastructure, jobs, education, or terrorism, LGBTQ+ Gen Zers stood out from their cisgender counterparts when it comes to prioritizing numerous progressive concerns, especially student debt, climate change, health care, and, especially, equal rights for marginalized groups (see fig. 13.2). Their prioritization of LGBTQ+ rights, for instance, is perhaps not as surprising because of their own identities as not straight. Given the strongly Democratic partisanship leanings of LGBTQ+ and, especially, noncisgender Gen Zers, it is also little surprise that they tend to prioritize issues pertaining to human rights.

It is still notable that Gen Z Americans who are trans or nonbinary are far more liberal on all of these issues compared with other LGBTQ+ Americans. Their prioritization of racial inequality, gender equality, and LGBT rights, in particular, are even higher than among LGBTQ+ Gen Z Americans writ large and may be key to understanding why nonbinary Gen Zers engage in politics at higher levels than others in their generation.

The Gender Spectrum and Political Behavior among Gen Z

In addition to questions regarding their gender identity, my 2019 National Gen Z Survey also asked Gen Zers to rate themselves with respect to their own self-perceived gender traits on a scale of 1 being most masculine and 10 being most feminine. Figure 13.3 shows the

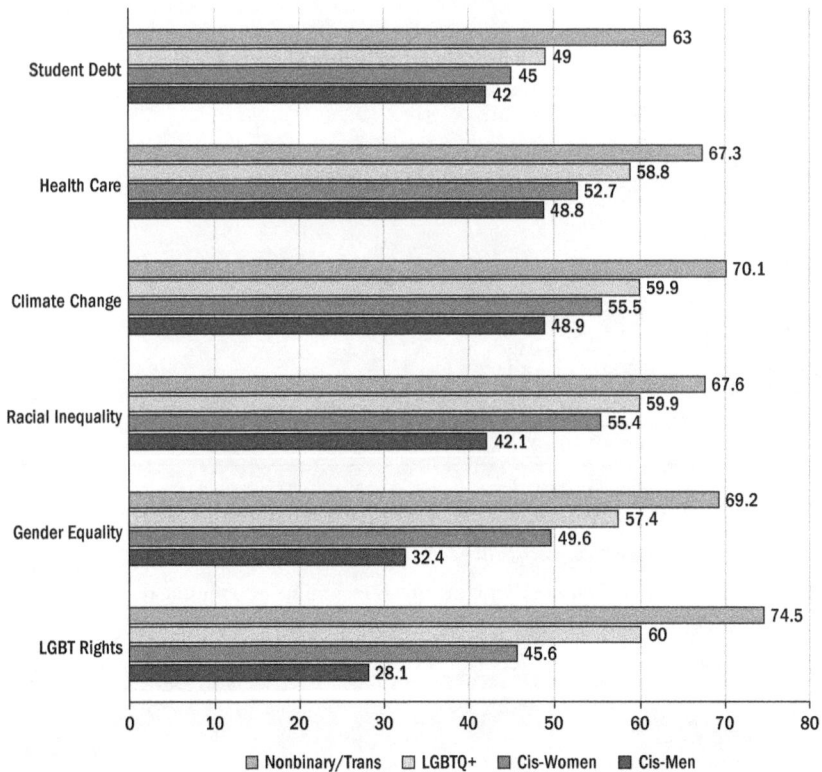

Figure 13.2: Percentage of Gen Z Americans who say the following are critical issues

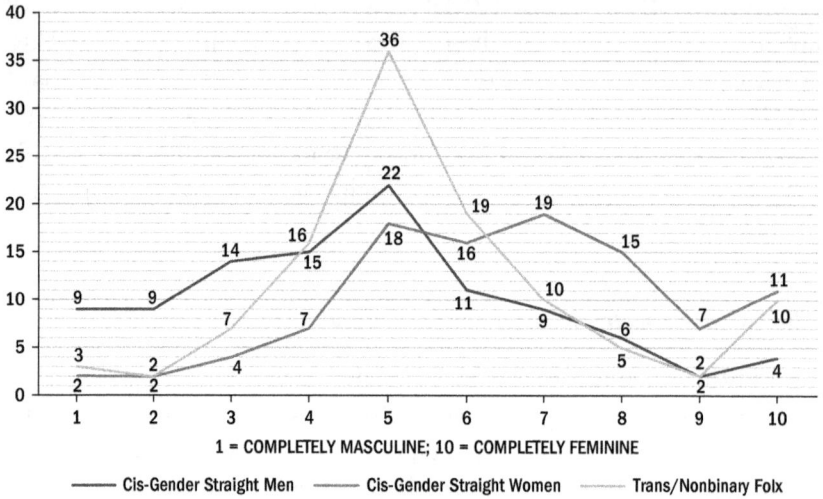

Figure 13.3: Percent of Gen Zers who identify as masculine or feminine on 10-point scale

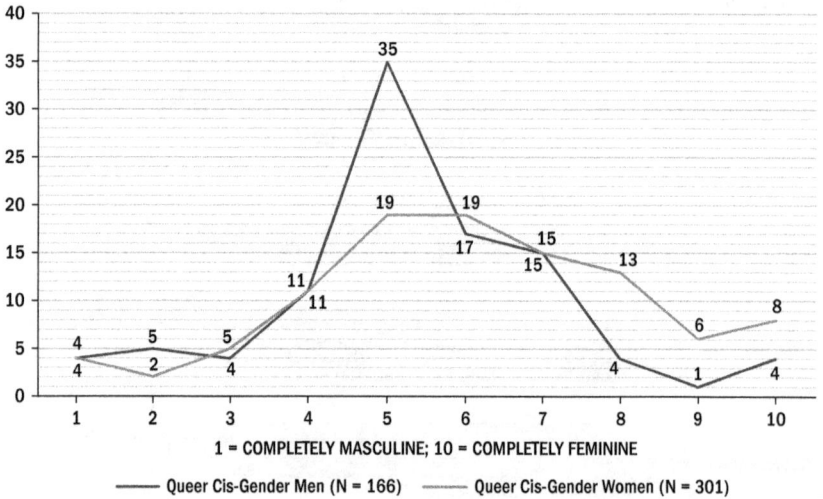

Figure 13.4: Percent of Gen Zers who identify as masculine or feminine on 10-point scale

distribution of scores for cisgender straight men, cisgender straight women, and trans/nonbinary Gen Zers; I also present the distribution of scores for LGBTQ+ Gen Zers who are cisgender male and female as a point of comparison in figure 13.4.

Turning first to figure 13.3, while the gender identity of trans/ nonbinary Gen Zers ranges from 1 to 10, the clear plurality chose the middle score of 5, which is at much higher levels than cisgender straight men and women. Similarly, figure 13.4 shows that 35 percent of LGBTQ+ cisgender men similarly place themselves at the score of 5, with a more respondents choosing scores closer to the most feminine option. By contrast, LGBTQ+ cisgender Gen Z women have a range of scores that is more balanced and more closely mirrors straight cisgender Gen Z women. Even Gen Z men who are straight and cisgender have a pretty dispersed range of values in terms of self-described gender identity, but they are the only group that has more self-rankings on the lower end (more masculine) than the higher end (more feminine).

How are such self-perceived gender traits linked to partisanship and political participation among Gen Z Americans? I've divided Gen Zers into predominately masculine identifiers (those who placed themselves 1 through 3 on the scale), feminine identifiers (those who place themselves 8 through 10 on the scale), and mixed identifiers (those who place themselves 4 through 7 in the scale). Among Gen Z Americans in total, there is a statistically significant relationship between self-professed gender traits and partisanship. As Gen Zers identify themselves with higher feminine traits, they are more likely to identify as Democrats: 50 percent of feminine Gen Zers are Democratic compared with 32 percent of feminine Gen Zers who are Republican.[4] Likewise, 32 percent of masculine Gen Zers identify as Democratic compared with 38 percent who identify as Republicans (see table 13.1).

Generation Z

Differences with respect to partisanship and self-described gender traits are more pronounced among LGBTQ+ Gen Z Americans than those who are cisgender, however. In all cases except those Gen Zers who are trans/nonbinary, likely due to the preponderance of Democrats

TABLE 13.1: Relationship between masculine-feminine traits and party identification among° Gen Z

	Democrats (Percentage)	Independents (Percentage)	Republican (Percentage)
All Gen Z Americans			
Masculine	32	30	38
Mixed	51	25	24
Feminine	50	18	32
Cisgender straight men (N = 896)*			
Masculine	32	24	44
Mixed	49	25	26
Feminine	38	18	44
Cisgender LGBTQ+ men (N = 165)#			
Masculine	42	46	13
Mixed	57	24	20
Feminine	79	7	14
Cisgender straight women (N = 769)*			
Masculine	27	46	27
Mixed	48	23	29
Feminine	50	16	34
Cisgender LGBTQ+ women (N = 300)#			
Masculine	30	47	23
Mixed	55	30	15
Feminine	61	26	13
Trans/nonbinary Gen Zers (N = 108)			
Masculine	54	31	15
Mixed	68	20	13
Feminine	50	25	25

in this groups, the relationship between gender traits and partisanship are statistically significant. Reading the row columns among each of those categories, we see, for instance, that there is a positive relationship among cisgender straight men between identifying as masculine and identifying as Republican: 32 percent identify as Democrats compared with 44 percent who identify as Republican. Yet cisgender straight Gen Z men who self-identify as more feminine are still slightly more likely to identify as Republican—38 percent to 44 percent, respectively. The relationship between gender traits and partisanship among Gen Z Americans who are cisgender and LGBTQ+, is much stronger: for instance, 79 percent of LGBTQ+ cisgender men who describe themselves as feminine are Democrats, as are 61 percent of LGBTQ+

cisgender women. Even among Gen Z Americans, then, the most gender-fluid of all generations, masculinity is linked to a greater likelihood of identifying as Republicans—a pattern found among Americans more generally (McDermott 2016).

When it comes to political participation, however, Gen Z bucks Monika McDermott's earlier research, which finds that masculinity is linked to higher levels of political engagement. Among Gen Z, it is actually Gen Z Americans who identify as more *feminine* who engage at significantly higher levels in the past year (3.97 political activities) compared with Gen Z Americans who identify as masculine (3.33 political activities).[5] Breaking those categories down into cisgender men, cisgender women, and nonbinary Americans, however, those self-identified traits are not at all linked to the political participation habits of cisgender men, who express pretty uniform levels of engagement, regardless of whether they see themselves primarily as masculine, feminine, or somewhere in between (see fig. 13.5). By contrast, identifying as more feminine drives Gen Z women to engage in politics at higher levels.[6] While the differences in terms of gender traits and gender identity appear the largest among trans/nonbinary Gen Zers, it is important to remember that the

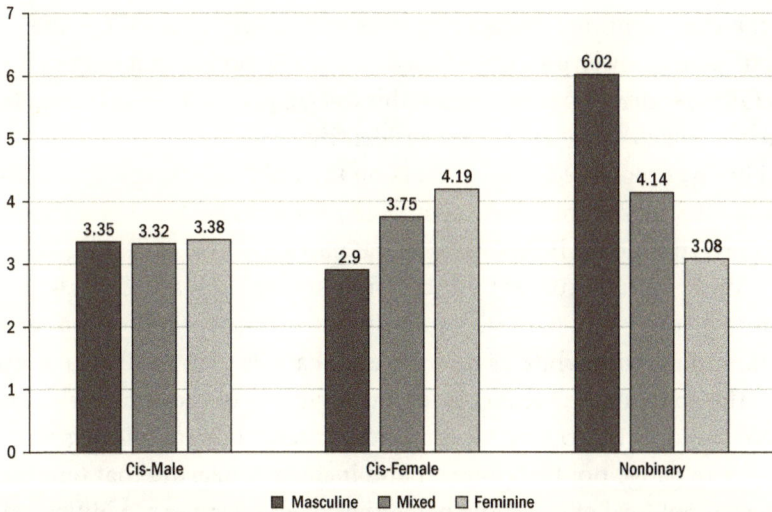

Figure 13.5: Mean number of political actions by gender identity and gender traits

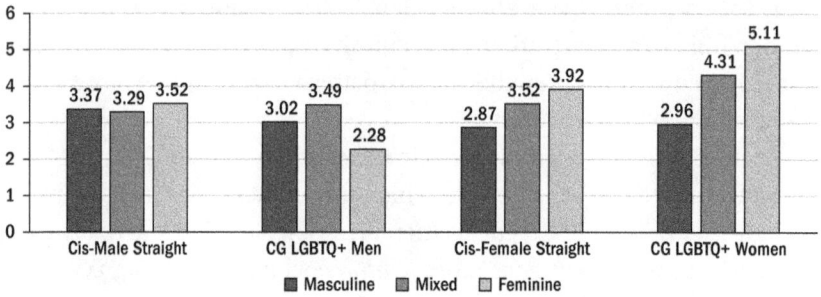

Figure 13.6: Mean level political engagement among cisgender Gen Z Americans by LGBTQ+ status and gender traits

vast majority of those Americans are in the "mixed" gender traits category among this group; just 13 (12 percent) identify as masculine leaning while 8 (7 percent) identify as feminine leaning, so these results should be interpreted with some caution.

Considering the relationship between gender traits and political engagement among cisgender Gen Z Americans by LGBTQ+ status, figure 13.6 shows that that the positive relationship between femininity and political engagement is even more pronounced among LGBTQ+ women, although it still exists among straight Gen Z women. While identifying as the most feminine category appears to lead Gen Z LGBTQ+ men to participate in fewer political actions, it is worth noting that only 14 Gen Z LGBTQ+ men (8 percent) are in this category; most LGBTQ+ men fall into the mixed category for gender identity.

Finally, I regressed gender traits on the political engagement scale, using OLS regression while controlling for a range of other variables that are commonly linked to political participation, including socioeconomic status (current educational status, education goals, and family income) and identities such as race/ethnicity (coded as a series of dummies, with white as the reference category) or LGBTQ+ status (see the appendix, table A13.2, for a description of these variables and their coding). I also control for whether respondents follow politics closely to gauge political interest and include a measure that taps into internal political efficacy, the belief that one understands politics, and external political efficacy, measured here as agreement with whether the political system responds to one's needs (in the model, the variable is coded such that higher levels indicates respondents are more likely to *disagree* with that sentiment). I include a measure of partisan strength (0 = pure independent; 1 = leaners or weak partisans; 2 = strong partisans) as well as political ideology (1 = very conservative; 7 = very liberal). Given that these respondents are young, I also asked them how many civic or social activities they engaged in while in high school, to see if they had developed any sort of organizing skills that might carry over into political participation. Following the work of Harhie Han (2009), which argues that Americans' "issue publics" are important for understanding political participation among Americans with lower socioeconomic status, I include a cumulative measure of the number of issues that respondents reported being critically important to them, which ranges from 0 to 14. I included measures that consider whether Gen Zers had been contacted by political parties, campaigns, or groups in the past year, as mobilization studies show that being asked to be involved in politics raises levels of overall political participation (Rosenstone and Hansen 1994). I also asked Gen Zers whether they had positive emotional reactions (feeling happy, enthusiastic, hopeful, or proud) or negative emotional reactions (feeling angry, nervous, afraid, or disgusted) about how things are going in the country these days, to tap into the role that emotions play in shaping political engagement levels (see, e.g., Valentino et al. 2018). Finally, I include a control for church attendance, again to capture whether civic engagement in one form spills over into political engagement overall for Gen Zers.

Figure 13.7 shows the results of those regression analyses, run separately for Gen Z women and men, in the form of a graph plot (all the variables have been normalized so that they range from 0 to 1, for ease of interpretation). In the full model (see the appendix, table A13.3), I find that self-reported gender traits are not significantly related to overall levels of political engagement once I control for the factors that are commonly linked to political participation among Americans. (I did not run a separate model for trans/nonbinary Gen Zers, as there are too few cases.) However, when I run separate models for Gen Z women and Gen Z men (all of whom are cisgender in these cases), the more Gen Z women identify as feminine, the higher levels of political engagement they undertake. Moving from the lowest to the highest value on the masculine/feminine scale results in .73 more activities on the political

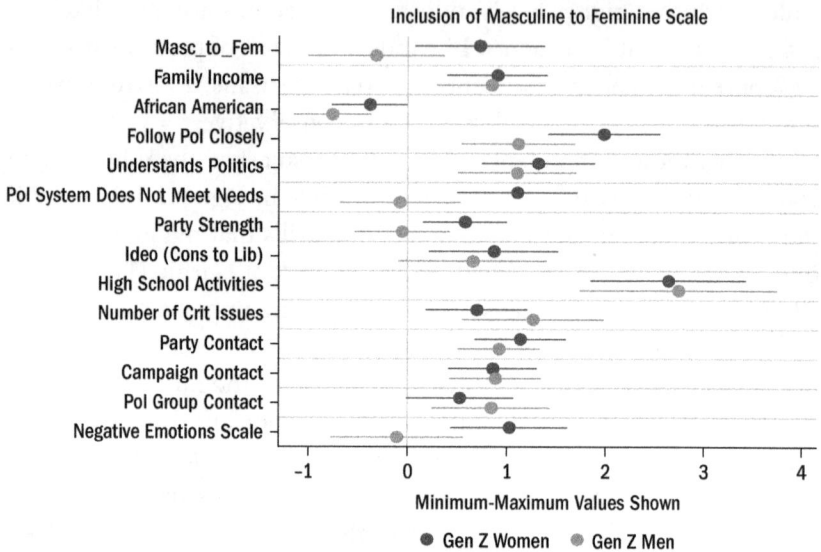

Figure 13.7: Political engagement model, inclusion of masculine to feminine scale

engagement scale. This positive bump can be seen in figure 13.7, at the top of the plot; in this version of the graph, I omit showing the independent variables that are not statistically significant; the full versions of the models can be found in the appendix (table A13.3). For Gen Z men, however, there is no significant relationship at all between femininity and political participation, as the plot shows. In contrast to previous research on the impact of gender traits on American political behavior, then, I find that, among Gen Z, placing oneself as more feminine is propelling higher levels of engagement among this nascent generation—but for cisgender women only.

Gender traits aren't the most important factor in explaining the political participation levels of Gen Z women, as the plots demonstrate. Interest in politics, family income, internal and external efficacy, past civic and organizational experience in high school, and identifying as a political liberal, in addition to having a negative emotional response to the state of the country, matter more to the overall participation levels of Gen Z women. But the relationship between feminine identity and political engagement is stronger than being a strong partisan or personally caring about a lot of political issues. That femininity is driving higher levels of political engagement among Gen Z women is an important and notable finding, considering that the opposite relationship exists among the public in past studies.

Toxic Masculinity and Political Engagement among Generation Z

Having considered the relationship between political participation and the impact of gender identity/sexual orientation and self-described gender traits among Generation Z, I lastly consider how attitudes *about* gender shape their political engagement. Borrowing a battery of questions concerning society's expectations for young men to behave in traditionally masculine ways used by a PRRI/MTV survey from 2018, I create a "toxic masculinity" scale. Specifically, I ask respondents if they agree or disagree that when society pressures men to behave in traditionally masculine ways, it results in six negative or "toxic" behaviors: prevents men from expressing their emotions in healthy ways; limits the type of friendships men can have with other men; leads men to treat women as weaker and less capable; and encourages sexual aggressiveness, violent behavior, and homophobic attitudes. I created a scale combining these six questions—those who score 0 would disagree with each of these assertions, and those who score 6 would agree with every assertion. The higher the score on the toxic masculinity scale, the more likely the respondent believes that societal pressure for men to behave in masculine ways has negative consequences. The scale's reliability is high (Cronbach's alpha = .773). The average score among young Americans is 3.66, with a relatively high standard deviation (1.92), so, while most young Americans agree that societal pressure for men to conform to masculine standards has some pernicious or toxic societal effects, there is a fairly wide distribution of responses.

Looking at the national average on the belief in toxic masculinity scale obscures significant differences based on both gender identity and sexual orientation (see fig. 13.8). Trans/nonbinary Gen Zers have the highest score when it comes to their views on whether there are toxic masculine pressures faced by men in American society at 4.74.[7] LGBTQ+ cisgender Gen Zers also have high higher scores on the scale than their straight counterparts, with LGBTQ+ women scoring 4.18 and LGBTQ+ men scoring 3.76. The outlying group here is cisgender

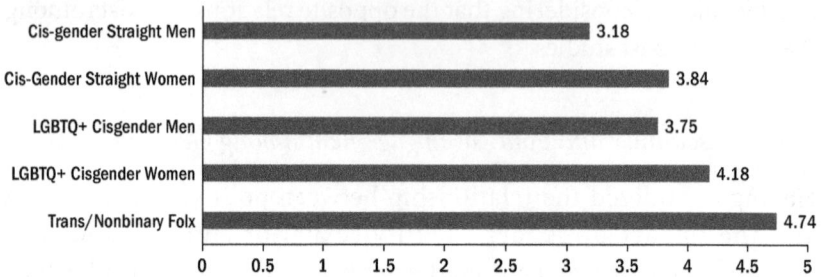

Figure 13.8: Toxic masculinity beliefs scores by gender, gender identity, and sexual orientation

straight men, who score 3.18, which is also far lower than the average score for cisgender straight women, whose average is 3.84.

Finally, I consider how negative views of toxic masculinity are linked to partisanship and political participation levels among Gen Z Americans. Looking at Gen Z nationally, there is a significant relationship between party identification and average toxic masculinity attitude scores. Republicans, perhaps not surprisingly, on average score a 3.03, while Independents score 3.35. Democrats are the most likely to think that pressure on men to act in traditionally masculine ways will yield the most negative effects on society, as their average score is 4.19.[8] These relationships also exist when I control for gender identity: for cisgender women, cisgender men, and nonbinary individuals, the higher their scores on the measure, the more likely they are to identify as Democrats. Finally, I also find a significant relationship between scores on the toxic masculinity scale and political engagement levels. Gen Z Americans who don't ascribe any negative behaviors to societal pressure for men to behave in traditionally masculine ways—those who score a 0 on the toxic masculinity scale—participated in an average of 2.61 political acts in 2019. By contrast, those with the highest score on the scale (6) engaged in an average of 4.56 political acts in 2019.

Returning to the regression model of political engagement among Gen Z Americans, adding the toxic masculinity belief scale reveals some important distinctions between the impact of gender identity, on the one hand, and beliefs about the negative stereotypes regarding masculinity, on the other, when it comes to the political participation levels of Gen Z Americans. (To avoid multicollinearity concerns, I removed the self-described gender traits variable from the model.) While gender identity was previously linked to the political engagement levels of Gen Z women, but not Gen Z men, attitudes about gender in the form of masculine pressure works to enhance participation levels for both Gen Z women *and* men, as shown in figure 13.9. (In this version of the graph, I omit showing the independent variables that are not statistically significant; the full versions of the models can be found in the appendix, table A13.4.). Normalizing the toxic masculinity scale such that the values range from 0 to 1, I find that moving from the belief that masculine pressures lead to no negative effects to the belief that such pressures lead to 6 negative effects results in a .536 increase in the number of political acts undertaken by Gen Z men in the past year (p = 053). For Gen Z women, the impact of believing masculine pressures result in negative or toxic results is even more pronounced, as moving from 0 to 1 on the normalized results in almost a full point increase (.918) on the political engagement scale even while controlling for a wide assortment of variables.

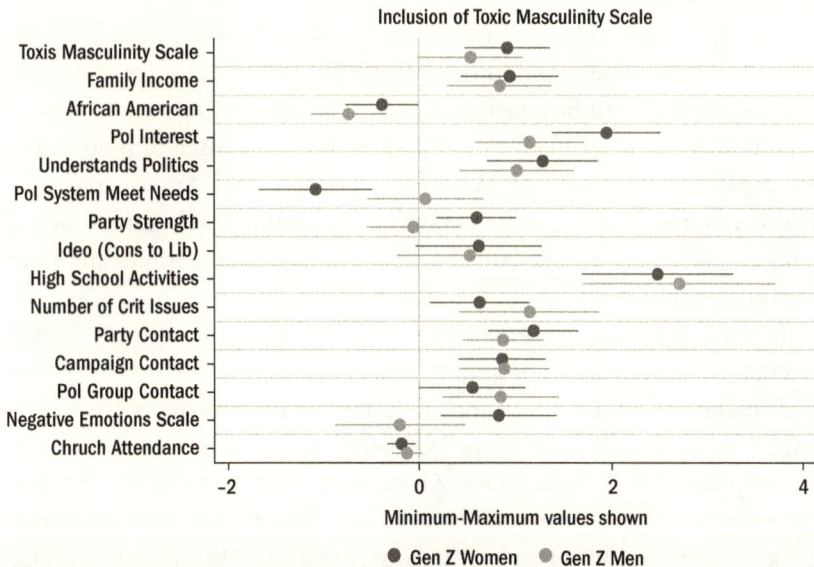

Figure 13.9: Political engagement model, inclusion of toxic masculinity scale

Conclusion

Generation Z is the most gender-fluid generation of Americans to date and is less accepting of traditional gender norms than older Americans. These attributes of Gen Z also spill over into their partisanship and to their decisions to participate in politics in ways that are unique to their generation. In what may be one of the first studies to compare the political choices of noncisgender Gen Zers to their cisgender counterparts, my research here finds that trans/nonbinary Gen Zers are far more likely to identify as Democrats, prioritize progressive concerns, and participate in politics at higher levels, even more than cisgender LGBTQ+ Gen Z Americans. Of course, this study only includes about one hundred cases of noncisgender Gen Zers, so future research needs to find ways to incorporate and measure this growing group of young Americans, as, at least in this case, the evidence suggests that identification as a gender minority may be propelling more engagement in politics. Given growing debates in state legislatures around the country concerning the rights of trans/nonbinary youth, and the medical treatment that they seek, consideration of the political views and attitudes of the marginalized group is more essential than ever.

A burgeoning body of scholarship is also beginning to consider the impact of masculine or feminine traits on the political choices of Americans, and earlier studies have concluded that masculinity traits among men and women is linked to Republican partisanship and higher levels of political engagement. When it comes to Gen Z Americans, masculinity is linked to Republican partisanship for both cisgender Gen Z women and men, straight and LGBTQ+, while femininity is linked to Democratic partisanship.

However, a greater propensity to identify as *feminine* leads Gen Z women to participate in politics at higher levels, which counters previous research. Gender traits appear to matter little to the political engagement level of Gen Z men. Why might this be the case? Political participation levels among Gen Z women are significantly higher than Gen Z men, which, historically, is a notable first (Deckman 2018). There are a variety of reasons that may help us understand this historic reverse gender gap in political participation, including the reemergence of the women's movement in wake of Donald Trump's election, the #MeToo Movement, and the election of younger, dynamic women to prominent political offices, such as congresswoman Alexandria Ocasio-Cortez, leading to an enhanced role-model effect for girls and young women (see Deckman and McDonald 2022; Campbell and Wolbrecht 2020). When the face of politics becomes more female, as it is for Generation Z, femininity is no longer a barrier to political engagement, and instead becomes a positive attribute for political engagement.

At the same time, Gen Z men are not immune to the shifting dynamics about gender stereotypes and what denotes acceptable masculine behavior in society today. Both Gen Z women and men who believe that societal pressure for men to conform to traditional masculinity results in negative or toxic behaviors, such as being emotionally less healthy, limiting friendships with men, or encouraging homophobia or sexism, are more likely to participate in politics. Part of this linkage is likely linked to the current political milieu, in which Gen Z is strongly committed to fighting for the rights of marginalized groups in society in an increasingly racially, ethnically, and LGBTQ+ society. Gen Z is the most diverse generation in American history on all these fronts, and concerns about toxic masculinity and gender rights are leading to new patterns and behaviors when it comes to political participation.

NOTES

1 Those activities include the following: discussed politics with family; discussed politics with friends; encourages others to vote; liked a political group or candidate online; signed a petition online; visited political websites; donated to a political candidate or cause; advocated for a political candidate or cause online; attended a political rally; wrote a letter to an elected official; talked to a legislator; attended a government meeting; served as a poll worker; ran for political office, including in school; applied to serve on a community board; or tried to influence how others' voted.

2 This difference is statistically significant (T = 4.59; p < .001).

3 Differences among trans/nonbinary, cisgender women and cisgender men are statistically significant (F = 12.51; p < .001).

4 These differences in terms of partisanship and self-identified gender traits among Gen Z Americans are statistically significant (Chi-Square = 63.89; p < .001).

5 T = 3.51; p < .001; the relationship between femininity and political participation remains significant when I regress the full ten-point gender trait scale onto the

political participation scale. Gen Z Americans who are in the middle category in terms of gender traits engaged in an average of 3.59 political activities.

6 $T = 3.75$; $p < .001$.

7 Differences among trans/nonbinary, cisgender women and cisgender men on the toxic masculinity scale are statistically significant ($F = 49.48$; $p < .001$).

8 Differences among Republicans, Independents, and Democrats on the toxic masculinity belief scores are statistically significant ($F = 82.21$; $p < .001$).

Conclusion

What Do We Know, and Where Do We Go from Here?

DAN CASSINO AND MONIKA L. MCDERMOTT

Donald Trump did not invent the use of masculinity in American politics, and the end of Trump's political career will not mean the end of the centrality of masculinity to understanding the political world. What Trump did was to make explicit and salient the undercurrents of masculinity in our political system, to force us to reckon with them in a new way and to highlight dynamics that had previously been easier to ignore.

Nearly every quantitative study in political science makes use of sex as a control variable. When researchers include this control—which might be as simple as a dummy variable for male or female, or a more nuanced variable, with categories for nonbinary or transgender people—they are acknowledging that gender matters, often without really thinking through what that means. When researchers control for sex, even if they arre using a variable labeled as "gender," they are not doing so because they are worried about confounds arising from reproductive organs, but rather because they recognize that society shapes the behaviors and attitudes of men and women in very different ways and are using sex categories as a blunt instrument to get at those differences.

Not too long ago, this might have seemed like a reasonable approach, but one of the many lessons of the past few years of US politics has been that gender matters. Yes, there is a mean difference in the political attitudes and behaviors of men and women, but, within those categories, as well as across them, there is also enormous variation. As gender, and especially masculinity, have become more salient, it has become more important to understand that within sex variation. In a word, we *must* understand gender better.

As the chapters in this book have amply shown, gender—as distinct from sex and sexuality—is a powerful explanatory variable in many aspects of American political life, from the behavior of candidates and voters to the way that children learn about politics and political leaders. Politicians consciously shape how they present themselves as masculine, and voters respond to these appeals. Masculinity is baked into the way that people understand themselves as social and political actors, and into their very identities—but it is also baked into our political system. So, in order to understand that political system, and how people behave within it, we need to understand masculinity.

What We Have Learned

There is no easy way to summarize the findings presented in this volume, but we can take away some broad conclusions.

Masculinity is central to how people understand the political world, shaping how schoolchildren see political leaders, how voters view candidates, and even what people know about American politics. We know that individuals learn about politics by building up from early observations, from parental input, what they experience in their communities, and even from political events that they experience. These foundational parts of our political histories shape the way that we view all subsequent political events, and the defense mechanisms of motivated reasoning and hot cognition make people loath to question or abandon them. To the list of foundational elements in our political perceptions, we can add masculinity. We learn about the gendering of politics early in our lives, and it shapes everything that comes afterward.

Masculinity is also a major fault line in political attitudes and behaviors. It shapes political ideology and efficacy and issue positions, and work on younger Americans shows that these fault lines are not going away anytime soon, and they may even become more relevant as time goes on. There is little disagreement about the importance of other social identities, like race, ethnicity and religion to political behavior, and it certainly seems that gender—as opposed to sex—has similarly important effects.

But, in addition to operating on the level of the individual, masculinity suffuses every level of American politics. Just as parties in American politics are cognitive constructs to voters and organizations for elections and organizational principles for officials within government, masculinities serve different functions and lead to different outcomes for voters and officials and in elections, but are present, and linked, nonetheless. For example, candidates make masculinity appeals, the attitudes and actions of voters may be driven by responses to candidate masculinity or even by voters' own desires to assert masculinities, and even the parties themselves are seen as masculine (Republican) or feminine (Democrat). Masculinities are not just an aspect of how we think about politics; they are part of the way that our political system is organized.

While there is an overriding internal logic to how masculinity operates in the political world, the ways in which people express those masculinities can be enormously fluid. Masculine gender identity can be expressed through politics differently for people, depending on their age group, or neighborhood, or racial group. There is not one set of political behaviors driven by masculinity, but a variety of attitudes and behaviors related to differences in other identities and social circumstances.

Anyone who has gotten this far into this volume should have an appreciation for how important it is for people to express their gender identities. It is fundamental to our social identities, and it turns out that politics is a powerful way for people—candidates and voters alike—to express their masculinity. Politics has the potent combination of being highly visible, and easily understood by others, meaning that expressions of masculinity made through political stances or actions are likely to be seen and understood by others. If gender is a performance, politics is a grand stage with a built-in audience that knows the play by heart.

Finally, as much progress as we have made toward women's representation in government, masculine traits and assertions of masculinity are still valued by both voters and candidates. Female candidates have to balance the way in which they present themselves in order to fit into deep-seated notions of what a leader looks and acts like, a dynamic that disadvantages women running for office. To understand the sex gap in representation, we have to look at it as a gender gap.

Where Do We Go Next?

But, as much as we have been able to establish about the role of masculinity in American politics, there is still a great deal of work to be done.

The most basic step that political science needs to take is simply to measure gender with more nuance than the blunt instrument of sex. There has been a reluctance to ask questions about masculinity and femininity on surveys, for fear that respondents would not understand them or would be offended by them, but these fears have not been borne out. There is also hesitation because measuring sex is easy and straightforward, while measuring gender is less so: there are many measures (as evidenced by the research in this volume), and anything beyond a simple, single question can be costly in survey research. Yet there is plenty of room for various ways of measuring gender, and part of the project of masculinity research in political science must be to weigh the costs and benefits of each of them, and how they might work better on different subsamples (unidimensional or multidimensional measures? Numbered scales or anchored options? Midpoints or not? First-person or third-person measures?) but any measurement of gender is better than none (i.e., sex alone).

One of the criticisms faced by researchers working on masculinities in politics is the way in which masculinity interacts with other, better understood, constructs widely used in political science. From a theoretical perspective, masculinity is distinct from social dominance orientation, or hostile sexism, or right-wing authoritarianism, but more and better data are needed to show exactly how it differs. Many of these constructs are likely to be correlated with each other, and, in some circumstances, for some populations, and when looking at some variables, they may be so tightly correlated as to make measuring all of them unnecessary. But we cannot make such judgments until we have the data to show the distinct effects of each on important variables of interest. It seems likely that masculinity—especially assertions of traditional masculinity coming from men—are part of a constellation of related attitudinal and behavioral constructs that include many other constructs from psychology, sociology, and political science. Charting out those relationships will not only help us to better understand the role of masculinities in political behavior, but it will also help us better understand those foundational concepts and where they come from.

Even when we have a more complete understanding of measurement, and how masculinities interact with other traits, we need to take intersectionality seriously. In many parts of social science, "intersectionality" is a buzzword that gets relegated to a paragraph in a book or article stating that the authors know that race and ethnicity and socioeconomic status and sexuality matter, but they are not really dealing with any of that here (once you start looking for those paragraphs, you find them everywhere). When we are studying masculinities, though—and that pluralization is important here—we cannot just hand-wave it away or throw in a control variable to deal with these concepts. There is a reason that sociologists generally talk about masculinities, rather than masculinity, because even though there are commonalities, the ways in which masculine gender identity is expressed across different subpopulations varies widely. Behaviors that are used to assert masculinity in some groups might be unrecognizable as such in other groups. Because expressions of masculinity are socially oriented, the social context in which they are found is profoundly important. This means that while getting items measuring masculinity onto major surveys is important, we should not stop there; we must explore how masculinity impacts political behavior in groups that are not sufficiently large to be represented in such surveys. This will almost certainly mean collaboration between qualitative and quantitative researchers, as researchers might not initially know what questions to even ask, but such work is necessary. Just as we cannot understand the how religion impacts political attitudes and behavior by only looking at Methodists, we cannot hope to fully understand how masculinities shape politics if we limit ourselves to the study of white, middle-class masculinities.

This points to another area critical to the development of the study of political masculinities: deepening connections between qualitative and quantitative research in the area. It is not enough to say that we believe that qualitative and quantitative work, when carried out rigorously, are of equal value. Rather, we have to make use of the often complementary strengths of the two approaches. Quantitative work can tell us what people are doing, and how many are doing it, building external validity, but ethnographic work can help us understand how people do things, and allow us to move from how to why, building internal validity. On their own, neither of these approaches is sufficient to build a complete picture of the role of masculinities in American politics, but by making use of experiments and surveys and content analyses and ethnographies— much as the researchers in this volume have done—we can build a more complete picture.

Some of the work that remains to be undertaken is on the cognitive side of political psychology and political behavior. Researchers working on political masculinities have variously looked at the traits that are considered masculine (as in instruments like the BSRI), people's assertions of masculinity (as in self-report scales), and the ways in which people express their masculinity (as in behavioral measures). These constructs are no doubt intertwined, but they are also theoretically distinct: What is the relationship between having certain behavioral and attitudinal traits that are considered masculine and claiming a masculine gender identity? How accurately can people report the presence of their own gendered traits? How do they filter into behaviors? We also have to contend with a distinction between transitory state-based masculinities, how people assert their gender identities in the moment, in response to stimuli that might not normally be present, and trait-based masculinities, which are theoretically more stable over time. The linkages between traits and states and expressions are no doubt complicated, and likely situational, but no more so than the impact of other identities on behaviors and attitudes that have been well studied in political psychology. By building up these connections and understandings, we can move closer to a unified understanding of political masculinities and ensure that all of the corners that individual researchers are studying can be pieced together into a unified whole.

But building up this deeper understanding is going to require that, as a discipline, we take theory seriously. Much as with intersectionality, researchers in political science too often see theory as something to be dispensed with so that we can get to the real purpose of our papers, presenting new findings or showing off a cool technique or a creative way of getting at a problem. But research in political masculinities shows the weakness of such an approach. It is easy enough for people who have never read Judith Butler to quote her saying that gender is a performance, that gender is constructed through behavior. Citing it and moving on does not require us to engage with the ideas, to read three hundred pages of *Gender Trouble* or *Undoing Gender*. But that idea, that people construct their gender through behavior, that gender arises from the interaction between the individual and the expectations of society, is crucial to the project of understanding political masculinities. Simply put, it may benefit us to draw from philosophy and humanities and gender theory in a way that political scientists are not normally asked to do in graduate school. The progress that we have made thus far has been based on the insights of scholars not just outside of political science, but outside of social science on the whole, and there is a great deal more to be mined from these works and disciplines. But we will not be able to get at those advancements until we read and engage with work that may be outside of our comfort zones.

In this, the study of political masculinities is going to be drawing on a long tradition in political science. In many ways, political science is an amalgam of ideas and methods from psychology and economics and sociology and philosophy applied to questions of how we should, and do, govern ourselves. By drawing on gender theory and sociology to build our understanding of political masculinities, we are following in that lineage. But we also have the opportunity to be additive and to give back to the disciplines that we are borrowing from. In US politics, we are living in a moment where gender, and especially masculinity, is suddenly salient to the polity in a way it simply has not been before. Trump, and Hillary Clinton, and the #MeToo movement, and gay rights, and trans visibility all mean that gender is becoming as important as other identities, like race, in shaping political behaviors and attitudes. Aside from whatever else that means for our society, for researchers in political masculinities, it is an opportunity. We have an unprecedented laboratory to study how masculinity is understood by individuals, how it is transmitted, and how it shapes behaviors. The careful study of political masculinities, then, will allow us to give back to our donor disciplines, to help them understand masculinities in ways that they otherwise would never be able to get at.

This book has been an early foray into the intersection of masculinity and American politics. Rather than just reflecting the state of the art, we have been trying to push it forward, using the same terminology, responding to what other researchers have found, and building a coherent subfield. Our hope is not that this book winds up being the last word on the subject, but, rather, that it becomes a jumping-off point for other researchers. The next phase of research should consider what has been established about gender and masculinity in US politics and apply it to well-established areas of study: activism, campaign contributions, reelections, campaign styles, governance and policy, and so on. As the acceptance of gender and masculinity as important aspects of American political life builds, our hope is that they will become as ubiquitous in political science as sex measures are now: something that is understood to be vital, even if it is not always the central focus of the research.

As political science comes to acknowledge and study the role of gender and masculinity in our political system, that understanding should seep into the work of pollsters and journalists who serve to link the polity and public officials, and, through them, into how the general public understands politics. And while that is important, it is not the most important outcome that we can hope for. As the work in this book has shown, once you start looking for how masculinity shapes politics, its influence becomes both obvious and inescapable, and so, too, are the inequities that it creates. By understanding the importance of masculinity in our political system, we can come to understand how it distorts that system, how it advantages or disadvantages people, and, with time, what we can do about it. The first step in fixing a problem is naming it—but there is a lot more work to be done.

ACKNOWLEDGMENTS

This volume began with a discussion between we two editors about how we thought the field of gender and politics research could use such a resource on the often underresearched field of masculinity in American politics. Little did we know we were far from the only scholars who felt that way. We created a sort of wish list of the scholars we thought could make substantial contributions to the volume, and we started reaching out. Much to our surprise and delight, everyone we initially contacted was also enthusiastic about the idea, and nearly all eventually chose to contribute their work. The result is this published compendium.

We owe our biggest debt of gratitude to these contributors in this volume. Throughout the process, our contributors have been creative, optimistic, and timely. The pieces presented here are top-notch research—from the best in the field—into the topic of masculinity in politics. The pieces stem from a variety of different fields and methodological approaches, making the end result, in our opinion, a valuable collection. We thank our contributors for their work, their enthusiasm, and their ability to meet deadlines. Someone once warned one of us that creating an edited volume like this was akin to herding cats; we are delighted to report that our experience was much easier than that.

Thanks are also due to the Midwest Political Science Association and its planners, and gender and politics section heads, for the 2022 annual meeting in Chicago. We were able to present two complete panels at the meeting, consisting of many of the chapters in this volume. The meeting was a valuable opportunity to bring our authors together to spark ideas, comment on each other's work, and raise a glass to the collaboration.

New York University Press—specifically Sonia Tsuruoka and the editorial board—are also due thanks for seeing the worth in this volume and wanting to invest in it. We would also like to thank the two anonymous reviewers for their positivity and helpful comments and suggestions. And special thanks go to Molly Mulvaney, an intrepid Fordham undergraduate who was willing to help with editorial fixes at a key stage of the process.

Finally, we each owe a debt of gratitude to our respective families. We are both lucky to have supportive, academic spouses who understand not only the topic we are studying but also the burden we undertook.

BIBLIOGRAPHY

Abramson, Paul R. 1972. "Political Efficacy and Political Trust among Black Schoolchildren: Two Explanations." *Journal of Politics* 34 (4): 1243–75.

Achen, Christopher H. 1975. "Mass Political Attitudes and the Survey Response." *American Political Science Review* 69 (4): 1218–31.

Acker, Joan. 1990. "Hierarchies, Jobs, Bodies: A Theory of Gendered Organizations." *Gender & Society* 4 (2): 139–58.

Adams, David. F. 2014. "Roman Catholic Males' Religiousness, Masculine Norms, and Attitudes toward Gay Men." PhD diss., Ball State University.

Agius, Christine, Annika Bergman Rosamond, and Catarina Kinnvall. 2020. "Populism, Ontological Insecurity, and Gendered Nationalism: Masculinity, Climate Denial, and covid-19." *Politics, Religion & Ideology* 21 (4): 432–50.

Ahmed, Osub, Shipla Phadke, and Diana Boesch. 2020. "Women Have Paid the Price for Trump's Regulatory Agenda." Center for American Progress. https://www .americanprogress.org.

Ainley, Vivien, Lara Maister, and Manos Tsakiris. 2015. "Heartfelt Empathy? No Association between Interoceptive Awareness, Questionnaire Measures of Empathy, Reading the Mind in the Eyes Task or the Director Task." *Frontiers in Psychology* 6: 554.

Alexander, Amy C., Catherine Bolzendahl, and Farida Jalalzai. 2018. *Measuring Women's Political Empowerment Across the Globe: Strategies, Challenges and Future Research*. New York: Springer.

Alexander, Amy C., Catherine Bolzendahl, and Lena Wängnerud. 2021. "Beyond the Binary: New Approaches to Measuring Gender in Political Science Research." *European Journal of Politics and Gender* 4 (1): 7–9.

Alexander, Amy C., Catherine Bolzendahl, and Patrik Öhberg. 2021. "Gender, Socio-Political Cleavages, and the Co-constitution of Gender Identities: A Multidimensional Analysis of Self-Assessed Masculine and Feminine Characteristics." *European Journal of Politics and Gender* 4 (1): 151–71.

Alexander, Deborah, and Kristi Andersen. 1993. "Gender as a Factor in the Attribution of Leadership Traits." *Political Research Quarterly* 46 (3): 527–45.

Alex-Assensoh, Yvette, and A. B. Assensoh. 2003. "Inner-City Contexts, Church Attendance, and African-American Political Participation." *Journal of Politics* 63 (3): 896–901.

Almond, Gabriel, and Sidney Verba. 1963. *The Civic Culture: Political Attitudes and Democracy in Five Nations*. Princeton, NJ: Princeton University Press.

Althusser, Louis. 1971. *Lenin and Philosophy and Other Essays*. New York: New Left.

Ananat, Elizabeth Oltmans, and Ebonya Washington. 2009. "Segregation and Black Political Efficacy." *Journal of Public Economics* 93 (5–6): 807–22.

Anderson, Eric. 2012. "Shifting Masculiities in Anglo-American Countries." *Masculinity and Social Change* 1 (1): 40–60.

Ansbacher, Heinz L., and Rowena R. Ansbacher. 1956. *The Individual Psychology of Alfred Adler*. New York: Basic Books.

Ashcraft, Karen Lee. 2022. *Wronged and Dangerous: Viral Masculinity and the Populist Pandemic*. Bristol: Policy.

Athenstaedt, Ursula. 2003. "On the Content and Structure of the Gender Role Self-Concept: Including Gender-Stereotypical Behaviors in Addition to Traits." *Psychology of Women Quarterly* 27 (4): 309–18.

Atkeson, Lonna R., and Ronald B. Rapoport. 2003. "The More Things Change the More They Stay the Same: Examining Gender Differences in Political Attitude Expression." *Public Opinion Quarterly* 50 (4): 1152–68.

Auster, Carol J., and Susan C. Ohm. 2000. "Masculinity and Femininity in Contemporary American Society: A Reevaluation Using the Bem Sex-Role Inventory." *Sex Roles* 43 (7–8): 499–528.

Azevedo, Flavio, John T. Jost, and Tobias Rothmund. 2017. "Making America Great Again: System Justification in the US Presidential Election of 2016." *Translational Issues in Psychological Science* 3 (3): 231–40.

Bäckström, Martin, and Fredrik Björklund. 2007. "Structural Modeling of Generalized Prejudice." *Journal of Individual Differences* 28 (1): 10–17.

Bakan, David. 1966. *The Duality of Human Existence*. Boston: Beacon.

Balch, George I. 1974. "Multiple Indicators in Survey Research: The Concept 'Sense of Political Efficacy.'" *Political Methodology* 1 (2): 1–43.

Baldega, Katherine. 2014. "Gender Differences in Willingness to Guess." *Management Science* 60 (2): 434–48.

Banwart, Mary Christine, and Kelly L. Winfrey. 2013 "Running on the Web: Online Self-Presentation Strategies in Mixed-Gender Races." *Social Science Computer Review* 31 (5): 614–24.

Barbee, Anita P., Michael R. Cunningham, Barbara A. Windstead, Valerian J. Derlega, Mary R. Gulley, Pamela A. Yankeelov, and Perri B. Druen. 1993. "Effects of Gender Role Expectations on the Social Support Process." *Journal of Social Issues* 49 (3): 175–90.

Barnes, Collin D., Ryan P. Brown, and Lindsey L. Osterman. 2012. "Don't Tread on Me: Masculine Honor Ideology in the US and Militant Responses to Terrorism." *Personality and Social Psychology Bulletin* 38 (8): 1018–29.

Barnes, Tiffany D., and Erin C. Cassese. 2017. "American Party Women: A Look at the Gender Gap within Parties." *Political Research Quarterly* 70 (1): 127–41.

Baron-Cohen, Simon, and Sally Wheelwright. 2004. "The Empathy Quotient: An Investigation of Adults with Asperger Syndrome or High-Functioning Autism, and Normal Sex Differences." *Journal of Autism and Developmental Disorders* 34 (2): 163–75.

Baron-Cohen, Simon, Sally Wheelwright, Jacqueline Hill, Yogini Raste, and Ian Plumb. 2001. "The 'Reading the Mind in the Eyes' Test Revised Version: A Study with

Normal Adults, and Adults with Asperger Syndrome or High-Functioning Autism." *Journal of Child Psychology and Psychiatry* 42 (2): 241–51.

Barr, Jason J., and Ann Higgins-D'Alessandro. 2007. "Adolescent Empathy and Prosocial Behavior in the Multidimensional Context of School Culture." *Journal of Genetic Psychology* 168 (3): 231–50.

Bartels, Larry. 2020. "Under Trump, Democrats and Republicans Have Never Been More Divided—on Nearly Everything." *Washington Post*, May 21, 2020. www.washingtonpost.com.

Batson, C. Daniel, Johee Chang, Ryan Orr, and Jennifer Rowland. 2002. "Empathy, Attitudes, and Action: Can Feeling for a Member of a Stigmatized Group Motivate One to Help the Group?" *Personality and Social Psychology Bulletin* 28 (12): 1656–66.

Bauer, Nichole M. 2015. "Emotional, Sensitive, and Unfit for Office: Gender Stereotype Activation and Support for Female Candidates." *Political Psychology* 36 (6): 691–708.

Bauer, Nichole M. 2017. "The Effects of Counter-Stereotypic Gender Strategies on Candidate Evaluations." *Political Psychology* 38 (2): 279–95.

Bauer, Nichole M. 2020. "Shifting Standards: How Voters Evaluate the Qualifications of Female and Male Candidates." *Journal of Politics* 82 (1): 1–12.

Bauer, Nichole M. 2020. *The Qualifications Gap: Why Women Must Be Better than Men to Win Political Office*. Cambridge: Cambridge University Press.

Bauer, Nichole M., and Colleen Carpinella. 2018. "Visual Communication and Candidate Evaluation: The Influence of Feminine and Masculine Images on Support for Female Candidates." *Political Research Quarterly* 71 (2): 395–407.

Bauer, Nichole M., and Martina Santia. 2022. "Going Feminine: Identifying How and When Female Candidates Emphasize Feminine and Masculine Traits on the Campaign Trail." *Political Research Quarterly* 75 (3): 691–705.

Bauer, Nichole M., Laurel Yong Harbridge, and Yanna Krupnikov. 2017. "Who is Punished? Conditions Affecting Voter Evaluations of Legislators Who Do Not Compromise." *Political Behavior* 39 (2): 379–400.

Bedolla, Lisa García, and Becki Scola. 2006. "Finding Intersection: Race, Class, and Gender in the 2003 California Recall Vote." *Politics & Gender* 2 (1): 5–27.

Bejarano, Christina. 2013. *The Latina Advantage: Gender, Race, and Political Success*. Austin: University of Texas Press.

Bejarano, Christina, and Wendy Smooth. 2022. "Women of Color Mobilizing: Sistahs Are Doing It for Themselves from GOTV to Running Candidates for Political Office." *Journal of Women, Politics & Policy* 43 (1): 8–24.

Beltran, Javier, Aina A. Gallego, Alba Huidobro, Enrique Romero, and Lluis Padro. 2020. "Male and Female Politicians on Twitter: A Machine Learning Approach." *European Journal of Political Research* 60 (1): 239–51.

Bem, Sandra L. 1974. "The Measurement of Psychological Androgyny." *Journal of Consulting and Clinical Psychology* 42 (2): 155–62.

Bem, Sandra L. 1978. *Bem Sex-Role Inventory–Short Form*. Palo Alto, CA: Consulting Psychologists Press.

Bem, Sandra L. 1979. "Theory and Measurement of Androgyny: A Reply to the Pedhazur-Tetenbaum and Locksley-Colten Critiques." *Journal of Personality and Social Psychology* 37 (6): 1047–54.

Bem, Sandra L. 1981. *A Manual for the Bem Sex Role Inventory*. Palo Alto, CA: Consulting Psychologists Press.

Bem, Sandra L. 1981. "Gender Schema Theory: A Cognitive Account of Sex Typing." *Psychological Review* 88 (4): 354–64.

Ben-Ghiat, Ruth. 2021. *Strongmen: Mussolini to the Present*. New York: W. W. Norton.

Bennett, Linda L. M., and Stephen Earl Bennett. 1989. "Enduring Gender Differences in Political Interest: The Impact of Socialization and Political Dispositions." *American Politics Quarterly* 17 (1): 105–22.

Berinsky, Adam J., Gregory A. Huber, and Gabriel S. Lenz. 2012. "Using Mechanical Turk as a Subject Recruitment Tool for Experimental Research." *Political Analysis* 20 (3): 351–68.

Beutel, Ann M., and Margaret Mooney Marini. 1995. "Gender and Values." *American Sociological Review* 60 (3): 436–48.

Bittner, Amanda, and Elizabeth Goodyear-Grant. 2017a. "Digging Deeper into the Gender Gap: Gender Salience as a Moderating Factor in Political Attitudes." *Canadian Journal of Political Science* 50 (2): 559–78.

Bittner, Amanda, and Elizabeth Goodyear-Grant. 2017b. "Sex Isn't Gender: Reforming Concepts and Measurements in the Study of Public Opinion." *Political Behavior* 39 (4): 1019–41.

Blair, Karen L. 2017. "Did Secretary Clinton Lose to a 'Basket of Deplorables'? An Examination of Islamophobia, Homophobia, Sexism, and Conservative Ideology in the 2016 US Presidential Election." *Psychology and Sexuality* 8 (4): 334–55.

Blair, R. J. R. 2005. "Responding to the Emotions of Others: Dissociating Forms of Empathy through the Study of Typical and Psychiatric Populations." *Consciousness and Cognition* 14 (4): 698–718.

Bledsoe, Timothy. 1986. "A Research Note on the Impact of District/At-Large Elections on Black Political Efficacy." *Urban Affairs Quarterly* 22 (1): 166–74.

Blinder, Scott, and Meredith Rolfe. 2018. "Rethinking Compassion: Toward a Political Account of the Partisan Gender Gap in the United States." *Political Psychology* 39 (4): 889–906.

Bobo, Lawrence D. 2017. "Racism in Trump's America: Reflections on Culture, Sociology, and the 2016 US Presidential Election." *British Journal of Sociology* 68: S85–104.

Bobo, Lawrence, and Franklin D. Gilliam. 1990. "Race, Sociopolitical Participation, and Black Empowerment." *American Political Science Review* 84 (2): 377–93.

Bock, Jarrod, Jennifer Byrd-Craven, and Melissa Burkley. 2017. "The Role of Sexism in Voting in the 2016 Presidential Election." *Personality and Individual Differences* 119:189–93.

Bocock, Robert. 1986. *Hegemony*. Chichester: Ellis Horwood.

Borah, Porismita, Erika Franklin Fowler, and Travis N. Ridout. 2018. "Television vs. YouTube: Political Advertising in the 2012 Presidential Election." *Journal of Information Technology & Politics* 15 (3): 230–44.

Bordo, Susan. 2004. *Unbearable Weight: Feminism, Western Culture, and the Body.* 2nd ed. Berkeley: University of California Press.

Bos, Angela L., Jill S. Greenlee, Mirya R. Holman, Zoe M. Oxley, and J. Celeste Lay. 2022. "This One's for the Boys: How Gendered Political Socialization Limits Girls' Political Ambition and Interest." *American Political Science Review* 116 (2): 484–501.

Bosselman, Beulah, and Bernard Skorodin. 1940. "Masculinity and Femininity in Psychotic Patients." *American Journal of Psychiatry* 97 (3): 699–702.

Bosson, Jennifer K., Joseph A. Vandello, and T. Andrew Caswell. 2013. "Precarious Manhood." In *The Sage Handbook of Gender and Psychology,* edited by Michelle K. Ryan and Nyla R. Branscombe, 115–130. Los Angeles, CA: Sage.

Box-Steffensmeier, Janet, Suzanna De Boef, and Tse-Min Lin. 2004. "The Dynamics of the Partisan Gender Gap." *American Political Science Review* 98 (3): 515–28.

Bracic, Ana, Mackenzi Israel-Trummel, and Allyson F. Shortle. 2019. "Is Sexism for White People? Gender Stereotypes, Race, and the 2016 Presidential Election." *Political Behavior* 41 (2): 281–307.

Brannon, Robert. 1976. "The Male Sex Role: Our Culture's Blueprint of Manhood, and What It's Done for Us Lately." In *The Forty-Nine Percent Majority: The Male Sex Role,* edited by. D. S. David and R. Brannon, 1–48. Reading, MA: Addison-Wesley.

Bridges, Tristan, and C. J. Pascoe. 2014. "Hybrid Masculinities: New Directions in the Sociology of Men and Masculinities." *Sociology Compass* 8 (3): 246–58.

Britton, Dana M. 2000. "The Epistemology of the Gendered Organization." *Gender & Society* 14 (3): 418–34.

Brown, Nadia. 2014. *Sisters in the Statehouse: Black Women and Legislative Decision Making.* New York: Oxford University Press.

Brown, Nadia, and Danielle Casarez Lemi. 2021. *Sister Style: The Politics of Appearance for Black Women Political Elites.* New York: Oxford University Press.

Brown, Nadia, and Sarah Allen Gershon. 2016. "Intersectional Presentations: An Exploratory Study of Minority Congresswomen's Websites Biographies." *Du Bois Review* 13 (1): 85–108.

Budgeon, Shelley. 2014. "The Dynamics of Gender Hegemony: Femininities, Masculinities, and Social Change." *Sociology* 48 (2): 317–34.

Buehler, Marilyn H. 1977. "Voter Turnout and Political Efficacy among Mexican-Americans in Michigan." *The Sociological Quarterly* 18 (4): 504–17.

Burns, Nancy, and Donald Kinder. 2012. "Categorical Politics: Gender, Race, and Public Opinion." In *New Directions in Public Opinion,* edited by Adam Berinsky, 139–67. New York: Routledge.

Burns, Nancy, Kay Lehman Schlozman, Ashley Jardina, Shauna Shames, and Sidney Verba. 2018. "What's Happened to the Gender Gap in Political Participation? How Might We Explain It?" In *100 Years of the Nineteenth Amendment: An Appraisal of Women's Political Activism,* edited by Lee Ann Banaszak and Holly J. McCammon, 69–104. New York: Oxford University Press.

Burns, Nancy, Kay Lehman Scholzman, and Sidney Verba. 2001. *The Private Roots of Public Action: Gender, Equality, and Political Participation*. Cambridge, MA: Harvard University Press.

Buss, Arnold H., and Mark Perry. 1992. "The Aggression Questionnaire." *Personality and Individual Differences* 63:452–59.

Butler, Judith. 1990. *Gender Trouble: Feminism and the Subversion of Identity*. New York: Routledge.

Butler, Judith. 2020. "Performative Acts and Gender Constitution: An Essay in Phenomenology and Feminist Theory." In *Feminist Theory Reader*, edited by Carole McCann, Seung-kyung Kim, and Emek Ergun, 353–61. New York: Routledge.

Cameron, James E. 2001. "Social Identity, Modern Sexism, and Perceptions of Personal and Group Discrimination by Women and Men." *Sex Roles* 45 (11): 743–66.

Campbell, Angus, Gerald Gurin, and Warren E. Miller. 1954. *The Voter Decides*. Evanston, IL: Row, Peterson.

Campbell, Angus, Philip E. Converse, Warren E. Miller, and Donald E. Stokes. 1960. *The American Voter*. Chicago: University of Chicago Press.

Campbell, David E., and Christina Wolbrecht. 2020. "The Resistance as Role Model: Disillusionment and Protest among American Adolescents after 2016." *Political Behavior* 42 (3): 1143–68.

Campi, Ashleigh. 2021. "Cultivating Authoritarian Submission: Race and Gender in Conservative Media." *Theory & Event* 24 (2): 456–82.

Campi, Ashleigh, and Jane Junn. 2019. "Racial Linked Fate and Gender in U.S. Politics." *Politics, Groups, and Identities* 7 (3): 654–62.

Cargile, Ivy A. M. 2016. "Latina Issues: An Analysis of the Policy Issue Competencies of Latina Candidates." In *Distinct Identities: Minority Women in U.S. Politics*, edited by Nadia E. Brown and Sarah A. Gershon, 134–50. New York: Routledge.

Cargile, Ivy A. M. 2023. "Stereotyping Latinas: Candidate Gender and Ethnicity on the Political Stage." *Politics, Groups, and Identities* 11 (2): 207–25.

Cargile, Ivy A. M., Jennifer Merolla, and Jean Reith Schroedel. 2016. "Intersectionality and Latino/a Candidate Evaluation." In *Latinas in American Politics*, edited by Sharon Navarro, Sharon Hernandez and Leslie A. Navarro, 39–60. London: Lexington.

Carian, Emily K., Alex DiBranco, and Chelsea Ebin. 2022. *Male Supremacism in the United States: From Patriarchal Traditionalism to Misogynist Incels and the Alt-Right*. New York: Routledge.

Carian, Emily K., and Tagart C. Sobotka. 2018. "Playing the Trump Card: Masculinity Threat and the U.S. 2016 Presidential Election." *Socius: Sociological Research for a Dynamic World* 4:1–6.

Carmines, Edward G., and Donald J. Baxter. 1986. "Race, Intelligence, and Political Efficacy." *Adolescence* 21 (82): 437–42.

Carpinella, Colleen M., Eric Hehman, Jonathan B. Freeman, and Kerri L. Johnson. 2016. "The Gendered Face of Partisan Politics: Consequences of Facial Sex Typicality for Vote Choice." *Political Communication* 33 (1): 21–38.

Carpinella, Colleen M., and Nichole M. Bauer. 2021. "A Visual Analysis of Gender Stereotypes in Campaign Advertising." *Politics, Groups, and Identities* 9 (2): 369–86.

Carroll, Susan J. 2006. "Voting Choices: Meet You at the Gender Gap." In *Gender and Elections: Shaping the Future of American Politics*, edited by Susan J. Carroll and Richard L. Fox, 74–96. Cambridge: Cambridge University Press.

Carter, Julian B. 2007. *The Heart of Whiteness: Normal Sexuality and Race in America, 1880–1940*. Durham, NC: Duke University Press.

Cartledge, Paul. 2013. "The *Machismo* of the Athenian Empire—Or the Reign of the *Phaulus*?" In *When Men Were Men: Masculinity, Power, and Identity in Classical Antiquity*, edited by Lin Foxhall and John Salmon, 54–67. New York: Routledge.

Cassese, Erin C., and Tiffany D. Barnes. 2019a. "Reconciling Sexism and Women's Support for Republican Candidates: A Look at Gender, Class, and Whiteness in the 2012 and 2016 Presidential Races." *Political Behavior* 41(3): 677–700.

Cassese, Erin C., and Tiffany D. Barnes. 2019b. "White Women and Party Loyalty in the 2016 Presidential Election." *Political Behavior* 41: 677–700.

Cassese, Erin C., and Mirya Holman. 2018. "Party and Gender Stereotypes in Campaign Attacks." *Political Behavior* 40: 785–807.

Cassese, Erin C., and Mirya R. Holman. 2019. "Playing the Woman Card: Ambivalent Sexism in the 2016 U.S. Presidential Race." *Political Psychology* 40 (1): 55–74.

Cassino, Dan. 2018. "Emasculation, Conservatism, and the 2016 Election." *Contexts* (17) 1: 48–53.

Cassino, Dan. 2020. "Moving Beyond Sex: Measuring Gender Identity in Telephone Surveys." *Survey Practice* 13 (1). doi.org/10.29115/SP-2020-0009.

Cassino, Dan. 2021. "Political Identity, Gender Identity or Both? The Political Effects of Sexual Orientation and Gender Identity." *European Journal of Politics and Gender* 4 (1): 79–91.

Cassino, Dan, and Yasemin Besen-Cassino. 2020a. "Of Masks and Men? Gender, Sex, and Protective Measures during COVID-19." *Politics & Gender* 16 (4): 1052–62.

Cassino, Dan, and Yasemin Besen-Cassino. 2020b. "Sometimes (But Not This Time), a Gun Is Just a Gun: Masculinity Threat and Guns in the United States, 1999–2018." *Sociological Forum* 35 (1): 5–23.

Cassino, Dan, and Yasemin Besen-Cassino. 2021. *Gender Threat: American Masculinity in the Face of Change*. Stanford, CA: Stanford University Press.

Castle, Jeremiah. 2019. "New Fronts in the Culture Wars? Religion, Partisanship, and Polarization on Religious Liberty and Transgender Rights in the United States." *American Politics Research* 47 (3): 650–79.

Caswell, T. Andrew, Jennifer K. Bosson, Joseph A. Vandello, and Jennifer G. Sellers. 2014. "Testosterone and Men's Stress Responses to Gender Threats." *Psychology of Men & Masculinity* 15 (1): 4–11.

Caughell, Leslie A. 2016. *The Political Battle of the Sexes: Exploring the Sources of Gender Gaps in Policy Preferences*. Lanham, MD: Rowman & Littlefield.

Center for American Women and Politics (CAWP). 2022. "Fact Sheet Archive on Women in Congress." cawp.rutgers.edu.

Chambers, David Wade. 1983. "Stereotypic Images of the Scientist: The Draw-A-Scientist Test." *Science Education* 67 (2): 255–65.

Chandler, Jesse, and Danielle Shapiro. 2016. "Conducting Clinical Research Using Crowdsourced Convenience Samples." *Annual Review of Clinical Psychology* 12:53–81.

Chaney, Carole Kennedy, R. Michael Alvarez, and Jonathan Nagler. 1998. "Explaining the Gender Gap in U.S. Presidential Elections." *Political Research Quarterly.* 51 (2): 311–39.

Chen, Anthony S. 1999. "Lives at the Center of the Periphery, Lives at the Periphery of the Center: Chinese American Masculinities and Bargaining with Hegemony." *Gender & Society* 13 (5): 584–607.

Cheryan, Sapna, Jessica S. Cameron, Zach Katagiri, and Benoit Monin. 2015. "Manning Up: Threatened Men Compensate by Disavowing Feminine Preferences and Embracing Masculine Attributes." *Social Psychology* 46:218–27.

Childs, Sarah. 2004. "A Feminised Style of Politics? Women MPs in the House of Commons." *British Journal of Politics and International Relations* 6 (1): 3–19.

Choi, Namok, Dale R. Fuqua, and Jody L. Newman. 2009. "Exploratory and Confirmatory Studies of the Structure of the Bem Sex Role Inventory Short Form with Two Divergent Samples." *Educational and Psychological Measurement* 69 (4): 696–705.

Choma, Becky L., and Yaniv Hanoch. 2017. "Cognitive Ability and Authoritarianism: Understanding Support for Trump and Clinton." *Personality and Individual Differences* 106:287–91.

Christiansen, Paul. 2017. *Orchestrating Public Opinion: How Music Persuades in Television Political Ads for US Presidential Campaigns, 1952–2016.* Amsterdam: Amsterdam University Press.

Christov-Moore, Leonardo, Elizabeth A. Simpson, Gino Coudé, Kristina Grigaityte, Marco Iacoboni, and Pier Francesco Ferrari. 2014. "Empathy: Gender Effects in Brain and Behavior." *Neuroscience & Biobehavioral Reviews* 46:604–27.

Clarke, Harold D., and Alan C. Acock. 1989. "National Elections and Political Attitudes: The Case of Political Efficacy." *British Journal of Political Science* 19 (4): 551–62.

Clayton, Dewey M., and Angela M. Stallings. 2000. "Black Women in Congress: Striking the Balance." *Journal of Black Studies* 30 (4): 574–603.

Clifford, Scott, Ryan M. Jewell, and Philip D. Waggoner. 2015. "Are Samples Drawn from Mechanical Turk Valid for Research on Political Ideology?" *Research & Politics* 2 (4).

Clifton, Derick. 2021. "50% of Gen Zers Believe Traditional Gender Norms Are Outdated." February 24. www.them.us.

Cochrane, Christopher. 2010. "Left/Right Ideology and Canadian Politics." *Canadian Journal of Political Science* 43 (3): 583–604.

Cochrane, Christopher. 2015. *Left, and Right: The Small World of Political Ideas.* Montreal: McGill- Queen's University Press.

Coffé, Hilde, and Catherine Bolzendahl. 2010. "Same Game, Different Rules? Gender Differences in Political Participation." *Sex Roles* 62 (5): 318–33.

Coffé, Hilde, and Catherine Bolzendahl. 2021. "Are All Politics Masculine? Gender Socialised Personality Traits and Diversity in Political Engagement." *European Journal of Politics and Gender* 4 (1): 113–33.

Cohn, Amy M., L. Alana Seibert, and Amos Zeichner. 2009. "The Role of Restrictive Emotionality, Trait Anger, and Masculinity Threat in Men's Perpetration of Physical Aggression." *Psychology of Men & Masculinity* 10:218–24.

Collins, Patricia Hill. 1990. *Black Feminist Thought: Knowledge, Consciousness and the Politics of Empowerment.* New York: Routledge.

Connell, R. W. 1987. *Gender and Power.* Cambridge: Polity.

Connell, R. W. 1995. *Masculinities.* Berkeley: University of California Press.

Connell, R. W. 2000. *The Men and the Boys.* Berkeley: University of California Press.

Connell, R.W. 2005. *Masculinities.* 2nd ed. Berkeley: University of California Press.

Connell, R. W., and James W. Messerschmidt. 2005. "Hegemonic Masculinity: Rethinking the Concept." *Gender & Society* 19 (6): 829–59.

Conroy, Meredith. 2015. *Masculinity, Media, and the American Presidency.* New York: Palgrave Macmillan.

Conroy, Meredith, and Sarah Oliver. 2020. *Who Runs? The Masculine Advantage in Candidate Emergence.* Ann Arbor: University of Michigan Press.

Constantinople, Anne. 1973. "Masculinity-Femininity: An Exception to a Famous Dictum?" *Psychological Bulletin* 80 (5): 385–407.

Converse, Philip E. 1972. "Change in the American Electorate." In *The Human Meaning of Social Change,* edited by Angus Campbell and Philip E. Converse, 263–337. New York: Russell Sage Foundation.

Converse, Philip E. 1990. "Popular Representation and the Distribution of Information." In *Information and Democratic Processes,* edited by J. A. Frerejohn and James H. Kuklinski, 369–88. Urbana: University of Illinois Press.

Copenhaver, Michael M., Steve J. Lash, and Richard M. Eisler. 2000. "Masculine Gender-Role Stress, Anger, and Male Intimate Abusiveness: Implications for Men's Relationships." *Sex Roles* 42 (5–6): 405–14.

Costa Jr., Paul T., Antonio Terracciano, and Robert R. McCrae. 2001. "Gender Differences in Personality Traits across Cultures: Robust and Surprising Findings." *Journal of Personality and Social Psychology* 81 (2): 322–31.

Courtenay, Will H. 2000. "Constructions of Masculinity and Their Influence on Men's Well-Being: A Theory of Gender and Health." *Social Science & Medicine* 50: 1385–401.

Craig, Stephen C., and Michael A. Maggiotto. 1982. "Measuring Political Efficacy." *Political Methodology* 8 (3): 85–109.

Craig, Stephen C., Richard G. Niemi, and Glenn E. Silver. 1990. "Political Efficacy and Trust: A Report on the NES Pilot Study Items." *Political Behavior* 12 (3): 289–314.

Crenshaw, Kimberlé. 1991. "Mapping the Margins: Intersectionality, Identity Politics, and Violence Against Women of Color." *Stanford Law Review* 43 (6): 1241–99.

Crowson, Howard M., and Joyce A. Brandes. 2017. "Differentiating Between Donald Trump and Hillary Clinton Voters Using Facets of Right-Wing Authoritarianism and Social-Dominance Orientation: A Brief Report." *Psychological Reports* 120 (3): 364–73.

Daddow, Oliver, and Isabelle Hertner. 2021. "Interpreting Toxic Masculinity in Political Parties: A Framework." *Party Politics* 27 (4): 743–54.

Dalton, Russell J. 2000. "Citizen Attitudes and Political Behavior." *Comparative Political Studies* 33 (6–7): 912–40.

Davis, Mark H. 1980. "A Multidimensional Approach to Individual Differences in Empathy." *Catalog of Selected Documents in Psychology* 10:85.

Dawson, Michael C. 1994. *Behind the Mule: Race and Class in African American Politics*. Princeton, NJ: Princeton University Press.

Dawson, Michael C. 2001. *Black Visions: The Roots of Contemporary African American Political Ideologies*. Chicago: University of Chicago Press.

Deason, Grace, Jill S. Greenlee, and Carrie A. Langer. 2015. "Mothers on the Campaign Trail: Implications of Politicized Motherhood on Women in Politics." *Politics, Groups, and Identities* 3 (1): 133–48.

Deaux, Kay, and Marianne LaFrance. 1998. "Gender." In *The Handbook of Social Psychology*, edited by Daniel Todd Gilbert, Susan T. Fiske and Gardner Lindzey, 788–827. New York: Oxford University Press.

de Boise, Sam. 2019. "Editorial: Is Masculinity Toxic?" *NORMA* 14 (3): 147–51.

Decety, Jean. 2011. "The Neuroevolution of Empathy." *Annals of the New York Academy of Sciences* 1231 (1): 35–45.

Declerck, Carolyn H, and Sandy Bogaert. 2008. "Social Value Orientation: Related to Empathy and the Ability to Read the Mind in the Eyes." *Journal of Social Psychology* 148 (6): 711–26.

Deckman, Melissa. 2016. *Tea Party Women: Mama Grizzlies, Grassroots Activists, and the Changing Face of the American Right*. New York: NYU Press.

Deckman, Melissa. 2018. "A New Poll Shows How Younger Women Could Help Drive a Democratic Wave." *Washington Post*, March 5. www.washingtonpost.com.

Deckman, Melissa, and Erin Cassese. 2021. "Gendered Nationalism and the 2016 US Presidential Election: How Party, Class, and Beliefs About Masculinity Shaped Voting Behavior." *Politics & Gender* 17 (2): 277–300.

Deckman, Melissa, and Jared McDonald. 2023. "Uninspired by Old, White Guys: The Mobilizing Factor of Younger, More Diverse Candidates for Gen Z Women." *Politics & Gender* 19 (1): 195–219.

Devine, Christopher. 2018. "Partisanship Runs Deep in America—Even among 'Independents.'" The Conversation, October 17. theconversation.com.

Devlin, L. Patrick. 1989. "Contrasts in Presidential Campaign Commercials of 1988." *American Behavioral Scientist* 32 (4): 389–414.

de Waal, Frans B. M. 2008. "Putting the Altruism Back into Altruism: The Evolution of Empathy." *Annual Review of Psychology* 59: 279–300.

Diekman, Amanda B., and Alice H. Eagly. 2000. "Stereotypes as Dynamic Constructs: Women and Men of the Past, Present, and Future." *Personality and Social Psychology Bulletin* 26 (10): 1171–88.

Diekman, Amanda B., and Monica C. Schneider. 2010. "A Social Role Theory Perspective on Gender Gaps in Political Attitudes." *Psychology of Women Quarterly* 34 (4): 486–97.

Diekman, Amanda B., and Sarah K. Murnen. 2004. "Learning to Be Little Women and Little Men: The Inequitable Gender Equality of Nonsexist Children's Literature." *Sex Roles* 50 (5–6): 373–85.

Dimock, Michael. 2019. "Defining Generations: Where Millennials End and Gen Z Begins." Pew Research Center, January 17. www.pewresearch.org.

DiMuccio, Sarah H., and Eric D. Knowles. 2020. "The Political Significance of Fragile Masculinity." *Current Opinion in Behavioral Sciences* 34:25–28.

DiMuccio, Sarah H., and Eric D. Knowles. 2021. "Precarious Manhood Predicts Support for Aggressive Policies and Politicians." *Personality and Social Psychology Bulletin* 47 (7): 1169–87.

DiMuccio, Sarah H., and Eric D. Knowles. 2023. "Something to Prove? Manhood Threats Increase Political Aggression among Liberal Men." *Sex Roles* 88:240–67.

Ditonto, Tessa M. 2017. "A High Bar or a Double Standard? Gender, Competence, and Information in Political Campaigns." *Political Behavior* 39 (2): 301–25.

Ditonto, Tessa M., Allison J. Hamilton, and David P. Redlawsk. 2014. "Gender Stereotypes, Information Search, and Voting Behavior in Political Campaigns." *Political Behavior* 36 (2): 335–58.

Dittmar, Kelly. 2015. *Navigating Gendered Terrain: Stereotypes and Strategy in Political Campaigns*. Philadelphia: Temple University Press.

Doherty, Erin. 2022. "The Number of LGBTQ-Identifying Adults in the US Is Soaring." Axios, February 19. www.axios.com.

Dolan, Kathleen. 2011. "Do Women and Men Know Different Things? Measuring Gender Differences in Political Knowledge." *Journal of Politics* 73 (1): 97–107.

Dolan, Kathleen. 2014. "Gender Stereotypes, Candidate Evaluations, and Voting for Women Candidates: What Really Matters?" *Political Research Quarterly* 67 (1): 96–107.

Dolan, Kathleen, and Michael A. Hansen. 2020. "The Variable Nature of the Gender Gap in Political Knowledge." *Journal of Women, Politics, & Policy* 41 (2): 127–43.

Donaldson, M. 1993. "What Is Hegemonic Masculinity?" *Theory and Society* 22:643–57.

Donnelly, Kristin, and Jean M. Twenge. 2017. "Masculine and Feminine Traits on the Bem Sex-Role Inventory, 1993–2012: A Cross-Temporal Meta-Analysis." *Sex Roles* 76 (9): 556–65.

Dow, Jay. 2009. "Gender Differences in Political Knowledge: Distinguishing Characteristics-Based and Returns-Based Differences." *Political Behavior* 31 (1): 117–36.

Ducat, Stephen J. 2004. *The Wimp Factor: Gender Gaps, Holy Wars, and the Politics of Anxious Masculinity*. Boston: Beacon.

Duckitt, John. 2001. "A Dual-Process Cognitive-Motivational Theory of Ideology and Prejudice." In *Advances in Experimental Social Psychology*, vol. 33, edited by Mark P. Zanna, 41–113. Cambridge: Academic Press.

Duerst-Lahti, Georgia. 2006. "Presidential Elections as Gendered Space." In *Gender and Elections: Shaping the Future of American Politics*, edited by Susan Carroll and Richard L. Fox, 12–42. Cambridge: Cambridge University Press.

Duerst-Lahti, Georgia, and Madison Oakley. 2018. "Presidential Elections: Gendered Space and the Case of 2016." In *Gender and Elections: Shaping the Future of American Politics*, edited by Susan Carroll and Richard L. Fox, 15–47. Cambridge: Cambridge University Press.

Duerst-Lahti, Georgia, and Rita Mae Kelly.1995. *Gender Power, Leadership, and Governance*. Ann Arbor: University of Michigan Press.

Dunaway, Johanna, Regina G. Lawrence, Melody Rose, and Christopher R. Weber. 2013. "Traits Versus Issues: How Female Candidates Shape Coverage of Senate and Gubernatorial Races." *Political Research Quarterly* 66 (3): 715–26.

Duverger, Maurice. 1955. *The Political Role of Women*. Paris: UNESCO.

Eagly, Alice H., Amanda B. Diekman, Mary C. Johannesen-Schmidt, and Anne M. Koenig. 2004. "Gender Gaps in Sociopolitical Attitudes: A Social Psychological Analysis." *Journal of Personality and Social Psychology* 87 (6): 796–816.

Eagly, Alice H., and Maureen Crowley. 1986. "Gender and Helping Behavior: A Meta-Analytic Review of the Social Psychological Literature." *Psychological Bulletin* 100 (3): 283–308.

Eagly, Alice H., and Steven J. Karau. 2002. "Role Congruity Theory of Prejudice Toward Female Leaders." *Psychological Review* 109 (3): 573–98.

Eagly, Alice H., and Wendy Wood. 2012. "Social Role Theory." *Handbook of Theories in Social Psychology* 2:458–76.

Eagly, Alice H., Wendy Wood, and Amanda B. Diekman. 2000. "Social Role Theory of Sex Differences and Similarities: A Current Appraisal." In *The Developmental Social Psychology of Gender*, edited by Thomas Eckes and Hanns M. Trautner, 123–74. Mahwah, NJ: Lawrence Erlbaum.

Eichenberg, Richard C. 2003. "Gender Differences in Public Attitudes toward the Use of Force by the United States, 1990–2003." *International Security* 28 (1): 110–41.

Eisenberg, Nancy, and Randy Lennon. 1983. "Sex Differences in Empathy and Related Capacities." *Psychological Bulletin* 94:100–131.

Eisler, R. M., and J. R. Skidmore. 1987. "Masculine Gender Role Stress: Scale Development and Component Factors in the Appraisal of Stressful Situations." *Behavior Modification* 11:123–36.

Eisler, R. M., J. R. Skidmore, and C. H. Ward. 1988. "Masculine Gender-Role Stress: Predictor of Anger, Anxiety, and Health-Risk Behaviors." *Journal of Personality Assessment* 52:133–41.

Elmer, Greg, and Anthony Burton. 2022. "Rebel Personalities: Canada's Far-Right Media." *First Monday* 27 (5). doi.org/10.5210/fm.v27i5.12546.

Engel, David, Anita Williams Woolley, Lisa X. Jing, Christopher F. Chabris, and Thomas Malone. 2014. "Reading the Mind in the Eyes or Reading between the Lines? Theory of Mind Predicts Collective Intelligence Equally Well Online and Face-To-Face." *PLOS ONE* 9 (12): e115212.

English, Ashley, Kathryn Pearson, and Dara Z. Strolovitch. 2019. "Who Represents Me? Race, Gender, Partisan Congruence, and Representational Alternatives in a Polarized America." *Political Research Quarterly* 72 (4): 785–804.

Erzeel, Silvia, and Ekaterina R. Rashkova. 2017. "Still Men's Parties? Gender and the Radical Right in Comparative Perspective." *West European Politics* 40 (4): 812–20.

Evans, Lorraine, and Kimberly Davies. 2000. "No Sissy Boys Here: A Content Analysis of the Representation of Masculinity in Elementary School Reading Textbooks." *Sex Roles* 42 (3): 255–70.

Fahey, Anna Cornelia. 2007. "French and Feminine: Hegemonic Masculinity and the Emasculation of John Kerry in the 2004 Presidential Race." *Critical Studies in Media Communication* 24:132–50.

Feldman, Stanley, Leonie Huddy, Julie Wronski, and Patrick Lown. 2020. "The Interplay of Empathy and Individualism in Support for Social Welfare Policies." *Political Psychology* 41 (2): 343–62.

Feldman, Stanley, and Marco R. Steenbergen. 2001. "The Humanitarian Foundation of Public Support for Social Welfare." *American Journal of Political Science* 45 (3): 658–77.

Feliciano, Cynthia, Belinda Robnett, and Golnaz Komaie. 2009. "Gendered Racial Exclusion among White Internet Daters." *Social Science Research* 38 (1): 39–54.

Ferguson, Ann Arnett 2020. *Bad Boys: Public Schools in the Making of Black Masculinity*. Ann Arbor: University of Michigan Press.

Ferguson, Thomas, Benjamin I. Page, Jacob Rothschild, Arturo Chang, and Jie Chen. 2020. "The Roots of Right-Wing Populism: Donald Trump in 2016." *International Journal of Political Economy* 49 (2): 102–23.

Finkel, Steven E. 1985. "Reciprocal Effects of Participation and Political Efficacy: A Panel Analysis." *American Journal of Political Science* 29 (4): 891–913.

Fischer, Ann R., David M. Tokar, Glenn E. Good, and Andrea F. Snell. 1998. "More on the Structure of Male Role Norms: Exploratory and Multiple Sample Confirmatory Analyses." *Psychology of Women Quarterly* 22 (2): 135–55.

Ford Dowe, Pearl K. 2020. "Resisting Marginalization: Black Women's Political Ambition and Agency." *PS: Political Science & Politics* 53 (4): 697–702.

Form, William H., and Joan Huber. 1971. "Income, Race, and the Ideology of Political Efficacy." *Journal of Politics* 33 (3): 659–88.

Fortin-Rittberger, Jessica. 2016. "Cross-National Gender Gaps in Political Knowledge: How Much Is Due to Context?" *Political Research Quarterly* 69 (3): 391–402.

Fowler, Erika Franklin, Michael M. Franz, and Travis N. Ridout. 2014. Political Advertising in 2010. Version 1.2. Middletown, CT: Wesleyan Media Project.

Fowler, Erika Franklin, Michael M. Franz, and Travis N. Ridout. 2015. Political Advertising in 2012. edited by Wesleyan Media Project. Middletown, CT.

Fowler, Erika Franklin, Michael M. Franz, and Travis N. Ridout. 2017. Political Advertising in 2014. edited by Department of Government at Wesleyan University Wesleyan Media Project. Middletown, CT.

Fowler, Erika Franklin, Michael M. Franz, Travis N. Ridout, and Laura M. Baum. 2019. Political Advertising in 2016. edited by Department of Government at Wesleyan University The Wesleyan Media Project. Middletown, CT.

Fowler, Erika Franklin, Michael M. Franz, Travis N. Ridout, and Laura M. Baum. 2020. Political Advertising in 2018. edited by Department of Government at Wesleyan University The Wesleyan Media Project. Middletown, CT.

Fowler, Derek J., Jennifer L. Merolla, and Abbylin H. Sellers. 2014. "Descriptive Representation and Evaluations of Government." *Politics, Groups, and Identities* 2 (1): 66–89.

Fraile, Marta. 2013. "Do Information-Rich Contexts Reduce Knowledge Inequalities? The Contextual Determinants of Political Knowledge in Europe." *Acta Political* 48 (2): 119–43.

Fraile, Marta, and Carolina de Miguel Moyer. 2021. "Risk and the Gender Gap in Internal Political Efficacy in Europe." *West European Politics* 45 (7): 1462–80.

Fraser, Barry J. 1978. "Development of a Test of Science-Related Attitudes." *Science Education* 62 (4): 509–15.

Frazer, Elizabeth, and Kenneth Macdonald. 2003. "Sex Differences in Political Knowledge in Britain." *Political Studies* 51 (1): 67–83.

Freeman, Jo. 1993. "Feminism vs. Family Values: Women at the 1992 Democratic and Republican Conventions." *PS: Political Science and Politics* 26 (1): 21–27.

Freud, Sigmund. [1915] 1949. *Three Essays on the Theory of Sexuality*. Translated by J. Strachey. London: Imago.

Fulton, Sarah A. 2012. "Running Backwards and in High Heels: The Gendered Quality Gap and Incumbent Electoral Success." *Political Research Quarterly* 65 (2): 303–14.

Funk, Carolyn L. 1996. "The Impact of Scandal on Candidate Evaluations: An Experimental Test of the Role of Candidate Traits." *Political Behavior* 18 (1): 1–24.

Funk, Carolyn L. 1997. "Implications of Political Expertise in Candidate Trait Evaluations." *Political Research Quarterly* 50 (3): 675–97.

Funk, Carolyn L. 1999. "Bringing the Candidate into Models of Candidate Evaluation." *Journal of Politics* 61 (3): 700–720.

Gale, Steven R. 1996. "Male Role Norm Endorsement and Acquaintance Sexual Aggression among College Students." PhD diss., Colorado State University.

Galea, Natalie, and Barbara Gaweda. 2018. "(De)constructing the Masculine Blueprint: The Institutional and Discursive Consequences of Male Political Dominance." *Politics & Gender* 14 (2): 276–82.

Gallagher, Kathryn E., and Dominic J. Parrott. 2011. "What Accounts for Men's Hostile Attitudes toward Women? The Influence of Hegemonic Male Role Norms and Masculine Gender Role Stress." *Violence against Women* 17:568–83.

García Bedolla, Lisa. 2005. *Fluid Borders: Latino Power, Identity, and Politics in Los Angeles*. Berkeley: University of California Press.

Gault, Barbara A., and John Sabini. 2000. "The Roles of Empathy, Anger, and Gender in Predicting Attitudes toward Punitive, Reparative, and Preventative Public Policies." *Cognition & Emotion* 14 (4): 495–520.

Gay, Claudine, Jennifer Hochschild, and Ariel White. 2016. "Americans' Belief in Linked Fate: Does the Measure Capture the Concept?" *Journal of Race, Ethnicity, and Politics* 1 (1): 117–44.

Gelb, Joyce. 1989. *Feminism and Politics: A Comparative Perspective*. Berkeley: University of California Press.

Gerring, John. 2011. *Social Science Methodology: A Unified Framework*. Cambridge: Cambridge University Press.

Gershon, Sarah Allen, Celeste Montoya, Christina Bejarano, and Nadia Brown. 2019. "Intersectional Linked Fate and Political Representation." *Politics, Groups, and Identities* 18 (2): 438–512.

Gershon, Sarah Allen, and Jessica Lavariega Monforti. 2021. "Intersecting Campaigns: Candidate Race, Ethnicity, Gender, and Voter Evaluations." *Politics, Groups, and Identities* 9 (3): 439–63.

Glick, Peter, and Susan T. Fiske. 1996. "The Ambivalent Sexism Inventory: Differentiating Hostile and Benevolent Sexism." *Journal of Personality and Social Psychology* 70 (3): 491–512.

Glick, Peter, and Susan T. Fiske. 1997. "Hostile and Benevolent Sexism: Measuring Ambivalent Sexist Attitudes toward Women." *Psychology of Women Quarterly* 21 (1): 119–35.

Gonzalez, Sylvia I., and Nichole M. Bauer. 2020. "Using Gender and Partisan Stereotypes to Evaluate Female Candidates." In *Politicking While Female: The Political Lives of Women*, edited by Nichole Bauer. Baton Rouge: Louisiana State University Press.

Goodman, Joseph K., Cynthia E. Kryder, and Amar Cheema. 2013. "Data Collection in a Flat World: Strengths and Weaknesses of Mechanical Turk Samples." *Journal of Behavioral Decision Making* 26 (3): 213–24.

Goodyear-Grant, Elizabeth. 2013. "Women Voters, Candidates, and Legislators: A Gender Perspective on Recent Party and Electoral Politics." In *Parties, Elections, and the Future of Canadian Politics*, edited by Amanda Bittner and Royce Koop, 119-39. Vancouver: University of British Columbia Press.

Goodyear-Grant, Elizabeth. 2019. "Candidates' Self-Presentation Strategies: Filling in the Gaps." In *Gendered Mediation: Identity and Image Making in Canadian Politics*, edited by Angelia Wagner and Joanna Everitt, 27–44. Vancouver: University of British Columbia Press.

Goodyear-Grant, Elizabeth, Melanee Thomas, Amanda Bittner, and Erin Tolley. 2021. "Women to the Left, Men to the Right? Updating the Sex Gap in Vote Choice in Canada." Presented at the Annual Conference of the Canadian Political Science Association, June 8.

Grant, John, and Fiona MacDonald. 2020. "The 'Alt' Right, Toxic Masculinity, and Violence." In *Turbulent Times, Transformational Possibilities? Gender and Politics Today and Tomorrow*, edited by Fiona MacDonald and Alexandra Dobrowolsky, 366–88. Toronto: University of Toronto Press.

Greig, Alan. 2019. "Masculinities and the Rise of the Far-Right Implications for Oxfam's Work on Gender Justice." Oxfam Research Backgrounder Series. www.oxfamamerica.org.

Grönlund, Kimmo, and Henry Miller. 2006. "The Determinants of Political Knowledge in Comparative Perspective." *Scandanavian Political Studies* 29 (4): 386–406.

Guariglia, Paola, Laura Piccardi, Flavio Giaimo, Sofia Alaimo, Giusy Miccichè, and Gabriella Antonucci. 2015. "The Eyes Test Is Influenced More by Artistic Inclination and Less by Sex." *Frontiers in Human Neuroscience* 9:292.

Guilford, J. P., and Howard G. Martin. 1943. *The Guilford-Martin Inventory of Factors G-A-M-I-N*. Beverly Hills, CA: Sheridan Supply.

Hacker, Jacob S., and Paul Pierson. 2020. *Let Them Eat Tweets: How the Right Rules in an Age of Extreme Inequality*. New York: Liveright.

Hallerback, Maria Unenge, Tove Lugnegård, Fredrik Hjärthag, and Christopher Gillberg. 2009. "The Reading the Mind in the Eyes Test: Test-Retest Reliability of a Swedish Version." *Cognitive Neuropsychiatry* 14 (2): 127–43.

Hammond, Matthew D., Chris G. Sibley, and Nikola C. Overall. 2014. "The Allure of Sexism: Psychological Entitlement Fosters Women's Endorsement of Benevolent Sexism over Time." *Social Psychological and Personality Science* 5 (4): 422–29.

Han, Hahrie. 2009. *Moved to Action: Motivation, Participation, and Inequality in American Politics*. Stanford, CA: Stanford University Press.

Hansen, Michael A., Jennifer L. Clemens, and Kathleen Dolan. 2022. "Gender Gaps, Partisan Gaps, and Cross-Pressures: An Examination of American Attitudes toward the Use of Force." *Politics & Gender* 18 (1): 273–95.

Harrington, Carol. 2021. "What Is 'Toxic Masculinity' and Why Does It Matter?" *Men and Masculinities* 24 (2): 345–52.

Harrison, Brian F., and Melissa R. Michelson. 2019. "Gender, Masculinity Threat, and Support for Transgender Rights: An Experimental Study." *Sex Roles* 80 (1–2): 63–75.

Hau, Caroline. 2015. "Tiger Mother as Ethnopreneur: Amy Chua and the Cultural Politics of Chineseness." *TRaNS: Trans-Regional and -National Studies of Southeast Asia* 3 (2): 213–37.

Hayes, Andrew F. 2018. *Introduction to Mediation, Moderation, and Conditional Process Analysis: A Regression-Based Approach*. New York: Guilford.

Hayes, Danny. 2005. "Candidate Qualities through a Partisan Lens: A Theory of Trait Ownership." *American Journal of Political Science* 49 (4): 908–23.

Hayes, Danny. 2011. "When Gender and Party Collide: Stereotyping in Candidate Trait Attribution." *Politics & Gender* 7 (2): 133–65.

Heilman, Madeline E., Caryn J. Block, and Richard F. Martell. 1995. "Sex Stereotypes: Do They Influence Perceptions of Managers?" *Journal of Social Behavior and Personality* 10 (4): 237–52.

Hershey, Marjorie Randon. 1977. "The Politics of Androgyny? Sex Roles and Attitudes toward Women in Politics." *American Politics Quarterly* 5 (3): 261–87.

Hess, Ursula, Reginald B. Adams Jr., Karl Grammer, and Robert E. Kleck. 2009. "Face Gender and Emotion Expression: Are Angry Women More like Men?" *Journal of Vision* 9 (12): 19.

Hesse, Monica. 2020. "The Weird Masculinity of Donald Trump." *Washington Post*, July 16. www.washingtonpost.com.

Hicks, William D., Carl E. Klarner, Seth C. McKee, and Daniel A. Smith. 2018. "Revisiting Majority-Minority Districts and Black Representation." *Political Research Quarterly* 71 (2): 408–23.

Himmelweit, Hilde T., Biberian, Marianne Jaeger, and Stockdale, Janet. 1978. "Memory for Past Vote: Implications of a Study of Bias in Recall." *British Journal of Political Science* 8 (3): 365–75.

Hinger, Sarah, and Brian Hauss. 2020. "The Trump Administration is Banning Talk About Race and Gender." American Civil Liberties Union. www.aclu.org.

Hodges, Sara D., and Daniel M. Wegner. 1997. "Automatic and Controlled Empathy." In *Empathic Accuracy*, 311–39. New York: Guilford.

Hoffman, Rose Marie. 2001. "The Measurement of Masculinity and Femininity: Historical Perspective and Implications for Counseling." *Journal of Counseling & Development* 79 (4): 472–85.

Holder, Aisha, Margo A. Jackson, and Joseph G. Poterotto. 2015. "Racial Microaggression Experiences and Coping Strategies of Black Women in Corporate Leadership." *Qualitative Psychology* 2 (2): 164–80.

Holman, Mirya R., Jennifer L. Merolla, and Elizabeth J. Zechmeister. 2011. "Sex, Stereotypes, and Security: An Experimental Study of the Effect of Crises on Assessments of Gender and Leadership." *Journal of Women, Politics & Policy* 32 (3): 173–92.

Holman, Mirya R., Jennifer L. Merolla, and Elizabeth J. Zechmeister. 2016. "Terrorist Threat, Stereotypes, and Candidate Evaluations." *Political Research Quarterly* 69 (1): 134–47.

Holman, Mirya R., Jennifer L. Merolla, and Elizabeth J. Zechmeister. 2022. "The Curious Case of Theresa May and the Public That Did Not Rally: Gendered Reactions to Terrorist Attacks Can Cause Slumps Not Bumps." *American Political Science Review* 116 (1): 249–64.

Holman, Mirya R., Jennifer L. Merolla, Elizabeth J. Zechmeister, and Ding Wang. 2019. "Terrorism, Gender, and the 2016 U.S. Presidential Election." *Electoral Studies* 61:1–8.

Holman, Mirya R., and Monica C. Schneider. 2018. "Gender, Race, and Political Ambition: How Intersectionality and Frames Influence Interest in Political Office." *Politics, Groups, and Identities* 6 (2): 264–80.

Holt, Cheryl L., and Jon B. Ellis. 1998. "Assessing the Current Validity of the Bem Sex-Role Inventory." *Sex Roles* 39 (11–12): 929–41.

Howell, Susan E., and Christine L. Day. 2000. "Complexities of the Gender Gap." *Journal of Politics* 62 (3): 858–74.

Huddy, Leonie. 2013. "From Group Identity to Political Cohesion and Commitment." In *The Oxford Handbook of Political Psychology*, edited by Leonie Huddy, David O. Sears, and Jack S. Levy, 737–73. New York: Oxford University Press.

Huddy, Leonie, Erin Cassese, and Mary-Kate Lizotte. 2008. "Gender, Public Opinion, and Political Reasoning." In *Political Women and American Democracy*, edited by Christina Wolbrecht, Karen Beckwith, and Lisa Baldez, 31–49. Cambridge: Cambridge University Press.

Huddy, Leonie, and Nayda Terkildsen. 1993. "Gender Stereotypes and the Perception of Male and Female Candidates." *American Journal of Political Science* 37 (1): 119–47.

Huddy, Leonie, and Nayda Terkildsen. 1993. "The Consequences of Gender Stereotypes for Women Candidates at Different Levels and Types of Office." *Political Research Quarterly* 46 (3): 503–25.

Huddy, Leonie, Romeo Gray, Stanley Feldman, and Elizabeth C. Connors. 2022. "Immigration Support: Does Immigrant Skill-Level Override the Effects of Racial and Ethnic Prejudice?" Paper presented at the annual meeting of the Midwest Political Science Association, Chicago, IL, April 7–10.

Hunt, Christopher John, Karen Gonsalkoraleand, and Stuart B. Murray. 2013. "Threatened Masculinity and Muscularity: An Experimental Examination of Multiple Aspects of Muscularity in Men." *Body Image* 10:290–99.

Hurtado, Aída, and Mrinal Sinha. 2016. *Beyond Machismo: Intersectional Latino Masculinities.* Austin: University of Texas Press.

Igielnik, Ruth. 2020. "Men and Women in the U.S. Continue to Differ in Voter Turnout Rate, Party Identification." Pew Research Center, August 18. www.pewresearch.org.

Igielnik, Ruth, Scott Keeter, and Hannah Hartig. 2021. "Behind Biden's 2020 Victory." Pew Research Center, June 30. https://www.pewresearch.org.

Ihme, Toni Alexander, and Markus Tausendpfund. 2018. "Gender Differences in Political Knowledge: Bringing Situation Back In." *Journal of Experimental Political Science* 5 (1): 39–55.

Iyengar, Shanto, and Sean J Westwood. 2015. "Fear and Loathing across Party Lines: New Evidence on Group Polarization." *American Journal of Political Science* 59 (3): 690–707.

Iyengar, Shanto, Yphtach Lelkes, Matthew Levendusky, Neil Malhotra, and Sean J. Westwood. 2019. "The Origins and Consequences of Affective Polarization in the United States." *Annual Review of Political Science* 22 (1): 129–46.

Jackman, Mary R. 1994. *The Velvet Glove: Paternalism and Conflict in Gender, Class, and Race Relations.* Berkeley: University of California Press.

Jakupcak, Matthew, David Lisak, and Lizabeth Roemer. 2002. "The Role of Masculine Ideology and Masculine Gender Role Stress in Men's Perpetration of Relationship Violence." *Psychology of Men & Masculinity* 3:97–106.

Jaramillo, Patricia. 2010. "Building a Theory, Measuring a Concept: Exploring Intersectionality and Latina Activism at the Individual Level." *Journal of Women, Politics & Policy* 31 (3): 193–216.

Jerit, Jennifer, and Jason Barabas. 2017. "Revisiting the Gender Gap in Political Knowledge." *Political Behavior* 39 (4): 817–38.

Johnson, Carol, and Blair Williams. 2020. "Gender and Political Leadership in a Time of COVID." *Politics & Gender* 16 (4): 943–50.

Johnson Carew, Jessica D. 2016. "How Do You See Me? Stereotyping of Black Women and How It Affects Them in an Electoral Context." In *Distinct Identities: Minority Women in U.S. Politics*, edited by Nadia Brown and Sarah Gershon, 111–31. New York: Routledge.

Johnston, Richard. 2019. "Affective Polarization in the Canadian Party System, 1988–2015." Paper presented at the annual meeting of the Canadian Political Science Association, Vancouver, BC, June 4.

Jones, Robert P., Daniel Cox, Molly Fisch-Friedman and Alex Vandermaas-Peeler. 2018. "Diversity, Division, Discrimination: The State of Young America." PRRI/MTV, March 17. https://www.prri.org.

Jordan-Zachary, Julia. 2007. "Am I a Black Woman or a Woman Who Is Black? A Few Thoughts on the Meaning of Intersectionality." *Politics & Gender* 3 (2): 256–63.

Jost, John T., and Mahzarin R. Banaji. 1994. "The Role of Stereotyping in System-Justification and the Production of False Consciousness." *British Journal of Social Psychology* 33 (1): 1–27.

Jost, John T., Melanie Langer, Vivienne Badaan, Flavio Azevedo, Edgardo Etchezahar, Joaquin Ungaretti, and Erin P. Hennes. 2017. "Ideology and the Limits of Self-Interest: System Justification Motivation and Conservative Advantages in Mass Politics." *Translational Issues in Psychological Science* 3 (3): e1–e26.

Juge, George E. 2013. "'Get Away From Me!' Implicit and Explicit Transphobia in Swedish-Speaking Men." Master's thesis, University of East Anglia.

Jungblut, Marc, and Mario Haim. 2023. "Visual Gender Stereotyping in Campaign Communication: Evidence on Female and Male Candidate Imagery in 28 Countries." *Communication Research* 50 (5): 561–83.

Junn, Jane. 2017. "The Trump Majority: White Womanhood and the Making of Female Voters in the U.S." *Politics, Groups, and Identities* 5 (2): 343–52.

Junn, Jane, and Natalie Masuoka. 2020. "The Gender Gap Is a Race Gap: Women Voters in US Presidential Elections." *Perspectives on Politics* 18 (4): 1135–45.

Kahn, Kim. F. 1996. *The Political Consequences of Being a Woman: How Stereotypes Influence the Conduct and Consequences of Political Campaigns*. New York: Columbia University Press.

Kamas, Linda, and Anne Preston. 2019. "Can Empathy Explain Gender Differences in Economic Policy Views in the United States?" *Feminist Economics* 25 (1): 58–89.

Karniol, Rachel, Rivi Gabay, Yael Ochion, and Yael Harari. 1998. "Is Gender or Gender-Role Orientation a Better Predictor of Empathy in Adolescence?" *Sex Roles* 39:45–59.

Karp, Jeffrey A., and Susan A. Banducci. 1999. "Political Efficacy and Participation in Nineteen Democracies: How Electoral Rules Shape Political Behavior." Paper presented at the Annual Conference of the American Political Science Association, Atlanta, GA, September 1.

Katz, Jackson. 2016. *Man Enough? Donald Trump, Hillary Clinton, and the Politics of Presidential Masculinity*. Northampton, MA: Interlink.

Kaufmann, Karen M. 2002. "Culture Wars, Secular Realignment, and the Gender Gap in Party Identification." *Political Behavior* 24 (3): 283–307.

Kaufmann, Karen M. 2006. "The Gender Gap." *PS: Political Science and Politics* 39 (3): 447–53.

Kaufmann, Karen, and John R. Petrocik. 1999. "The Changing Politics of American Men: Understanding the Sources of the Gender Gap." *American Journal of Political Science* 43 (3): 864–87.

Kawahara, Debra M. 2007. "Asian American Women Leaders: The Intersection of Race, Gender, and Leadership." In *Women and Leadership: Transforming Vision and Diverse Voices*, edited by Jean Lau Chine, Bernice Lott, Joy K. Rice, and Janis Sanchez-Hucles, 297–313. Hoboken, NJ: Blackwell.

Keller, Jared. 2018. "The (Coming) End of Toxic Masculinity." *Pacific Standard*, January 10. psmag.com.

Kenski, Kate, and Kathleen Hall Jamieson. 2000. "The Gender Gap in Political Knowledge: Are Women Less Knowledgeable than Men about Politics?" In *Everything You Think You Know about Politics . . . and Why You're Wrong*, edited by K. H. Jamieson, 83–89. New York: Basic Books.

Kevins, Anthony, and Stuart N. Soroka. 2018. "Growing Apart? Partisan Sorting in Canada, 1992–2015." *Canadian Journal of Political Science* 51 (1): 103–33.

Khorashad, Behzad S., Simon Baron-Cohen, Ghasem M. Roshan, Mojtaba Kazemian, Ladan Khazai, Zahra Aghili, Ali Talaei, and Mozhgan Afkhamizadeh. 2015. "The 'Reading the Mind in the Eyes' Test: Investigation of Psychometric Properties and Test–Retest Reliability of the Persian Version." *Journal of Autism and Developmental Disorders* 45 (9): 2651–66.

Kimmel, Michael. 1994. *Manhood in America: A Cultural History*. Oxford: Oxford University Press.

Kimmel, Michael. 2006. *Manhood in America: A Cultural History*. 2nd ed. New York: Free Press.

Kimmel, Michael. 2013. *Angry White Men: American Masculinity at the End of an Era*. New York: Nation Books/Perseus.

Kimmel, Michael S., and Michael A. Messner. 1992. *Men's Lives*. 2nd ed. New York: Macmillan.

Kinder, Donald R. 1986. "Presidential Character Revisited." In *Political Cognition*, edited by Richard R. Lau and David O. Sears, 233–55. Hillsdale, NJ: Lawrence Erlbaum.

Kirkland, Rena, Eric Peterson, Crystal Baker, Stephanie Miller, and Steven Pulos. 2013. "Meta-Analysis Reveals Adult Female Superiority in 'Reading the Mind in the Eyes Test.'" *North American Journal of Psychology* 15:449–58.

Klatch, Rebecca E. 1987. *Women of the New Right*. Philadelphia, PA: Temple University Press.

Kleiman, Michael B. 1976. "Trends in Racial Differences in Political Efficacy: 1952 to 1972." *Phylon (1960–)* 37 (2): 159–62.

Klein, Ethel. 1984. *Gender Politics: From Consciousness to Mass Politics*. Cambridge, MA: Harvard University Press.

Klofstad, Casey A., Rindy C. Anderson, and Stephen Nowicki. 2015. "Perceptions of Competence, Strength, and Age Influence Voters to Select Leaders with Lower-Pitched Voices." *PLOS ONE* 10 (8): e0133779.

Knafo, Ariel, Alessandra C. Iervolino, and Robert Plomin. 2005. "Masculine Girls and Feminine Boys: Genetic and Environmental Contributions to Atypical Gender Development in Early Childhood." *Journal of Personality and Social Psychology* 88 (2): 400–412.

Koch, Jeffrey W. 2000. "Do Citizens Apply Gender Stereotypes to Infer Candidates' Ideological Orientations?" *Journal of Politics* 62 (2): 414–29.

Koenig, Anne M. 2018. "Comparing Prescriptive and Descriptive Gender Stereotypes about Children, Adults, and the Elderly." *Frontiers in Psychology* 9:1086.

Koenig, Anne M., Alice H. Eagly, Abigail A. Mitchell, and Tiina Ristikari. 2011. "Are Leader Stereotypes Masculine? A Meta-Analysis of Three Research Paradigms." *Psychological Bulletin* 137 (4): 616–42.

Kosakowska-Berezecka, Natasza, Tomasz Besta, Krystyna Adamska, Michal Jaśkiewicz, Pawel Jurek, and Joseph A. Vandello. A. 2016. "If My Masculinity Is Threatened I Won't Support Gender Equality? The Role of Agentic Self-Stereotyping in Restoration of Manhood and Perception of Gender Relations." *Psychology of Men & Masculinity* 17:274–84.

Krieg, Gregory. 2016. "Donald Trump Defends Size of His Penis." CNN Politics, March 4. www.cnn.com.

Krook, Mona Lena. 2020. *Violence against Women in Politics*. Vol. 28. New York: Oxford University Press.

Krumpal, Ivar. 2013. "Determinants of Social Desirability Bias in Sensitive Surveys: A Literature Review." *Quality & Quantity* 47 (4): 2025–47.

Krupnikov, Yanna, and Nichole M. Bauer. 2014. "The Relationship between Campaign Negativity, Gender, and Campaign Context." *Political Behavior* 36 (1): 167–88.

Kurtzleben, Danielle. 2016. "Trump and the Testosterone Takeover of 2016." NPR, October 1. www.npr.org.

Kuteleva, Anna, and Sarah J. Clifford. 2021. "Gendered Securitization: Trump's and Putin's Discursive Politics of the COVID-19 Pandemic." *European Journal of International Security* 6 (3): 301–17.

Lane, Robert E. 1959. *Political Life: Why and How People Get Involved in Politics*. New York: Free Press.

Laurent, Sean M., and Sara D. Hodges. 2009. "Gender Roles and Empathic Accuracy: The Role of Communion in Reading Minds." *Sex Roles* 60 (5–6): 387–98.

Laustsen, Lasse, and Alexander Bor. 2017. "The Relative Weight of Character Traits in Political Candidate Evaluations: Warmth Is More Important than Competence, Leadership, and Integrity." *Electoral Studies* 49:96–107.

Lawless, Jennifer L. 2004. "Women, War, and Winning Elections: Gender Stereotyping in the Post–September 11th Era." *Political Research Quarterly* 57 (3): 479–90.

Lawrence, E. J., P. Shaw, D. Baker, S. Baron-Cohen, and A. S. David. 2004. "Measuring Empathy: Reliability and Validity of the Empathy Quotient." *Psychological Medicine* 34 (5): 911–20.

Lay, J. Celeste, Mirya R. Holman, Angela L. Bos, Jill S. Greenlee, Zoe M. Oxley, and Allison Buffett. 2021. "TIME for Kids to Learn Gender Stereotypes: Analysis of Gender and Political Leadership in a Common Social Studies Resource for Children." *Politics & Gender* 17 (1): 1–22.

Leaper, Campbell, and Stephanie R. Van. 2008. "Masculinity Ideology, Covert Sexism, and Perceived Gender Typicality in Relation to Young Men's Academic Motivation and Choices in College." *Psychology of Men and Masculinity* 9 (3): 139–53.

Lee, Marilyn C. 1952. "Relationship of Masculinity-Femininity to Tests of Mechanical and Clerical Abilities." *Journal of Applied Psychology* 36 (6): 377–80.

Lefevre, Carmen E., Gary J. Lewis, Timothy C. Bates, Milena Dzhelyova, Vinet Coetzee, Ian J. Deary, and David I. Perrett. 2012. "No Evidence for Sexual Dimorphism of Facial Width-to-Height Ratio in Four Large Adult Samples." *Evolution and Human Behavior* 33 (6): 623–27.

Levant, Ronald F. 1992. "Toward the Reconstruction of Masculinity." *Journal of Family Psychology* 5 (3–4): 379–402.

Levant, Ronald F. 2011. "Research in the Psychology of Men and Masculinity Using the Gender Role Strain Paradigm as a Framework." *American Psychologist* 66 (8): 765–76.

Levant, Ronald F., David J. Wimer, Christine M. Williams, K. Bryant Smalley, and Delilah Noronha. 2009. "The Relationships between Masculinity Variables, Health Risk Behaviors, and Attitudes toward Seeking Psychological Help." *International Journal of Men's Health* 8 (1): 3–21.

Levant, Ronald F., Linda S. Hirsch, Elizabeth Celentano, Tracy M. Cozza, Susan Hill, Mary Maceachern, Nadine Marty, and John Schnedeker. 1992. "The Male Role: An Investigation of Contemporary Norms." *Journal of Mental Health Counseling* 14 (3): 325–37.

Levant, Ronald F., Richard G. Majors, and Michelle L. Kelley. 1998. "Masculinity Ideology among Young African American and European American Women and Men in Different Regions of the United States." *Cultural Diversity and Mental Health* 4 (3): 227–36.

Levant, Ronald F., Ryon McDermott, Mike C. Parent, Nuha Alshabani, James R. Mahalik, and Joseph H. Hammer. 2020. "Development and Evaluation of a New Short Form of the Conformity to Masculine Norms Inventory (CMNI-30)." *Journal of Counseling Psychology* 67 (5): 622–36.

Liekefett, Luisa, and Julia C. Becker. 2022. "Low System Justification Is Associated with Support for Both Progressive and Reactionary Social Change." *European Journal of Social Psychology* 52 (7): 1015–30.

Lippa, Richard A. 2016. "Biological Influences on Masculinity." In *APA Handbook of Men and Masculinities*, edited by Joel Y. Wong and Stephen R. Wester, 187–209. Washington, DC: American Psychological Association.

Liu, William M. 2002. "Exploring the Lives of Asian American Men: Racial Identity, Male Role Norms, Gender Role Conflict, and Prejudicial Attitudes." *Psychology of Men and Masculinity* 3 (2): 107–18.

Lizotte, Mary-Kate. 2017. "Gender, Partisanship, and Issue Gaps." *Analyses of Social Issues and Public Policy* 17 (1): 379–405.

Lizotte, Mary-Kate. 2018. "Attitudes toward Women and the Influence of Gender on Political Decision Making." *Oxford Research Encyclopedia of Politics* 1–28. doi. org/10.1093/acrefore/9780190228637.013.771.

Lizotte, Mary-Kate. 2019. "Authoritarian Personality and Gender Differences in Gun Control Attitudes." *Journal of Women, Politics & Policy* 40 (3): 385–408.

Lizotte, Mary-Kate. 2020. *Gender Differences in Public Opinion: Values and Political Consequences*. Philadelphia, PA: Temple University Press.

Lizotte, Mary-Kate, and Andrew H. Sidman. 2009. "Explaining the Gender Gap in Political Knowledge." *Politics & Gender* 5 (2): 127–51.

Lombard, Ella, Jovenia Azpeitia, and Sapna Cheryan. 2021. "Built on Uneven Ground: How Masculine Defaults Disadvantage Women in Political Leadership." *Psychological Inquiry* 32 (2): 107–16.

Lovenduski, Joni. 2005. *Feminizing Politics*. Cambridge: Polity.

Lu, Alexander, and Y. Joel Wong. 2013. "Stressful Experiences of Masculinity among US-Born and Immigrant Asian American Men." *Gender & Society* 27 (3): 345–71.

Lublin, David. 1999. "Racial Redistricting and African-American Representation: A Critique of 'Do Majority-Minority Districts Maximize Substantive Black Representation in Congress?'" *American Political Science Review* 93 (1): 183–86.

Ludlow, Larry H., and James R. Mahalik. 2001. "Examining the Conformity to Masculine Norms Inventory." *Journal of Applied Measurement* 2 (3): 205–26.

Lupia, Arthur. 2015. *Uninformed: Why People Seem to Know So Little about Politics and What We Can Do about It*. Oxford: Oxford University Press.

Luskin, Robert C., and John G. Bullock. 2011. "'Don't Know Means Don't Know': DK Responses and the Public's Level of Political Knowledge." *Journal of Politics* 73 (2): 547–57.

Maass, Anne, Mara Cadinu, Gaia Guarnieri, and Annalisa Grasselli. 2003. "Sexual Harassment under Social Identity Threat: The Computer Harassment Paradigm." *Journal of Personality and Social Psychology* 85:853–70.

Macdonald, Fiona, and Alexandra Dobrowolsky. 2020. *Turbulent Times, Transformational Possibilities? Gender and Politics Today and Tomorrow*. Toronto: University of Toronto Press.

Magliozzi, Devon, Aliya Saperstein, and Laurel Westbrook. 2016. "Scaling Up: Representing Gender Diversity in Survey Research." *Socius* 2 (1). doi. org/10.1177/2378023116664352.

Mahalik, James R., Benjamin D. Locke, Larry H. Ludlow, Matthew A. Diemer, Ryan P. J. Scott, Michael Gottfried, Gary Freitas. 2000. "Development of the Conformity to Masculine Gender Roles Scale." Paper presented at the *Annual Meeting of the American Psychological Association*, Washington, DC, August 4–8.

Majors, Richard, and Janet Mancini Billson. 1993. *Cool Pose: The Dilemma of Black Manhood in America*. New York: Simon & Schuster.

Mangum, Maurice. 2003. "Psychological Involvement and Black Voter Turnout." *Political Research Quarterly* 56 (1): 41–48.

Mansell, Jordan, Allison Harell, Melanee Thomas, and Tania Gosselin. 2022. "Competitive Loss, Gendered Backlash, and Sexism in Politics." *Political Behavior* 44:455–76.

Manza, Jeff, and Clem Brooks. 1998. "The Gender Gap in U.S. Presidential Elections: When? Why? Implications?" *American Journal of Sociology* 103 (5): 1235–66.

Markus, Gregory. B., 1982. "Political Attitudes During an Election Year: A Report on the 1980 NES Panel Study." *American Political Science Review* 76 (3): 538–60.

Marx Ferree, Myra. 2020. "The Crisis of Masculinity for Gendered Democracies: Before, during, and after Trump." *Sociological Forum* 35 (S1): 898–917.

Mason, Lilliana. 2018. *Uncivil Agreement: How Politics Became Our Identity*. Chicago: University of Chicago Press.

McClain, Paula D., Jessica D. Johnson Carew, Eugene Walton Jr., and Candis S. Watts. 2009. "Group Membership, Group Identity, and Group Consciousness: Measures of Racial Identity in American Politics?" *Annual Review of Political Science* 12: 471–85.

McCue, Clifford P., and J. David Gopoian. 2000. "Dispositional Empathy and the Political Gender Gap." *Women & Politics* 21 (2): 1–20.

McCusker, Michael G., and M. Paz Galupo. 2011. "The Impact of Men Seeking Help for Depression on Perceptions of Masculine and Feminine Characteristics." *Psychology of Men and Masculinity* 12 (3): 275–84.

McDermott, Monika L. 2016. *Masculinity, Feminity, and American Political Behavior*. New York: Oxford University Press.

McDermott, Ryon C., Kyle M. Brasil, Nicholas C. Borgogna, Jennifer L. Barinas, April T. Berry, and Ronald F. Levant. 2021. "The Politics of Men's and Women's Traditional Masculinity Ideology in the United States." *Psychology of Men & Masculinities* 22 (4): 627–38.

McDermott, Ryon C., Nicholas C. Borgogna, Joseph H. Hammer, April T. Berry, and Ronald F. Levant. 2020. "More Similar Than Different? Testing the Construct Validity of Men's and Women's Traditional Masculinity Ideology Using the Male Role Norms Inventory-Very Brief." *Psychology of Men & Masculinities* 21 (4): 523–32.

McDermott, Ryon C., Ronald F. Levant, Joseph H. Hammer, Nicholas C. Borgogna, and Daniel K. McKelvey. 2019. "Development and Validation of a Five-Item Male Role Norms Inventory Using Bifactor Modeling." *Psychology of Men & Masculinities* 20 (4): 467–77.

Messerschmidt, James W. 2012. "Engendering Gendered Knowledge: Assessing the Academic Appropriation of Hegemonic Masculinity." *Men and Masculinities* 15 (1): 56–76.

Messerschmidt, James W. 2018. "Multiple Masculinities." In *Handbook of the Sociology of Gender*, eds. Barbara J. Risman, Carissa M. Froyum, and William J. Scarborough. Springer.

Messerschmidt, James W. 2019. "Hidden in Plain Sight: On the Omnipresence of Hegemonic Masculinities." *Masculinities: A Journal of Identity and Culture* 12: 14–29.

Messerschmidt, James W. 2021. "Donald Trump, Dominating Masculine Necropolitics, and COVID-19." *Men and Masculinities* 24 (1): 189–94.

Messner, Michael A. 1998. "The Limits of 'The Male Sex Role': An Analysis of the Men's Liberation and Men's Rights Movements' Discourse." *Gender & Society* 12 (3): 255–76.

Messner, Michael A. 2007. "The Masculinity of the Governator: Muscle and Compassion in American Politics." *Gender & Society* 21 (4): 461–80.

Michalska, Kalina J., Katherine D. Kinzler, and Jean Decety. 2013. "Age-Related Sex Differences in Explicit Measures of Empathy Do Not Predict Brain Responses Across Childhood and Adolescence." *Developmental Cognitive Neuroscience* 3: 22–32.

Michelson, Melissa R. 2000. "Political Efficacy and Electoral Participation of Chicago Latinos." *Social Science Quarterly* 81 (1): 136–50.

Miller, Andrea L., and Eugene Borgida. 2019. "The Temporal Dimension of System Justification: Gender Ideology Over the Course of the 2016 Election." *Personality and Social Psychology Bulletin* 45 (7): 1057–67.

Miller, David I., Kyle M. Nolla, Alice H. Eagly, and David H. Uttal. 2018. "The Development of Children's Gender-Science Stereotypes: A Meta-Analysis of 5 Decades of U.S. Draw-A-Scientist Studies." *Child Development* 89 (6): 1943–55.

Miller, Melissa K. 2019. "Who Knows More About Politics? A Dual Explanation for the Gender Gap." *American Politics Research* 47 (1): 174–88.

Mondak, Jeffery J., and Mary R. Anderson. 2003. "A Knowledge Gap or a Guessing Game? Gender and Political Knowledge." *Public Perspective* 14 (1): 6–9.

Mondak, Jeffrey J., and Mary R. Anderson. 2004. "The Knowledge Gap: A Reexamination of Gender-Based Differences in Political Knowledge." *The Journal of Politics* 66 (2): 492–512.

Mondak, Jeffery J., and Damarys Canache. 2004. "Knowledge Variables in Cross-National Social Inquiry." *Social Science Quarterly* 85 (3): 539–58.

Monteith, Margo J., and Laura K. Hildebrand. 2020. "Sexism, Perceived Discrimination, and System Justification in the 2016 US Presidential Election Context." *Group Processes and Intergroup Relations* 23 (2): 163–78.

Moore, Aaron J., and David Dewberry. 2012. "The Masculine Image of Presidents as Sporting Figures: A Public Relations Perspective." *Sage Open* 2 (3).

Morrell, Michael E. 2003. "Survey and Experimental Evidence for a Reliable and Valid Measure of Internal Political Efficacy." *The Public Opinion Quarterly* 67 (4): 589–602.

Morrell, Michael E. 2005. "Deliberation, Democratic Decision-Making, and Internal Political Efficacy." *Political Behavior* 27 (1): 49–69.

Moskowitz, David A., and Trevor A. Hart. 2011. "The Influence of Physical Body Traits and Masculinity on Anal Sex Roles in Gay and Bisexual Men." *Archives of Sexual Behavior* 40 (4): 835–41.

Mudde, Cas. 2007. *Populist Radical Right Parties in Europe*. Cambridge: Cambridge University Press.

Mudde, Cas. 2017. *The Populist Radical Right: A Reader*. London: Routledge.

Mudde, Cas, and Cristobal Rovira Kaltwasser. 2017. *Populism: A Very Short Introduction*. Oxford: Oxford University Press.

Murnen, Sarah K., Carrie Wright, and Gretchen Kaluzny. 2002. "If 'Boys Will Be Boys,' Then Girls Will Be Victims? A Meta-Analytic Review of the Research That Relates Masculine Ideology to Sexual Aggression." *Sex Roles* 46 (11): 359–75.

Mutz, Diana C. 2018. "Status Threat, Not Economic Hardship, Explains the 2016 Presidential Vote." *Proceedings of the National Academy of Sciences of the United States of America*. 115 (19): E4330–39.

Neville-Shepard, Meredith. 2021. "Masks and Emasculation: Populist Crisis Rhetoric and the 2020 Presidential Election." *American Behavioral Scientist* 68 (1): 97–111.

Newman, Benjamin J., Todd K. Hartman, Patrick L. Lown, and Stanley Feldman. 2015. "Easing the Heavy Hand: Humanitarian Concern, Empathy, and Opinion on Immigration." *British Journal of Political Science* 45 (3): 583–607.

Newport, Frank. 2009. "Women More Likely to Be Democrats, Regardless of Age." Gallup, June 12. news.gallup.com.

Niemi, Richard G., Stephen C. Craig, and Franco Mattei. 1991. "Measuring Internal Political Efficacy in the 1988 National Election Study." *American Political Science Review* 85 (4): 1407–13.

Norrander, Barbara. 1999. "The Evolution of the Gender Gap." *Public Opinion Quarterly* 63 (4): 566–76.

Norrander, Barbara. 2003. "The Intraparty Gender Gap: Differences between Male and Female Voters in the 1980–2000 Presidential Primaries." *PS: Political Science and Politics* 36 (2): 181–86.

Nylund-Gibson, Karen, and Andrew Young Choi. 2018. "Ten Frequently Asked Questions about Latent Class Analysis." *Translational Issues in Psychological Science* 4 (4): 440–61.

O'Connor, Cliodhna, and Helene Joffe. 2020. "Intercoder Reliability in Qualitative Research: Debates and Practical Guidelines." *International Journal of Qualitative Methods* 19:1–13.

Olderbak, Sally, Oliver Wilhelm, Gabriel Olaru, Meghan W. Brenneman, and Richard D. Roberts. 2015. "A Psychometric Analysis of the Reading the Mind in the Eyes Test: Toward a Brief Form for Research and Applied Settings." *Frontiers in Psychology* 6. doi.org/10.3389/fpsyg.2015.01503.

Oliver, J. Eric, and Wendy M. Rahn. 2016. "Rise of the Trumpenvolk: Populism in the 2016 Election." *Annals of the American Academy of Political and Social Science* 667 (1): 189–206.

Oliver, Sarah, and Meredith Conroy. 2020. *Who Runs? The Masculine Advantage in Candidate Emergence*. Ann Arbor: University of Michigan Press.

Oliver, William. 1989. "Black Males and Social Problems: Prevention through Afrocentric Socialization." *Journal of Black Studies* 20 (1): 15–39.

Ondercin, Heather L. 2017. "Who Is Responsible for the Gender Gap? The Dynamics of Men's and Women's Democratic Macropartisanship, 1950–2012." *Political Research Quarterly* 70 (4): 749–61.

Ondercin, Heather L., and Daniel Jones-White. 2011. "Gender Jeopardy: What Is the Impact of Gender Differences in Political Knowledge on Political Participation?" *Social Science Quarterly* 92 (3): 675–94.

Oxley, Zoe M., Mirya R. Holman, Jill S. Greenlee, Angela L. Bos, and J. Celeste Lay. 2020. "Children's Views of the American Presidency." *Public Opinion Quarterly* 84 (Spring): 141–57.

Palmer, Carl L. and Rolfe D. Peterson. 2020. "Toxic Mask-ulinity: The Link between Masculine Toughness and Affective Reactions to Mask Wearing in the COVID-19 Era." *Politics & Gender* 16 (4): 1044–51.

Pardo, Mary. 1990. "Mexican American Women Grassroots Community Activists: 'Mothers of East Los Angeles.'" *Frontiers* 11:1–7.

Parent, Mike C., and Bonnie Moradi. 2011. "An Abbreviated Tool for Assessing Conformity to Masculine Norms: Psychometric Properties of the Conformity to Masculine Norms Inventory-46." *Psychology of Men & Masculinity* 12 (4): 339–53.

Parent, Mike C., Teresa D. Gobble, and Aaron Rochlen. 2019. "Social Media Behavior, Toxic Masculinity, and Depression." *Psychology of Men & Masculinities* 20 (3): 277–87.

Parrott, Dominic J. 2009. "Aggression toward Gay Men as Gender Role Enforcement: Effects of Male Role Norms, Sexual Prejudice, and Masculine Gender Role Stress." *Journal of Personality* 77:1137–66.

Pascoe, C. J. 2003. "Multiple Masculinities? Teenage Boys Talk about Jocks and Gender." *American Behavioral Scientist* 46:1423–38.

Pascoe, C. J. 2005. "'Dude, You're a Fag': Adolescent Masculinity and the Fag Discourse." *Sexualities* 8 (3): 329–46.

Pascoe, C. J. 2007. *Dude, You're a Fag: Masculinity and Sexuality in High School*. Berkeley: University of California Press.

Pascoe, C. J. 2017. "Who Is a Real Man? The Gender of Trumpism." *MCS-Masculinities and Social Change* 6 (2): 119–41.

Pateman, Carol. 1989. *The Disorder of Women: Democracy, Feminism, and Political Theory*. Cambridge: Polity.

Paxton, Pamela Marie, and Melanie M. Hughes. 2018. "Gender and Politics in the 2016 U.S. Election and Beyond." *Socius: Sociological Research for a Dynamic World* 4. doi.org/10.1177/2378023118763844.

Paxton, Pamela Marie, Melanie M. Hughes, and Tiffany Barnes. 2020. *Women, Politics, and Power: A Global Perspective*. Lanham, MD: Rowman & Littlefield.

Pearson, Elizabeth. 2019. "Extremism and Toxic Masculinity: The Man Question Re-Posed." *International Affairs* 95 (6): 1251–70.

Pelligra, Vittorio. 2011. "Empathy, Guilt-Aversion, and Patterns of Reciprocity." *Journal of Neuroscience, Psychology, and Economics* 4 (3): 161–73.

Peralta, Robert L., Jennifer L. Steele, Stacey Nofziger, and Michael Rickles. 2010. "The Impact of Gender on Binge Drinking Behavior among U.S. College Students Attending a Midwestern University: An Analysis of Two Gender Measures." *Feminist Criminology* 5 (4): 355–79.

Petersen, Michael Bang, Daniel Sznycer, Leda Cosmides, and John Tooby. 2012. "Who Deserves Help? Evolutionary Psychology, Social Emotions, and Public Opinion about Welfare." *Political Psychology* 33 (3): 395–418.

Petrocik, John R. 1996. "Issue Ownership in Presidential Elections, With a 1980 Case Study." *American Journal of Political Science* 40 (3): 825–50.

Petrocik, John R., William L. Benoit, and G. J. Hansen. 2003. "Issue Ownership and Presidential Campaigning, 1952–2000." *Political Science Quarterly* 118 (4): 599–626.

Pew Research Center. 2018. "An Examination of the 2016 Electorate, Based on Validated Voters." Pew Research Center, August 9. www.people-press.org.

Pfeffer, Carla A., Christabel L. Rogalin, and Cari A. Gee. 2016. "Masculinities through a Cross-Disciplinary Lens: Lessons from Sociology and Psychology." *Sociology Compass* 10:652–72.

Phillips, Anne. 1998. *Feminism and Politics*. New York: Oxford University Press.

Phua, Voon Chin. 2007. "Contesting and Maintaining Hegemonic Masculinities: Gay Asian American Men in Mate Selection." *Sex Roles* 57 (11): 909–18.

Pleck, Joseph H. 1981. *The Myth of Masculinity*. Cambridge, MA: MIT Press.

Pleck, Joseph H. 1995. "The Gender Role Strain Paradigm: An Update." In *A New Psychology of Men*, edited by Ronald F. Levant and William S. Pollack, 11–32. New York: Basic Books/Hachette.

Pleck, Joseph H., Freya L. Sonenstein, and Leighton C. Ku. 1994. "Attitudes toward Male Roles among Adolescent Males: A Discriminant Validity Analysis." *Sex Roles* 30 (7): 481–501.

Pollock, Philip H., III. "The Participatory Consequences of Internal and External Political Efficacy: A Research Note." *Western Political Quarterly* 36 (3): 400–409.

Powell, Gary N., D. Anthony Butterfield, and Xueting Jiang. 2018. "Why Trump and Clinton Won and Lost: The Roles of Hypermasculinity and Androgyny." *Equality, Diversity, and Inclusion: An International Journal* 37 (1): 44–62.

Prado, Luis Antonio. 2004. "Patriarchy and Machismo: Political, Economic and Social Effects on Women." Master's thesis, California State University, San Bernardino.

Pratto, Felicia, Jim Sidanius, and Shana Levin. 2006. "Social Dominance Theory and the Dynamics of Intergroup Relations: Taking Stock and Looking Forward." *European Review of Social Psychology* 17 (1): 271–320.

Prentice, Deborah A., and Erica Carranza. 2002. "What Women and Men Should Be, Shouldn't Be, Are Allowed to Be, and Don't Have to Be: The Contents of Prescriptive Gender Stereotypes." *Psychology of Women Quarterly* 26 (4): 269–91.

Preston, Stephanie D., and Frans B. M. de Waal. 2002. "Empathy: Its Ultimate and Proximate Bases." *Behavioral and Brain Sciences* 25 (1): 1–20.

Preuhs, Robert R., and Eric Gonzalez Juenke. "Latino US State Legislators in the 1990s: Majority-Minority Districts, Minority Incorporation, and Institutional Position." *State Politics & Policy Quarterly* 11 (1): 48–75.

Ranehill, Eva, and Roberto A. Weber. 2022. "Gender Preference Gaps and Voting for Redistribution." *Experimental Economics* 25 (3): 845–75.

Ratliff, Kate A., Liz Redford, John Conway, and Colin T. Smith. 2019. "Engendering Support: Hostile Sexism Predicts Voting for Donald Trump over Hillary Clinton in the 2016 U.S. Presidential Election." *Group Processes and Intergroup Relations* 22 (4): 578–93.

Reidy, Dennis E., Colleen A. Sloan, and Amos Zeichner. 2009. "Gender Role Conformity and Aggression: Influence of Perpetrator and Victim Conformity on Direct Physical Aggression in Women." *Personality and Individual Differences* 46:231–35.

Reidy, Dennis E., Danielle S. Berke, Brittany Gentile, and Amos Zeichner. 2014. "Man Enough? Masculine Discrepancy Stress and Intimate Partner Violence." *Personality and Individual Differences* 68:160–64.

Reidy, Dennis E., Joanne P. Smith-Darden, Kai S. Cortina, Roger M. Kernsmith, and Poco D. Kernsmith. 2015. "Masculine Discrepancy Stress, Teen Dating Violence, and Sexual Violence Perpetration among Adolescent Boys." *Journal of Adolescent Health* 56:619–24.

Reidy, Dennis E., Kathryn A. Brookmeyer, Brittany Gentile, Danielle S. Berke, and Amos Zeichner. 2016. "Gender Role Discrepancy Stress, High-Risk Sexual Behavior, and Sexually Transmitted Disease." *Archives of Sexual Behavior* 45:459–65.

Relman, Eliza. 2019. "The Most Disparaging Nicknames Trump Used for His Political Enemies and Former Allies." *Business Insider*, June 7. www.businessinsider.com.

Reynolds-Dobbs, Wendy, Kecia M. Thomas, and Matthew S. Harrison. 2008. "From Mammy to Superwoman: Images That Hinder Black Women's Career Representation." *Journal of Career Development* 35 (2): 129–50.

Ridgeway, Cecilia L. 2011. *Framed by Gender: How Gender Inequality Persists in the Modern World.* New York: Oxford University Press.

Ridgeway, Cecilia L., and Shelley J. Correll. 2004. "Unpacking the Gender System: A Theoretical Perspective on Gender Beliefs and Social Relations." *Gender & Society* 18 (4): 510–31.

Risman, Barbara J. 2004. "Gender as a Social Structure: Theory Wrestling with Activism." *Gender & Society* 18 (4): 429–50.

Ritter, Gretchen. 2007. "Gender and Politics over Time." *Politics and Gender* 3 (3): 386–97.

Roberts, Damon C., and Stephen M. Utych. 2020. "Linking Gender, Language, and Partisanship: Developing a Database of Masculine and Feminine Words." *Political Research Quarterly* 73 (1): 40–50.

Rodgers, Harrell R., Jr. "Toward Explanation of the Political Efficacy and Political Cynicism of Black Adolescents: An Exploratory Study." *American Journal of Political Science* 18 (2): 257–82.

Rodrigues, Sarina M., Laura R. Saslow, Natalia Garcia, Oliver P. John, and Dacher Keltner. 2009. "Oxytocin Receptor Genetic Variation Relates to Empathy and Stress Reactivity in Humans." *Proceedings of the National Academy of Sciences* 106 (50): 21437–41.

Rosenstone, Steven J., and John Mark Hansen. 1993. *Mobilization, Participation, and Democracy in America*. New York: Longman.

Rosenwasser, Shirley Miller, and Jana Seale. 1988. "Attitudes toward a Hypothetical Male or Female Presidential Candidate—A Research Note." *Political Psychology* 9 (4): 591–98.

Rosenwasser, Shirley Miller, and Norma G. Dean. 1989. "Gender Role and Political Office: Effects of Perceived Masculinity/Feminity of Candidate and Political Office." *Psychology of Women Quarterly* 13 (1): 77–85.

Rothwell, Valerie, Gordon Hodson, and Elvira Prusaczyk. 2019. "Why Pillory Hillary? Testing the Endemic Sexism Hypothesis Regarding the 2016 U.S. Election." *Personality and Individual Differences* 138:106–8.

Rubarth, Scott. 2014. "Competing Constructions of Masculinity in Ancient Greece." *Athens Journal of Humanities and Arts* 1 (1): 21–32.

Rubin, Henry. 2003. *Self-Made Men: Identity and Embodiment among Transsexual Men*. Nashville, TN: Vanderbilt University Press.

Rudolph, Thomas J., Amy Gangl, and Dan Stevens. "The Effects of Efficacy and Emotions on Campaign Involvement." *Journal of Politics* 62 (4): 1189–97.

Rueckert, Linda, Brandon Branch, and Tiffany Doan. 2011. "Are Gender Differences in Empathy Due to Differences in Emotional Reactivity?" *Psychology* 2 (6): 574–78.

Sabin, Gerald, and Kyle Kirkup. 2019. "Competing Masculinities and Political Campaigns." In *Mediation of Gendered Identities in Canadian Politics*, edited by Angelia Wagner and Joanna Everitt, 45–64. Vancouver: University of British Columbia Press.

Saez, Pedro A., Adonaid Casado, and Jay C. Wade. 2010. "Factors Influencing Masculinity Ideology among Latino Men." *Journal of Men's Studies* 17 (2): 116–28.

Sanbonmatsu, Kira. 2002. "Gender Stereotypes and Vote Choice." *American Journal of Political Science* 46 (1): 20–34.

Sanchez, Gabriel R., and Jason L. Morin. 2019. "The Effect of Descriptive Representation on Latinos' Views of Government and of Themselves." *Social Science Quarterly* 92 (2): 483–508.

Santia, Martina, and Nichole M. Bauer. 2022. "The Intersection of Candidate Gender and Ethnicity: How Voters Respond to Campaign Messages from Latinas." *International Journal of Press/Politics* 28 (4): 975–94.

Schaffner, Brian F., Matthew McWilliams, and Tatishe Nteta. 2018. "Understanding White Polarization and the 2016 Presidential Vote: The Sobering Role of Racism and Sexism." *Political Science Quarterly* 133 (1): 9–34.

Schermerhorn, Nathaniel E. C., Theresa K. Vescio, and Kathrine A. Lewis. 2022. "Hegemonic Masculinity Predicts Support for US Political Figures Accused of Sexual Assault." *Social Psychological and Personality Science* 14 (5): 475–86.

Schilt, Kristen. 2006. "Just One of the Guys? How Transmen Make Gender Visible at Work." *Gender & Society* 20 (4): 465–90.

Schilt, Kristen, and Laurel Westbrook. 2015. "Bathroom Battlegrounds and Penis Panics." *Contexts* 14 (3): 26–31.

Schippers, Mimi. 2007. "Recovering the Feminine Other: Masculinity, Femininity, and Gender Hegemony." *Theory and Society* 36 (1): 85–102.

Schlesinger, Mark, and Caroline Heldman. 2001. "Gender Gap or Gender Gaps? New Perspectives on Support for Government Action and Policies." *Journal of Politics* 63 (1): 59–92.

Schlozman, Kay Lehman, Nancy Burns, and Sidney Verba. 1994. "Gender and the Pathways to Participation: The Role of Resources." *Journal of Politics* 56 (4): 963–90.

Schneider, Monica C., and Angela L. Bos. 2014. "Measuring Stereotypes of Female Politicians." *Political Psychology* 35 (2): 245–66.

Schneider, Monica C., and Angela L. Bos. 2019. "The Application of Social Role Theory to the Study of Gender in Politics." *Political Psychology* 40 (S1): 173–213.

Schneider, Monica C., and Angela L. Bos. 2023. "The Political Psychology of Gender." In *Oxford Handbook of Political Psychology*, 3rd ed., edited by Leonie Huddy, David O. Sears, Jack S. Levy, and Jennifer Jerit, 694–732. New York: Oxford University Press.

Schocker, Jessica B., and Christine Woyshner. 2013. "Representing African American Women in U.S. History Textbooks." *Social Studies* 104 (1): 23–31.

Schrock, Douglas, and Michael Schwalbe. 2009. "Men, Masculinity, and Manhood Acts." *Annual Review of Sociology* 35:277–95.

Scott, Jamil, Nadia Brown, Lorrie Frasure, and Diane Pinderhughes. 2021. "Destined to Run? The Role of Political Participation on Black Women's Decision to Run for Elected Office." *National Review of Black Politics* 2 (1): 22–52.

Segal, Lynne. 1993. "Changing Men: Masculinities in Context." *Theory and Society* 22 (5): 625–41.

Setzler, Mark, and Alixandra B. Yanus. 2018. "Why Did Women Vote for Donald Trump?" *PS: Political Science and Politics* 51 (3): 523–27.

Shapiro, Robert Y., and Harpreet Mahajan. 1986. "Gender Differences in Policy Preferences: A Summary of Trends from the 1960s to the 1980s." *Public Opinion Quarterly* 50 (1): 42–61.

Sharrow, Elizabeth A., Dara Z. Strolovitch, Michael T. Heaney, Seth E. Masket, and Joanne M. Miller. 2016. "Gender Attitudes, Gendered Partisanship: Feminism and Support for Sarah Palin and Hillary Clinton among Party Activists." *Journal of Women, Politics & Policy* 37 (4): 394–416.

Shook, Natalie J., Holly N. Fitzgerald, Shelby T. Boggs, Cameron G. Ford, Patricia D. Hopkins, and Nicole M. Silva. 2020. "Sexism, Racism, and Nationalism: Factors Associated with the 2016 U.S. Presidential Election Results?" *Plos One* 15 (3): e0229432.

Silva, Tony. 2017. "Bud-Sex: Constructing Normative Masculinity among Rural Straight Men That Have Sex With Men." *Gender & Society* 31 (1): 51–73.

Silva, Tony. 2023. "Masculinity, Femininity, and Reported Paranormal Beliefs." *Journal for the Scientific Study of Religion* 62 (3): 709–22.

Simien, Evelyn M. 2006. *Black Feminist Voices in Politics*. Albany: State Univeristy of New York Press.

Singer, Tania, and Claus Lamm. 2009. "The Social Neuroscience of Empathy." *Annals of the New York Academy of Sciences* 1156 (1): 81–96.

Skevrin, Annette E. 2015. "Success Factors for Women of Color Information Technology Leaders in Corporate America." PhD diss., College of Management and Technology.

Smith, James A., Annette Braunack-Mayer, Gary Wittert, and Megan Warin. 2007. "'I've Been Independent For So Damn Long!': Independence, Masculinity, and Aging in a Help Seeking Context." *Journal of Aging Studies* 21 (4): 325–35.

Smith, Tom W. 2006. *Altruism and Empathy in America: Trends and Correlates*. Chicago: National Opinion.

Smooth, Wendy. 2006. "Intersectionality in Electoral Politics: A Mess Worth Making." *Politics & Gender* 2 (3): 400–414.

Soszynski, Michael, and Ryan Bliss. 2023. "Demographic and Measurement Differences between Text-to-Web and Phone Survey Respondents." Survey Practice 16 (1). https://www.surveypractice.org/article/85141-demographic-and-measurement-differences-between-text-to-web-and-phone-survey-respondents.

Spence, Janet T. 1993. "Gender-Related Traits and Gender Ideology: Evidence for a Multifactorial Theory." *Journal of Personality and Social Psychology* 64 (4): 624–35.

Spence, Janet T., Robert Helmreich, and Joy Stapp. 1974. "Personal Attributes Questionnaire." *JSAS Catalog of Selected Documents in Psychology* 4:1–42.

Spisak, Brian R., Peter H. Dekker, Max Krüger, and Mark van Vugt. 2012. "Warriors and Peacekeepers: Testing a Biosocial Implicit Leadership Hypothesis of Intergroup Relations Using Masculine and Feminine Faces." *PLOS ONE* 7 (1): e30399.

Spreng, Nathan R., Margaret C. McKinnon, Raymond A. Mar, and Brian Levine. 2009. "The Toronto Empathy Questionnaire: Scale Development and Initial Validation of a Factor-Analytic Solution to Multiple Empathy Measures." *Journal of Personality Assessment* 91(1): 62–71.

Stanaland, Adam, and Sarah Gaither. 2021. "'Be a Man': The Role of Social Pressure in Eliciting Men's Aggressive Cognition." *Personality and Social Psychology Bulletin* 47 (11): 1596–611.

Stephens-Davidowitz, Seth. 2017. *Everybody Lies: Big Data, New Data, and What the Internet Can Tell Us about Who We Really Are*. New York: HarperCollins.

Stokes-Brown, Atiya Kai. 2009. "The Hidden Politics of Identity: Racial Self-Identification and Latino Political Engagement." *Politics & Policy* 37 (6): 1281–305.

Stolle, Dietlind, Marc Hooghe, and Michele Micheletti. 2005. "Politics in the Supermarket: Political Consumerism as a Form of Political Participation." *International Political Science Review* 26 (3): 245–69.

Stout, Christopher T., Katherine Tate, and Meghan Wilson. 2021. "Does Black Representation Matter? A Review of Descriptive Representation for African Americans in Legislative Offices." *National Review of Black Politics* 2 (1): 2–21.

Strolovitch, Dara Z., Janelle S. Wong, and Andrew Proctor. 2017. "A Possessive Investment in White Heteropatriarchy? The 2016 Election and the Politics of Race, Gender, and Sexuality." *Politics, Groups, and Identities* 5 (2): 353–63.

Strong, Edward K. 1936. "Interests of Men and Women." *Journal of Social Psychology* 7 (1): 49–67.

Stryker, Sheldon, and Richard T. Serpe. 1994. "Identity Salience and Psychological Centrality: Equivalent, Overlapping, or Complementary Concepts?" *Social Psychology Quarterly* 57 (1): 16–35.

Swain, Randall D. 2018. "Negative Black Stereotypes, Support for Excessive Use of Force by Police, and Voter Preference for Donald Trump during the 2016 Presidential Primary Election Cycle." *Journal of African American Studies* 22 (1): 109–24.

Sweet-Cushman, Jennie. 2022. "Legislative vs. Executive Political Offices: How Gender Stereotypes Can Disadvantage Women in Either Office." *Political Behavior* 44:411–34.

Talbot, Kirsten, and Michael Quayle. 2010. "The Perils of Being a Nice Guy: Contextual Variation in Five Young Women's Constructions of Acceptable Hegemonic and Alternative Masculinities." *Men and Masculinities* 13:255–78.

Tate, Charlotte Chucky, Jay N. Bettergarcia, and Lindsay M. Brent. 2015. "Re-assessing the Role of Gender-Related Cognitions for Self-Esteem: The Importance of Gender Typicality for Cisgender Adults." *Sex Roles* 72 (5): 221–36.

Terman, Lewis M., and Catharine Cox Miles. 1936. *Sex and Personality: Studies in Masculinity and Femininity.* New York: McGraw-Hill.

Thomas, Stucky D., Geralyn M. Miller, and Linda M. Murphy. 2008. "Gender, Guns, and Legislating: An Analysis of State Legislative Policy Preferences." *Journal of Women, Politics, & Policy* 29 (4): 477–95.

Thompson, Edward H., and Kate M Bennett. 2015. "Measurement of Masculinity Ideologies: A (Critical) Review." *Psychology of Men & Masculinity* 16 (2): 115–33.

Thompson, Edward H., and Joseph H. Pleck. 1986. "The Structure of Male Role Norms." *American Behavioral Scientist* 29 (5): 531–43.

Thompson, Edward H., Joseph Pleck, and David Ferrera. 1992. "Men and Masculinities: Scales for Masculinity Ideology and Masculinity-Related Constructs." *Sex Roles* 27 (11–12): 573–607.

Torgrimson, Britta N., and Christopher T. Minson. 2005. "Sex and Gender: What Is the Difference?" *Journal of Applied Physiology* 99 (3): 785–87.

Tuathail, Gearóid Ó. 2003. "'Just out Looking for a Fight': American Affect and the Invasion of Iraq." *Antipode* 35 (5): 856–70.

Twenge, Jean M. 1997. "Changes in Masculine and Feminine Traits over Time: A Meta-Analysis." *Sex Roles* 36 (5): 305–25.

Unger, Rhoda K., and Mary Crawford. 1993. "Sex and Gender—The Troubled Relationship between Terms and Concepts." *Psychological Science* 4 (2): 122–24.

Unnever, James D., and Cecilia Chouhy. 2021. "Race, Racism, and the Cool Pose: Exploring Black and White Male Masculinity." *Social Problems* 68 (2): 490–512.

Valentino, Nicholas A., Ted Brader, Eric W. Groenendyk, Krysha Gregorowica, and Vincent L. Hutchings. 2011. "Election Night's Alright for Fighting: The Role of Emotions in Political Participation." *Journal of Politics* 73 (1): 156–70.

van Anders, Sari M. 2013. "Beyond Masculinity: Testosterone, Gender/Sex, and Human Social Behavior in a Comparative Context." *Frontiers in Neuroendocrinology* 34 (3): 198–210.

Vandello, Joseph A., and Jennifer K. Bosson. 2013. "Hard Won and Easily Lost: A Review and Synthesis of Theory and Research on Precarious Manhood." *Psychology of Men & Masculinity* 14:101–13.

Vandello, Joseph A., Jennifer K. Bosson, Dov Cohen, Rochelle M. Burnaford, and Jonathan R. Weaver. 2008. "Precarious Manhood." *Journal of Personality and Social Psychology* 95 (6): 1325–39.

van der Pas, Daphne, Loes Aaldering, and Angela L. Bos. 2023. "Looks Like a Leader: Measuring Evolution in Gendered Politician Stereotypes." *Political Behavior*. doi: 10.1007/s11109-023-09888-5.

van Elsas, Erika J., Emily M. Miltenburg, and Tom W. G. van der Meer. 2016. "If I Recall Correctly: An Event History Analysis of Forgetting and Recollecting Past Voting Behavior." *Journal of Elections, Public Opinion, and Parties* 26 (3): 1–20.

Vavreck, Lynn, and Douglas Rivers. 2008. "The 2006 Cooperative Congressional Election Study." *Journal of Elections, Public Opinion, and Parties* 18 (4): 355–66.

Vellante, Marcello, Simon Baron-Cohen, Mariangela Melis, Matteo Marrone, Donatella Rita Petretto, Carmelo Masala, and Antonio Preti. 2013. "The 'Reading the Mind in the Eyes' Test: Systematic Review of Psychometric Properties and a Validation Study in Italy." *Cognitive Neuropsychiatry* 18 (4): 326–54.

Verba, Sidney, Nancy Burns, and Kay Lehman Schlozman. 1997. "Knowing and Caring about Politics: Gender and Political Engagement." *Journal of Politics* 59 (4): 1051–72.

Verba, Sidney, Kay Lehman Schlozman, and Henry E. Brady. 1995. *Voice and Equality: Civic Voluntarism in American Politics*. Cambridge, MA: Harvard University Press.

Vescio, Theresa K., Kristine A. Schlenker, and Joshua G. Lenes. 2010. "Power and Sexism." In *The Social Psychology of Power*, edited by Ana Guinote and Theresa K. Vescio, 363–80. New York: Guilford.

Vescio, Theresa K., and Nathaniel E. C. Schermerhorn. 2021. "Hegemonic Masculinity Predicts 2016 and 2020 Voting and Candidate Evaluations." *Proceedings of the National Academy of Sciences* 118 (2): e2020589118.

Vinkenburg, Claartje, Marloes L. van Engen, Alice H. Eagly, and Mary C. Johannesen-Schmidt. 2011. "An Exploration of Stereotypical Beliefs about Leadership Styles: Is Transformational Leadership a Route to Women's Promotion?" *Leadership Quarterly* 22 (1): 10–21.

Vonk, Jennifer, Patricia Mayhew, and Virgil Zeigler-Hill. 2016. "Gender Roles, Not Anatomical Sex, Predict Social Cognitive Capacities, Such as Empathy and Perspective-Taking." In *Psychology and Neurobiology of Empathy*, edited by Douglas F. Watt and Jaak Panksepp, 187–209. Hauppauge, NY: Nova Biomedical.

Wade, Jay C., and Chris Brittan-Powell. 2001. "Men's Attitudes toward Race and Gender Equity: The Importance of Masculinity Ideology, Gender-related Traits, and Reference Group Identity Dependence." *Psychology of Men and Masculinity* 2 (1): 42–50.

Walter, Sheryl L., Scott E. Seibert, Daniel Goering, and Ernest H. O'Boyle. 2019. "A Tale of Two Sample Sources: Do Results from Online Panel Data and Conventional Data Converge?" *Journal of Business and Psychology* 34 (4): 425–52.

Ward, Jane. 2015. *Not Gay: Sex between Straight White Men*. New York: New York University Press.

Warner, Tara D, and Shawn Ratcliff. 2021. "What Guns Mean: Who Sees Guns as Important, Essential, and Empowering (and Why)?" *Sociological Inquiry* 91 (2): 313–46.

Warner, Tara D., Tara Leigh Tober, Tristan Bridges, and David F. Warner. 2022. "To Provide or Protect? Masculinity, Economic Precarity, and Protective Gun Ownership in the United States." *Sociological Perspectives* 65 (1): 97–118.

Watts, Sarah. 2003. *Rough Rider in the White House: Theodore Roosevelt and the Politics of Desire*. Chicago: University of Chicago Press.

Weaver, Jonathan R., Joseph A. Vandello, and Jennifer K. Bosson. 2013. "Intrepid, Imprudent, or Impetuous? The Effects of Gender Threats on Men's Financial Decisions." *Psychology of Men and Masculinity* 14:184–91.

Weeks, Ana Catalano, Bonnie M. Meguid, Miki Caul Kittilson, and Hilde Coffé. 2022. "When Do Männerparteien Elect Women? Radical Right Populist Parties and Strategic Descriptive Representation." *American Political Science Review* 117 (2): 421–38.

Weinschenk, Aaron C., and Christopher T. Dawes. 2019. "Moral Foundations, System Justification, and Support for Trump in the 2016 Presidential Election." *Forum* 17 (2): 195–208.

Welch, Susan, and John Hibbing. 1992. "Financial Conditions, Gender, and Voting in American National Elections." *Journal of Politics* 54 (1): 197–213.

West, Candace, and Don H. Zimmerman. 1987. "Doing Gender." *Gender & Society* 1 (2): 125–51.

Westbrook, Laurel, and Aliya Saperstein. 2015. "New Categories Are Not Enough." *Gender & Society* 29 (4): 534–60.

Whitaker, Lois Duke. 2008. *Voting the Gender Gap*. Urbana: University of Illinois Press.

Whitley, Bernard E. 2001. "Gender-role Variables and Attitudes toward Homosexuality." *Sex Roles* 45 (11/12): 691–721.

Wilhelm, Mark Ottoni, and René Bekkers. 2010. "Helping Behavior, Dispositional Empathic Concern, and the Principle of Care." *Social Psychology Quarterly* 73 (1): 11–32.

Willer, Robb, Christabel Rogalin, Bridget Conlon, and Michael T. Wojnowicz. 2013. "Overdoing Gender: A Test of the Masculine Overcompensation Thesis." *American Journal of Sociology* 118:980–1022.

Wilson, Bianca D. M., and Ilhan H. Meyer. 2021. "Nonbinary LGBTQ Adults in the United States." Williams Institute, June. williamsinstitute.law.ucla.edu.

Winer, Canton. 2021. "Sex Roles and the Erasure of Women From Conversations about Gender Oppression: The Case of #BoysDanceToo." *Men and Masculinities* 24 (5): 842–61.

Winer, Canton. 2022. "'The Queers Hate Me Because I'm Too Butch': Goldilocks Masculinity Among Non-Heterosexual Men." *Sexualities* 27 (4): 1053–73.

Winter, Nicholas J. G. 2010. "Masculine Republicans and Feminine Democrats: Gender and Americans' Explicit and Implicit Images of the Political Parties." *Political Behavior* 32 (4): 587–618.

Wolak, Jennifer. 2022. "Conflict Avoidance and Gender Gaps in Political Engagement." *Political Behavior* 44:133–56.

Womick, Jake, Tobias Rothmund, Flavio Azevedo, Laura A. King, and John T. Jost. 2019. "Group-based Dominance and Authoritarian Aggression Predict Support for Donald Trump in the 2016 US Presidential Election." *Social Psychological and Personality Science* 10 (5): 643–52.

Wright, Joshua D., and Victoria M. Esses. 2019. "It's Security, Stupid! Voters' Perceptions of Immigrants as a Security Risk Predicted Support for Donald Trump in the 2016 US Presidential Election." *Journal of Applied Social Psychology* 49 (1): 36–49.

Zaki, Jamil. 2014. "Empathy: A Motivated Account." *Psychological Bulletin* 140 (6): 1608–47.

Zaki, Jamil, and Kevin Ochsner. 2013. "Neural Sources of Empathy: An Evolving Story." In *Understanding Other Minds: Perspectives from Developmental Social Neuroscience*, 3rd ed., edited by Simon Baron-Cohen, Helen Tager-Flusberg, and Michael Lombardo, 214–32. New York: Oxford University Press.

Zalewski, Marysia, and Jane L. Parpart. 2019. *The "Man" Question in International Relations*. New York: Routledge.

Zaller, John. 1992. *The Nature and Origins of Mass Opinion*. Cambridge: Cambridge University Press.

Zurbriggen, Eileen L. 2010. "Rape, War, and the Socialization of Masculinity: Why Our Refusal to Give Up War Ensures That Rape Cannot Be Eradicated." *Psychology of Women Quarterly* 34 (4): 538–49.

ABOUT THE CONTRIBUTORS

NICHOLE M. BAUER is an Associate Professor of Political Communication in the Department of Political Science and the LSU Manship School of Mass Communication. Her research investigates the persistence of women's underrepresentation in the United States. She is the recipient of the 2020 LSU Rainmaker Award and the 2019 LSU Alumni Association Rising Faculty Research Award. She is the author of *The Qualifications Gap: Why Women Must be Better than Men to Win Political Office* (2020, Cambridge University Press). Her research is published in a variety of journals, including the *Journal of Politics, Political Psychology, Political Behavior, Politics & Gender,* and *Politics, Groups, and Identities,* among other outlets.

AMANDA BITTNER is Professor of Political Science and Director of the Gender and Politics Laboratory at Memorial University. Her books include: *Platform or Personality? The Role of Party Leaders in Elections* (2011, Oxford University Press); and the edited volumes *Parties, Elections, and the Future of Canadian Politics* (2013, UBC Press), and*Mothers and Others: The Impact of Family Life on Politics* (2017, UBC Press); and the textbook *Essential Readings in Canadian Government and Politics* (2016, Emond Montgomery). In 2022 she was inducted into the Royal Society of Canada's College of New Scholars, Artists, and Scientists.

CATHERINE BOLZENDAHL is Professor of Sociology and Director of the School of Public Policy at Oregon State University. In addition to numerous peer-reviewed journal articles, she has two coauthored two books: *Counted Out: Same-Sex Relations and Americans' Definitions of Family* (2010, Russell Sage Foundation) and the edited volume *Measuring Women's Political Empowerment across the Globe* (2018, Palgrave Macmillan).

ANGELA L. BOS is Dean and Professor in the School of Public Service at Boise State University. Dr. Bos publishes research on gender and political leadership and creates public-facing scholarship to improve women's representation in our public institutions. Her research is published in journals such as the *American Political Science Review, Political Psychology*, and *Political Communication.*

IVELISSE CUEVAS-MOLINA is Assistant Professor of Political Science at Fordham University. Her research interests include Latinx politics, Puerto Rican politics in the US mainland, and survey methodology. Her work has been published in *Political Research Quarterly, American Politics Research, Journal of Racial and Ethnic Politics*, and *Centro Journal.*

MELISSA DECKMAN, PhD, is CEO of Public Religion Research Institute. A political scientist who studies gender, religion, and political behavior, she is the author of more than two dozen peer-reviewed articles and five books, including *Tea Party Women: Mama Grizzlies, Grassroots Activists, and the Changing Face of the American Right* (2016, NYU Press) and *The Politics of Gen Z: How the Youngest Voters Will Shape Our Democracy* (2024, Columbia University Press), which examines the impact of gender and sexuality on the political choices of this nascent generation.

SARAH H. DIMUCCIO is a Senior Consultant at Mannaz A/S.

ELIZABETH GOODYEAR-GRANT is a Professor of Political Studies at Queen's University (Canada). Her books and edited volumes include *Gendered News: Media Coverage and Electoral Politics in Canada* (2013, UBC Press), which won the 2016 Pierre Savard Award from the International Council for Canadian Studies, and *Women, Power, and Political Representation: Canadian and Comparative Perspectives* (2021, University of Toronto Press). Since 2016, she has served as the Director of the Canadian Opinion Research Archive.

JILL S. GREENLEE is an Associate Professor in Politics and Women's, Gender & Sexuality Studies at Brandeis University. She is the author of *The Political Consequences of Motherhood* (2014, University of Michigan Press) and articles in numerous journals, such as *American Politics Research*; *American Political Science Review*; *Political Behavior*; *Politics and Gender*; *Political Behavior*; *Political Psychology*; *Politics, Groups, and Identities*; *P.S.*; and *Public Opinion Quarterly*.

MIRYA R. HOLMAN is Associate Professor at the Hobby School of Public Affairs at the University of Houston. She is the author of *Women in Politics in the American City* (2014; Temple University Press), coauthor of *The Power of the Badge* (2024, University of Chicago Press), and coeditor of *Good Reasons to Run* (2020, Temple University Press).

LEONIE HUDDY is a Distinguished Professor of Political Science at Stony Brook University. She is coeditor (with David O Sears, Jack Levy, and Jennifer Jerit) of *The Oxford Handbook of Political Psychology* (3rd ed.; 2023, Oxford University Press), and coauthor (with Stanley Feldman and George Marcus) of *Going to War in Iraq: When Citizens and the Press Matter* (2015, University of Chicago Press). She is past president of the International Society of Political Psychology (ISPP) and serves on the Board for the American National Election Studies.

DAVID R. JONES is Professor of Political Science at Baruch College and the Graduate Center, City University of New York. He specializes in American politics, the US Congress, and methodology. He is the author of *Political Parties and Policy Gridlock in American Government* (2001, Edwin Mellen) and coauthor of *Americans, Congress, and Democratic Responsiveness: Public Evaluations of Congress and Electoral Consequences* (2009, University of Michigan Press). His research has been published in many scholarly journals, such as the *American Journal of Political Science*, the *Journal of Politics*, and the *Political Research Quarterly*.

ERIC D. KNOWLES is Associate Professor of Psychology at New York University.

EUGENE B. LEE-JOHNSON is an Assistant Professor in the Department of Political Science and Geography at the Nelson Mandela College of Government and Social Sciences at Southern University and

Agricultural & Mechanical College. Eugene's primary research interests lie within American politics and how political behaviors and group identity are structured by race and gender, specifically looking at Black women in leadership roles. Eugene combines social movement literature and gender and politics literature to understand what vehicles of change Black women value the most.

J. Celeste Lay is a Professor of Political Science at Tulane University. She researches American political behavior, especially political socialization and public opinion about public policy. She is the author of *Public Schools, Private Governance: Education Reform and Democracy in New Orleans* (2022, Temple University Press), which chronicles the transformation of the city's school system into an all-charter system run by private boards. She has also published several other articles in peer-reviewed journals and another monograph.

Maggie K. Martin is a Doctoral Candidate in the department of Political Science at Stony Brook University.

Zoe M. Oxley is William D. Williams Professor of Political Science at Union College. Her books include *Public Opinion: Democratic Ideals, Democratic Practice* (2020, Congressional Quarterly), now in its fourth edition. She is a teacher and scholar of gender politics, public opinion, political psychology, and political socialization.

Christina Pao is a PhD student in Sociology and Social Policy at Princeton University, and they are affiliated with the Office of Population Research. Their work has been in academic journals such as *Electoral Studies* and *Socius* and in news outlets such as the *Washington Post*. They are committed to public-facing work and have been awarded a Truman Scholarship (2019) and Rhodes Scholarship (2020)

Carl L. Palmer is an Associate Professor in the Department of Politics and Government at Illinois State University. Prior to joining Illinois State he was a Rooney Center Postdoctoral Research Associate at the University of Notre Dame. He received his PhD from the University of California, Davis, and specializes in political psychology and political behavior. His research has appeared in *Frontiers in Political Science*; *Politics & Gender*; *Politics, Groups, and Identities*; and the *Journal of Politics*, among others.

ROLFE DAUS PETERSON is an Associate Professor of Political Science at Susquehanna University. He received his PhD from the University of California at Davis and studies political behavior and political psychology. His recent research has been published in *Social Science Quarterly*; *Politics and the Life Sciences*; the *Journal of Elections, Parties, and Public Opinion*; and *American Politics Research*.

DAN QI is a Visiting Assistant Professor in the Political Science Department at Reed College. Her main research area is political behavior and identity politics, especially in election studies, Asian American politics, and immigration politics. She has been active in research, with papers published in scholarly journals, including *Political Behavior, PS: Political Science & Politics*, and *Social Science Quarterly*. Dan is the recipient of the 2021 Center for American Women and Politics (CAWP) Research Grant and the 2023 Bernard Goldhammer Grants for Research on Economics and Natural Resources.

NATE ROUNDY recently graduated from the University of Cambridge with a PhD in Politics and International Studies. Their work focuses on survey research design and LGBTQ+ politics. They are affiliated with the Cambridge-YouGov Centre for Public Opinion Research.

NATHANIEL E. C. SCHERMERHORN is a Lecturer at the University of Essex. His research focuses on the ways in which individuals, groups, and institutions maintain and reinforce the existing status quo.

JACOB F. H. SMITH is Assistant Professor of Political Science at Fordham University. Jacob's research focuses on Congress, elections, public policy, and disability and politics. Jacob is the author of *Minority Party Misery: Political Powerlessness and Electoral Disengagement* (2021, University of Michigan Press)). He is currently working on his second book "Waves of Discontent: Electoral Volatility, Public Policymaking, and the Health of American Democracy."

THERESA K. VESCIO is Professor of Psychology at Penn State.

TARA WARNER is Associate Professor of Criminal Justice at the University of Alabama at Birmingham. She is also an Associate Director of UAB Social Science and Justice Research, where she leads the Violence Prevention and Reduction core.

CANTON WINER is Assistant Professor of Sociology and Gender/Sexuality Studies at Northern Illinois University. His research has appeared in *Sociology Compass*, *Sociological Inquiry*, *Sexualities*, the *Journal of Homosexuality*, and *Men and Masculinities*, among other journals. His upcoming work explores asexuality's generative potential for the sociology of gender, the sociology of sexuality, and feminist and queer theory.

ABOUT THE EDITORS

DAN CASSINO is Professor of Government and Politics at Fairleigh Dickinson University. His books include *Gender Threat: American Masculinity in the Face of Change* (2021, Stanford University Press) and the textbook *Social Research Methods by Example* (2023, Routledge), now in its second edition, both with Yasemin Besen-Cassino. Since 2020, he has served as the Executive Director of the FDU Poll.

MONIKA L. McDERMOTT is Professor of Political Science at Fordham University. She researches political psychology, voting, and gendered influences in politics. She coauthored the book *Americans, Congress, and Democratic Responsiveness* (2009; University of Michigan Press), and she is the author of *Masculinity, Femininity, and American Political Behavior* (2016, Oxford University Press). Her scholarly articles have appeared in a wide range of political science journals, including the *American Journal of Political Science* and the *Journal of Politics*.

INDEX

ableist stereotypes: masculinity and, 76–78; research on, 6, 84–92, *87, 91*; in society, 78–84, 92–94
abortion attitudes, 138–39
acquired brain injury, 83–84
activism: #MeToo movement, 23, 33, 236, 239, 255, 263; in United States, 263–64; voting behavior and, 241–42, 255n1
Adler, Alfred, 13–14
advertising data, 65–70, *66,* 75n6
African American identity. *See* Black identity
age: partisanship/party ID and, *242*; political participation and, 235–37, 241–42, 245, 247–55; scholarship on, 185n4. *See also* Generation Z
agency, communion and, 15–16
agentic/instrumental (masculine) traits: analysis of, 56–57; in BSRI, *52, 54*; children and, 58n4; communal traits and, 43; hegemonic masculinity and, 56; measurement of masculinity/femininity and, 94n1; political interest and, *55,* 55–56; political leadership and, 112–13; scholarship on, 41–45, 47, 49–58
aggression: dominance masculinity and, 158; hegemonic masculinity and, 153; hyper-aggression, 154; in liberal men, 148–52, *151*; masculinity

and, 142; from precarious masculinity/manhood, 145–48; toughness and, 1, 21, 32, 49–50, 60–61, 66, 68; types of, 143–45
Amazon, 113
American National Election Study (ANES), 171, 180
analysis of variance, 134
Anderson, Rindy C., 26
andreia, 12–13
androgyny, 18
ANES. *See* American National Election Study
anti-Black racism, 112
anti-femininity, 22
anxiety, 142–43, 152–53
Asch, A., 84
Asian identity: Black identity and, 121, 123–24; Latino/a/x identity and, 70–73, *71, 72*; research on, 72–73; scholarship on, 51, *51*; stereotypes of, 73; for women, 59, 75n7. *See also* race/ethnicity
Asperger's Syndrome, 191

Bäckström, Martin, 198
Bakan, David, 15–16
Baron-Cohen, Simon, 192
Beatty, Joyce, 67
behavior, surveys on, 113–20, *114, 117–20*
behavioral aggression, 144–45. *See also* aggression

www.ingramcontent.com/pod-product-compliance
Lightning Source LLC
Chambersburg PA
CBHW031139020426
42333CB00013B/450